D0208565

MAXIM GORKY

MAXIM GORKY

A POLITICAL BIOGRAPHY

TOVAH YEDLIN

PRAEGER

Westport, Connecticut
London

Library of Congress Cataloging-in-Publication Data

Yedlin, Tova.
    Maxim Gorky : a political biography / Tovah Yedlin.
      p. cm.
    Includes bibliographical references and index.
    ISBN 0–275–96605–4 (alk. paper)
      1. Gorky, Maksim, 1868–1936—Political and social views.
    2. Gorky, Maksim, 1868–1936. 3. Authors, Russian—20th century
Biography. 4. Communism and literature—Soviet Union. I. Title.
PG3465.Z9P699 1999
891.78'309—dc21
[B]   99–14383

British Library Cataloguing in Publication Data is available.

Copyright © 1999 by Tovah Yedlin

All rights reserved. No portion of this book may be
reproduced, by any process or technique, without the
express written consent of the publisher.

Library of Congress Catalog Card Number: 99–14383
ISBN: 0–275–96605–4

First published in 1999

Praeger Publishers, 88 Post Road West, Westport, CT 06881
An imprint of Greenwood Publishing Group, Inc.
www.praeger.com

Printed in the United States of America

The paper used in this book complies with the
Permanent Paper Standard issued by the National
Information Standards Organization (Z39.48–1984).

10 9 8 7 6 5 4 3 2 1

Copyright Acknowledgments

The author and publisher gratefully acknowledge permission for use of the following material:

From "The Letters of Maksim Gor'kij to V. F. Xodasevič, 1922–1925," translated and edited
by Hugh McLean in *Harvard Slavic Studies, vol. I.* Copyright © 1953 by the President and
Fellows of Harvard College. Reprinted by permission of Harvard University Press.

TO MISHA
in loving memory.

CONTENTS

ACKNOWLEDGMENTS

Having been involved for many years in the study of Gorky and his political career, I can no longer recall all the people who helped me find sources, gave advice, and answered questions concerning one or another event of Gorky's life and actions.

The work in many libraries and archives where I searched for materials was in each case made possible by the kind and helpful attitude of the staff. Of particular importance for the present study were the materials found in the Library of Congress; the Helsinki Library in Finland; the Columbia University Library; the Bakhmetev Archive in New York; the Hoover Institution in Stanford, California; the Slavic Studies Library at the University of Illinois at Champaign-Urbana; the Slavonic Department of the New York Public Library; and, last but not least, the M. Gorky Institute of World Literature in Moscow.

In the last few years I have become indebted to the following people for their help and assistance in the work on the political biography of Gorky: my late colleague and friend R. H. McNeal and V. S. Barakhov, M. V. Dmitriev, R. C. Elwood, K. Holden, A. Hornjatkevyč, L. V. Kuzmitcheva, M. Mote, J. Ould, H. Solomon, L. A. Spiridonova, J. Willman, and A. Zelnikov. To M. Carter and to A. Tulchinsky and V. Ourdeva, graduate students in the Division of Slavic Studies of the University of Alberta, many thanks for their technical help. I owe a special word of thanks to G. Olson and D. Rees for their invaluable help in the work of editing the manuscript. I am very grateful to two members of the Greenwood Publishing Group, Ms. L. Robinson, copyeditor, and Ms. H. Straight, production editor, for their superb work in preparing the manuscript for publication. Of course, any errors or omissions are entirely my responsibility.

INTRODUCTION

Maxim Gorky was and remains a hard man to know. After more than a quarter of a century of studying his works and his pronouncements and trying to understand the different roads he traveled during the crucial period in Russian history, one is left with many questions.

Gorky's life spanned two centuries. He was born during the reign of Alexander II, known as the Tsar Liberator, seven years after the aboliton of serfdom. He died in a totalitarian Soviet Union, with Stalin at its helm. Gorky is also that rarity, a famous writer without a biography. Although millions of copies of his works, literary and publicist, including a voluminous correspondence have been published and some unpublished sources have been available, a comprehensive biography of Gorky has never been written. How shall we explain that no attempts have been made, either in the Soviet Union or in the West to write an honest Gorky biography, comprehensive and free from political bias?

Some important pieces of evidence were buried during the Stalin era, and the published essays, correspondence, and his allegedly complete works were censored by the removal of unwanted evidence. Paragraphs have been deleted or altered, and dates and names have often been omitted. All this made such a biography impossible to write. The inability of Soviet scholars to undertake the rather difficult task may be traced to the creation of a "Gorky myth." The myth took its beginning with the writer's first return to Russia from his second exile in 1928. In that myth, Gorky was hailed as "the first proletarian writer," as an unwavering friend of Lenin, and later as the faithful follower of Stalin and his policies. It was acknowledged that the author of the *Pesnia o burevestnike* (The Song of the Stormy Petrel) who in his writing issued the call for revolution had erred in October 1917, when he first rejected the Revolution, but had later recanted. It was within the framework of the myth that one was permitted to write about Gorky's life and work as if the man were subsumed in the story. In examining the Soviet record of works on Gorky we will find that his literary legacy was discussed, albeit within the framework allowed. As to Gorky's revolutionary path and involvement in the political life of tsarist Russia and then of the Soviet Union, little of substance was written. The exception was the book *Gor'kii-revoliutsioner* (Gorky the Revolutionary), authored by V. A. Bazarov (Rudnev) and published in 1929. Rudnev was purged in 1931, in the trial of the Mensheviks; his work, considered not politically correct, was buried in the archives. Therein appeared a number of one-volume biographies of Gorky, written within the permitted limits. These portrayals of Gorky were rather superficial or simply not true.

Gorky lived in the West and travelled widely. He had maintained close contact with many of the left-leaning intellectual élite, and as a result some of his writings and correspondence found its way to archives, university libraries, and private collections brought west by Russian émigrés. Until the period of glasnost' (1985–1991), these sources were unavailable to scholars in the Soviet Union, given the controls imposed by the state.

Today we know more about Gorky than we did a few years ago, as a result of revelations and debates that have been taking place since the period of glasnost'. Essays and articles began appearing in periodicals and newspapers in Russia; major works authored by writers and literary critics also were published.

Among works recently published in the West on Gorky is Nikolaus Katzer's *Maksim Gorkijs Weg in die russische Sozialdemokratie*, a scholarly political biography of Gorky to the year 1907. But by and large the new works published in the West in recent years are written by literary critics, often with an emphasis on the philosophical and psychological elements of Gorky the writer and the thinker.

The present study is a political biography of Gorky. Much of the material used consists of Gorky's works, mainly literary and publicistic, his rich epistolary legacy, published for the first time and important for our understanding of Gorky in the prelude and postlude of the Revolution. Only recently released was the Gorky-Stalin correspondence for the period 1929–1931. Similarly, the contacts with G. Yagoda, head of the infamous Unified State Political Administration (OGPU) have been documented in letters from 1928 to 1935. The material is arranged in chronological order. The work consists of nine chapters. In Chapters 1 and 2 Gorky's early life and his introduction to the ideologies of populism and Marxism are discussed. Chapter 3, entitled "Gorky and The Revolution of 1905," describes Gorky's active participation in the events and emphasizes his genuinely revolutionary spirit. The chapter ends with Gorky's leaving the country in the face of imminent arrest in December 1905. Gorky's unsuccessful mission to the United States aimed at collecting funds for the revolution, which he believed was to continue, and at winning the sympathy of the Americans for his cause is the theme of Chapter 4.

Chapter 5 is devoted to describing the details of Gorky's life on the island of Capri. Unable to return to Russia, Gorky settled on the island of Capri where he spent the years of 1906 to 1913. The Capri period was an important milestone in Gorky's life. It was during that period that Gorky became for a while an ally of Lenin, the high point of that friendly association being Gorky's attendance, with a consultative voice, at the Fifth Congress of the Russian Social Democratic Workers' Party (RSDWP) in 1907. The alliance of the two men ended with a break in relationship with Lenin and the beginning of Gorky's temporary alliance with Bogdanov and the *Vperëd* group of the RSDWP.

War and Revolution is the topic of Chapter 6. It is here that one learns about Gorky's stand toward World War I, his cautious acceptance of the February Revolution, and his strong opposition to the Revolution of October 1917. In this chapter are discussed three important developments: Gorky's arrival at some *modus vivendi* with Lenin and the Bolsheviks, Gorky's devotion to the task of saving Russia's cultural inheritance and the remaining members of the intelligentsia, and his departure for the West in 1921.

Gorky remained in the West from 1921 to 1928. The years of emigration were spent for the most part in Italy; in the quiet of Sorrento he was able to devote his time to the vocation he held dear, that of a writer. The events of 1921 to 1928 are the theme of Chapter 7.

The last, most tragic years of Gorky's life were spent in Stalin's Russia, where he would become an icon and submit to the regime for reasons that are explained within the documentation available. This constitutes the content of Chapter 8.

The concluding chapter, titled "Gorky: For and Against," contains a short summary of an ongoing debate in Russia on the question of "Whither Gorky in our century's history?" The debate centers on questions concerning Gorky's political ideology, his relationship with Stalin, and the "why" of Gorky's compliance with the policies of Stalinism. Interpretations of the causes of Gorky's death remain controversial, for even in the environment of glasnost' certain questions remained unanswered.

Work on the political biography of Gorky demanded a selective approach. Thus, a detailed analysis of Gorky the philosopher and the literary artist is omitted; nor is his religious thinking discussed in depth. The events of Gorky's private life have been given attention only when these appear to affect Gorky's political activity. Similarly, no attempt has been made to include a psychological analysis of Gorky's personality.

In the present work, an attempt is made to separate Gorky from the "myth" of the man and, by using sources recently made available, to present an honest portrayal of Gorky the political activist, with all his oscillations and inconsistencies. The aim is to contribute to the understanding of this interesting and sometimes perplexing life, which merged with the general history of the Soviet system, particularly in the years 1928 to 1936. It is to be remembered that even though Gorky was a writer first and foremost and a political or national figure second, he became involved in the political life of his country because of his abiding, if frequently naive and almost blind commitment to a radical "change" that would, he believed, inevitably bring a better future for his people.

CHAPTER 1

GORKY—THE FORMATIVE YEARS

I have come into the world to disagree.

M. Gor'kii, *Pesn' starogo duba*

Maxim Gorky or "Maxim the Bitter," the first so-called proletarian writer, was born Aleksei Peshkov on March 16, 1868,[1] in the old city of Nizhnii Novgorod. At the time, Nizhnii Novgorod had forty thousand inhabitants of mixed ethnic origin. Within a quarter of a century the population more than doubled, reaching ninety thousand in 1890. The rise in population was the direct result of the increased pace of industrialization that followed the emancipation of the peasants in 1861. At the beginning of the 1890s there were in Nizhnii Novgorod 311 industrial enterprises employing a total of 13,775 workers, with the Sormovo shipyards as the most important industrial enterprise.[2] Nizhnii Novgorod, like other Russian provincial cities in the nineteenth century, was for the majority of its inhabitants a squalid swamp of poverty and ignorance. The administration was poor and city amenities were primitive. The daily newspaper *Nizhegorodskii birzhevoi listok* (The Nizhegorod Financial Page) often reported the brutal beating of wives, the deserting of children, and the excess of cheap and wild entertainment.[3]

Gorky, like his friend V. I. Lenin, could not pride himself on having had a proletarian background. On his passport he was designated as *meshchanin* (burgher) and inscribed as member of the painters' guild. He belonged by birth to that class of Russian society that he came later to criticize, ridicule, and despise. His mother, Varvara Vasil'evna Kashirina, was the only daughter of Vasilii Vasil'ev Kashirin, who at the time of Gorky's birth was the prosperous owner of a dye-shop. Beginning as a Volga barge man, Kashirin had worked himself up to the position of fore-man and, having saved enough money, moved to Nizhnii Novgorod, where together with his two sons, Mikhail and Iakov, he established his shop. With money came honors: and Kashirin was chosen foreman of the dyers' guild, became a member of the city duma, and lived in a two-story house in the better section of the city. The ambition of the elder Kashirin to marry his daughter into the nobility suffered a severe blow when Varvara Ka-shirina eloped with Maksim Savateevich Peshkov, a newcomer to the town without family or connections. He had come from the city of Perm' and had been educated by his godfather in the art of carpentry.

Gorky's paternal grandfather had served in the army of Nicholas I and had risen to officer rank. But because of cruelty towards his subordinates, he was discharged and exiled to Siberia. Given the severe discipline in the army of Nicholas I, one can easily draw a very unflattering portrait of the old Peshkov. Maksim Savateevich, after several attempts to escape the tu-telage of his father, was befriended and educated by his godfather. The hard "school of life" did not seem to have scarred this capable, happy young man, whom the old Akulina Kashirina, Gorky's grandmother, ap-parently loved more than her own sons.[4]

Maksim Savateevich was a very skillful craftsman and only a few years after his marriage received the post of dock master in the city of Astrakhan', where he settled in 1871 with his wife and son. He was entrusted with the building of a triumphal arch to welcome Tsar Alexander II, and his work-manship showed great artistic ability.[5] An epidemic of cholera that swept through Astrakhan' from August to October 1871 affected the Peshkov household.[6] First to contract the dreaded disease was Aleksei, whom his father nursed back to health. Maksim Savateevich fell ill shortly after and did not recover. After his death Varvara Vasilievna Peshkova, with Aleksei and his infant brother, left Astrakhan' for Nizhnii Novgorod to rejoin her family. The infant died on the way.[7] On their arrival, Peshkova submitted a request for membership in the Nizhnii Novgorod painters' guild, classi-fying herself as a *meshchanka* of the Perm' province.[8]

The impact that the growing industrialization had upon the small crafts-man was well illustrated in the fortunes of the Kashirin household. At the time of his daughter's arrival, the economic situation of Kashirin had de-teriorated rapidly. This was not an uncommon phenomenon. According to statistical data, within a period of less than twenty years, the number of dye-shops in Nizhnii Novgorod declined from 136 to five.[9] Life in the Ka-shirin household was one of constant discord, and the environment was far removed from that of Gorky's father's home in Astrakhan'.[10] Gorky wrote later that he remembered life in his grandfather's house as a "grim fairy tale told by a good but painfully truthful genius."[11]

Gorky never wrote much about his mother's influence upon him. From his autobiography one can infer that he had a very deep love for her but that she resented his presence, blaming him for her misfortune, and that there never was an understanding between mother and son. After his father's death Gorky watched the slow disintegration of his mother's proud and strong personality, her unhappy marriage to "one from the gentry," the death of a son from that marriage, and her death from tuberculosis at the age of thirty-four.[12]

The only bright ray in the depressing and cruel life of the Kashirin family was provided by the grandmother, Akulina Ivanovna Kashirina. The daughter of a serf, she was trained in the art of lace-making and was famous both for her craftsmanship and her superior ability to retell folk-tales. She belonged to a peculiar Russian class of *skaziteli*, or narrators of folk-tales, and was a source of inspiration for her grandson.[13] Not satisfied with merely repeating the tales and songs, Akulina Ivanovna often composed her own. Gorky, who considered his grandmother his dearest confidant, later recalled the songs and ballads he learned from her:

It seems that until she came into my life I was as if asleep, hidden in the dark. But she appeared and woke me up, led me out into the light, tied all around me one unbroken thread, wove it into a multi-colored lace and became at once my friend for life, the closest, the dearest and the most understanding. Her selfless love for all creations enriched and fortified me for a hard life ahead.[14]

Except for the brief period of his mother's influence, Gorky's education was in the hands of the old Kashirin. His grandfather tried to rule the family with an iron fist in accord with the ancient code of Russian family life as written in the *Domostroi*. He taught young Aleksei Old Church Slavonic on the basis of the *Psaltyr'* and the prayer-book, as it was taught in the times of Moscow Rus'.[15] Gorky was enrolled in a parish school at the age of nine. One bright episode of his school days was the visit of Episcop Krisanov of Nizhnii Novgorod, who on examining the student was astonished by his remarkable ability to read, to recite prayers, and to retell folk tales.[16] At the end of his last term in school Gorky was awarded a certificate and a book prize, which he soon sold to provide his ill grandmother with money to buy food.[17] Aleksei's formal education ended rather abruptly at the age of ten because his now impoverished grandparents were unable to support him. His certificate, under the column "education," read: "did not finish school because of poverty."[18] The old and embittered Kashirin, having lost his wealth and with it his place in society, turned young Aleksei out of the house, remarking that he was "not a medal to hang around his neck" and that he had to fend for himself.[19] Thus began for Gorky the years of apprenticeship, later vividly described in the second volume of his autobiography *V liudiakh* (In the World).[20]

When Gorky began his apprenticeship in 1878, the economic situation in Russia was marked by a catastrophic decline of the small craft industries. At the same time machine industry was not developing rapidly enough to absorb the influx of the country population migrating to the cities. Thus, the pressure upon the worker became greater, and the unemployed and unskilled swelled the ranks of the *bosiaki*.[21] It was easy enough to lose oneself among these people, and great strength of character was required to withstand the pressure of the environment to which the young Aleksei Peshkov was exposed. He often wondered how he had succeeded in resisting the temptation to follow the line of least resistance and to become one of the inhabitants of the Millionka district in Nizhnii Novgorod.[22] Strong character and exceptional ability were, no doubt, decisive factors, but some attempt was made also by his grandparents to find him a place where he could learn a trade or a vocation.

His apprenticeship began in the shoe-store of the merchant L. M. Porkhunov, where Aleksei had to fulfill a double task of working in the store and helping out with the household chores. The experiment proved unsuccessful. He fared not much better when transferred to his uncle Sergeev, to learn the trade of draftsman. He had neither the ability to draw nor the desire to learn the trade. Besides, he disliked the oppressive atmosphere of the Sergeev household, where he felt people led dull lives devoid of any meaning. He ran away from Sergeev and found a place as a cook's helper on the Volga steamer "Dobryi."[23] The important influence upon him during this period was that of his superior, the cook Mikhail Antonov Smuryi, a retired noncommissioned officer and a great lover of books.[24]

The most popular books in Russia at that time were the sentimental French novels of the eighteenth century. Also, an important role in the education of the Russian reading public was played by the *tolstye zhurnaly* (thick journals), biweekly publications, and daily newspapers. Gorky himself had only occasional opportunities to read these. Having finished with the French writers, of whom he found Balzac the most interesting, Gorky began reading the Russian classics: Pushkin, Lermontov, Turgenev, and Dostoevsky, who opened for him the world of his own, the Russian people.[25]

He was thirteen years old when the activities of the People's Will culminated in the assassination of Tsar Alexander II. Gorky was unaware of the background to the regicide. Occupied with the sole task of survival and confined by the environment in which he was forced to live, he had little opportunity to learn about revolutionary movements. A prolonged ringing of bells announced to the Russian people the death of the tsar. Asked by

Gorky the reason for the tsar's assassination, the confused and frightened Sergeev answered, "that these are things forbidden to be discussed."[26]

Gorky's further efforts to find a place in society included his apprenticeship in an icon shop and work as a construction foreman for the Nizhnii Novgorod fair project. The work in the icon shop was monotonous, but the young apprentice tried to dispel the boredom of his fellow workers by readings and improvisations of theater-like performances. He met with little success.[27] Having left the icon shop, Gorky found that the position of a construction foreman afforded him the opportunity to meet craftsmen, most of whom were of peasant background. They had left their native villages to seek a better life in the city and often drifted away to join the homeless band in the Millionka district. It was this dreadful waste of human potential that concerned young Gorky, and he expressed these reflections on the social life of Russia when he wrote: "It is terrible to think how many good people perished in my lifetime. . . . All people wear out and die, this is natural; but nowhere do people wear out so quickly . . . as here, in our Rus'."[28]

He described his mood during this particular period thus: "At the age of fifteen I felt very unsure here on earth; everything seemed to be swaying under my feet . . . I was seeking and longing for some kind of truth, as hard and as straight as a sword."[29]

Gorky's religious experiences at the time were limited to what he had observed in his grandparents' home. He discovered very soon that his grandmother and grandfather prayed to two different gods. The God of Akulina Ivanovna was kind, merciful, and forgiving. Old Kashirin approached God with fear and trepidation; his God was omnipotent, stern, and vengeful. Little wonder that the sensitive Gorky found more affinity with the God of his grandmother.[30] Observing closely the life of people he met during the years of apprenticeship, Gorky saw the discrepancy between their religious beliefs and their secular practices and was repelled by their hypocrisy. In his autobiography he later wrote that he liked to go to church for its splendor and that the scent of incense reminded him of a fairy tale, but he seldom prayed:

It was uncomfortable to pray to grandmother's God repeating grandfather's prayers and weeping psalms; I was certain that grandmother's God would not have liked it, as I did not. Also, the prayers were all printed in books, and therefore God must have known them off by heart as all literate people did.[31]

In time, Gorky came to believe that the way out of the oppressive environment in which he lived was not through religion but through the acquisition of knowledge. Encouraged by one of his student friends, N. Evreinov,

Gorky left for Kazan', arriving there in the fall of 1884 with the aim of entering the university.[32]

His arrival in Kazan' coincided yet with another severe economic depression, which sent thousands of workers into the streets. Those still employed were working under appalling conditions. The period saw a serious strike movement, beginning with the strike in the Morozov factories in 1885. Approximately one-sixth (ca. 20,000) of the population of Kazan' lived the lives of *bosiaki*, and among them was the young Aleksei Maksimovich Peshkov. "I liked them," wrote Gorky later, "and according to the logic of my experiences it would have been natural for me to have joined them."[33] He lived for a while in the house of Evreinov and later shared one bed in a half-demolished house in the Marusovka district (a poor variant of the Latin Quarter) with another student, Gurii Pletnev.[34] The trying experiences of the Kazan' period convinced Gorky "that man is being molded by the struggle against his environment."[35] His dreams of entering the university were quickly shattered, and even the career of a village schoolteacher was out of reach because of the lack of money and of the difficulty in mastering the Russian grammar; only a strong desire to get to something better kept him afloat.[36] One can say that Gorky's conscious individualism and his interest in men able to fight their environment dated back to the Kazan' period. It was this latent interest that would later draw him to Lenin.

The formative years of Gorky's childhood and early youth now came to a close. From his birth in Nizhnii Novgorod in 1868, through his early years in the home of his grandparents, during his brief public school career, and while he was working at various apprenticeships, he was gaining experience and forming the attitudes that were to appear in the mature Gorky.

Ten years had passed since the famous "movement to the people," in which young men and women went into the villages to spread the gospel of the populists.[37] This gospel contained an ardent faith in the peasant commune, the belief that the *mir* (village commune) would provide the basic political unit for Russia's future social order and that the *artel'* (artisans' cooperative) was the best possible institution to conduct business and trade. It emphasized the unlimited potential of the *narod* (the people), who alone had the ability to affect the regeneration of Russian society. At the time of Gorky's arrival in Kazan', populism was spent as a social movement. Alexander III, guided by his tutor, the Ober-Procurator of the Holy Synod, K. P. Pobedonostsev, had begun a policy of repression, which he carried out consistently during the thirteen years of his reign. By 1883, all the twenty-four members of the executive committee of the People's Will responsible for the assassination of the tsar had been imprisoned or executed. The main journal of the populists, *Otechestvennye zapiski* (Annals of the Fatherland), was closed. Finally, in 1884, repressive measures were introduced in the field of education. Nevertheless, the activities of the populists continued, centered now on different goals.

The populists abandoned the idea that a revolutionary transformation of the political, social, and economic order could be achieved in Russia in the near future. Instead, they turned toward evolutionary work. This involved study in discussion "circles" and welfare work among the people. This was the period of *malye dela* (small deeds). Led by the dean of the movement, writer and publicist N. K. Mikhailovskii, many of the populists departed from the idolatry worship of the *narod* and from the idea of the "repentant nobleman," which stressed the debt incurred by the upper classes to the common man whom they had long exploited. Instead, Mikhailovskii put forward a critical approach toward the *narod* and advocated the idea that service to the people was to emanate from a sense of honor rather than of debt. But the belief that Russia could bypass the stage of capitalism and proceed to socialism based on the commune and the *artel'* still remained central to the creed. The *narodovol'tsy*, the members of the People's Will who succeeded in escaping from exile, returned to carry out essentially the same work as the populists, often meeting in the same circles.

Gorky was introduced to the work of the populists by A. S. Derenkov, whose home served as a meeting place in Kazan' for students and other interested members of the movement. The Derenkov family owned a grocery store that was in fact a cover for conspiratorial work, for behind it was a library well-stocked with illegal literature. For Peshkov, meeting Derenkov and other populists was, he wrote, important: "For the first time I saw people whose interests lay beyond the everyday care to satisfy their own needs, people who knew the life of the toiling masses, and who believed in the necessity and the possibility to change that life."[38] Some of the populists he met still believed in the inherent goodness and beauty of the *narod*. They stressed the importance of the peasant commune for the future of Russia and insisted that the Russian man was by nature *artel'nyi* (collectivist). It was necessary, maintained the populists, to expand the rights of the commune so that more people could join it. Although Gorky knew little of the life of the village, he favored the idea that the road to a better way of life was as simple as the populists portrayed it. It lay in joining a peasant commune.[39] Yet the question of whether the Russian man was a collectivist by nature remained unsolved for him. The problem that occupied Gorky all his life, the conflict between the individual and society, was made more acute, but remained unresolved by the social and political theories to which he was introduced in Kazan'.[40]

The picture of the commune as painted by the populists was in fact far removed from reality.[41] The Marxists, who came to dispute the populist ideology, maintained that the commune was in a state of disintegration. Peshkov was little acquainted with the controversy and eagerly accepted the ideas of the populists, but he could readily see the difficulties in trying to implement them: "We had to understand the peasant, this was most important. The idea was being preached by our literature . . . but a program of work was lacking."[42] He began taking part in self-education circles, an activity stimulated by government's repression in the field of education. There was also strict censorship. Among the forbidden books were the works of H. Spencer, N. A. Dobroliubov, D. I. Pisarev, N. K. Mikhailovskii, and N. G. Chernyshevskii. Many of the important journals were withdrawn. Libraries such as the one run by the Derenkov family were essential.[43]

The work in the circles centered around the reading of forbidden literature, followed by discussion. The members were also required to write papers. The meetings took place twice a week, and often as many as twenty members were present, the majority of whom were students. There Peshkov met a teacher named A. V. Chekin and a revolutionary, S. G. Somov, with whom he was later associated in Nizhnii Novgorod. One participant recalled the work in a Kazan' circle thus:

We assembled twice a week and we read. We started with the book of Golovachev, *Desiat' let reform* (Ten Years of Reform); we continued with Chernyshevskii's writing on [John Stuart] Mill, the articles of Lavrov, works of V. Vorontsov, and some of the writings of Marx in the articles edited by Ziber.[44]

The first assignment entrusted by Pletnev to the newcomer was to inform a certain party about an arrest in the Marusovka.[45] Although Gorky tried to convince his friend to initiate him in the more active clandestine work, he was unsuccessful. Thus encounters with the populists were not without pain for Gorky. He did not like being typecast as "a son of the people" and "felt as a pariah among them."[46] Some of the students reminded him of the sectarian dogmatists of the Volga region, whom he resented for their fanaticism.[47]

Gorky disliked reading Mill with the commentaries of Chernyshevskii because he failed to understand the arguments. However, he learned these lessons in economics in a practical way when working as a baker's aid in the shop of Vasilii Semenov.[48] For three rubles a month, he worked an unspecified number of hours, which left him with little time for reading or attendance at meetings. He later wrote that he became a Marxist not because he read the works of Marx but because of the lessons he was taught by the baker Semenov. The work in the bakery provided him with an opportunity to meet workers of peasant background who spoke with hatred about life in the countryside, thus contradicting his mentors, the populists. Leaving Semenov after an unsuccessful attempt to organize a strike at the shop, Gorky was employed in a bakery opened by the populists for the purpose of raising funds for clandestine activities. He, experienced now in the trade and trusted by the populists, was made manager.[49] The following description of the bakery was found in the report by the gendarmerie:

An enterprise opened with highly suspicious aims, the essence of which was impossible to determine. The shop was used as a meeting place for young students, who among other things occupied themselves with the reading of tendentious literature for the purpose of self-education . . . in which Aleksei Peshkov also participated.[50]

One of the most significant meetings that he attended during this period involved the discussion of G. V. Plekhanov's *Nashi raznoglasiia* (Our Differences), which was directed against the populists. The meeting was stormy and Plekhanov was branded a traitor by the majority of the participants. At that meeting, Gorky met N. E. Fedoseev, who was later credited with having organized the first Marxist circle in Kazan'.[51]

As populism began to be disputed, Marxist ideas came to influence sections of the Russian intelligentsia in the 1880s. Plekhanov's *Nashi raznoglasiia* was a pioneer work, in which Marxist thought was applied to Russian reality. His main tenets were that Russia had no distinct path of development from other countries, that capitalism had already begun in Russia, that the Russian peasant was not socialist by nature, and that the disintegration of the peasant commune was an indisputable fact. He advocated the establishment of a workers' party to be led by the revolutionary-minded intelligentsia, and in 1883 he founded in Geneva the first Russian Marxist organization, the Group for the Liberation of Labor. Among the writers who tried to present Marxist ideas to the Russian public were P. B. Struve and M. I. Tugan-Baranovskii. Both were later termed "Legal Marxists" to denote their emphasis on legal (as opposed to clandestine) means of spreading Marxist ideas. In 1899, V. I. Ul'ianov (better known as Lenin) published his first work, *Razvitie kapitalizma v Rossii* (Development of Capitalism in Russia), which dealt with the growth of capitalism in Russia.

Marxist circles were beginning to emerge as early as 1891, and in 1895 the Union for the Struggle for the Emancipation of the Working Class was formed in St. Petersburg. There is no evidence to support the assumption that Gorky was particularly interested at that time in the controversy between the Marxists and the populists. It is obvious that until the turn of the century he was primarily influenced by populist ideology. There is little evidence that Gorky came into contact with Russian liberals or members of the *zemstva*. A baker's environment was far removed from that of the progressively minded segment of the gentry, the mainstay of the liberal ideology at the time.

Conflicts of personal nature—the news of the death of his beloved grandmother and his failure to fulfil the aim that had brought him to Kazan'—

resulted in an attempted suicide in 1887.[52] Following recovery he was afforded the opportunity to learn about the actual work of the populists in
the village of Krasnovidovo when the populist M. A. Romas, impressed by
the personality of Peshkov, offered him a job in his store there.[53] The work
of education and propaganda that Romas conducted among a small circle
of peasants in the village did not follow the orthodox pattern of populism,
for he did not preach the idea that the peasant commune is the prototype
of the future socialist order or that collectivity was ingrained in the Russian
peasant, or that the peasant brought up by the commune should now be
prepared for revolutionary struggle. Instead, Romas wanted to educate the
peasant to organize and to protest against the arbitrariness of the police
and the administration. He wanted a democratically elected government
and political reforms.[54] United against Romas were the government authorities and the wealthy peasants of the village. After a period of six
months, these two groups forced Romas and Peshkov to leave. The peasants burned down the store, and the two propagandists were nearly killed.[55]
For Gorky, the unsuccessful experiment in Krasnovidovo was a severe
blow. It undermined his trust in the doctrine of the populists, and he became disillusioned with the peasants. From close observation, he came to
the conclusion that peasants were distrustful and unfriendly, "always afraid
of something," and that there was "something lupine in them."[56] He disliked life in the village, which he described as gloomy and joyless.[57] His
deep-seated distrust and criticism of the Russian peasantry, born from the
experience in Krasnovidovo, remained with him all his life and was later
expressed in his work *O russkom krest'ianstve* (On the Russian Peasantry),
written in 1922.

The Kazan' period ended for Gorky with the failure of the experiment
in Krasnovidovo. Although he had not succeeded in obtaining a formal
education, the years spent there were not lost.[58] The meetings in Derenkov's
store and in the bakery laid the foundations for Gorky, the *obshchestven-
nik*, "the social reformer." It evoked in him the realization of a close tie
with the life of the lower strata of Russian society and imbued him with
hope that life could be changed. Moreover, he met people who had sincere
intentions to change that life. "I often thought," wrote Gorky years later,
"that I heard my own unspoken thoughts in the words of the students, and
I regarded them with admiration, as a captive who was promised freedom."[59] He realized that the life of an individual could be changed only
with the transformation of the whole social and economic order. To the
problem of how this could be done, he had no answer. He questioned the
validity of the idealization of the *narod*, in spite of the fact that he was
trying to believe that such people existed in Russia. It was impossible for
him to accept blindly political theories handed down from above. He had
a peculiar way of perceiving abstract ideas and always tried first to relate
the abstract to some concrete phenomenon and only then to proceed to

apply inductive reasoning. This may be best illustrated in Gorky's understanding of the concept of the *narod*. He wrote:

When they spoke of the *narod*, I felt with astonishment and distrust in myself that on this point I could not think the way these people thought. For them the *narod* was an embodiment of wisdom, spiritual beauty, and benevolence, a god-like creature . . . I did not know that kind of *narod*. I have met carpenters, stone masons . . . I knew Iakov, Osip, Grigorii . . . but [the populists] spoke of the consubstantial *narod* and put themselves somewhat lower in dependence of its will.[60]

Gorky's years of wandering began in 1888 and lasted for five years. During this period, as he journeyed aimlessly from Kazan' to the Caspian to the Volga-Don region, he sought his place in life and attempted to assert his independence. He also sought the proper revolutionary path among the welter of radical ideologies then crying for followers in Russia. It was only in 1892 that he began to turn his attention seriously to his literary work, which ultimately became his principal occupation.

In the fall of 1888, he arrived at the shores of the Caspian Sea, where he worked in a fishermen's cooperative, and later in the year got work on the Griaze-Tsaritsynskaia railroad. There he succeeded in making contact with a number of political exiles. The management of the railroad, troubled by persistent thievery, engaged political exiles, who after their return from Siberia had been prevented from reestablishing themselves at their previous places of domicile. Thus the work on the railroad afforded Gorky an opportunity to meet with former members of revolutionary movements,[61] and to participate in circles that were organized by these political exiles.[62] By the spring of 1889, the work of "small deeds" became more difficult as a result of the tighter grip by the gendarmerie. Gorky now thought to establish an agricultural commune together with his newly acquired friends. He set out for Iasnaia Poliana, the estate of L. N. Tolstoy to ask for a grant of land. Tolstoy was not at home, but his wife, Sof'ia Andreevna, gave Gorky some tea and buns and told him that lately many homeless wanderers had been trying to see her husband and that Russia was full of such shady individuals.[63] The Tolstoyan agrarian communes had emerged in 1886. Their members were faithful followers of Tolstoy's teachings and set as their goals self-perfection and nonresistance to evil. Self-perfection, according to the teachings of Tolstoy, could only be achieved through close contact with the soil and physical labor. There is no evidence that Gorky accepted Tolstoy's ideas. He understood "Tolstoyanism" in a special way. For him the agrarian colony served practical rather than ideal means: to escape the life he led, to find a place where he would belong, and be able to ponder the question of what he wanted to accomplish in life.[64] That he was not ready to sit back and work toward self-perfection alone is evident

in the first poem he wrote while working at Krutaia station. Titled *Pesn'*
starogo duba (Song of the Old Oak), it says: "I have come into this world
to disagree."[65] The poem expressed the author's conviction that a supreme
effort on the part of the people was necessary in order to resurrect the
world "soaked in tears and blood."[66] Following his visit to Iasnania Poliana, he sent Tolstoy a letter requesting a grant of land and advice, which
remained unanswered. Similarly, his attempts to approach other populist
writers such as N. E. Karonin-Petropavlovskii and Gleb Uspenskii, who
advocated the establishment of agricultural communes by the intelligentsia,
were unsuccessful.[67] Following a brief stay in Kazan', Gorky returned to
Nizhnii Novgorod in the summer of 1889, after an absence of close to five
years.[68]

Nizhnii Novgorod in 1889 was a more exciting place than when Gorky
had left it. The unrest at several of the universities, including the University
of Kazan', brought a number of political exiles to the city. Some of the
exiles were Gorky's former friends: the schoolteacher Chekin, dismissed
from his position for political unreliability, and Somov.[69] Both Chekin and
Somov were under police surveillance, as was their apartment, where
Gorky now settled as a third member of the "commune." Revolutionary
activity still centered around the circles of the populists and the *naro-*
dovol'tsy. Three prominent members of the populist movement directed
their work in the city: the writer V. G. Korolenko; the head of the Department of Statistics, N. F. Annenskii; and a writer and medical doctor
employed by the *zemstvo*, S. I. Elpatevskii. Each in his own way was trying
to enlist the support of the progressive sections of the intelligentsia. Gorky
soon joined the circle led by Chekin. The program of study did not differ
much from that followed by the circles in Kazan'. Additions to the reading
list included F. Lassalle's *Rechi i Stat'i* (Speeches and Articles), Mikhailovskii's work *Chto takoe progress* (What Is Progress), P. L. Lavrov's *Istori-*
cheskie pis'ma (Historical Letters), and the *Communist Manifesto* of K.
Marx.[70] An interesting description of the young Aleksei Peshkov shortly
after his arrival is given by one of the members of the circle, Osip Vol-
zhanin:

He was tall, stooped, dressed in a coat-like jacket and high polished boots. His face
was ordinary, "plebeian," with a homely duck-like nose. By his appearance he
could easily have been taken for a worker or a craftsman. The young man sat on
the window sill, and swinging his long legs, spoke strongly emphasizing the letter
"O" . . . We listened with great delight to his stories, though Somov, an implacable
"political," disapproved of the stories and the behaviour of the young man. In his
opinion, the latter occupied himself with trifles.[71]

His first arrest by the tsarist police took place in October 1889. The
authorities in Nizhnii Novgorod, having discovered a new inhabitant in the

apartment of Chekin and Somov, followed Gorky's moves closely. General Poznanskii, the head of the local gendarmerie, suspected that Gorky was used by Chekin and Somov in spreading revolutionary propaganda. Dissatisfied with the reports of the local agents, Poznanskii asked for information about Peshkov from Tsaritsyn, Kazan', and Saratov. The answer indicated the extent to which he had now become politically suspect. The reply from Kazan' stated that Aleksei Peshkov had lived there from April 1887 to June 1888, further stating that Peshkov had been employed in the bakery of Derenkov, which served as a meeting place for members of revolutionary circles.[72] In addition, the report contained information about a search carried out in the house of a schoolteacher, N. A. Shcherbatova, a former associate of Peshkov at the time of his work in the bakery and a close friend of Mariia, Derenkov's sister. Among the papers of Shcherbatova were two items belonging to Peshkov, one a notebook containing handwritten passages from an article by Lavrov and the other *Sistematicheskii ukazatel' luchshikh knig i zhurnal'nykh statei 1856–1883 gg.* (An Index of Better Books and Articles Published in 1856–1883.) The report also made mention of Peshkov's several visits to Kazan'. For General Poznanskii the evidence showed that Peshkov provided a link between the politically suspect of Kazan' and of Nizhnii Novgorod.[73] Following a series of investigations, Gorky was arrested, but he was soon released for lack of sufficient grounds to detain him.[74] However, it was decided that Peshkov was definitely politically suspect, and he was put under police surveillance.[75]

The importance of Chekin's circle and Peshkov's participation in it was further confirmed when a dossier on Akim Chekin was found in the state archives of Georgia. The papers found there indicated that Chekin's circle had connections with other populist circles in the country. There was also evidence of close ties between Chekin's group and the populist leaders in Nizhnii Novgorod, Korolenko, and Annenskii.[76]

Although the police accounts made Gorky appear a revolutionary, his work in the circles of the populists was that of "small deeds." In fact, the whole period was that of small deeds, the slogan being "ours is not the time of great feats."[77] "Down with ideas" was the slogan of many of the members of the intelligentsia. Many of them believed that progress was predetermined by the course of history, deeming it unnecessary for them to try to effect change.[78] Gorky disagreed. He thought that the solution to the problem was greater immersion of the intelligentsia in the work of the people.[79]

An important event in Gorky's life during this period was his meeting with V. G. Korolenko, a prominent writer and a leader of the populists in Nizhnii Novgorod.[80] More than any other literary figure of the time, Korolenko extended a helping hand to Gorky, who long considered himself Korolenko's pupil. He sought from Korolenko an answer to the question of "What is to be done?" and advice on his first literary efforts. Korolenko subjected Gorky's work to severe criticism and advised him to write about his experiences. To the question of "What was to be done?" Korolenko answered that the thing most needed was justice, which he understood to mean the struggle against the vestiges of serfdom, which was to be led by the intelligentsia. The road to a better life was through evolutionary work of the "small deeds" kind.[81] Gorky, while not satisfied with Korolenko's answer, retained close ties with the writer.

In 1891 Gorky left Nizhnii Novgorod to escape the environment of petty squabbles and ideological sectarianism, similar that of the Kazan' circles.[82] In the autumn of that year he arrived in Tiflis (Tbilisi) after wandering through the Ukraine, Bessarabia, and the Crimea.[83] What exactly had brought him to Tiflis? Gorky later wrote that in the spring of 1891, depressed and lonely and unable to adapt himself to the environment of "the cultural people of Nizhnii Novgorod," he had set out on foot to go to France; unsuccessful in carrying out the plan, he ended up in Tiflis.[84] Here he made contact with some of his former friends from Nizhnii Novgorod, among whom was Olga Kaminskaia, the object of his first love; Gorky's arrival there could be thus explained. Yet this fact alone cannot account for the presence of several other members of Chekin's circle in Tiflis. One must infer that there were contacts between the populists of Nizhnii Novgorod and Tiflis.

Tiflis at the beginning of the 1890s was a thriving and fast-growing industrial center. Gorky found employment as a painter in one of the railway shops. He soon came in contact with political exiles and joined one of the circles led by them. The members were populists in orientation and confined their activities to study and discussion of current social and political problems. Gorky, with fellow worker Fedor Afanas'ev, organized a "commune" that served as a meeting place for students and workers but was of no significance in terms of revolutionary agitation. In a letter to his friend of the Kazan' days, Pletnev, Gorky noted: "I am sprinkling decent little ideas from the water pail of enlightenment with perceptible results."[85] Since Peshkov, the addressee, and others mentioned in the letter were under police surveillance, the letter was intercepted by the police and resulted in an inquiry sent from St. Petersburg concerning Peshkov's activities. The reply from Tiflis contained information about Peshkov, his work, and his association with Afanas'ev, mentioning also his role in conducting discussion groups among the students. It informed St. Petersburg that Peshkov was still under police surveillance.[86]

His literary work began in 1892, and from the middle of that decade it became his main occupation. While this latter period was marked by Gorky's diminished interest in revolutionary work, he still belonged to several circles, was twice arrested, and by virtue of his association with "politically unreliable elements," was under constant surveillance by the police.

In the autumn of 1892, Gorky left Tiflis for Nizhnii Novgorod. Before his departure, the name "Maksim Gor'kii" (Maxim the Bitter) appeared for the first time in the Tiflis newspaper *Kavkaz* (Caucasus), where his story *Makar Chudra* was published. It was based on the folk tales Gorky had heard during his wanderings through Bessarabia and the Crimea. He had been encouraged to set these down in writing by A. M. Kaliuzhnyi, in whose house he stayed after the Afanas'ev commune disbanded. Kaliuzhnyi, an exiled populist, recognized the young man's ability and asked him to write the stories he was able to tell so well.[87]

The intangible influence of Gorky the writer and publicist had now begun. A keen observer of Russian life, he could not, by virtue of his character and experiences, become a passive onlooker and painter of that life. In his idea of the writer's involvement in the social, political, and economic problems facing Russia, he was close to writers such as Tolstoy and Korolenko. Gorky, first instinctively and then philosophically came to regard literature as a weapon of social struggle. His contribution to Russian literature of the period was the realistic portrayal of life of the lowest strata of the Russian society. The heroes of his stories were the *bosiaki*, in whose souls Gorky had discovered the "spark of God." By their very existence and the stubbornness of their protest, they demanded a place in the society from which they felt alienated. Gorky did not ask for charity or help for his heroes, since he believed in their own power to fight for a better life. In his writings, which took many literary forms, Gorky painted a dark picture of society; his message then was easily detected. The order that had allowed such injustices, brutality, and ignorance had to be destroyed. Yet nowhere in his works did Gorky indicate what was to follow the destruction of the old order. Gorky's revolutionary ideology lay in his insistence on the inevitability of radical change in Russian society.[88]

Unlike the populist writers who made the peasant the center of their literature, Gorky drew his heroes from the cities. V. A. Desnitskii, Gorky's friend, biographer, and associate in the Capri school for underground party workers, commented on the *bosiatskii* period of Gorky's literary work:

We, the young Marxists, were interested in Gorky. . . . Evident in his early writings was a refreshing departure of the talented writer from the village to the city, from the traditional peasant of populism to the man of the city, even if only the *bosiak* and not the worker, but the *bosiak* with his contempt for the stagnant, old mode of life was for us a welcome herald of the new.[89]

His works began to appear in journals and newspapers of the provincial cities of Kazan', Samara, and Nizhnii Novgorod. With Korolenko's help some of the stories were published in the populist organ *Russkoe bogatstvo* (Russian Wealth). It is a myth, however, that Gorky became a famous writer overnight. In the year after the appearance of *Makar Chudra*, none of his works was published. Forced to work as a copyist for the lawyer A. I. Lanin, Gorky lived in great want. It was Korolenko who consistently supported the young writer, forever interceding on his behalf with editors and publishers in order to promote his works. Gorky later called that period in his life the *Vremia Korolenko* (The Time of Korolenko).[90] Occupied with the task of finding the necessary means of existence for himself and his common-law wife, Ol'ga Kaminskaia, Gorky had little time for involvement in revolutionary activity, but still the tsarist police did not relax its surveillance.[91]

One of the means to reach the Russian people and to criticize the life of the Russian provincial city was through journals and newspapers. With the general upward trend of the Russian economy in the last decade of the century, the number of newspapers and periodicals grew.[92] Gorky's career as journalist started in Samara in 1895, where he began writing for the *Samarskaia gazeta* (Samara Gazette). His task was to write a daily column in the section *Ocherki nabroski* (Essays and Sketches) and feuilletons that appeared under the title *Mezhdu prochim* (By the Way).[93] At the time of Gorky's arrival in Samara in February 1895, *Samarskaia gazeta* was edited by a journalist exiled from St. Petersburg, B. N. Asheshov. Gorky wrote under a mysterious pseudonym, "Iegudiel Khlamida,"[94] criticizing the exploitation of the workers, the arbitrariness of the authorities, corruption, and the dullness of the everyday life of the citizens of Samara. He tried to fight the battle of the poor by means of the newspaper, openly opposing the eviction of workers from one of the districts, which would have sent them into the slums. At another time he criticized the treatment of the workers by the owners of the mills. Even Korolenko asked Gorky for moderation in his criticism.[95]

Within a period of fourteen months Gorky published close to thirty stories and poems, 416 daily commentaries in *Ocherki i nabroski*, 185 feuilletons, and a number of articles. In March 5, 1895, Gorky's *Pesnia o sokole* (Song of the Falcon), written "in praise of the madness of the brave," appeared in the *Samarskaia gazeta* and became a favorite poem of the revolutionary intelligentsia.[96] In writing about the life of the Russian people, Gorky grew more and more pessimistic.[97] His criticism of society continued unabated. The rival newspaper, *Samarskii vestnik* (Samara Messenger), began publishing articles against him and went as far as to brand him decadent. Gorky decided to leave Samara. Plagued by poor health and financial difficulties as well as by dissension in the editorial office of the newspaper, he left for Nizhnii Novgorod, where he settled with his newly married wife, Ekaterina Pavlovna Volzhina. There, on Korolenko's recommendation, he began writing for the *Nizhegorodskii listok* (Nizhegorod Page) and also got a contract with the *Odesskie novosti* (Odessa News) to report on the forthcoming Nizhnii Novgorod fair.

The fair, the first to be held in the city since 1882, afforded an opportunity to widen the scope of his writings on political, social, and economic issues. He wrote under the pseudonym "Pacatus" (Peaceful), but still the note of criticism did not disappear from his publications. His contributions to *Nizhegorodskii listok* also meant a certain identification with the ideology of the populists, since the newspaper was dominated by them. The influence of the populists had grown since the disastrous famine of 1891. L. B. Krasin, one of the Marxist pioneers active in Nizhnii Novgorod and later a prominent member of the Russian Social Democratic Workers' Party (RSDWP), wrote of the predominant influence in the city of the populists, who tried to rally the support of the progressive-minded sectors of public opinion.[98] At the same time the number of Marxist circles increased.[99]

Gorky's attitude towards the populists during this period is difficult to define. The difficulty is increased by the complicated and often contradictory ideology of the young writer.[100] One critic of his ideas at the time noted: "[T]hat those who say 'that inherent to Gorky was a revolutionary mood and socialist ideals,' ignore the influence of the populists and see in Gorky an opponent of the ideology of populism from the very beginning of his career."[101]

In a way, Gorky's writings on the Nizhnii Novgorod fair published in *Nizhegorodskii listok* and *Odesskie novosti* show his stand towards the populist ideas in the 1890s.[102] He discussed the main tenets of the populists, developed them according to his own view of the contested issues, and although disagreeing with some of the aspects of their doctrine, identified with their ideology. He thus found a place for himself in their camp.[103] *Beglye zametki* (Brief Notes), published in *Nizhegorodskii listok*, are a mixture of journalism and literature whereby Gorky expressed his views on the question of the future of capitalism in Russia, on the small craft industries, on trade, on tariffs, on foreign investments, on culture, and on labor.

The problem of the future of capitalism in Russia was still a controversial issue between the Marxists and the populists. Closely connected with it was the problem of the place of small craft industries in the economic and social life of the country. Rejecting the Marxist dogma of inevitability in economic development, the populists stressed, as something distinctly Russian, the importance of the preservation of the old system of small craft industries organized in the form of the *artel'*. Gorky seemed to have sided with them on this issue, although his concern was perhaps motivated by aesthetic rather than economic considerations. He wanted protection for native arts and crafts and deplored the failure of the zemstva to help preserve them. Yet he readily admitted that there were certain areas of manufacture which the native craftsmen should leave for the manufacturer. Echoing the populists, he demanded both financial and vocational assistance for the small craft industry.[104] Gorky criticized the exaggerated notion of the "greatness" of Russia's industrial development, emphasizing rather its backwardness.[105] He voiced his criticism of increased foreign investments and considered Russia's low cultural level to be the main obstacle to economic development of the country.[106] He was opposed to S. I. Witte's policies of protectionism, which he considered to be an additional burden on the consumer with a low income. He further expressed dissatisfaction with the power the machine was acquiring over man. While the populists wanted to stop the advent of the machine, condemning all technical progress as evil, Gorky's main concern was with the fact that the machine was becoming a new means of exploitation.[107] He deplored the disregard that the organizers of the fair had shown toward the Russian worker, whose part in the economic development of the country went unacknowledged. Gorky saw the solution as having both the worker and the peasant led by the intelligentsia, stressing the beneficial influences of the educated stratum of the city dwellers and the officials of the *zemstva*.[108]

In May of 1898, Gorky found himself again in prison. The case of Fedor Afanas'ev, his friend from the Tiflis "commune," had come up in 1897. In a search of Afanas'ev's apartment, among the articles and proclamations, the Tiflis gendarmerie found a signed photograph of Gorky. Afanas'ev tried unsuccessfully to deny acquaintance with Gorky, but the authorities demanded Gorky's immediate arrest and transfer to Tiflis. A report sent to the Nizhnii Novgorod office of the gendarmerie on April 26, 1898, enumerated a series of Gorky's "crimes," including his membership in the Tiflis "commune" and allegations that Peshkov conducted propaganda of a social democratic nature during his stay there.[109] He was sent under police escort to Tiflis and imprisoned in Metekhskii fortress. In his testimony, he disassociated himself from Afanas'ev.[110] V. A. Posse, a journalist and publisher, succeeded in obtaining the intervention of N. A. Tagantsev, a member of the State Council. Because of a lack of evidence and the strong action taken by his friends, he was soon released. In August 1898, Gorky returned to Nizhnii Novgorod.[111] The Tiflis office of the gendarmerie, trying to justify its actions, continued to draw up accusations against him. The St. Petersburg police, however, remained unconvinced.[112]

Posse, who had earlier recognized the potential of the young writer and had helped to publish some of his works in the monthly review *Novoe slovo* (New Word), was instrumental in the publication of a collection of Gorky's stories. The book appeared in the fall of 1898 and marked the beginning of Gorky's success as a writer.[113]

The year 1898 was also important in the history of the RSDWP, for it was in March of that year that the first congress of the party took place in Minsk. There is no indication in Gorky's correspondence that he was aware of the event. In any case, it did not appear any more important at the time than the other organizational meetings of various parties that had been taking place during the second half of the nineteenth century. That it was an important event in the history of Russia no one at that time could have foreseen.

NOTES

1. The following practice has been adopted with regard to dates: until Gorky's departure in 1906, dates are given in the old style, according to the Julian calendar in force in tsarist Russia and then in the Soviet Union until February 14, 1918; for the period from 1906 to 1913, the dates appear here in both the old style and the new (according to the Gregorian calendar in use in the West). From Gorky's return in December 1913 and until February 1918, the old style alone is used. From the latter date, the new style alone is used. A slight departure from this method is to be found in the footnotes, where dates of newspapers are often given in both styles.

2. S. Murashov, *Leninskaia "Iskra" i Nizhegorodskaia organizatsiia bol'shevikov* (Moscow, 1956), 9.

3. I. A. Gruzdev, *Gor'kii i ego vremia, 1868–1896*, 3rd ed. (Moscow, 1962), 20; see also M. Gor'kii, *Sobranie sochinenii v tridtsati tomakh*, vol. 13 (Moscow, 1949–1955), 19–81. Hereafter referred to as *Sobranie sochinenii*.

4. Gor'kii, *Sobranie sochinenii*, vol. 13, 158.

5. Evidence now available indicates that Alexander II did not visit, but only passed through Astrakhan' in 1871. *Astrakhanskii spravochnyi listok*, 125 (1871), quoted in Gruzdev, *Gor'kii i ego vremia*, 7, 555.

6. *Astrakhanskie gubernskie vedomosti*, quoted in Gruzdev, *Gor'kii i ego vremia*, 7.

7. Gor'kii, *Sobranie sochinenii*, vol. 13, 41.

8. A. Belozerov, "Iz molodykh let Maksima Gor'kogo," *Novyi mir* 3 (1926): 115–116.

9. *Pomiatnye knizhki Nizhegorodskoi gubernii na 1847, 1855 i na 1865 Gody*, quoted in Gruzdev, *Gor'kii i ego vremia*, 9. The reason for the decline in the number of dye-shops was the advent of factory-made goods.

10. Gor'kii, *Sobranie sochinenii*, vol. 13, 41.

11. Gruzdev, *Gor'kii i ego vremia*, 11.

12. Gor'kii, *Sobranie sochinenii*, vol. 13, 201.

13. Gruzdev, *Gor'kii i ego vremia*, 11.

14. Gor'kii, *Sobranie sochinenii*, vol. 13, 15. See also Gruzdev, *Gor'kii i ego vremia*, 12; Gor'kii, *Sobranie sochinenii*, vol. 30, 33.

15. Gor'kii, *Sobranie sochinenii*, vol. 13, 66.

16. Gor'kii, *Sobranie sochinenii*, vol. 13, 179–181.

17. Gor'kii, *Sobranie sochinenii*, vol. 13, 196.

18. Gor'kii, *Sobranie sochinenii*, vol. 13, 516; Il'ia Gruzdev, *Gor'kii*, 2nd. ed. (Moscow, 1960), 12.

19. Gor'kii, *Sobranie sochinenii*, vol. 13, 202.

20. Gor'kii, *Sobranie sochinenii*, vol. 13, 203–511.

21. *Delo* 2 (1879): 174, quoted in Gruzdev, *Gor'kii i ego vremia*, 15.

22. The Millionka district in Nizhnii Novgorod was the habitat of the *bosiaki*.

23. Gor'kii, *Sobranie sochinenii*, vol. 13, 277.

24. Gor'kii, *Sobranie sochinenii*, vol. 22, 270–271.

25. Gor'kii, *Sobranie sochinenii*, vol. 13, 357.

26. Gor'kii, *Sobranie sochinenii*, vol. 13, 337.

27. Gor'kii, *Sobranie sochinenii*, vol. 13, 358–365.

28. Gor'kii, *Sobranie sochinenii*, vol. 13, 358–365.

29. Gruzdev, *Gor'kii i ego vremia*, 55; Gor'kii, *Sobranie sochinenii*, vol. 13, 504.

30. Gor'kii, *Sobranie sochinenii*, vol. 13, 85.

31. Gor'kii, *Sobranie sochinenii*, vol. 13, 266–267.

32. The date of Gorky's arrival in Kazan' has been erroneously quoted as 1885, 1886, and 1887. It has been established, however, on the basis of events that took place while Gorky was there, that he arrived in the autumn of 1884. See Gruzdev, *Gor'kii i ego vremia*, 585: Akademiia Nauk SSSR. *Letopis' zhizni i tvorchestva A. M. Gor'kogo*, 4 vols. (Moscow, 1958–1960, 39. Hereafter referred to as *Letopis'*.

33. P. Maksimov, *Vospominaniia o Gor'kom: Perepsika i vstrechi* (Moscow, 1956), 13.

34. G. A. Pletnev (1864–1922), a student at Kazan' University, was also connected with the circles of the populists and later with the Marxist circle of N. E. Fedoseev. Gorky settled with Pletnev in the Marusovka district in October 1884. See Gor'kii, *Sobranie sochinenii*, vol. 13, 520.

35. V. Rudnev, *Gor'kii revoliutsioner* (Moscow, 1929), 4; Gor'kii, *Sobranie sochinenii*, vol. 13, 516.

36. Rudnev, *Gor'kii revoliutsioner*, 4.

37. James H. Billington, in his work *Mikhailovsky and Russian Populism* (London, 1958), 120, sees in populism a deeply religious basis: "No inner understanding of this impassioned movement of secular protest is possible without an appreciation of its deeply religious basis . . . populism can be said to represent for Russia a unique form of protesting if not Protestant Christianity."

38. Gor'kii, *Sobranie sochinenii*, vol. 13, 535–536.

39. Gor'kii, *Sobranie sochinenii*, vol. 13, 586–587; vol. 28, 5–6.

40. Rudnev, *Gor'kii revoliutsioner*, 5.

41. Gruzdev, *Gor'kii i ego vremia*, 101.

42. Gor'kii, *Sobranie sochinenii*, vol. 13, 348.

43. Gruzdev, *Gor'kii i ego vremia*, 10; A. S. Derenkov, "Iz vospominanii o velikom pisatele," *M. Gor'kii v vospominaniiakh sovremennikov*, ed. A. S. Miasnikov (Moscow, 1955), 79; Gor'kii, *Sobranie sochinenii*, vol. 13, 532–538.

44. Gruzdev, *Gor'kii i ego vremia*, 111.

45. Gor'kii, *Sobranie sochinenii*, vol. 13, 526–537.

46. Gor'kii, *Sobranie sochinenii*, vol. 13, 536.

47. Gor'kii, *Sobranie sochinenii*, vol. 13, 535.

48. Rudnev, *Gor'kii revoliutsioner*, 12; Gruzdev, *Gor'kii i ego vremia*, 112.

49. Gor'kii, *Sobranie sochinenii*, vol. 13, 553.

50. Bor. N-skii [Boris Nikolaevskii], "'Pervoe prestuplenie' M. Gor'kogo," *Byloe* 16 (1921): 177. The organization of populists in Kazan' conducted its work in a highly conspiratorial manner. The members of the various circles were students of Kazan' University and the Theological Academy. The participants of these circles, having completed their course of study, usually left Kazan' to organize circles in

other centers of the Volga region. The organization was established in 1884 but started to decline by 1889. It ceased to function in 1892. The majority of its members became *Kulturtraegers* and later, with the revival of the revolutionary movement, joined the Socialist Revolutionaries or the Constitutional Democrats. Evidently, both Derenkov's bakery and the store of Romas in Krasnovidovo were affiliated with the populists in Kazan'. See I. S. Mitskevich, *Revoliutsionnaia Moskva* (Moscow, 1940), 45; N. Ia. Bykhovskii, "Bulochnik Aleksei Maksimovich Peshkov i kazan'skaia revoliutsionnaia molodezh' kontsa 80-kh godov," *Byloe* 34 (1926): 212–214.

51. N. E. Fedoseev was a prominent revolutionary Marxist. He died in 1898 at the age of twenty-eight, having spent eight years in prison and exile. Lenin valued Fedoseev's work and felt that his role in spreading Marxist ideas was of great importance. V. I. Lenin, *Polnoe sobranie sochinenii*, 5th ed., 55 vols. (Moscow, 1958–1965), XLV, 324–335; M. G. Grigor'ev, "Vospominaniia o Fedoseevskom kruzhke v Kazani," *Proletarskaia revoliutsiia* 8.20 (1923): 61.

52. Gor'kii, *Sobranie sochinenii*, vol. 13, 585; Gruzdev, *Gor'kii i ego vremia* 132.

53. N-skii, "Pervoe prestuplenie M. Gor'kogo," 186.

54. Romas later joined the party of *Narodnoe pravo*. Organized toward the end of the 1880s, the *Narodnoe pravo* (The People's Right) insisted that people's rights were political as well as social and economic. The members of this group emphasized the importance of political freedom as the prerequisite for the establishment of socialism. By 1894 the police had succeeded in seizing the press and arresting most of the leaders. The party was destroyed before it began to function. Billington, *Mikhailovsky*, 158–159.

55. N-skii, "Pervoe prestuplenie M. Gor'kogo," 185–186; Gor'kii, *Sobranie sochinenii*, vol. 13, 624–628.

56. Gor'kii, *Sobranie sochinenii*, vol. 13, 604.

57. Rudnev, *Gor'kii revoliutsioner*, 24.

58. In his literary work, the Kazan' period is portrayed in the stories *Khoziain* and *Byvshie liudi* and in the autobiographical work *Moi universitety*.

59. Rudnev, *Gor'kii revoliutsioner*, 15; Gor'kii, *Sobranie sochinenii*, vol. 13, 536.

60. Gor'kii, *Sobranie sochinenii*, vol. 13, 538. See also Rudnev, *Gor'kii revoliutsioner*, 24.

61. Gruzdev, *Gor'kii i ego vremia*, 181.

62. See V. Rudnev, "Gor'kii revoliutsioner," *Novyi mir* 3 (1928): 191; *Arkhiv*, vol. II, 100–103; A. Kaun, "Maxim Gorky and the Tsarist Police," *Slavonic and East European Review* 8 (1930): 643.

63. *A. M. Gor'kii i V. G. Korolenko: Perepiska, stat'i, vyskazyvaniia* (Moscow, 1957), 134–135; Gruzdev, *Gor'kii i ego vremia*, 214–216, 635–638.

64. Gruzdev, *Gor'kii i ego vremia*, 27.

65. Gor'kii, *Sobranie sochinenii*, vol. 24, 489.

66. Gruzdev, *Gor'kii i ego vremia*, 214.

67. See Gruzdev, *Gor'kii i ego vremia*, 241, 636–638; Gor'kii, *Sobranie sochinenii*, vol. 28, 5–6. For details on N. E. Karonin-Petropavlovskii (1853–1892), see Gor'kii, *Sobranie sochinenii*, vol. 10, 289, 292–293.

68. The police reported that according to secret information: "Aleksei Peshkov

in the last days of May was for a short while in Kazan', but the aim of his visit as well as the place he stayed at was impossible to determine." Tsentrarkhiv, *Revoliutsionnyi put' Gor'kogo* (Moscow, 1933), 21.

69. Gorky wrote later of Somov that he was a typical "nihilist" who believed in the power of physical sciences and wanted to apply the laws of physics to social psychology. N-skii, "Pervoe prestuplenie M. Gor'kogo," 184–186.

70. Mitskevich, *Revoliutsionnaia Moskva*, 49.

71. Gruzdev, *Gor'kii i ego vremia*, 220–221.

72. The police in Kazan' obviously had no record on Gorky for the period 1884–1887. Gorky arrived in Kazan' in the fall of 1884.

73. Tsentrarkhiv, *Revoliutsionnyi put' Gor'kogo*, 19–21; N-skii, "Pervoe prestuplenie M. Gor'kogo," 174–186; Rudnev, *Gor'kii revoliutsioner*, 31–32. See also B. Piradov, "K istorii rannikh sviazei A. M. Gor'kogo" (Gruziia, 1891–1892)," *Stat'i o Gor'kom: Sbornik* (Moscow, 1957), 2–89.

74. Tsentrarkhiv, *Revoliutsionnyi put' Gor'kogo*, 18–19.

75. Evidently, Somov was connected with the newly founded Marxist circle of Fedoseev in Kazan', and his arrest was a direct result of the uncovering by police of the activities of that circle. N. L. Sergeevskii, "Fedoseevskii kruzhok 1888–1889 gg.," *Krasnaia letopis'* 7 (1923): 296. Gorky called Fedoseev a "capable student of Somov." Gruzdev, *Gor'kii i ego vremia*, 229.

76. Piradov, "K istorii," 4, 8.

77. Gor'kii, *Sobranie sochinenii*, vol. 24, 424.

78. Gor'kii, *Sobranie sochinenii*, vol. 15, 25.

79. Gor'kii, *Sobranie sochinenii*, vol. 13, 306; vol. 15, 26–27.

80. V. G. Korolenko (1853–1921) was a prominent member of the populist movement and one of the most socially minded writers of the period. He was also the editor of *Russkoe bogatstvo* (Russian Wealth).

81. *Gor'kii i Korolenko* 158–59; Gor'kii, *Sobranie sochinenii*, vol. 15, 15, 30, 31.

82. Gor'kii, *Sobranie sochinenii*, vol. 15, 103.

83. Gor'kii, *Sobranie sochinenii*, vol. 17, 185, 205; vol. 15, 34–35.

84. Rudnev, *Gor'kii revoliutsioner*, 194. Piradov, "K istorii," 8; E. Zamyslovskaia, "Iz vospominanii," *Gor'kii v vospominaniiakh sovremennikov*, A. S. Maksimov, ed. (Moscow, 1955), 144.

85. Gor'kii, *Sobranie sochinenii*, vol. 28, 6–7; Tsentrarkhiv, *Revoliutsionnyi put' Gor'kogo*, 26–27.

86. Tsentrarkhiv, *Revoliutsionnyi put' Gor'kogo*, 28–29. Two other letters intercepted by police were found in Rostov on the Don. One of them referred to a "visit of shining buttons." Aesopian language for the police. Tsentrarkhiv, 40.

87. A. M. Kaliuzhnyi, "Staryi drug (Vospominaniia o Gor'kom)," *Izvestiia* 28 March 1938, 73; A. Nestorova, "M. Gor'kii i A. M. Kaliuzhnyi," *M. Gor'kii: Materialy i issledovaniia*, vol. 1, V. A. Desnitskii, ed.; vol. 2, S. D. Balukhatyi and V. A. Desnitskii, eds.; vol. 3, S. D. Balukhatyi and V. A. Desnitskii, eds.; vol. 4, V. A. Desnitskii and K. D. Muratova, eds. 4 vols.; vol. 1 (Moscow-Leningrad, 1934–1951), 229. Gorky never forgot his help, and thirty years later wrote to Kaliuzhnyi: "You were the first person to have forced me to look at myself seriously. I am indebted to you for the fact that for thirty years now I have been serving Russian literature." Gor'kii, *Sobranie sochinenii*, vol. 29, 446–447.

88. Melkhior de Vogüe, *Maksim Gor'kii* (St. Petersburg, 1902), 24–46.

89. Rudnev, *Gor'kii revoliutsioner*, 38. Gorky wrote later that his predilection to write about the *bosiak* was caused by the desire to portray "unusual people" and not those of the *meshchane*. Gor'kii, *Sobranie sochinenii*, vol. 24, 498.

90. *Gor'kii i Korolenko*, 134–160.

91. L. M. Farber, "Novye materialy ob M. Gor'kom, 1896–1903," *Gor'kovskie chteniia 1961–1963* (Moscow, 1964), 290.

92. N. M. Lisovskii, *Bibliografiia*, as quoted in Gruzdev, *Gor'kii i ego vremia*, 472.

93. Tsentrarkhiv, *Revoliutsionnyi put' Gor'kogo*, 25.

94. A. Kaun maintains that according to a legend Iegudiel Khlamida was "an apocriphal priest, the only one of the twelve priests at the trial of Jesus to pronounce him not guilty." A. Kaun, *Maxim Gorky and His Russia* (London, 1932), 236.

95. Gor'kii, *Sobranie sochinenii*, vol. 23, 23, 43; K. Muratova, *M. Gor'kii: "Mezhdu prochim"* (Kuibyshev, 1941), 311; Gor'kii, *Sobranie sochinenii*, vol. 23, 23, 26, 37, 71; I. Gruzdev, "Literaturnaia bursa M. Gor'kogo," *Novyi mir* 4 (1928): 159–161.

96. The Soviet historian E. Iaroslavskii, at an evening devoted to the memory of Gorky in 1941, said that shortly after its publication, *Pesnia o sokole* was distributed in millions of copies. He further stated that "the two poems, *Pesnia o sokole* and *Pesnia o burevestnike*, had no less revolutionary influence upon the masses than the leaflets of the various revolutionary party committees." Tsentrarkhiv, *Revoliutsionnyi put' Gor'kogo*, 10. See also Gruzdev, *Gor'kii i ego vremia*, 450.

97. *Gor'kii i Korolenko*, 45.

98. Murashov, *Leninskaia "Iskra,"* 16.

99. M. G. Grigoriev, "Marksisty v Nizhnem 1888–1894 gg.," *Proletarskaia revoliutsiia* 4 (27) (1924): 96; Murashov, *Leninskaia "Iskra,"* 16.

100. Farber, "Novye materialy," 75–76, asserts that Gorky accepted the Marxist creed during that period. See also V. Borshchukov, "U istokov sotsialistichekogo realizma," in *Stat'i o Gor'kom: Sbornik*, 89–202, *passim*.

101. I. K. Kuzmichev, "Gor'kii publitsist i narodnik," *Uchennye zapiski Gor'kovskogo pedagogicheskogo instituta* (Gor'kii, 1961), 19.

102. Gor'kii, *Sobranie sochinenii*, vol. 23, 139–255.

103. I. Gruzdev, "Gor'kii i kapitalizm," *Oktiabr'* 2 (1934): 168–87.

104. Gor'kii, *Sobranie sochinenii*, vol. 23, 146.

105. Gor'kii, *Sobranie sochinenii*, vol. 23, 198–221.

106. Gor'kii, *Sobranie sochinenii*, vol. 23, 221.

107. Gor'kii, *Sobranie sochinenii*, vol. 23, 159, 160.

108. Kuzmichev, "Gor'kii publitsit," 34.

109. Tsentrarkhiv, *Revoliutsionnyi put' Gor'kogo*, 29.

110. Tsentrarkhiv, *Revoliutsionnyi put' Gor'kogo*, 32–36.

111. Tsentrarkhiv, *Revoliutsionnyi put' Gor'kogo*, 36, 38; V. A. Posse, *Moi zhiznennyi put'* (Moscow, 1929), 146–147.

112. E. Klein, "Gor'kii i tiflisskaia zhandarmeria," in *Katorga i ssylka* 6 (43) (1928): 7–19; Rudnev, *Gor'kii revoliutsioner*, 35.

113. By the end of 1903 close to half a million volumes of Gorky's works had appeared in print. See N. I. Stechkin, *Maksim Gor'kii* (St. Petersburg, 1904), 3.

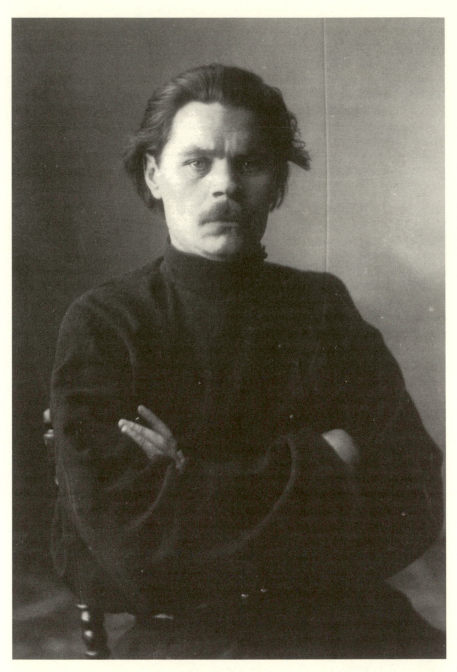

M. Gorky—The Nizhnii Novgorod Period 1901–1902. Reproduced courtesy of Gorky Archives of the Institute of World Literature, Moscow.

CHAPTER 2

THE SUCCESSFUL WRITER AND THE FLEDGLING REVOLUTIONARY

Young man—a person with a program has somehow always reminded me of a log.

Materialy i issledovaniia, II, 179

To the question whether Gor'kii was, during the Nizhegorodskii period, a fully consistent Social Democrat, in accordance with theory, I have to answer—as strange as it may seem—both yes and no. . . . Why? If this should serve as a suitable answer, it can be explained on the basis of his stormy nature, the equanimity which he had shown during those years towards pure theory, towards theoretical discussions, and finally, in that he is a wonderful artist not only in his creation but also in life.

V. A. Desnitskii, *M. Gor'kii*, 47

In Gorky's life, the years 1898–1904 were important ones in his career as a writer and publicist, and it was during this period that he began to participate more actively in revolutionary work, especially in the work of the Social Democrats (SDs). He was still unable to identify himself fully with one particular ideology and readily extended his assistance to other parties and causes. These years are often referred to as the Nizhegorodskii period, since on his return from Tiflis, Gorky settled in Nizhnii Novgorod.

The publication in 1898 of the first volume of his short stories made Gorky one of the most read and discussed writers in the country. Some criticized his choice of heroes and themes, but others saw in his works something new and refreshing. Gorky emerged as the champion of the underdog; his stories were seen as a protest against the existing social and economic order and as a revolt of the individual rising to defend his rights. He continued to be closely watched by the authorities. There is little doubt that they would have liked to have taken stronger measures against the rebellious writer, but Gorky's great popularity precluded this kind of action. Revolutionary work did not take all of Gorky's time, but the artist's stormy nature prevented him from following consistently one narrow path. His friend, Posse, the publisher of the journal *Zhizn'* (Life), described a meeting between Gorky and a student during the unrest at the University of St. Petersburg in 1901. Gorky was questioned by the student about his allegiance to a particular party program. Looking owlishly at his guest, he replied, "A person with a program has somehow always reminded me of a log."[1] In the first years of the Nizhegorodskii period, he devoted much of his time to educational and welfare work. Lenin had once expressed his doubts as to the possibility of saving Russia through work in committees on illiteracy. Yet Gorky was doing just that kind of work among the people of Nizhnii Novgorod, appearing at lectures, conducting discussions, building libraries, and organizing educational and welfare societies.[2] In the Russia of the early 1900s this work was of great importance, but whether it could solve the basic ills of Russian society was another question.

Russian society at the turn of the century was facing a number of problems of a political, economic, and social nature. As the century industrialized at an accelerated pace, the autocratic rule of Nicholas II became more irrelevant; and the tsar, after his ascension to the throne, had quickly dispelled all hopes of reform. With the assistance of foreign investors, rapid strides were made in industrialization. The growth of machine industry brought in its wake all the social ills characteristic of early stages of an industrial revolution. Plagued by unemployment, the lack of adequate housing, and absence of effective labor laws, for his protection, the worker was paying a high price for Russia's growth as an industrial power. The situation in Nizhnii Novgorod was no different from that in other industrial cities of the empire.[3]

The triumph of industrialization in the form of private and state capitalism made discussion between the populists and the Marxists obsolete. The populists' argument that capitalism could be bypassed in an agrarian country such as Russia and that industry could be built by socialism was no longer plausible. The Marxists were attracting few from the ranks of the populists but were winning a number of followers from among the uncommitted intelligentsia.

Gorky, at the beginning of Nizhegorodskii period, remained aloof from revolutionary work. Having emancipated himself from the tutelage of the populists, he preferred to remain independent of the Social Democrats, the

Socialist Revolutionaries (SRs), and the various shades of liberals who were organizing during this period. His work as a writer, publicist, and publisher occupied most of his time, and he was eagerly sought as a contributor to journals and newspapers. In 1898, the journal *Zhizn'* began to appear, and in November of that year, Gorky was invited to write for it.[4] His association with *Zhizn'* continued until the journal was closed in 1901.

During his first visit to St. Petersburg in 1899, he was introduced to the intellectual elite of the capital: the leading Legal Marxists, P. B. Struve and M. I. Tugan-Baranovskii, and a number of other prominent writers. But these encounters proved a disappointment. Gorky criticized the futility of discussions about the relative merits of Marxism and populism (which were still going on) and the irrelevancy of these to the problems and needs of the people. Reporting to Chekhov on the visit, he commented:

I do not understand all this. I will tell you that I do not think much of the Petersburg journalists. I think that all their parties are a thing of little importance. These people are far more motivated by egotistic aims than by the desire to build a new free life on the debris of the old, the narrow.[5]

Not endowed by nature with diplomatic ability, Gorky did not hesitate, during a banquet arranged in his honor by Posse, to voice openly his criticism of the intelligentsia and of contemporary literature. Replying to a highly laudatory speech in his honor, he answered by insulting the distinguished audience with "among the blind, the one-eyed is king" (*na bezrybie i rak ryba*).[6] One observer noted that "at the banquet" Gorky "exploded" loudly, abusing those things before which people have been accustomed "to burn incense" and branding the intelligentsia and men of letters as bourgeois, stagnant, and vulgar, like the lowest of the low.[7] Those present were outraged by such "blasphemy," but to the writer of the these comments, Gorky's words seemed like a revolutionary call. Gorky's resentment of the intelligentsia was also caused by personal considerations, for he was never made to feel an equal among them. Writing to his wife about the St. Petersburg visit, Gorky remarked that "they [the intelligentsia] came to look at me as if I were an alligator, or a person with two heads."[8] His ambivalent attitude towards the intelligentsia was to remain with him all his life: On one hand he was drawn toward them, because he believed that they had the power to lead the Russian people toward freedom, but on the other he was repelled by their failings and hurt by their condescending treatment of him.[9]

Gorky, the writer and journalist, emerged during this period as a champion against injustice, arbitrariness of police, and all forms of curtailment of men's freedom. One of his concerns was the treatment of Jewish citizens in the Russian empire. In an open letter to A. S. Suvorin, editor of the influential paper *Novoe vremia* (New Times), Gorky condemned the paper's stand on the famous Dreyfus case. This was followed by the little-known sketch, *Pogrom*, written in 1901. In a savagely realistic manner, it portrays an anti-Semitic riot that Gorky had witnessed in Nizhnii Novgo-rod in 1887.[10] His further endeavors on behalf of the Jews included attempts to publish works by Jewish writers, providing financial support to needy Jews in the Pale of Settlement, and paying for the education of a number of Jewish students.[11] In 1902, he adopted Zinovii Sverdlov, one of these students, in order to facilitate the boy's entry into the conservatory.[12] Gorky's further condemnation of the treatment of the Jews in Russia came after the Kishinev pogrom, which was carried out by the "Black Hundreds" with the quiet consent of the police in the spring of 1903. It left forty-five dead and several hundred wounded, evoking cries of indignation both at home and abroad. In an article entitled "Po povodu Kishenevskogo po-groma" (On the Kishinev Pogrom), Gorky condemned the actions of the Russian people, the government, and the "enlightened" circles of society.[13]

It was during the Nizhegorodskii period that he formulated his strongly humanistic philosophy in the work *Chelovek* (Man) and his play *Na dne* (The Lower Depths). "Man," wrote Gorky, "is everything. He even created God.... Man's ability to achieve perfection is infinite."[14] One of the greatest needs of man was freedom of thought and expression, a need of far greater importance than freedom of movement.[15] This philosophy did not solve for him the question of God and His place in the life of man. His feelings on the matter are expressed in correspondence with friends. To V. S. Miroliubov, he wrote, "You see, I understand and value religious feelings, the passion of seeking God. I know the power of that passion. We will be indebted to its creative work for the renewal of life."[16] Emphasizing the inherent need for God, Gorky wrote Chekhov, "I have the feeling that people are stupid. They need God so that they can live more easily and yet they reject Him and ridicule those who affirm God.... God is necessary, Anton Pavlovich. What do you think?"[17]

Gorky himself queried the existence of God, and in writing to L. Andreev in January 1902, he expressed his doubts thus: "There is no God, Leonid; there is a dream about Him, there is an external, unsatisfied striving in one way or another to explain life to oneself. God is a convenient explanation of all that happens around, and that is all."[18] At the end of the letter, there is an indication that Gorky was devising his own solution to this dilemma: "We will create for ourselves a God, a great one, a wonderful and joyful one."[19] He reaffirmed that only man exists and that man created God in his image. "How can you accept something foreign," wrote Gorky to Posse, "when you are yourself God ... and the source of all wisdom and all evil?"[20] It is difficult to ascertain whether Gorky was acquainted at the time with the philosophy of Feuerbach, who differed from Marx and Lenin by stressing that religious beliefs are inherent in the nature of man and therefore necessary. It seems that Gorky accepted the idea of the necessity of religious experience, but he sought it outside organized religion and later went to the extent of trying to create his own.

In criticizing the various religious societies that were emerging in Russia at the turn of the century (notably the mystical god-seekers of D. Merezhkovskii), Gorky attacked the hypocrisy of their beliefs and used the opportunity to voice his criticism of the political system of Russia. Thus he questioned the need for a Christ in a society where the policeman was ruler and the need for a church to instill discipline when there were Cossacks to perform that task.[21] His quest for a religion persisted, beginning with the experiences in his grandparents' house and extending to his encounters with members of the Orthodox Church, sectarians, hermits and holy men and to the last stage, that of god-building. In the last stage, in spite of an effort to make god-building rational, it appeared as a confused and mystical faith.

In 1901, Gorky's active involvement in revolutionary work began. The department of the police received special information from one of its agents, who reported that "Peshkov, as many others, is successfully combining legal work with conspiratorial activity."[22] A letter, intercepted by the police in 1901, noted that "Gorky is now becoming a social reformer of the new and young Russia."[23] Gorky had established contact with revolutionary circles and had overcome his negative attitude towards Marxism, even though he did not become an orthodox Marxist.[24] He attended illegal meetings in the offices of *Zhizn'*. When the journal was closed by the authorities, its editor, Posse, remarked that this was a result of Gorky's actions rather than his publications in the journal; the police acknowledged that one of the reasons for the closure of *Zhizn'* was that many of its contributors were politically suspect. Special mention was made of Peshkov and his friends, the writers S. G. Skitalets and E. N. Chirikov.[25] Referring again to Peshkov, the police reported that revolutionary life in Nizhnii Novgorod, at a standstill during his absence, had again revived. Together with Skitalets, Gorky was accused of propagandizing the workers of Sormovo.[26]

Many of Gorky's activities at this time were connected with the Marxists and his leanings toward Marxism became known among his populist friends. Korolenko, on meeting his wayward pupil after a lapse of five years, queried him about being a Marxist. Gorky replied that he was coming close to it.[27] To the populist poet P. Iakubovich (Melshin), he admitted that he read *Iskra* (Spark) and found it interesting. His road to Marxism, like his road to populism, was practical and emotional rather than scientific. Perhaps he, like P. B. Akselrod, one of the founders of Russian Social Democratic Workers' Party (RSDWP) saw in Marxism "A liberating force for living and suffering men."[28] Programs that demanded only political reforms could not satisfy Gorky. He would, if necessary, be ready to assist liberals bring out a change in Russia's method of government, but the sine qua non of a new system had to include economic and social change as well. Although he helped them on occasion, he could not join the Socialist Revolutionaries (SR) because of his deep-seated distrust of the peasant and his dislike of the SR's use of terror.[29]

The RSDWP, which based its hope for the future on the worker, was the party of social and economic change. Thus Gorky shared more affinity with it than with any of the other parties that emerged at that time. Gorky was well acquainted with most of the members of the first committee of the RSDWP in Nizhnii Novgorod, although he himself was not a member. The party leadership exploited Gorky's sentiments by enlisting his assistance in the publication of the *Iskra*, which was both an ideological and organizational center. The paper was smuggled into Russia, reprinted in specially established printing shops, and then distributed among the party committees. By 1901, nearly a dozen agents of *Iskra* lived in Russia and were directed from abroad by Lenin, I. O. Martov, and N. K. Krupskaia. Thus mimeograph machines and printing shops were important for the publication of *Iskra*. At one point the Nizhnii Novgorod committee of the RSDWP asked Gorky to acquire a mimeograph machine with his friends Skitalets and Z. Sverdlov, member of the committee. A close watch by the police through the offices of the gendarmerie in St. Petersburg was established. Soon Gorky was arrested along with Skitalets and Sverdlov.[30] Under section 1035 of the Criminal Code, Gorky was accused of "drawing up, printing and distributing proclamations aimed at inciting the workers to anti-government activities in April and May of this year."[31] A search of Gorky's and his colleagues' apartments did not uncover any incriminating evidence since neither the mimeograph nor the revolutionary proclamations were found. Instead, a so-called revolutionary poem, "To the Tunes of the Marseillaise," and a copy of the *Oproverzhenie pravitel'stvennogo soobshcheniia sostavlennoe M. Gor'kim* (Denial of the Government's Communiqué Written by M. Gorky) were seized among Gorky's papers.[32]

The "Denial" was a result of Gorky's involvement and concern with student affairs and the actions of the government. It was Gorky's protest against the stand taken by the authorities at a student demonstration on March 4, 1901, near the Kazan' Cathedral in St. Petersburg. This demonstration was a manifestation of growing student unrest and dissatisfaction with university policy. Discontent had increased after the government published, in July 1899, the "Temporary Regulations." According to these, students could be punished for demonstrating against the authorities by being drafted into the army regardless of their circumstances. Sharp student protests took place when, in December 1900, 183 students of Kiev University were drafted for taking part in a student meeting.[33] Gorky was greatly concerned over the issue and wrote extensively about what he considered to be a violation of the rights of the individual, and he asked that his influential friends intercede on behalf of the Kiev students.[34]

Gorky witnessed the student demonstration at Kazan' Cathedral of March 4, 1901. He later described it in a letter to his wife:

It is five o'clock in the evening. I have just returned from the demonstration at the Kazan' *sobor*. It began at twelve o'clock and is still continuing. The crowd is huge— 12,000 to 15,000. Of these, 2,000 to 3,000 are actively participating in the demonstration, while the rest are sympathizers. I cannot tell you all about it, for I am overwrought. . . . [The Cossacks] lashed with whips in the *sobor* and on the parvis . . . among those beaten were Annenskii and Peshekhonov. . . . There were thirteen dead . . . close to one thousand were arrested, among them Struve and Tugan-Baranovskii.[35]

Following the events, a protest against the actions of the authorities was signed by forty-three prominent writers and journalists. Among the signatories was Gorky.[36] In response to the publication of a distorted official report on the demonstration, Gorky wrote his "Denial of the Government's Communiqué."[37] It read:

We declare that on March 4, the police were stationed on the Nevskii . . . and did not prevent the people from gathering in front of the cathedral. . . . We declare that the police and the Cossacks had been secretly stationed since early morning in private courtyards and that Kleigels [general and military governor of St. Petersburg] was planning a trap for the students. . . . We believe that the students were provoked by the police to assemble, and that the leaflets and the invitations issued to the students originated in the offices of the Okhrana. . . . We declare that the Cossacks and not the students were first to start the scuffle, . . . that the Cossacks grabbed women by their hair and beat them with whips. . . . The writers Peshekhonov and Annenskii were beaten in the presence of Prince Viazemskii, a member of the State Council. . . . Society must protest police terror and the murder of its children.[38]

On the basis of the "Denial" and other incriminating evidence, Gorky was imprisoned in April 1901. After spending a month in the Nizhnii Novgorod prison, he was released on grounds of poor health[39] and because of the intercedings of his influential friends, among them L. N. Tolstoy. His release from prison, however, did not mean complete freedom. He was put under house arrest, his correspondence was scrutinized, and he was forbidden to reside in Nizhnii Novgorod.[40]

Because Gorky was too dangerous to be ignored, yet too popular to be dealt with harshly, the tsarist government seemed at a loss in handling his case. The proofs of Gorky's popularity were the many demonstrations in Nizhnii Novgorod by workers and members of the intelligentsia who protested the forced exile of the writer. Lenin wrote an article, "Nachalo demonstratsii" (The Beginning of the Demonstration) in which he condemned the action taken by the authorities against Gorky, whose only crime lay in the defense of free speech.[41] Exiled from Nizhnii Novgorod, Gorky was allowed to go to the Crimea in order to restore his health, which had deteriorated greatly during his imprisonment. The authorities, apprehensive of other demonstrations similar to the one in Nizhnii Novgorod, forbade him to stop in Moscow and instructed the governors of the provinces that lay on Gorky's route to take all necessary measures in order to prevent any kind of demonstration. The authorities, however, were unsuccessful in carrying out these orders, since crowds greeted Gorky with cries "Long live Gorky, the bard of Freedom exiled without investigation or trial."[42]

On his return from the Crimea, Gorky settled in Arzamas, a provincial town south of Nizhnii Novgorod. Police surveillance continued. His home was closely watched, and agents sent detailed reports on his activities to the offices of the gendarmerie.[43] Gorky continued his educational work among the people in the countryside and retained close contact with some of the members of the Nizhnii Novgorod committee of the RSDWP. He gave assistance several times to the cause of the Party. One of these occasions concerned the defense of the leaders of the Sormovo demonstration who were imprisoned and awaiting trial. This demonstration, which took place on May 1, 1902, involved more than 5,000 workers and resulted in numerous arrests. Gorky extended considerable financial help for the defense of those arrested.[44]

The RSDWP was, at this time, mostly interested in obtaining Gorky's financial help, since its income from membership dues was not sufficient to cover growing expenditures. The transporting, reprinting, and distribution of the *Iskra* required considerable sums of money, thus making the Party dependent on benefactors sympathetic to the cause.[45] A. I. Helphand, a Party member under the name of Parvus, devised a plan to provide the Party with funds. In the summer of 1902, he established in Munich the *Verlag*, a publishing house with a dual purpose: to protect abroad the rights of Russian authors and to bring funds to the Party. The protection of the rights of Russian authors could only be achieved through the publication of small editions of Russian works in Germany, thus establishing a claim for legal protection that was otherwise lacking, because Russia was not a member of the Bern copyright convention of 1886. To draw Gorky into the project, Helphand traveled to Russia in the summer of 1902. He met with Gorky at the railway station in Sevastopol and suggested that the Party receive some of the funds from Gorky's royalties from the sale of his works abroad. According to the agreement concluded between Helphand on behalf of *Verlag* and Gorky on behalf of the *Znanie* publishing house, Helphand was to look after Gorky's copyrights in Western Europe and receive twenty percent of the profit from sales of his works. The remainder was to be apportioned between Gorky and the Party at a ratio of twenty-five percent for Gorky and seventy-five percent for the Party. The enterprise, however, proved to be a failure. Neither Gorky nor the Party received the money, since it was either spent by Helphand or lost when the *Verlag* went bankrupt. Efforts to salvage something from this project dragged on for years, and the matter was in fact never cleared up.[46]

A further attempt to obtain Gorky's assistance was made by the members of the Moscow committee of the RSDWP in October 1902. The Moscow office of the Okhrana included in its report the contents of an intercepted letter that described that meeting.[47] It told of Gorky's expressed sympathy towards the RSDWP, his recognition of *Iskra* as the best of the revolutionary papers, and Gorky's offer of financial help. The letter detailed further the agreement concluded with Gorky concerning funds. Gorky promised to contribute to the Party a yearly sum of 5,000 rubles, of which 4,000 were earmarked for *Iskra*. Gorky indicated that he wanted to stay in contact with the people he had met and hoped that he would be able to enlist the assistance of his wealthy and influential friends. At the meeting, he donated a sum of 400 rubles to the Party treasury.[48]

His work on behalf of the RSDWP was in some measure due to the contacts with M. F. Andreeva, the actress of the Moscow Art Theatre and later Gorky's second (common-law) wife. Gorky and Andreeva met in 1900 in the Crimea during the tour of the Moscow Art Theatre. By 1902, he was spending much of his time in the capitals, and when in Moscow he was a frequent visitor in Andreeva's home. She assumed leading roles in his plays. A published collection of Andreeva's memoirs, letters, and documents explains little of the complicated question of their relationship, which has received only brief mention in the Soviet works on Gorky. Andreeva is referred to as Gorky's second wife by a civil marriage contracted in 1904. But this information is misleading, for Gorky was never formally divorced from his first wife, E. P. Peshkova. He and his first wife parted in 1904 but remained close friends to the day of Gorky's death. E. Peshkova retained custody of their two children, son Maxim and daughter Ekaterina (Katia). Since Gorky could not be married to Andreeva, she remained, in fact, Gorky's common-law wife until after the October Revolution. Soviet writers are rather hesitant to admit this fact for fear of tarnishing Gorky's image. Gorky and Andreeva were in contact with some of the members of the RSDWP as early as 1902, and from 1903 on they carried out together certain tasks on behalf of the Party. Much like Gorky's, Andreeva's work consisted of organizing fund-raising concerts, participating in the illegal organization of the Red Cross, safeguarding illegal literature, and securing passports and jobs for party members in hiding: "My part was a very minor one—I collected and obtained funds for the Party and fulfilled those tasks which were entrusted to me by the more experienced and important members of the Party. That was all."[49]

Examining closely Gorky's work for the RSDWP during this period, one finds that it was of considerable importance. Desnitskii, a member of the Nizhegorodskii committee of the RSDWP, characterized Gorky's work thus:

Gorky's assistance to the Party took different forms. It consisted of financial help systematically paid every month, technical assistance in the establishment of printing shops, organizing transport of illegal literature, arranging for meeting places, and supplying addresses of people who could be helpful.[50]

Gorky did not strive to assume any official position within the ranks of the Party and remained by and large on its fringes. A writer first, he expanded his talents to encompass an ever-growing field of activity including playwriting, editorial work, and publishing. He could not surrender his freedom to the hierarchy of a party machine, nor did he wish to become involved in questions of party theory and program. It is of interest that the famous split in 1903 at the Second Party Congress, which resulted in the emergence of two factions, the Bolsheviks and the Mensheviks, found no echo in Gorky's writings.[51]

The year 1904 brought to a close the Nizhegorodskii period in Gorky's life. He moved to St. Petersburg, where he retained contacts with Party members and with the transfer of illegal literature. The offices of the Okhrana carefully documented all Gorky's moves and recorded his contributions and services to the Party.[52]

The disastrous war with Japan, which began in February 1904, increased the revolutionary mood and activity in the country. Gorky's attitude toward the war was not different from that of wide sections of the Russian population. The slogan "the worse the better" was a common cry, indicating that the greater the defeats at the front, the greater the probability that the tsar and his government would be compelled to grant concessions to the people. Gorky ridiculed the attitude of some of the members of the ruling classes who considered the revolutionary upsurge in the country as the work of "some 10,000–15,000 rebels who incited the Russian people."[53] He was greatly concerned over the loss of life and the suffering that the war was causing.

As disaster followed disaster at the front, the possibility of government concession was growing, but Gorky was still rather skeptical about the kind of reforms the government would be ready to grant. He considered reforms granted from above to be useless and not long lasting—a fact that, he maintained, the Russians should have learned from their history.[54] Doubting the successful outcome of the demands for reforms presented by the liberals, Gorky nevertheless wrote for the liberal newspapers and journals, following with interest the work of some of the more active zemstvos.[55] The ambivalence of Gorky's attitude towards liberal reforms becomes obvious: he maintained that he had no faith in reforms granted from above, yet he seemed to be satisfied with the progress the liberals were making and even enthusiastic about the success of the meetings of the zemstva.[56] Perhaps Gorky's stand could be best explained by his desire to see first a change in Russia's system of government that would lead to further reforms, and he welcomed the involvement of the educated and influential sectors of the Russian society in the cause of such reforms.

The years from 1898 to 1904 marked Gorky's great triumph, for not only was he one of the most widely read writers in Russia, but he was known as well to many Western European audiences. Through the medium of writing he became a spokesman for the lower class of the Russian society. It was as if Gorky and the Russian proletariat had been born at the same time. His writings contained a bitter indictment of the ineptness, servility, and narrow-mindedness of the *meshchanstvo*. At the same time he praised mankind, whose powers and possibilities he saw as limitless. In writing to Andreev, in December 1901, Gorky maintained that the times required literature to be full of joy, of life, and of the heroic; he felt that literature, as an art, had to be of service to man, fostering belief in oneself and in the ultimate triumph of truth. It was this conviction that lay behind the fact that so much of Gorky's literary work had a political significance. The role of art, according to Gorky, was not only to satisfy mankind's aesthetic needs but also to help its strivings to break the old and to build the new forms of existence.[57] Perhaps the best definition of what Gorky considered to be the task of literature is contained in his letter to the writer N. D. Teleshov:

The aim of literature is to help man to understand himself, to strengthen the trust in himself, and to develop in him the striving towards truth; it is to fight meanness in people, to learn how to find the good in them, to awake in their souls shame, anger, courage; to do all in order that man should become nobly strong.[58]

Among Gorky's works completed in the Nizhegorodskii period, in addition to a number of short stories, were two novels, *Foma Gordeev* and *Troe* (The Three); three plays, *Meshchane* (The Burghers), *Na dne* (The Lower Depths), and *Dachniki* (The Summer Folk); and, of special significance to the revolutionary intelligentsia, the poem "Pesnia o burevestnike" (The Song of the Stormy Petrel).[59] Together with the previously written "Pesnia o sokole" this poem was read, recited, and often included in revolutionary leaflets. Gorky was now dubbed "the herald of the oncoming storm" (*bureglashatel'*).

In the novel *Foma Gordeev*, Gorky described the nascent class of the Russian bourgeoisie, portraying that class as degenerate. In the novel *Troe*, he wrote of three men seeking their place in life; only one, the hero, found fulfillment among the workers. The play *Meshchane*, as the title indicates, depicted the self-satisfied, narrow-minded environment of the *meshchan-stvo*. In juxtaposition to the *meshchanin*, the worker is a "new" man full of energy and optimism and capable of effecting the desired change in Russian society. Even though the authorities regarded the play as tendentious, it was passed by the censor. Performances in the provincial cities were often accompanied by demonstrations.[60]

Na dne, written also during this period, was first performed in December 1902 in Moscow, and quickly became a very popular play in the repertoire of theaters at home and abroad. Its theme—the utmost degradation of human lives—was placed in juxtaposition with the concept of the greatness of man and his search for truth.[61] A third play, *Dachniki*, which contained a bitter indictment of the bourgeois intelligentsia, was first performed in 1904. In spite of the fact that both the author and the play were booed by the audience, Gorky called the premiere of *Dachniki* the best day of his life because the people who had so strongly objected to the theme of the play had apparently understood the message he was trying to convey.[62]

Gorky's popularity was enhanced by the so-called incident with the Imperial Academy of Sciences, that took place in the spring of 1902. Within a period of a few months, he was elected an honorary member of the Academy; the elections were then canceled, the procedure for future elections was altered, and Gorky was asked to return the official notification of the election; the tsar found it necessary to intervene.

The "incident" began in February 1902 when, during a meeting of the department of literature of the Imperial Academy, Maxim Gorky's name was included in the list of candidates for academy membership submitted to the chairman. According to tradition, it was customary to choose as candidates men of maturity and moderate political views. Thus, by the standards set by the Academy, Gorky did not fit into the community, for he was just thirty-four years old, had been engaged in literary work for a period of only ten years, was classified as a mere *meshchanin* and a member of the painters' guild, was politically suspect, and finally, had been accused of "rebellion against higher authorities."[63]

Nonetheless, his candidacy was sponsored by three members of the Academy: the writer V. G. Korolenko, the literary critic V. V. Stasov, and K. K. Arsenev of the journal *Vestnik Evropy* (The Messenger of Europe). When the votes were counted Gorky had received the highest number. The results came as a surprise to the electors, the press, and the government. Gorky's election was an indication of his great popularity. The official communiqué concerning the election was published in the *Pravitel'stvennyi vestnik* (The Government Herald) and an announcement of Gorky's election appeared in the newspaper *Novoe vremia* (New Times).[64] Following the official announcement, the chairman sent Gorky a personal letter that read: "My sincere appreciation of your work prompts me to nominate you as an active member of the oldest Russian literary society, which once saw in its ranks Pushkin and Gogol, and at present is proud to include Leo Tolstoy as a member."[65] It is important to note that the police added a comment on the newspaper clipping that announced Gorky's election: "Brought to testify on the accusation of conducting revolutionary propaganda among the workers and is under special police surveillance."[66]

The Minister of the Interior, N. M. Sipiagin, submitted to Tsar Nicholas the announcement of Gorky's election to the Imperial Academy along with a statement of the police on his political unreliability. The Tsar wrote in the margin (in his usual laconic style), "Most surprising!"[67] and proceeded to take steps to nullify the election. In a letter addressed to the Minister of Education, P. S. Vannovskii, Nicholas II wrote on March 5, 1902:

The announcement of the election of Gorky as a member of the Imperial Academy of Sciences had upon me, as upon all right-thinking Russians, a most distressing effect. What the wise men were guided by in that election is difficult to understand. Neither Gorky's age nor his works provide enough ground to warrant his election to such an honorary title. Much more serious is the circumstance that he is under police surveillance. And the Academy is allowing, in our troubled times, such a person to be elected! I am deeply dismayed by all this and entrust to you to announce that on my orders, the election of Gorky is to be cancelled. I hope somehow to sober the heads of the members of the Academy.[68]

Involved in the case were the President of the Academy, the Minister of Interior, the Minister of Education, the head of the department of literature of the Academy, the editor of the influential newspaper *Grazhdanin* (Citizen), and the Tsarina. The authorities were greatly concerned about the warm response Gorky's election received in the provinces.[69] The *Saratovskii vestnik* (Saratov Herald) wrote that the secret of Gorky's success lay in the fact that he was both a member and a spokesman of the new social class that was emerging in Russia. Nevertheless, on March 13 *Pravitel'stvennyi vestnik* published an announcement that "[I]n view of the circumstances unknown to the general meeting of the department of literature of the Imperial Academy of Sciences, the election of Aleksei Maksimovich Peshkov (pseudonym Maksim Gor'kii) . . . is declared null and void."[70]

Shortly afterward, the major newspapers in the country carried the news of the nullification of Gorky's election. In order to defend itself against rising criticism, the department of literature of the Academy declared that anyone accused of political unreliability was not eligible for an official post in the Academy. Many prominent writers and friends of Gorky voiced their protest against the actions of the Academy. Korolenko resigned his membership in August and Chekhov in September, while the dean of the Russian writers, Tolstoy, maintained that since he did not consider himself a member of the Academy, he saw no need to take any action whatsoever. Finally, in May 1902, the statutes of the Academy were changed, making it necessary for the president to have the list of candidates approved by the authorities before an election could take place.[71]

Nicholas's light dismissal of Gorky's works had little influence on the attitude of the literary critics. In trying to explain Gorky's meteoric rise to fame, the critic D. V. Filosofov, who was no friend of Gorky's, wrote that the passion for Gorky's works had a psychological explanation, for they appeared at a time when Russia had just begun to awake, touching the deep chords of human nature that met with immediate response. After the appearance of the first edition of Gorky's stories, the critic A. L. Lipovskii wrote in *Russkii vestnik* (Russian Messenger):

There is no journal or newspaper that has not written about him [Gorky]; he is the object of discussion among old and new readers . . . the multitude of critical essays devoted to the work of the young writer that have appeared within one year point to the importance of that writer.[72]

The dean of the populists, Mikhailovskii, wrote that Gorky's talent and power of observation were beyond doubt, but that the major flaw in his works was his unfavorable portrayal of peasant life. The symbolist poet N. Minskii also sensed Gorky's talent and considered the main theme of his works to be the desire for an elemental kind of freedom. An attempt was made by critics to find in Gorky's works the influence of the German philosopher F. Nietzsche[73]; such influence Gorky denied vehemently: "The accusation that I was influenced by Nietzsche is unjust; I was a man from the masses, and the creed of masters which Nietzsche preached in his philosophy did not entice me."[74]

A vituperative attack on Gorky's works was contained in the work *Maksim Gor'kii*, by N. I. Stechkin, who deplored Gorky's great popularity. Stechkin considered Gorky's writings to be a revolutionary torch, and Gorky a herald of destruction. He concluded that if Gorky's influence prevailed, a new *pugachevshchina* would follow.[75] Following Stechkin, the literary critic Melkhior de Vogue branded Gorky an anarchist who had no principles.[76] Opposing Stechkin and others who stressed the destructive aspects of Gorky's writings were critics who considered Gorky an outstanding writer with constructive political views. To this group of critics, his writings were not merely an expression of a new morality of *bosiachestvo* mingled with some aspects of social democracy.[77] Some critics tried to see in Gorky's works an attempt to portray the true Russian character, maintaining that his heroes, the *bosiaki*, bore the inherent characteristics of the Russians and expressed their insatiable rebelliousness. Since in every Russian, including the educated, there rested the spirit of Mikhail Bakunin, it was easy for Russians to understand Gorky and to be influenced by his writings.[78] Gorky in his writings followed the tradition established by writers such as Chernyshevskii, Dobroliubov, and Korolenko, giving expression to social protest against existing conditions. Through the portrayal and bitter indictment of Russian life and the belief in the infinite ability of man to accomplish great deeds, Gorky contributed in no small measure to the awakening of the spirit of the Russian people.

The end of the Nizhegoroskii period marked a new beginning for Gorky, both in his personal life and in his revolutionary work. Within the six years spent in Nizhnii Novgorod he became a famous writer whose works were read at home and abroad; he had means and influence; and he was sought by the various political parties and groups in Russia. Gradually, he came closer to the RSDWP. In 1917, he wrote in the newspaper *Novaia zhizn'* (New Life) that for seventeen years he had considered himself a Social Democrat but that he had never refused aid to other parties. Meanwhile, the situation in Russia was characterized by an increasing revolutionary mood, but the government was unable to control the revolutionary tide. Again, Gorky refused to remain a passive onlooker and soon found himself immersed in the events that culminated in the Revolution of 1905.

NOTES

1. V. A. Posse, *Moi zhiznennyi put'* (Moscow, 1929), 242; S. D. Balukhatyi and V. A. Desnitskii (eds.), *M. Gor'kii: Materialy issledovaniia*, II, 179.

2. V. Rudnev, *Gor'kii revoliutsioner* (Moscow, 1929), 39. For Gorky's educational and welfare work during this period, see Gor'kii, *Sobranie sochinenii*, vol. 28, 94–95, 143, 146–147, 475, 570.

3. V. P. Fadeev, *Revoliutsionnoe dvizhenie v Nizhnem Novgorode i Nizhego-rodskoi gubernii, 1900–1904 gg.* (Moscow, 1957), 8. There were in the city and in the suburbs close to 500 factories employing a labor force of 40,000 workers. The average wage of the Nizhnii Novgorod worker was under 176 rubles a year, and was lower than that paid in the larger centers such as Moscow and St. Petersburg.

4. *Zhizn'*, a literary, scientific, and political journal, was an organ of the Legal Marxists.

5. Gor'kii, *Sobranie sochinenii*, vol. 28, 56.

6. Akademiia Nauk SSSR, *Arkhiv A. M. Gor'kogo* (Moscow, 1939–1995), V: 66–67. Hereafter referred to as *Arkhiv*.

7. Tsentrarkhiv, *Revoliutsionnyi put' Gor'kogo* (Moscow, 1933), 41; Rudnev, *Gor'kii revoliutsioner*, 42, as cited in A. Kaun, *Maxim Gorky and His Russia* (London, 1932), 319.

8. *Arkhiv*, V: 66.

9. The exception was the period after the October Revolution, when Gorky felt that it was his duty to save as many of the intelligentsia as he could, both for humanitarian considerations and because they constituted a cultural element in a sea of ignorance. For the intelligentsia, Gorky appeared at that time as the only spokesman on their behalf, and even then he was subject to much criticism and abuse (see Chapter 6).

10. The riots began on June 7, 1887, on the allegation that the Jews had kidnapped a Christian child. See I. A. Gruzdev, *Gor'kii i ego vremia, 1868–1896*, 3rd ed. (Moscow, 1962), 586–594; *Materialy i issledovaniia*, I, 23–31.

11. Gor'kii, *Sobranie sochinenii*, vol. 27, 183, 200.

12. Zinovii Sverdlov (Peshkov) died recently in France. He was the twin brother of Yakov Sverdlov, a well-known Bolshevik. Zinovii Peshkov rose to the rank of general in the French army and before his retirement was the French Ambassador to Japan. Gorky retained contact with Zinovii all his life.

13. The article remained unpublished in Russia. A hectographic copy found its way into Gorky's police dossier. See Tsentrarkhiv, *Revoliutsionnyi put' Gor'kogo*, 80–82; "Daty zhizni i deiatel'nosti A. M. Gor'kogo," *Krasnyi arkhiv* 5 (78) (1936): 56. See also Boris Souvarine, "Gorky, Censorship and the Jews," in *Dissent* 1 (1965): 83–85.

14. Gor'kii, *Sobranie sochinenii*, vol. 28, 101–102.

15. Gor'kii, *Sobranie sochinenii*, vol. 28, 102. A. Serebrov [A. N. Tikhonov], *Vremia i liudi: Vospominaniia 1898–1905* (Moscow, 1960), 153.

16. Gor'kii, *Sobranie sochinenii*, vol. 28, 222.

17. *Gor'kii i Chekhov: Perepiska, stat'i, vyskazyvaniia* (Moscow, 1951), 83.

18. *M. Gor'kii i L. Andreev: Neizdannaia perepiska* (Moscow, 1956), 369.

19. *Gor'kii i Andreev*, 369.

20. Gor'kii, *Sobranie sochinenii*, vol. 28, 170.

21. Gor'kii, *Sobranie sochinenii*, vol. 28, 211–212.

22. Rudnev, *Gor'kii revoliutsioner*, 197.

23. Rudnev, *Gor'kii revoliutsioner*, 197.

24. Posse, *Moizhiznennyi put'*, 242.

25. Tsentrarkhiv, *Revoliutsionnyi put' Gor'kogo*, 51. Gorky had contributed at least 4,000 rubles.

26. Sormovo was a suburb of Nizhnii Novgorod.

27. *Gor'kii i Korolenko: Perepiska, stat'i, vyskazyvaniia* (Moscow, 1957), 175.

28. Quoted in L. Schapiro, *The Communist Party of the Soviet Union* (London, 1960), 9.

29. There are indications and allusions in Gorky's correspondence to the fact that his first wife, E. Peshkova, was closely connected with the party of the Socialist Revolutionaries. This fact is glossed over in Soviet publications. Peshkova died in 1965 and became in the Soviet Union a part of the "Gorky myth." To admit that the wife of the first proletarian writer was a Socialist Revolutionary would have been heresy.

30. Gor'kii, *Sobranie sochinenii*, vol. 28, 155, 490. See also *Letopis'*, I: 237.

31. L. M. Farber, "Gor'kii Nizhegorodskikh let," *Gor'kovskie chteniia, 1959–1960* (Moscow, 1962), 158–159; Gor'kii, *Sobranie sochinenii*, vol. 28, 238–239; Murashov, *Leninskaia "Iskra,"* 55; Fadeev, *Revoliutsionnoe dvizhenic*, 360–361.

32. Tsentrarkhiv, *Revoliutsionnyi pui' Gor'kogo*, 71–72.

33. *M. Gor'kii: Materialy i issledovaniia*, II, 221; Gruzdev, *Gor'kii*, 136.

34. Gor'kii, *Sobranie sochinenii*, vol. 28, 151, 153. See also A. Svobodov, "Gor'kii i studencheskoe dvizhenie 1901 goda," *Katorga i ssylka*, no. 35 (1927): 68–77. For Lenin's reaction, see V. I. Lenin, *Polnoe sobranie sochineii*, 5th edition (Moscow, 1958–1965), IV, 388–393. Hereafter referred to as *PSS*.

35. Gor'kii, *Sobranie sochinenii*, vol. 28, 156–157.

36. *M. Gor'kii: Materialy i issledovaniia*, II, 221–222; Farber, "Gor'kii Nizhegorodskikh let," 148; *Arkhiv*, V: 79; Posse, *Moi zhiznennyi put'*, 224–225.

37. Tsentrarkhiv, *Revoliutsionnyi put' Gor'kogo*, 43–44; Belozerov, "Iz molodykh let Maksima Gor'kogo," *Novyi mir* (Moscow), no. 3, 1926: 122–123.

38. Tsentrarkhiv, *Revoliutsionnyi put' Gor'kogo*, 44–45.

39. Tsentrarkhiv, *Revoliutsionnyi put' Gor'kogo*, 58–59.

40. Tsentrarkhiv, *Revoliutsionnyi put' Gor'kogo*, 60; Belozerov, "Iz molodykh let Maksima Gor'kogo," 127.

41. Lenin, *PSS*, V, 370.

42. E. D. Kuskova, "Obeskrylennyi sokol," *Sovremennyia zapiski XXXV* (Paris, 1928): 327. See also Tsentrarkhiv, *Revoliutsionnyi put' Gor'kogo*, 63–65; Belozerov, "Iz molodykh let Maksima Gor'kogo," 131; Gruzdev, *Gor'kii*, 142.

43. *Gor'kii i Andreev*, 151; Gor'kii, *Sobranie sochinenii*, vol. 28, 255, 256; L. M. Farber, "Revoliutsionnoe okruzheniie A. M. Gor'kogo v Nizhnem Novgorode (1901–1904)," *Gor'kovskie chteniia: k 100-letiu so dnia rozhdeniia pisatelia* (Moscow, 1968), 99–128.

44. A Soviet critic noted that Gorky was informed about the forthcoming demonstration. This is most unlikely. Under the conditions of conspirational work, such a step would have endangered the undertaking. In addition, Gorky was not a member of either the committee or the Party. Farber, "Gor'kii Nizhegorodskikh let," 156; Gor'kii, *Sobranie sochinenii*, vol. 28, 248–249; see also Lenin, *PSS*, VI, 251.

45. Schapiro, *Communist Party*, 40.

46. See Z. A. B. Zeman and W. B. Scharlau, *The Merchant of Revolution: The Life of Alexander Israel Helphand (Parvus), 1867–1924* (London, 1965), 69–70; Levitas, Moskalev, and Fingerit, *Revoliutsionnye tipografii v Rossii 1860–1917* (Moscow, 1962), 176; *Lenin i Gor'kii*, 241.

47. Tsentrarkhiv, *Revoliutsionnyi put' Gor'kogo*, 76–77. See the letter of Lenin to P. B. Akselrod of July 9, 1901, Lenin, *PSS*, XLVI, 123.

48. Tsentrarkhiv, *Revoliutsionnyi put' Gor'kogo*, 76–79; Rudnev, *Gor'kii revoliutsioner*, 54; Serebrov, *Vremia i liudi*, 162–165; Murashov, *Leninskaia "Iskra,"* 63; *Iz istorii organizatsii moskovskoi organizatsii VKP (b)* (Moscow, 1947), 91; Farber, *Gor'kii v Nizhnem*, 151, 188, 189.

49. *M. F. Andreeva: Perepiska, vospominaniia, stat'i*, ed. by A. P. Grigorieva and S. V. Shirina, 2nd ed. (Moscow, 1963), 348.

50. V. Desnitskii, "Vospominaniia o Gor'kom," in *Gor'kii v vospominaniiakh sovremennikov*, M. S. Miasnikov, ed. (Moscow, 1955), 131.

51. Murashov maintains that the reason of Gorky's unawareness of the split was caused by lack of information, since no delegates from Nizhnii Novgorod were present at the Second Congress. See Murashov, *Leninskaia "Iskra,"* 147.

52. Farber, "Novye materialy," 291; Rudnev, *Gor'kii revoliutsioner*, 208; Tsentrarkhiv *Revoliutsionnyi put' Gor'kogo*, 80.

53. Gor'kii, *Sobranie sochinenii*, vol. 28, 302, 313–314, 534.

54. *Arkhiv*, V: 126.

55. Gor'kii, *Sobranie sochinenii*, vol. 28, 335, 336, 337, 545.

56. Gor'kii, *Sobranie sochinenii*, vol. 28, 337.

57. *M. Gor'kii: Materialy i issledovaniia*, II, 248; Gor'kii, *Sobranie sochinenii*, vol. 28, 125, 216.

58. N. D. Teleshov, "Vospominaniia o Maksime Gor'kom," in *Gor'kii v vospominaniiakh sovremennikov*, 187.

59. "Pesnia o burevestnike" was first written as part of a story, *Vesennie melodii*. The censor forbade the publication of the story, but strangely enough the poem was allowed to appear in print.

60. N. M. Sipiagin, the Minister of Interior, informed the Grand Duke Sergei Romanov, the Governor General of Moscow, that he had sent Prince Shakhovskoi, the head of the department on publications, to attend a dress rehearsal of the play *Meshchane* and to censure the parts which he found harmful. During the performance the theatre was guarded by gendarmerie mounted on horseback M. *Gor'kii: Materialy i issledovaniia*, II, 164–165; Gruzdev, *Gor'kii*, 147–148; Tsentrarkhiv, *Revoliutsionnyi put' Gor'kogo*, 75.

61. At first the censors forbade the play from being performed. After negotiations it was allowed to be staged by the Moscow Art Theatre. Tsentrarkhiv, *Revoliutsionnyi put' Gor'kogo*, 79–80. Gor'kii, *Sobranie sochinenii*, vol. 28, 282–283; Rudnev, *Gor'kii revoliutsioner*, 57.

62. Gor'kii, *Sobranie sochinenii*, vol. 28, 333–334; *Arkhiv*, V: 137–139; *Letopis'*, I: 491.

63. M. Gor'kii, "Materialy sobrannye departamentom politsii s primechaniiami Gor'kogo," *Byloe* 12 (1918): 193–199.

64. Tsentrarkhiv, *Revoliutsionnyi put' Gor'kogo*, 73.

65. Quoted in Kaun, *Maxim Gorky and His Russia*, 334.

66. Tsentrarkhiv, *Revoliutsionnyi put' Gor'kogo*, 73.

67. "'Bolee chem original'no.' Sluchai s Maksimom Gor'kim," *Byloe* 1 (23) (1917): 84.

68. Tsentrarkhiv, *Revoliutsionnyi put' Gor'kogo*, 73–74. Gorky was officially invited to join the Academy of Sciences in 1917.

69. N. Kozmin, "Maksim Gor'kii i Imperatorskaia Akademiia Nauk," *Istorik marksist* 4 (1941): 55.

70. Tsentrarkhiv, *Revoliutsionnyi put' Gor'kogo*, 74–75.

71. For a discussion of this "incident" see Kozmin, 53–72; Tsentrarkhiv, *Revoliutsionnyi put' Gor'kogo*, 73–75; A. P. Chekhov, *Polnoe sobranie sochinenii* (Moscow, 1950), vol. 19, 325; M. Gor'kii, "Materialy sobrannyie departamentom politsii s primechaniiami Gor'kogo," 193–199; Gor'kii, *Sobranie sochinenii*, vol. 28, 238–239; Rudnev, "Gor'kii-revoliutsioner," *Novyi mir* 3 (1928): 205–206.

72. I. Eventov, "Gor'kii v otsenke dooktiabr'skoi bol'shevistskoi kritiki," in *Materialy i issledovaniia*, IV, 186.

73. Eventov, "Gor'kii v otsenke," 186–189.

74. M. *Gor'kii: Materialy i issledovaniia*, II, 168. For more information on the question of Nietzsche's influence on Gorky's early works see "U istokov mifa," in N. E. Krutikova, *V nachale veka* (Kiev, 1978); M. Gel'rot, "Nitsshe i Gor'kii," in *Maksim Gor'kii: Pro et Contra* (St. Petersburg, 1997); an excellent summary is in Nikolaus Katzer's *Maksim Gor'kijs Weg in die russische Sozialdemokratie* (Wiesbaden, 1990), 110–121.

75. N. I. Stechkin, "Maksim Gor'kii" in *Maksim Gor'kii: Pro et Contra* (St. Petersburg, 1997), 617.

76. Melkhoir de Voguë, *Maksim Gor'kii* (St. Petersburg, 1902), 40.

77. V. Kedrov, *V chem istinnoe znachenie tvorchestva Maksima Gor'kogo* (St. Petersburg, 1904).

78. E. Mart, "Maxim Gorki," *Sozialistische Monatshefte*, 7 (1901): 731–736.

CHAPTER 3

GORKY AND THE REVOLUTION OF 1905

Yes, Russia is awakening. This is a fact the importance of which no prophet can foretell.

Gor'kii, *Sobranie sochinenii*, vol. 28, 348

History can be painted anew only with blood.

Gor'kii, *Sobranie sochinenii*, vol. 28, 383

The events of January 9, 1905, marked the beginning of a revolution. During this revolution, for the first time in the history of modern Russia, hundreds of thousands of people took part in a genuine mass movement against the government. As the unrest in the country continued, the number of revolutionary parties grew, drawing into their ranks prominent members of Russian society. Among these was Gorky, who had established a reputation as one of the most influential writers in Russia and whose name was well known abroad. His collected works went through seven editions, and the play *Na dne*, staged with great success by the Moscow Art Theater in 1902, was reprinted fourteen times in a period of one year. N. Valentinov, his friend of many years, left a description of Gorky as he knew him in 1905: "His face did not have the stern look of later years. His hair was not short brushed. He wore a Russian style shirt, wide trousers tucked in tall boots."[1] Valentinov further commented that the style of his clothes was similar to that worn by members of the *meshchane*, the very class he criticized in his writings.

At that time Gorky was close to the Russian Social Democratic Workers' Party (RSDWP), and had wealthy and influential friends, among whom was the millionaire cotton manufacturer, Savva Morozov, who later donated large sums of money for the support of the *Iskra*.

Following the split in the ranks of the RSDWP into Bolshevik and Menshevik factions, Lenin and the Bolsheviks were relegated to a weaker position. The Menshevik *Iskra* group commanded a majority in the Party Council.[2] By the summer of 1904, Lenin, though technically still a member, was in fact excluded from the work of the Central Committee. He was determined to effect the calling of a Party congress, as well as to launch a separate, Bolshevik newspaper, the future *Vperëd* (Forward). In August 1904, at a conference in Geneva, a rival Central Committee emerged. It later was to call itself the "Bureau of the Committees of Party Majority," with Lenin at its helm. The call for a third congress met no response at this time.[3] As for the newspaper, the main obstacle to its operation was lack of funds. The Bolshevik faction turned to Gorky for financial support. The efforts of the Bolsheviks to secure Gorky's financial aid for *Vperëd* becomes evident from an exchange of letters between Lenin, Krupskaia, and the members of the St. Petersburg party organization, A. A. Bogdanov, R. S. Zemliachka, and M. M. Litvinov. In the correspondence, they referred to Gorky under the conspiratorial names of "G.," "Bukva," and "belletrist." Zemliachka went as far as to assert that "Gorky definitely has come over to our side and considers Lenin as the man capable of leading of proletariat."[4] Lenin reaffirmed the urgency of obtaining financial aid during the first months of the appearance of *Vperëd* and recognized that the position of the "majority" was very vulnerable and likely to suffer an irreparable blow in case the publication did not materialize. He asked them to "squeeze out [money] from Gorky, even if only a little at a time."[5] A. A. Lopukhin, the head of the police department in St. Petersburg, reported on Gorky's assistance to *Vperëd* and mentioned that a certain Bogdanov was a middleman in the transfer of money sent by Aleksei Peshkov for the publication of the revolutionary newspaper *Vperëd*.[6]

Gorky's literary talents were also sought by the Bolsheviks. Shortly after the announcement appeared concerning the publication of *Vperëd*, M. N. Liadov, a member of the Party, was sent from Geneva to recruit correspondents for the newspaper. Liadov approached Gorky, and he later wrote: "I told Gorky of Ilich's request to help us financially and with writings; he promised to do all possible."[7] Krupskaia also advised M. Litvinov to obtain from Gorky materials for publication in the newspaper.[8] On December 17, 1904, Gorky took part in a meeting of the St. Petersburg Bolshevik organization attended by A. I. Ulianov-Elizarova (Lenin's sister), S. I. Gusev, A. A. Bogdanov, Desnitskii, and A. F. Voitkevich, all prominent members of the faction. "As far as I remember, we discussed the question of legal and illegal publications," wrote Voitkevich.[9] It seems that Gorky, by his attendance at meetings of the Party, was now acquainted with the problems facing the Bolshevik faction. But to claim that he was "all on their side" would be to ignore Gorky's other commitments and the help extended during the same period to the Socialist Revolutionaries and even anarchists.[10] Moreover, the beginning of the Revolution of 1905 found him in contact with the liberals.

At the end of 1904, the zemstvo liberals and the members of the Union of Liberation were actively engaged in organizing banquets, drafting resolutions, and submitting petitions. Gorky took part in the campaign. He divided his time between Moscow and St. Petersburg and occasionally travelled to other parts of the country, to lecture or to attend to business of a political nature. He participated in a banquet arranged by the lawyers on November 20, 1904, where, together with 676 others present, he signed a resolution,[11] one that demanded a reorganization of the system of government, the calling of a constituent assembly, and an amnesty for all political prisoners. That same evening, Gorky appeared at a meeting in Pavlova Hall held under the chairmanship of his friend Korolenko. Gorky delivered a fiery address asking the people to resort to violence if necessary in the struggle against the autocratic government of Nicholas II. Said Gorky: "If on November 29, there should be a demonstration in the streets, we will not let ourselves be whipped or trampled upon. We will have to use our revolvers, daggers, and even our teeth in the struggle; any other way of demonstrating will produce no effect."[12] Hopeful that the government would grant a constitution without the people resorting to violence, Gorky helped agitate for the constitution. A mood of optimism permeated his letters. He wrote that within a period of four months a constitution would be issued.[13] His sympathies lay with the left wing of the liberals, which demanded a constituent assembly elected by universal suffrage. News about the growing unrest in the cities and in the countryside seem to have given Gorky a great deal of satisfaction. He did not, however, approve of terrorist activities. Relating the events of students' demonstrations in St. Petersburg and in Moscow, he criticized the tactics of the Socialist Revolutionaries.[14] At the end of December 1904, Gorky left St. Petersburg for the Christmas holidays, planning to return there to present a series of lectures.[15] Events of great magnitude prevented Gorky from carrying out his plans.

The strike that began at the Putilov works on January 3 did not at first forecast the momentous events of the Revolution of 1905. The growing mood of unrest among the workers organized by the priest Georgii A. Gapon compelled him to present their grievances to the tsar. Thus emerged the idea of the procession and petition of January 9. When Gorky arrived in St. Petersburg on January 4, he learned from the newspapers as well as from certain people about the forthcoming procession to the Winter Palace.[16] Gorky understood from messages received that the workers were loyal and that the petition contained no call to revolution. He tried, however, to convince the organizers of the folly of their undertaking and stressed the importance of inquiring from the authorities whether they would be admitted to the tsar. They replied that Gapon had submitted a request to the Minister of the Interior and that the fact that the workers were given permission to organize preliminary meetings in preparation for the procession proved that the authorities' attitude was favorable.[17] Gorky however had obtained information that the authorities were determined not to allow the workers to proceed as they planned. He felt that a clash between the workers and the army was imminent. In the evening of January 8, he went to the editorial office of the newspaper *Nashi dni* (Our Days), where he met a gathering of people discussing the forthcoming procession.[18] Most of the gathered there were populists and liberals who, allied with this newspaper's views, chose a delegation to meet with the Minister of the Interior, to ask that necessary measures be taken to prevent a clash between the workers, the police, and the army.[19] The populist-liberal delegation included Gorky, whose name was considered to be a great asset. Others in the delegation were men of letters and respected professionals.[20]

The delegation was dispatched to Prince P. D. Sviatopolk-Mirskii, Minister of the Interior, to ask that he refrain from sending the army into the streets of St. Petersburg on January 9 and that the workers be given an opportunity to present their petition to the tsar. Unsuccessful in their effort to meet with Sviatopolk-Mirskii, the delegates approached the deputy minister in charge of police, General-Major K. N. Rydzevskii, only to be told that the matter was not in his jurisdiction. The meeting with the chairman of the committee of ministers, S. Iu. Witte, was also unsuccessful. The delegates were informed that both the tsar and Sviatopolk-Mirskii were well aware of the situation. To Witte's statement "that the opinion of the ruling circles differs widely from that of the delegates," Gorky replied: "We request that you inform the ruling circles that if blood is shed tomorrow, they will pay dearly for it."[21] Gorky's connection with this delegation was a result of his fear of possible bloodshed, not a determination to be revolutionary or the delegation's desire to merely use his name.

On the morning of January 9, the workers began marching from various districts toward the Winter Palace. Gorky met the procession coming from the Vyborg Quarter. Suddenly, by the Troitsky bridge, the army opened fire: according to initial reports, there were sixty killed or wounded. One witness, a party member, E. Zamyslovskaia, wrote in her memoirs that Gorky was among the workers who assembled by the Admiralty passage:

He was approaching the crowd. The workers were retreating as if to make a passage for him. He silently gripped my hand, then proceeded forward, straight into the lines of the police. . . . After his departure the infantry lined up into two rows. The first volley was heard, then the second, the third. . . . The unarmed crowd retreated. Where Gorky was at that time nobody knew.

Gorky's next appearance was at a meeting in the Public Library, which had been arranged the previous evening in the editorial offices of *Nashi dni*. He delivered a short but inspiring speech, and as a result a collection was taken for the benefit of families of the victims of the shootings.[22] Gorky later described the behavior of the army toward the crowds: "They were fired upon without any warning. . . . I have myself seen three people killed and nineteen wounded, among them three women."[23] He further wrote that he would soon publish a report on the events preceding January 9, so that the people of Russia and the nations of Western Europe would learn the truth. Immediately after the procession, its central figure, Gapon, found refuge with Gorky.

Gapon by some miracle remained alive; he is in my house asleep. He now says that there is no tsar anymore, no church and no God. . . . This is a man who has great influence upon the workers of the Putilov works. He has a following of close to 10,000 men who believe in him as in a saint. . . . He will lead the workers on the true path.[24]

Gorky obviously had no prior knowledge of Gapon's ties with the Okhrana and had much confidence in the ability of the charismatic priest.

The ruthless suppression by the authorities of the demonstration on January 9 made a strong impact on Gorky and changed his stand from moderate to radical. "History," wrote Gorky, "can be painted anew only with blood."[25] In a letter to Andreev he explained that under certain conditions there was no other choice but revolution:

Do not despair my friend! It is not worth it! Two hundred black eyes will not paint Russian history over in a brighter colour; for that, blood is needed, much blood. . . . Do not cry unnecessarily! All goes the way it should. Life has been built on cruelty and force. For its reconstruction, it demands cold calculated cruelty—that is all! They kill? It is necessary to do so! Otherwise what will you do? Will you go to Count Tolstoy and wait with him?[26]

Gorky's growing radicalism aroused Andreev's suspicion: "Be careful of Maksim's judgment," wrote Andreev, "he has become very straightforward and in some ways a fanatic."[27] Gorky's radical stand was reflected in the declaration that he wrote in response to the events of January 8 and 9:

I wrote it on January 9, 1905, at 3 o'clock in the afternoon as soon as I had returned from the streets, shaken by the sight of the wounded and the excitement of the panic-stricken crowds. The declaration was written to be sent to the Minister

of the Interior and to St. Petersburg newspapers with the hope that some of the
newspapers would print it despite its strongly-worded content.[28]

He intended to make the declaration public only after the other members
had approved.[29] With that in mind, he gave the declaration to one of the
delegates, Attorney E. Kedrin, for him to read, correct, and sign. Gorky
spent the next day meeting people and discussing the situation in the capital. His apartment was closely watched by the police, who reported that
many "unknown persons" were visiting Gorky. In the evening he left for
Riga. Upon his arrival he was arrested, returned to St. Petersburg, and
confined in the Peter and Paul Fortress.[30] Together with other members of
the delegation, Gorky was accused of belonging to a committee conspiring
to overthrow the existing government.[31] Another charge (the authorship of
the declaration) was laid after Kedrin was arrested on January 11, and the
draft of the declaration was seized.

   Gorky denied membership in a conspiratorial committee, but he admitted
being the author of the declaration.[32] Kedrin also denied membership in an
anti-government committee and added that he would never have signed the
document drafted by Gorky: "It is unthinkable that one could overthrow
the government either through workers' strikes or student riots. I could not
imagine that any clear thinking individual could find himself in a committee
which would aim to overthrow the autocracy."[33] The historian N. I. Kareev
wrote that he resented the declaration's reference to himself and other
members of the delegation as "the undersigned." Other members felt the
same way, indicating the widening gulf between Gorky and the liberals.
The declaration found among Kedrin's papers was unsigned.[34]

   The echo of events of January 9, 1905, resounded through Russia, and
Gorky's involvement was widely publicized. Prince Constantine Romanov
noted in his diary on January 13, 1905: "I have heard that Maksim Gor'kii
is implicated in inciting the people to revolt, and that he managed to go
into hiding when the army prevented the workers from achieving their
aim."[35] On January 12, 1905, an anonymous letter was sent to the editorial
offices of *Vperëd* in which special mention was made of Gorky's arrest.
The news was also reported in leaflets of the St. Petersburg committee of
the RSDWP.[36] On the completion of the investigation, the accusatory act
stated that Gorky had "drafted a declaration calling for the overthrow of
the existing order."[37] During the interrogation, Gorky admitted that he was
radical in his thinking, but he denied active connection with any revolutionary parties. He also denied that he had given financial help to the cause
of the revolution. He further stated that he did not know much about
financial matters, which he left to his publishers.[38]

   Gorky's arrest and confinement produced outcries both at home and
abroad. Among the protesters were the workers of the industrial enterprises
of St. Petersburg, the Obukhov works, the Semianikovski ship-building

yards, and others. A demonstration took place in a theater in Kiev, during the performance of the play *Dachniki*. The demonstrators asked for Gorky's freedom, calling for the overthrow of the autocracy, shouting "Freedom for Gorky, the fighter for liberty!"[39] Similar demonstrations took place in other cities. A campaign for Gorky's release was started by his friends. The *Literaturnyi fond* (Literary Fund Society)[40] approached General Trepov, newly appointed governor general of St. Petersburg for support. Trepov replied that *Literaturnyi fond* had no right to intervene in cases such as Gorky's. Protests came from students of the Riga Politechnique, and a petition for Gorky's release was sent to the Russian Minister of the Interior from the editorial offices of the *Berliner Tageblatt* that contained 269 signatures of Germany's foremost scientists and men of letters.[41] Official representatives of the Russian government in Rome, Brussels, Lisbon, Berlin, and Paris received numerous protests, declarations, and petitions asking for Gorky's release. In France, the noted writer Anatole France wrote that Gorky belonged not to Russia alone but to the whole world. A letter signed by Henri Poincaré, Aristide Briand, Anatole France, and artists Rodin and Monet was sent to Gorky expressing their support. Also protesting against Gorky's imprisonment were Czechs, Britons, and Americans. The Writers' Club wired Nicholas II from New York City asking for Gorky's freedom.

The tsarist government could ill afford the publicity given abroad to Gorky's case. The publicity, as well as the mounting revolutionary mood in the country, compelled the authorities to release him from prison. He was freed after a bail of 10,000 rubles was put up by his publisher, K. P. Piatnitskii.[42] But the case was not closed. Gorky in fact wanted to be brought to court; he wanted to explain to Europe why "I am a revolutionary and what were the motives for my crimes against the existing order."[43] Following the events of "Bloody Sunday," when the question of the involvement of the intelligentsia became especially important, Gorky wrote of his disappointment with their response to the revolutionary events: "The future historian will start his work with the following statement: 'The first day of the Russian revolution was the day of the moral collapse of the Russian intelligentsia'; this is my impression on the basis of their speeches and actions."[44] In the play *Deti solntsa* (Children of the Sun), written in prison, he tried to convey the idea that the meaning of life was to "serve the revolution." This could be achieved only by men who had faith in it, and not by those "whose blood was polluted by pessimism."[45] Gorky found himself immersed in the growing revolutionary movement. He disagreed with the dean of the Russian writers, L. N. Tolstoy, concerning the justifiability of revolution. In *"Pis'mo Grafu Tolstomu"* (A Letter to Count Tolstoy), Gorky maintained that the revolution in Russia was not caused by a few thousand alienated workers stirred by propaganda, as Tolstoy saw it, but by a growing mass of workers and peasants who wanted to live like human beings. He thought that Tolstoy was wrong in condemning the people's struggle for freedom:

You are wrong when you say that the peasant needs only land; here you contradict the Gospel, which you consider to be the source of pure wisdom. It says there that man lives not by bread alone, and you know yourself that the Russian people, besides wanting land, want to be able to think and to worship as they wish, and you know that for that reason only they are sent to Siberia.[46]

He further expressed his disillusionment with Tolstoy's stand:

During these difficult days when blood is being shed on the soil of your motherland, and honest and brave men and women are dying for the right to live like human beings, you, whose words are eagerly listened to by the whole world, find it right to repeat your philosophical idea "that the moral perfectibility of the individual is the meaning of life for all men!" Can a man occupy himself with his moral perfectibility at times when men and women are being shot in the streets of our cities and it is forbidden to gather up the wounded?[47]

The situation in the country was deteriorating rapidly; Gorky, not allowed to remain in St. Petersburg, chose Finland for his temporary home. He settled in Kuokkala, carefully watching the developments. He occupied himself with writing articles, raising funds, and aiding the RSDWP in its attempts to acquire arms.[48] His home in Kuokkala became a meeting place for Party members, who came to ask for financial help.[49] Among his visitors were both Bolsheviks and Mensheviks.[50] Although not involved in the internal problems of the RSDWP, Gorky after January 9 sided with the Bolsheviks.

In Finland, he began several fund-raising campaigns.[51] On Gorky's initiative a publishing house was established abroad to replace the now bankrupt *Verlag* of Helphand. The profits from it were to go to the Bolshevik faction of the RSDWP. Lenin instructed V. D. Bonch-Bruevich, a Party member, to meet with Gorky and to make the necessary arrangements. Gorky supplied the initial capital. In July 1905, work began on the establishment of *Demos* in Geneva; the editorial board consisted of E. D. Stasova, Bonch-Bruevich, R. P. Abramov, and Ladyzhnikov.[52] *Demos* subsequently published the works of Gorky, Chirikov, Skitalets, and other members of the *Znanie* group. Within a few months, *Demos* was transferred to Berlin, where it existed under the name *Bühnen und Buchverlag russischen Autoren I.P. Ladyzhnikov Teatral'noe i knizhnoe izdatel'stvo I. P. Ladyzhnikov* (Theater and Book Publishing House I. P. Ladyzhnikov).[53] Gorky also assisted the RSDWP in its efforts to secure arms for the militia units set up in 1905. Called *boevye druzhiny* (fighting detachments), they were in fact loosely organized, badly trained, and poorly equipped units (knives, daggers, rifles, homemade bombs). The fighting detachments were to counteract the Black Hundreds.[54] In the summer of 1905, an effort was made to establish a training center for these *druzhiny* in Kuokkala, but the project was abandoned when plans for it were uncovered by the police.[55] The geographical location of Gorky's home in Kuokkala, which was situated close to the Gulf of Finland, made it possible for him to extend help to the Technical Group of the Central Committee, which provided arms for the fighting detachments.[56]

The members of the Bolshevik faction of the RSDWP tried to use Gorky's influence in order to obtain a share in the shipment of arms and ammunition transported aboard the ship *John Grafton*. The initiator of the plan to bring arms and ammunition to the revolutionary parties in Russia was a Finnish activist, Konni Zilliacus. He was backed in his enterprise by Japanese money.[57] Zilliacus planned to have the arms transported to the Gulf of Finland and then shipped to St. Petersburg. The Socialist Revolutionaries were to be the recipients and the distributors of the precious cargo. Also involved in the undertaking was Gapon, who, after the events of January 9, succeeded with Gorky's assistance in escaping abroad. Anxious to benefit from the enterprise, Lenin and N. E. Burenin met with Gapon in Geneva to discuss the transfer of arms to the Bolshevik faction. Since no agreement was reached in Geneva, Burenin and Gapon went to London in order to discuss the matter with the representative of the SR's N. V. Chaikovskii. The latter was in close collaboration with Zilliacus. Again, the negotiations met with little success. Meanwhile the *John Grafton* sailed for Russia. The Bolsheviks made one more attempt to meet with Gapon. This time Gorky was invited to attend the meeting. He was smuggled out of Kuokkala to the summer home of A. Torngren, a Finnish friend of Russian revolutionaries. Gorky, traveling by train and by cart, arrived at the meeting place only to find that Gapon had not come.[58] No arrangements were made to receive the cargo of the *John Grafton*. On August 26 (September 8), the *John Grafton* ran aground on a reef in the Gulf of Bothnia, north of the town of Pietarsaari. In the end the ship was blown up. The bulk of the cargo was lost at sea.[59]

Since Gapon played an important role in the revolutionary events of 1905, in which Gorky was also involved, the further contact between them and Gorky's evaluation of Gapon is of interest. In a letter written to Gapon in the summer of 1905, Gorky commented on Gapon's plan to found a workers' party in Russia without the participation of the intelligentsia. Gorky considered Gapon's intentions to separate the proletariat from the revolutionary intelligentsia as harmful, since it would result in a loss of leadership for the workers.[60] In an account by A. E. Karelin, a member of Gapon's "Assembly of Russian Factory Workers," mention is made of Gapon's attitude towards Gorky. "Gapon," wrote Karelin, "held Gorky in great esteem, and often told the leaders of the various groups that 'if Gorky

tells you something, listen to him.'"[61] Not mentioning Gapon's escape, Karelin stressed the fact that in spite of efforts for Gapon and Gorky to meet
after January 9, the meeting never took place.

In 1906, while in the United States, Gorky wrote the essay *Pop Gapon*
(The Priest Gapon).[62] In it Gorky described in great detail Gapon's career
and ideas, making clear the differences between his views and those of
Gapon, especially with regard to the role of the revolutionary intelligent-
sia.[63] In the essay there is no reference to Gapon being an agent of the
Okhrana.[64] Gorky was apparently unaware of Gapon's execution by the
SRs at approximately that time.

The growing revolutionary tide in the country compelled the government
to consider seriously the question of reforms. The result was the projected
Bulygin Duma of August 1905, conceived as a consultative body. It met
with criticism and indignation from wide sections of the population. Gorky
condemned the proposed Duma and severely criticized P. N. Miliukov, the
leader of the Kadets, whom he mistakenly believed had supported the Bulygin Duma.[65] The Bulygin Duma, as is known, became a dead letter. In
following the developments in the country, Gorky spoke with great enthusiasm of the emergence of the peasant on the Russian political scene. The
All Peasant Congress under the leadership of the Socialist Revolutionaries,
which met in Moscow on July 31, 1905, won Gorky's praise: "The Congress was something unexpected, of surprising power, and awakened consciousness."[66] This belief in the power of the peasant seems to be very
significant in Gorky's ideological development at that time. The same idea
was expressed in an interview with the correspondent of *Birzhevye vedomosti* (News of the Bourse), V. Reginin.[67] Gorky emphasized the importance of wide representation in a Duma and rejected the notion that the
masses were politically dormant and culturally ignorant: "People who
think," wrote Gorky, "that the peasants are unable to take an active part
in the social and political life of the country do not know the peasants."[68]
When confronted with the question of how the uneducated peasants would
be able to overcome the technical difficulties of election procedures, Gorky
replied that he was strongly convinced that the procedure of elections was
something that the Russian people acquired through history, mentioning
veche and the rural assemblies.[69] It seems that this was the only time that
Gorky put his faith in the peasant. He may have realized that the workers
alone, who constituted a small percent of the population, could not carry
out a successful revolution. The leadership in the revolutionary struggle
was to be left to the worker: "I have lived and worked among the working
class; I know its soul, and I know that only that class is capable of building
on earth the Kingdom of Justice. Only that class can create a new kind of
life, a life guided by reason and enlightenment."[70] An alliance of the worker

and the revolutionary intelligentsia with the participation of the peasantry was Gorky's hope for the success of the revolution.

The revolutionary events that continued forced the tsar to issue the October Manifesto. One of the provisions in the Manifesto was the establishment of a Duma, where both workers and peasants were to be represented. The October Manifesto satisfied only the party of the center, the "Union of October 17th," which emerged soon after the issuance of the Manifesto. The Right thought that the concessions went too far, the Left that they did not go far enough. Gorky regarded the October Manifesto as a step forward toward a constitutional government; but, at the same time, he considered the progress made by the workers, in their struggle for political and social change, of far greater importance than the Manifesto. In his appeal *K rabochim vsekh stran* (To the Workers of All Countries), he contended that the concessions were extracted from the government by the workers.[71]

With the rise of the revolutionary tide, the various political parties increased the number of their publications. Gorky's abilities as writer and publicist were used to further the cause of the revolution. From August to October 1905, an illegal workers' newspaper appeared in Moscow, *Rabochii* (The Worker). One of the contributors was Gorky, whose articles appeared under the name *Tretii* (Third). The articles, entitled *"Pis'ma k rabochim"* (Letters to Workers) were extremely critical of the existing order.[72] His poems *Pesnia o sokole* and *Pesnia o burevestnike*, forbidden by the censor since 1903, were reprinted and distributed in thousands of copies.[73] Gorky helped to found the first legal Bolshevik newspaper, *Novaia zhizn'*.[74] The newspaper was published in St. Petersburg from October 27 to December 3, 1905, when it was closed on the order of the government. Gorky had written already in July to one of the members of the *Znanie* group, the writer E. Chirikov, on the desirability of establishing a newspaper and mentioned the names of prospective members of the editorial board.[75] Since the prospects for obtaining a permit from the government were not very promising, Andreeva contacted the symbolist poet N. M. Minskii, not politically suspect, who could procure a permit to publish a daily newspaper without preliminary censorship. Subsequently, an agreement was reached between Minskii and the Bolsheviks that the paper would be edited jointly by Minskii and Gorky and published by Andreeva. Among the participants were Lenin, A. V. Lunacharskii, Bogdanov, and foreign socialists K. Kautsky, P. Lafarge, K. Liebknecht, and R. Luxemburg.[76] After Lenin's arrival on November 7, he became, from the sixth issue on, the sole editor. The editorial offices were located on the Nevsky Prospekt, in what Liadov described as luxurious quarters.[77] In October, Gorky transferred 15,000 rubles to Litvinov for the needs of the newspaper.[78] The appearance of the first issue of *Novaia zhizn'* was a great success. This was the first legal RSDWP-Bolshevik newspaper, and the program of the party

appeared on the first few pages.[79] G. Alekinskii, a member of the RSDWP
at that time and Gorky's friend, wrote that Gorky had wanted it to be
accessible to writers of all affiliations. To support this view, he mentioned
the participation in *Novaia zhizn'* of K. D. Balmont, a symbolist poet and
of the original owner of the paper, Minskii. Here was Gorky, not the fanatic Social Democrat of Lenin's style.

During his involvement with *Novaia zhizn'*, Gorky allegedly met with
Lenin for the first time. Alekinskii wrote that a meeting between Gorky
and Lenin took place on November 27, 1905, in the editorial offices of
Novaia zhizn', at which Gorky strongly disagreed with Lenin.[80] Others
close to the two men further elaborate upon this meeting.[81] On the agenda
were the events in Moscow, matters connected with the newly founded
Bolshevik daily *Bor'ba* (Struggle) and the question of the editorial policy
of *Novaia zhizn'*.[82] Lenin insisted that Minskii's further participation on
the board of *Novaia zhizn'* had to cease because he had no connection with
the Party. Gorky opposed this idea, but Lenin eventually had his way. The
question of Gorky's royalties, which had been appropriated by Helphand,
was also discussed. It was decided that Helphand should be forced to renounce his rights to Gorky's works and repay the money he had taken.
Gorky wrote to Ladyzhnikov in the latter part of December that he had
agreed to arbitration and that either he or Lenin would meet with Helphand.[83] However, no meeting with Helphand materialized, and nothing
was accomplished in the attempt to receive from him the money he appropriated.[84] Yet, after the death of Lenin, Gorky wrote in the essay "V. I.
Lenin," published in 1924, that their first encounter took place in 1907 at
the time of the Fifth Party Congress. It seems peculiar that a man as obser-
vant as Gorky should forget the 1905 meeting. Subsequently, in 1934,
Gorky wrote to the Marx-Engels Institute acknowledging the 1905 meeting
with Lenin: "I and Desnitskii were called by Krasin to come to St. Petersburg. [December 10, 1905, n. s.] We told Vladimir Ilich, Rumiantsev and
Krasin about the situation in Moscow. I arrived ill, running a high fever
and therefore remembered the event rather dimly, so that I hesitated to
mention it in my reminiscences about V. I. Lenin."[85] Because this acknowledgment was written in 1934 when Gorky was being closely watched, it is
possible that he admitted to the 1905 meeting to accommodate the Party
historians.

The publication of *Novaia zhizn'* was not without problems. In spite of
the October Manifesto, which granted the citizens of Russia freedom of
speech, several issues of the newspaper were confiscated. The post office
refused to accept subscriptions for the paper, and Minskii was called to
court. Later, proceedings were started against Andreeva.[86] The news office
was closed on December 3 because of the printing of the so-called Financial
Manifesto.[87] Gorky wrote a series of articles in *Novaia zhizn'* entitled *Zametki o meshchanstve* (Notes on Philistinism), giving a general outline of

the history of the Russian people and the role of the *meshchanstvo* in it.[88] *Meshchanstvo* represented many things, but particularly the mentality of the ruling classes. This mentality, Gorky contended, was caused by the institution of private property. Private property led man to be concerned with only himself. He further wrote that the ruling classes had always been the oppressors of the people, whom they did not understand, love, or consider. He ridiculed the efforts of the populists who wanted to educate the people hurriedly without understanding their basic needs. Gorky considered the belief in the uniqueness of the Russian peasant to be a cover-up for the policy of oppression pursued by the ruling class. Following the lead of the Bolsheviks, he joined in condemning the liberals. They were, as far as he was concerned, a helpless lot, always at the tail end of the revolutionary struggle of the masses, but only too happy to step in and to make use of the gains achieved by the masses.

Gorky's participation in the first legal Bolshevik newspaper and his writings raised storm of criticism. The *Russkii vestnik* (Russian Messenger), which characterized Gorky's poem *Chelovek* of 1904 as a call to revolution and a criminal proclamation, now regarded Gorky as "the leader and even the architect of the revolutionary movement."[89] The most severe indictment came from N. Berdiaev, who called the *Zametki o meshchanstve* "Hooliganism and an insult to the immortal idea of aestheticism."[90] In November and December 1905, Gorky published in *Novaia zhizn'* and in the Moscow *Bor'ba* two articles entitled *"Po povodu"* (On the Occasion). The first was written in defense of the poet Bal'mont, who, in the opinion of the literary groups associated with the liberal intelligentsia, committed a grave error in publishing his poems in a proletarian newspaper. The second, which appeared in *Bor'ba*, was an open attack upon those who were protesting against the ever-growing revolutionary deeds of the masses of workers and peasants.[91]

It was Gorky's conviction that the granting of certain liberties and the establishment of a Duma without far-reaching social and economic reforms would not provide a satisfactory solution for the ills of the Russian people. His conception of the "how" of a successful revolution is evident from a discussion between Gorky and the liberal academician Tarakhanov. He asked Gorky how he envisioned the very moment of the overthrow, the capture of power. "Well," said Gorky, "we will capture the arsenal, we will take over the general staff, the telegraph and the banks."[92] But what was to follow he did not state.

The rising revolutionary temper in the country did not diminish with the issuance of the October Manifesto. In Moscow the unrest was felt more than in other centers. The SDs had a majority in the Moscow Soviet, and their revolutionary propagandists were extremely active. There was also action of the right-wing extremists, which brought forth a reaction on the part of the workers to combat it, and preparations were made for an uprising.[93] Liadov gave an account of the preparedness of the armed militiamen, the *boevye druzhiny*, and estimated the number of Bolsheviks at 300. The SRs, according to their own estimates, also had approximately 300 men. The Mensheviks had 100 and the independent Caucasian student druzhina counted 150 men; there were close to 200 unaffiliated militiamen. Thus, in all, there were one thousand reliable men eager to fight.[94] Liadov, V. L. Shantser ("Marat"), and M. I. Vasiliev-Yuzhin, members of the inner group of the Moscow committee of the Social Democrats, were to lead the uprising. Several prominent leaders of the Social Democrats were arrested on the evening of December 7, among them Vasiliev and Shantser, but in spite of this setback the Social Democrats went on with their plans. The forces confronting the workers consisted of two thousand regular police, a division of gendarmes, and six thousand more men under arms.[95]

The uprising began on December 7 and lasted ten days. It was called under the guise of a general political strike; subsequently, a state of emergency was declared by the newly appointed Governor-general F. V. Dubasov. The appearance of barricades in the streets, the partisan tactics applied by the insurgents, and the apathy of the soldiers were all factors favoring the uprising. But, without question, the major drawback was lack of leadership and coordination between the various groups and parties. Liadov later wrote:

It was our misfortune that the Party was not prepared to lead an all-Russian uprising in 1905. The revolutionary ardour of both the peasants and the workers, shown in the years of 1905–1906, because of the lack of central organization, invariably had to take the form of isolated, uncoordinated local uprisings.[96]

On December 17, the last stronghold of the insurgents, Presnia, a working class district in the western part of Moscow, surrendered.[97] The uprising resulted in the death of approximately one thousand men; many more were wounded.

The December uprising found Gorky in Moscow. Never again was he to be so actively involved in the work of revolution as he was at this time. He believed intensely in the ultimate victory of the revolution.[98] He was in close contact with the Central Committee of the RSDWP in St. Petersburg and, when asked to appear at a meeting organized by the Moscow Committee, replied that he could do it only on the instruction of the Central Committee.[99] In order to protect Gorky from a possible attack by right-wing extremists, the Bolsheviks arranged that Gorky and his apartment be guarded by a Caucasian *boevaia druzhina*. From the very outset of the uprising, Gorky's apartment became a meeting place for Party members as well as an arms depot.[100] The shortage of arms, felt strongly by insurgents, was remedied by the manufacture of homemade bombs, and Gorky's apartment served as a laboratory.[101] To facilitate the production Gorky established close contact with Krasin, who supplied fuses ingeniously hidden in boxes of candies.[102] Krasin called also on P. Zalomov, at that time one of the organizers of the *boevye druzhiny* in the Zamoskvorechie district of Moscow, to assist Gorky in the preparation of bombs.[103] In his reminiscences, Zalomov wrote: "Gorky in 1905 was in the centre of preparation for the armed uprising. Thanks to his influence and connections he collected hundreds of thousands of rubles for the cause."[104] The money raised by Gorky did not reach "hundreds of thousands," but it certainly amounted to tens of thousands of rubles.[105] The high morale of the people surprised Gorky, for he wrote to Piatnitskii on December 10, "The morale of the people is absolutely wonderful! By God, I did not expect anything like it. Wonderful spirit!"[106] He had, it seems, no illusions about the immediate outcome of the uprising, but his hopes were that the victory of the government would not be long lasting.[107]

For Gorky the important factor was the participation of the rank and file not affiliated with any party. He liked the spontaneous response of the masses who, in his estimation, could free themselves through a conscious effort. This view he expressed in the article *Po povodu moskovskikh sobytii* (On the Moscow Events), written immediately after the collapse of the Moscow uprising and published in *Molodaia Rossiia* (Young Russia).[108] Evident in it is his enmity toward the tsarist government and his confidence in the power of the people: "Many may think that it was active members of the parties who started erecting the barricades; this of course is very flattering but not entirely true. It was the ordinary citizen, the man without any party affiliation whatsoever who started building them and this is the crux of the matter."[109] On December 17, Party members informed Gorky that it was imperative for him to leave Moscow immediately. That same evening he and Andreeva left for St. Petersburg and from thence went to Finland. The tsarist police, who had long followed Gorky's revolutionary work, arrived at his Moscow apartment shortly after his departure. On December 20, a search was carried out in his St. Petersburg flat.[110]

A word is in order here concerning Gorky's formal political affiliation. Only indirect evidence is available to prove that Gorky joined the Social Democrats in 1905. It is still a controversial issue, and since there were no party membership cards at that time, no material evidence is available. According to Gorky's biographer, A. Kaun, Gorky was never a member of any party.[111] This statement, however, is challenged. It appears that Gorky joined the RSDWP in the latter half of 1905.[112] In support of that contention is Gorky's letter of November 26, 1909, to L. A. Sulerzhitskii. There Gorky wrote that he became a member of the RSDWP a year after Chekhov's death (which had occurred in July 1904) and had never been expelled from it, as a newspaper article had recently intimated.[113] The question of his Party membership is still being debated.

His activities during the year 1905 were proof of his disillusionment with reforms granted from above and of his firm belief that only force could change the hateful system. His enthusiasm and participation in the revolutionary events of 1905 stimulated him to identify himself with revolutionaries. He offered financial assistance and his literary talent to the Bolshevik faction of the RSDWP. He was instrumental in launching the first legal Bolshevik newspaper, *Novaia zhizn'*. The year had begun with Gorky's participation in the delegation to the ministers, where he found himself among the liberal-minded representatives of the intelligentsia. It ended with Gorky's active involvement in the December uprising in Moscow. The members of the Bolshevik faction welcomed Gorky's increased participation and entrusted him with a mission to go abroad in order to win friends and obtain funds for the revolution.

NOTES

1. N. Valentinov (N. V. Volskii), "Vstrechi s Gor'kim," *Novyi zhurnal* 78 (1965): 120. N. Valentinov (N. V. Volskii, 1879–1964), economist, publicist, and member of the RSDWP from 1904, was a Menshevik. He was an editor and author of articles and the book *Young Lenin*. He died in Paris.

2. Established during the Second Congress of the RSDWP, the Party Council consisted of five members, of whom four were appointed by the Central Committee and the Central Organ and the fifth was elected by the Central Organ.

3. The Congress met in April 1905.

4. "Perepiska N. Lenina i N. K. Krupskoi s Peterburgskoi organizatsiei," *Proletarskaia revoliutsiia* 3 (38) (1925): 25–26.

5. "Perepiska Lenina i Krupskoi," 30.

6. *Letopis'*, I: 49. Lopukhin's report on Gorky's financial support of Vperëd was sent to the police department during Gorky's imprisonment in the Peter and Paul fortress in order to bring additional evidence against the accused. See "A. M. Gor'kii i sobytiia 9 Ianvaria 1905 g. v Peterburge," *Istoricheskii arkhiv* I (1955): 106–107.

7. M. N. Liadov. *Iz zhizni partii v 1903–1907 godakh: vospominaniia* (Moscow, 1956), 68.

8. "Perepiska N. Lenina i N. K. Krupskoi s M. M. Litvinovym," *Proletarskaia revoliutsiia* 2 (37) (1925): 84.

9. *Letopis'*, I: 496; Akademiia Nauk SSSR, *M. Gor'kii v epokhu revoliutsii 1905–1917 godov: materialy, vospominaniia, issledovaniia* (hereinafter referred to as *Gor'kii v epokhu revoliutsii: Materialy*) (Moscow, 1957), 128.

10. V. Rudnev, "Gor'kii revoliutsioner," *Novyi mir* 3 (1928): 214.

11. Gor'kii, *Sobranie sochinenii*, vol. 28, 338; Rudnev, "Gor'kii revoliutsioner," 213.

12. *Letopis'*, I: 492.

13. Gor'kii, *Sobranie sochinenii*, vol. 28, 338, 339.

14. Gor'kii, *Sobranie sochinenii*, vol. 28, 342–343.

15. Gor'kii, *Sobranie sochinenii*, vol. 28, 342–343.

16. *Arkhiv*, IV: 174; See also I. Eventov, *Gor'kii v Peterburge-Leningrade* (Leningrad, 1956), 69; Tsentrarkhiv, 86–91.

17. Tsentrarkhiv, *Revoliutsionnyi put' Gor'kogo*, 88; I. Eventov, *Gor'kii v Peterburge Leningrade*, 69.

18. I. Eventov, "Gor'kii v 1905 godu," *Zvezda* 3 (1955): 129.

19. Rudnev, *Gor'kii revoliutsioner*, 63; *Letopis'*, I: 502.

20. The delegation included V. A. Miakotin, N. F. Annenskii, attorney E. Kedrin, the academician K. Arsenev, I. V. Gessen, V. I. Semevskii, the historian N. I. Kareev, and a worker, Dmitri Kuzin, a member of Gapon's "Assembly of Russian Factory Workers." Tsentrarkhiv, *Revoliutsionnyi put' Gor'kogo*, 88; D. Gogol, "Maksim Gor'kii v Petropavlovskoi krepost," *Katorga i ssylka* 8–9 (1932): 8.

21. M. Gor'kii, "Savva Morozov," *Oktiabr'* 6 (1941): 12. See also Gor'kii, *Sobranie sochinenii*, vol. 28, 346–348; V. Nevskii, "Ianvarskie dni v Peterburge 1905," *Krasnaia letopis'* 1 (1922): 37; Gruzdev, *Gor'kii*, 2d ed., 157. The members of the delegation later insisted that the discussion (with Witte) did not have the character of threats, but rather was an expression of apprehension.

22. *Letopis'*, I: 504. Gorky's impressions of the day were later described in the sketch *9-oe Ianvaria* (The 9th of January), a literary interpretation of the events that was published abroad in 1907, and in the novel *Klim Samgin*, written in the 1920s and 1930s.

23. Gor'kii, *Sobranie sochinenii* vol. 28, 347.

24. Gor'kii, *Sobranie sochinenii* vol. 28, 347. P. Rutenberg, the Socialist Revolutionary who tried to draw Gapon into the ranks of the SRs, wrote about the encounter between Gorky and Gapon immediately after the January 9 demonstration. "In the evening of January 9th, Gapon sat in the study of Maksim Gor'kii asking him 'What should we do now, Aleksei Maksimovitch?' Gorky came close, looked at Gapon . . . answered: 'Well, we have to go on . . . even if we should die. . . . ' But to the question as to what was to be done, Gorky had no answer." See P. Rutenberg, "Delo Gapona," *Byloe* 2 (24) (1917): 13.

25. Gor'kii, *Sobranie sochinenii*, vol. 28, 383.

26. Quoted in *Gor'kii v epokhu revoliutsii: Materialy*, 303, from a photostat loaned to A. I. Ovcharenko by I. S. Zilberstein. Lenin, like Gorky, regarded the Revolution as a turning point in Russian history. See "Chto proiskhodit v Rossii, Lenin, *PSS*, IX, 207–209.

27. *Gor'kii i Andreev*, 582.

28. M. Gor'kii, *Ranniaia revoliutsionnaia publitsistika*, ed. by S. M. Breitburg (Moscow, 1938), 127.

29. Gor'kii, *Sobranie sochinenii*, vol. 23, 335–336; *Leninskii sbornik*, XXVI, 128.

30. D. Gogol, "Maksim Gor'kii v Petropavlovskoi Kreposti," 9; "A. M. Gor'kii i sobytiia 9 ianvaria 1905 g. v Peterburge," *Istorieheskii arkhiv* no. 1 (Moscow, 1955), 94.

31. Tsentrarkhiv, *Revoliutsionnyi put' Gor'kogo*, 84.

32. I. M. Novich, *Gor'kii v epokhu pervoi russkoi revoliutsii* (Moscow, 1960), 101–103. After their arrest, the members of the delegation were classified according to their party affiliations. It is of interest that the writer Peshkov (Gor'kii) was classified as liberal. Gogol "Maksim Gor'kii v Petropavlovskoi kreposti," 8.

33. Novich, *Gor'kii v epokhu revoliutsii*, 95–96; *Tsentral'nyi gosudarstvennyi istoricheskii arkhiv* (Moscow, 1905), 31–34.

34. Novich, *Gor'kii v epokhu revoliutsii*, 95–96; "A. M. Gor'kii i sobytiia 9 ianvaria 1905 g. v Peterburge, Document 8 in *Nachalo pervoi russkoi revoliutsii, Istoricheskii arkhiv*, no. 1 (Moscow, 1955), 102–103.

35. "Iz Dnevnika Konstantina Romanova," *Krasnyi arkhiv* 2 (43) (1930), 108.

36. Akademiia Nauk SSSR, *Nachalo pervoi russkoi revoliutsii* 84, 154.

37. Rudnev, *Gor'kii revoliutsioner*, 66.

38. Rudnev, "Gor'kii-revoliutsioner," *Novyi mir*, 215.

39. Tsentrarkhiv, *Revoliutsionnyi put' Gor'kogo*, 100; *Letopis'*, I: 515.

40. Gruzdev, *Gor'kii*, 160–161. Established in 1859 in St. Petersburg, *Literaturnyi fond* was a benevolent society to assist needy writers.

41. Rudnev, *Gor'kii revoliutsioner*, 67; *Leninskii sbornik*, XXVI, 255; *Letopis'*, I: 510–513.

42. *Arkhiv*, IV: 177, 198.

43. Gor'kii, *Sobranie sochinenii*, vol. 28, 353–354. See also "A. M. Gor'kii i sobytiia 9 ianvaria 1905 goda, v Peterburge," 112; Gruzdev, *Gor'kii*, 163; *Arkhiv*, IV: 177.

44. Gor'kii, *Sobranie sochinenii*, vol. 28, 347.

45. *M. Gor'kii: Materialy i issledovaniia*, III, 287. For an evaluation of *Deti solntsa* see L. K. Dolgopolov, "Vokrug 'detei solntsa,' " in Akademiia Nauk SSSR, *M. Gor'kii i ego sovremenniki* (Leningrad, 1968), 79–109.

46. Gor'kii, *Sobranie sochinenii*, vol. 28, 359. Gorky's letter was a reply to an article written by Tolstoy commenting on the events that were taking place in Russia. Tolstoy's view was that political struggle only hampered progress. The only means to destroy all evil on earth was the moral and religious perfectability of the individual. Gorky sent the letter to K. P. Piatniskii and asked him to forward it to Iasnaia Poliana. The letter was, however, never sent to Tolstoy. See Gor'kii, *Sobranie sochinenii*, vol. 28, 554.

47. Gor'kii, *Sobranie sochinenii*, vol. 28, 359–360.

48. Rudnev, *Gor'kii revoliutsioner*, 68.

49. S. Malyshev, "M. Gor'kii v rabochem dvizhenii," *Prozhektor* 13 (1928): 8; Gor'kii, *Sobranie sochinenii*, vol. 28, 559.

50. Gor'kii, *Sobranie sochinenii*, vol. 28, 372–373.

51. Liadov, "Iz zhizni partii," 71; *Letopis'*, I: 542–543.

52. V. D. Bonch-Bruevich, "Moi vstrechi s Gorkim," *Novyi mir* 5 (1928): 187–190; *Leninskii sbornik*, XVI, 197.

53. *Leninskii sbornik*, XVI, 297; XXVI, 438. In a letter to Ladyzhnikov, Gorky wrote that he planned to send 5,000 rubles during the months of September and October for the expenditures of *Demos*. Gor'kii, *Sobranie sochinenii*, vol. 28, 389; Bonch-Bruevich, "Moi vstrechi," 187.

54. On the importance of the *boevye druzhiny*, see J.L.H. Keep, *The Rise of Social Democracy in Russia* (London, 1963), 173.

55. For more details see S. M. Pozner, ed., *Pervaia boevaia organizatsiia bol'shevikov 1905–1907 gg: stat'i, vospominaniia i dokumenty* (Moscow, 1934).

56. See letter by N. E. Burenin addressed to the Institute of World Literature, dated October 7, 1951, and quoted in *Gor'kii v epokhu revoliutsii: Materialy*, 132;

E. Stasova, "Iz vospominanii, in *Gor'kii v epokhu revoliutsii 1905–1907 godov*, 71; Gor'kii, *Sobranie sochinenii*, vol. 27, 387.

57. Michael Futrell, *Northern Underground: Episodes of Russian Revolutionary Transport and Communications through Scandinavia and Finland, 1863–1917* (London, 1963), 66.

58. *Pervaia boevaia organizatsiia bol'shevikov 1905–1907 gg.*, 54–55; Posse, *Moi zhiznennyi put'* (Moscow, 1929), 383–384; *Gor'kii v epokhu revoliutsii: Materialy*, 63–64; *Leninskii sbornik*, V: 538–539; *Letopis'*, I: 541, 547. It appears from the account contained in "The Voyage of the *John Grafton*" that Gapon was in fact only a convenient figurehead in the whole undertaking. See Futrell, *Northern Underground*, 67.

59. Involved in the *John Grafton* episode were also the provocateurs Azef and Zhitomirskii. *Gor'kii v epokhu revoliutsii: Materialy*, 64. For more details on *John Grafton* see *Pervaia boevaia organizatsiia bol'shevikov 1905–1907 gg.*, 110–111, 259–283; M. N. Liadov and S. M. Pozner, eds., *Leonid Borisovich Krasin: Gody podpolia. Sbornik vospominanii, statei i dokumentov* (Moscow, 1928), 237 ff.; N. Krupskaya, *Memories of Lenin (1893–1917)* (Bournemouth, 1942), 87; Futrell, *Northern Underground*, 66–84.

60. *Lenin i Gor'kii*, 411.

61. A. E. Karelin, "Deviatoe Ianvaria i Gapon," *Krasnaia letopis'* 1 (1922): 113, 114.

62. *Arkhiv*, VI: 223.

63. Novich, *Gor'kii v epokhu revoliutsii*, 297.

64. M. Gor'kii, "Pop Gapon," *Arkhiv* VI: 14–21; For more details about Gapon's contact with the authorities and Witte in particular, see "Pis'mo Gapona," *Krasnyi arkhiv* 2 (9) (1925): 294–297.

65. Gor'kii, *Sobranie sochinenii*, vol. 28, 379.

66. Gor'kii, *Sobranie sochinenii*, vol. 28, 382–383.

67. *Birzhevye vedomosti*, 8888 (June 22, 1905), quoted in *Gor'kii v epokhu revoliutsii: Materialy*, 288.

68. *Gor'kii v epokhu revoliutsii: Materialy*, 288.

69. *Gor'kii v epokhu revoliutsii: Materialy*, 288, 289.

70. Gor'kii, *Sobranie sochinenii*, vol. 23, 395.

71. Gor'kii, *Sobranie sochinenii*, vol. 28, 393; Novich, *Gor'kii v epokhu revoliutsii*, 119.

72. For a detailed analysis of style and content of "Pis'ma k rabochim," and Gorky's other journalistic writings of the period, see Novich, *Gor'kii v epokhu revoliutsii*, 236–250; A. Ovcharenko, *Publitsistika M. Gor'kogo* (Moscow, 1961), 186–242.

73. Tsentrarkhiv, *Revoliutsionnyi put' Gor'kogo*, 8–9.

74. In his essay "Kak voznikla *Novaia zhizn'*," L. Krasin wrote that Gorky was one of the main architects of the paper. Novich, *Gor'kii v epokhu revoliutsii*, 124. See also Gor'kii, *Sobranie sochinenii*, vol. 28, 390; *Arkhiv*, V: 168, 165; *Letopis'*, I: 557.

75. Gor'kii, *Sobranie sochinenii*, vol. 28, 375; *Letopis'*, I: 538–39; Among the members were N. A. Rozhkov, a historian at one time sympathetic to the Bolsheviks; P. P. Rumiantsev, a member of the Central Committee of the RSDWP; Bogdanov, a very active member of the party; and I. I. Stepanov-Skvortsov, a Bolshevik,

later the editor of *Izvestiia* (News). See also Dietrich Grille, *Lenins Rivale* (Cologne, 1966), 54–55.

76. Rudnev, *Gor'kii revoliutsioner*, 69; *Leninskii sbornik*, V: 523.

77. Both Liadov and Bogdanov objected to the unnecessary expenditure. See Liadov, "Iz zhizni partii," 112.

78. It is evident from the police record of the imprisoned manufacturer N. P. Shmidt that Gorky asked Shmidt for a loan of 15,000 rubles. This was the money which Gorky transferred to M. Litvinov. See I. Kublanov, "M. Gor'kii i Dekabr'skoe vosstanie," *Istorik marksist* 6 (1941): 6; Gor'kii, *Sobranie sochinenii*, vol. 23, 400; Novich, *Gor'kii v epokhu revoliutsii*, 167; Rudnev, *Gor'kii revoliutsioner*, 70; *Letopis'*, I: 553; *Leonid Krasin: Gody podpolia*, 263; *Gor'kii v epokhu revoliutsii: Materialy*, 62.

79. The first edition was sold out very quickly, and toward the evening the price of a single copy rose to three rubles. Liadov, "Iz zhizni partii," 113.

80. Grégoire Alexinsky, *La vie amère de Maxime Gorki* (Grenoble, 1950), 157–158.

81. V. A. Desnitskii, *A. M. Gor'kii: Ocherki zhizni i tvorchestva* (Moscow, 1959), 97; M. F. Andreeva, "Vstrechi s Leninym," in *Gor'kii v vospominaniiakh sovremennikov*, 43–44. J. Eventov, *Gor'kii v Peterburge-Leningrade* (Leningrad, 1956), 104; Gruzdev, *Gor'kii*, 2d ed. (Moscow, 1960), 165.

82. Alexinsky, *La vie amère de Maxime Gorki*, 158; M. Levin, "Lenin v Peterburge v 1905 godu," *Voprosy istorii* 1 (1955): 9–10; Liadov, "Iz zhizni partii," 148; Novich, *Gor'kii v epokhu revoliutsii*, 225–226; *Letopis'*, I: 565–566. See also Gorky's letter to V. Sorin, in *Gor'kii v epokhu revoliutsii*, 65–66.

83. Gor'kii, *Sobranie sochinenii*, vol. 28, 401–402; *Arkhiv*, VII: 131–132, 294.

84. Gor'kii, *Sobranie sochinenii*, vol. 28, 573: A. B. Zeman and W. B. Scharlau, *The Merchant of Revolution: The Life of Alexander Helphand (Parvus) 1867–1924* (London, 1965), 70.

85. Gor'kii, *Sobranie sochinenii*, vol. 17, 475; See also *Lenin i Gor'kii*, 291, 423; *Gor'kii v epokhu revoliutsii: Materialy*, 65.

86. Rudnev, *Gor'kii revoliutsioner*, 70.

87. The Manifesto called for the overthrow of the tsarist government, a refusal to pay taxes, and the withdrawal of money from savings accounts. It declared that triumphant revolution would not recognize the loans contracted by the tsarist government for the purpose of fighting its own people. The Manifesto was signed by the Petersburg Soviet of Workers, the Central Committee of the RSDWP, and the Peasants' Union. Gor'kii, *Sobranie sochinenii*, vol. 28, 571.

88. M. Gor'kii, "Zametki o meshchanstve," *Novaia zhizn'* 1, October 27, 1905; 4, October 30, 1905; 12, November 13, 1905; 18, November 20, 1905. "Zametki o meshchanstve" is generally referred to as "Notes on Philistinism."

89. *Russkii vestnik* 12 (1905): 591, quoted in Eventov, *Gor'kii v Peterburge-Leningrade*, 106.

90. N. Berdiaev, "Revoliutsiia i kultura," *Poliarnaia zvezda* 2 (1905): 148–149, quoted in Eventov, *Gor'kii v Peterburge-Leningrade*, 109.

91. Gor'kii, *Sobranie sochinenii*, vol. 23, 372.

92. S. Marshak, "Tri vstrechi," in *Gor'kii v vospominaniiakh sovremenikov*, 148.

93. Gor'kii, *Sobranie sochinenii*, vol. 28, 392.

94. Liadov, "Iz zhizni partii," 131.

95. Keep, *Rise of Social Democracy*, 251–52. For more details see Liadov, "Iz zhizni partii," 243–257.

96. Liadov, "Iz zhizni partii," 141.

97. Located in Presnia was the factory of N. P. Shmidt, which was destroyed during the uprising. Shmidt, a nephew of Savva Morozov and a member of the RSDWP, had transferred through Gorky considerable sums of money for the Party. See n. 78.

98. Gor'kii, *Sobranie sochinenii*, vol. 28, 388–389.

99. S. I. Mitskevich, *Revoliutsionnaia Moskva* (Moscow, 1940), 377.

100. *1905 god v Moskve*, in Akademiia Nauk SSSR, *Nachalo pervoi russkoi revoliutsii, ianvar'-mart 1905 goda*. N. S. Trusova, A. A. Novoselskii and L. N. Pushkarev (eds.) (Moscow, 1955), 125; Gor'kii, *Sobranie sochinenii*, vol. 28, 527; F. I. Drabkina, "V dni Dekabr'skogo vosstaniia," in *Gor'kii v epokhu revoliutsii*, 92–97. Drabkina arrived in Moscow to recruit members for the Fourth (Unity) Congress of the RSDWP, which was to begin on December 10 in St. Petersburg. Because of the railway strike and the revolutionary situation in the cities, the Congress was postponed. Instead, an all-Bolshevik conference took place in Tammerfors (December 12–17). Gorky did not attend. See Institut Marksa-Engelsa-Lenina-Stalina, *Kommunisticheskaia partiia Sovetskogo Soiuza v rezoliutsiiakh i resheniiakh s"ezdov, konferentsii i plenumov TsK, 1898–1924* (hereinafter referred to as *KPSS v rezoliutsiiakh*) (7th ed., Moscow, 1954), I: 96.

101. V. Desnitskii, *A. M. Gor'kii: Ocherki zhizni i tvorchestva*, 99; *Letopis'*, I: 567, 570, 571; I. Kublanov, "Maksim Gor'kii: Dekabr'skoe vosstanie," *Istorik Marksist*, no. 6 (1941), 6. Gorky wrote about his experiences in the production of bombs in the sketch "Mitia Pavlov."

102. V. Kolbert, "Vospominaniia," in *Gor'kii v epokhu revoliutsii*, 80; K. P. Piatnitskii, "M. Gor'kii i vremia moskovskikh barrikad 1905 g.," *Krasnaia gazeta* 160, June 12, 1928.

103. P. A. Zalomov, "Moi vstrechi s Gorkim," *Pravda* 172, June 24, 1936: 2; *Letopis'*, I: 564.

104. P. A. Zalomov, "Burevestnik revoliutsii," *Gor'kii v vospominaniiakh sovremennikov*, 169.

105. Kublanov, "Maksim Gor'kii: Dekabr'skoe vosstanie," 4.

106. Gor'kii, *Sobranie sochinenii*, vol. 28, 399–401. See also *Arkhiv*, IV: 192, 193.

107. Gor'kii, *Sobranie sochinenii*, vol. 28, 401.

108. Gor'kii, *Sobranie sochinenii*, vol. 23, 373–376, 451.

109. Gor'kii, *Sobranie sochinenii*, vol. 23, 373.

110. *Letopis'*, I: 572, 573; *Gor'kii v epokhu revoliutsii*, 157.

111. A. Kaun, *Maxim Gorky and His Russia* (London, 1932), 407.

112. *Lenin i Gor'kii*, 11, 411–412.

113. Gor'kii, *Sobranie sochinenii*, vol. 29, 99–100. See also A. I. Spiridovich, *Istoriia bolshevizma v Rossii: ot vozniknoveniia do zakhvata vlasti, 1883–1903–1917* (Paris, 1922), 200–201; *Lenin i Gor'kii*, 383; Gor'kii, *Sobranie sochinenii*, vol. 29, 524–525.

CHAPTER 4

GORKY'S MISSION TO THE UNITED STATES

Well, Leonid, here is where you must visit. I mean it. It is such an amazing fantasy of stone, glass, and iron, a fantasy constructed by crazy giants, monsters longing after beauty, stormy souls full of wild energy. All these Berlins, Parises, and other "big" cities are trifles in comparison with New York. Socialism should first be realized here—that is the first thing you think of, when you see the amazing houses, machines, etc. (April 11, 1906)
Letters of Gorky and Andreev: 1899–1912, 85

America, in spite of all, is a wonderful country; it is a volcano of human energy.
Gor'kii, *Sobranie sochinenii*, vol. 23, 392–393

Gorky's mission to the United States is significant in that it marked his entry on the international scene as a political figure. Arranged with some help by the Bolshevik faction of the Russian Social Democratic Workers' Party (RSDWP), the mission was evidence of the efforts by the Bolsheviks to use Gorky's name and influence to obtain abroad badly needed funds. Gorky, by going to the United States, assumed the role of a political activist and propagandist for the Russian revolution for the first and last time in his political career. The events as they developed in the United States proved that Gorky was ill-suited for that role. However, the visit was important as, having observed closely the economic inequalities prevalent under the capitalist system, he became, as he wrote, a nonconformist socialist. During his stay in the United States he wrote the novel *Mat'* (Mother). Going with him to the United States was N. E. Burenin, a member of the Technical Group of the Central Committee.[1] According to Burenin, the question of Gorky's mission to the United States came up in 1906, when he was forced to leave Russia. Burenin mentioned that Lenin attached great importance to the projected undertaking.[2] The choice of Gorky as an emissary of the revolution was not surprising. The main consideration was his great popularity abroad, evident from the reaction to his imprisonment in January 1905. Andreeva, his common-law wife, went with him, and her presence contributed in no small measure to the failure of the mission.

Preceding his departure, Gorky spent some time in Finland. There, on Krasin's instructions, he helped to organize and participated in concerts and meetings in order to raise funds.[3] There he began his journalistic writings on the revolution. The first article was written in the form of an appeal entitled "K rabochim vsekh stran" (To the Workers of All Countries) and was sent for publication to the major papers of the socialist parties in Western European countries.[4] Written in a highly inflammatory style, the appeal announced to the world that a revolution had begun in Russia and bitterly criticized the policy of the tsarist government. The style of the appeal was similar to the style of the Bolshevik leaflets of the time and included slogans such as "long live the proletariat," "long live the workers of all countries who alone produce the wealth of nations," and "long live socialism—the religion of the workers."[5]

His departure from Finland on February 12 (25), 1906, was quite sudden. "I did not expect to leave so soon," he wrote E. Peshkova, "and there is so much to do that I must sit day and night and write letters."[6] He explained that he was warned by the Finnish "activists" that the tsarist authorities were demanding his extradition and that Saltz, the chief of police of Helsingfors, had a warrant for his arrest but hesitated to carry out the order because of Gorky's great popularity with the people of Finland. His itinerary included Germany, France, and England, but the main destination was the United States. His aim was to win friends for the revolution, to obtain funds, and to prevent the tsarist government from securing a foreign loan.[7]

Gorky's first stop en route to the United States was Berlin. The reception in the German capital was cordial, especially on the part of the leaders of the German Social Democratic party, A. Bebel, K. Kautsky, and K. Liebknecht. Gorky appeared at literary evenings and apparently raised some money for the Bolsheviks.[8] Not unlike A. Herzen, who, more than a half century before, had made a similar trip to escape the regime of Nicholas I, Gorky was disappointed with what he saw in Western Europe. He was repulsed by the Prussians' love of law: "The law is a fetish here, a religion. This is why the Prussian is so repulsive and stupid. Only a revolution could save this self-satisfied race from spiritual death. But they do not want a revolution."[9] On hearing of Trepov's visit to Prussia to learn about its parliamentary institutions, he commented, "A nice parliament we are going to have! Prussia is similar to Russia not only in the sound of her name, but in some other aspects also."[10] He expressed his fear that the Duma would be as useless for the Russians as the Prussian parliament was for Prussia.

Gorky's next stop was Switzerland, where he met with his friend Andreev. It was there that he wrote a bitter indictment of the tsarist government entitled "Ne davaite deneg russkomu pravitel'stvu" (Not One Penny for the Russian Government).[11] Money, he said, should not be given to a government of oppression, to a government that, several times in history, had used its millions to suppress the struggle for freedom in other countries. Gorky warned the governments of Western Europe that, given Russia's difficult economic situation, the money could not be repaid.[12] From Switzerland, he traveled to France, where he had many friends, among them the writer Anatole France, an executive member of the "League of Friends of the Russian People" and one of the first to protest against Gorky's imprisonment in January 1905. In a letter addressed to A. France, Gorky repeated his faith in the great potential of his people and, like a Slavophile of the nineteenth century, extolled the "wonderful soul" of the Russians. He asked France to use his influence in order to prevent the granting of a loan to the tsarist government.[13] It was after his arrival in the United States that Gorky learned that the tsarist government had successfully concluded its negotiations for a loan from France. In a pamphlet, *Prekrasnaia Frantsiia* (La Belle France), he expressed his bitter feelings over France's betrayal of the principles of liberty and freedom. The tone of the pamphlet, similar to other publicist writings of the period, was militant, uncompromising, and full of emotion.[14] Was he that naive to believe that his written words would influence the powers that were, Russia or France?

On March 23 (April 5), 1906,[15] Gorky, Andreeva, and Burenin left Cherbourg for the United States. From all appearances it could have been assumed that his mission to the United States would be a success. The progressive segments of American society were opposed to the Russian autocracy, its disastrous war with Japan, and its policy of dealing harshly with the participants of the revolution. Ever since "Bloody Sunday," Gorky's name had appeared often on the pages of the American newspapers. During his imprisonment, the editors and publishers of *Century* had been ready to support the action of the *Berliner Tageblatt* to free Gorky. Another advantage was his literary popularity. Many of his works had been translated into English, and enjoyed a wide reading public. His involvement in the political and social problems of Russia was also known to some sectors of American society. An article by C. Brinton entitled "Career of Maxim Gorky" had appeared in *Everybody's Magazine* a year before

Gorky's arrival in the United States.[16] Following a brief discussion of Gorky's career as a writer, Brinton turned to Gorky, the social reformer. He maintained that Gorky had become involved in the social-political problems of Russia through coincidence rather than through conviction; immediately after the publication of his stories, he was approached by the three leading political parties: the Nationalists, the Marxists, and the Conservatives. (Since the author mentions that the Nationalists had discovered Gorky, one can surmise that by the Nationalists, Brinton meant the populists, *narodniki*). Through natural affinity, Gorky had drifted into the camp of the liberty-loving Marxists. The Marxists had made much of their new prophet, his articles were widely read, and thousands of his photographs were sold. And yet, continued Brinton, Gorky finds it difficult to see himself as a reformer or a prophet, in spite of his dedicated work. "For serious minds," concluded the author, "Gorky's ethics remain too primitive. He professes no specific doctrine; he offers no valid panacea."[17]

Among the writers and journalists, an attempt was made to organize a campaign to collect funds for the revolution. Ernest Poole, writer and journalist, and some of the members of the "A" Club of writers, among whom were Jack London, Mark Twain, Upton Sinclair, and the journalist Leroy Scott, were determined to make Gorky's mission a success.[18] An American welcoming committee was organized, consisting of prominent personalities in the field of letters, with Mark Twain as chairman. Twain's sympathies with the Russian cause were expressed even before Gorky's arrival in a letter to the Socialist Revolutionary N. V. Chaikovskii, who also was on a mission to collect funds for his own party, the SRs. It read:

My sympathies are with the Russian revolution, of course. . . . Government by false promises, by lies, by treachery, and by the butcher-knife, for the aggrandizement of a single family of drones and its idle and vicious kin, has been born quite long enough in Russia, I should think. And it is to be hoped that the roused nation, now rising in its strength, will presently put an end to it and set up a republic in its place.[19]

To launch the campaign, a stag dinner for fifteen was planned for April 11 (March 29), the day after Gorky's arrival. A reception was arranged by the millionaire socialist Gaylard Wilshire, the owner and editor of the *Wilshire Magazine*. Invited guests included H. G. Wells, who was visiting the United States at that time, and professors Charles Beard and Franklin Giddings. Receptions and mass meetings were planned in New York and other cities by liberal, socialist, and labor groups and organizations. "To millions of Americans," wrote Poole, "Gorky's name had become a symbol of the cause of Russian freedom then so popular over here."[20] There were rumors that Gorky might be invited to the White House. Thus, everything seemed to promise a successful campaign.

It was not long however, before factors emerged that were to bring about the failure of Gorky's mission. The rivalry between the liberal segments of American society and the American socialists resulted in these two groups working at cross purposes: "The Russian party wanted to avail itself of his [Gorky's] literary prestige to secure funds from the rich and the fashionable, and the American socialists wished to exploit him as one of the great intellectuals of their party."[21] There was another serious obstacle to Gorky's mission. The word "revolution" itself was still popular, but an understanding of the Russian revolution, as Gorky saw it, was lacking. John Martin, Gorky's host on Staten Island and a Fabian socialist, noted:

It was not within human power to stir the American mind to the purposes of the revolution as Maxim Gorky understood them. For even among those who, despite all criticism, ardently continued to support Gorky's cause, there existed at the time no other image of the Russian revolution, than that of a political change.[22]

Political change meant the establishment in Russia of a liberal and constitutional order. The message was delivered to American audiences by the eminent Russian historian P. N. Miliukov, who the year before visited the United States. For the Americans this was the choice they could support.[23] An important factor that contributed to the failure of Gorky's mission was the attitude of the Russian embassy, which branded Gorky a dangerous "social revolutionist" and insisted that it was wrong to have a money-raising campaign for the purchase of arms that could be used against a friendly government. Unable to prevent Gorky's entry into the United States, the Russian embassy prepared information concerning his common-law wife, knowing that puritanical America would neither honor nor respect someone who dared to break the accepted and sanctified convention of marriage. The members of the welcoming committee learned that Andreeva was coming with Gorky. They also learned that the Russian embassy was in possession of photographs of Gorky's "deserted" wife and children and of his "mistress" and that the Russian ambassador, Baron Rosen, planned to give these to the press in order to upset the campaign from its beginning. To prevent the action of the embassy, the members of the "A" Club decided that Gorky should move to the "A" Club and that Andreeva should occupy a suite in the Belleclaire Hotel reserved for them by Wilshire. There was also a suggestion that Gorky should occupy the reserved suite in the Belleclaire Hotel and that Andreeva go to Staten Island to stay with John Martin and his wife.[24] All this was to be communicated to Gorky immediately after his arrival.

When on April 10 (March 28), 1906, the ship *Kaiser Wilhelm der Grosse*, docked at Hoboken, crowds in the thousands were awaiting her arrival. The *New York Times* reported that "the reception given to Gorky rivaled with that of Kossuth and Garibaldi."[25] On his arrival, Gorky stated that he was happy that his long-cherished dream to come to the free land of America had come true.[26] One of the first people to meet Gorky was Zinovii Peshkov, his adopted son. Others present were representatives of the Socialist party, delegates of the Socialist Labour Party, and former members of the Bund.[27] Immediately, members of the "A" Club warned Burenin of the Russian embassy's plan. They asked Burenin to persuade Gorky to change the arrangements made for his and Andreeva's accommodation, but Gorky refused.[28] Leroy Scott approached the representatives of the press, who apparently knew that Andreeva was not Gorky's legal wife, and tried to explain the difficulties encountered by anyone trying to obtain a divorce in the Greek Orthodox Church. Scott asked that Gorky's private life be kept out of the press.

The reception in the "A" Club took place as scheduled. Poole wrote about Gorky's appearance and the impression he made upon the audience. Gorky, lean and gigantic, dressed in a blue blouse and black trousers tucked into high boots, held all spellbound by the stories, which in his low deep voice, he told through Ivan Narodnyi to old Mark Twain.[29] Twain, in his address, expressed sympathy with the Russian cause and asked the Americans to respond generously to the plea for aid for the revolution. In his reply, Gorky pointed out that the revolution in Russia was not over and spoke of the importance of financial assistance.[30] A program for future receptions was outlined, including a dinner for the New York literary circle and a meeting in Boston planned by Alice Stone Blackwell, a noted American suffragette. Arthur Brisbane of Hearst's *Evening Journal* wrote an editorial in support of Gorky's mission. It was to appear in all of Hearst's papers across the country.[31] The same evening, April 11 (March 29), at Wilshire's reception, Gorky met H. G. Wells. There, Gorky gave an interview in which he blamed the anarchy in Russia on the policy of the tsarist government and that of S. Witte in particular. Commenting on his reception in the United States, he said that he felt that he had come to a country of friends.[32]

On April 13 (March 31), a reception was held in Gorky's suite in the Belleclaire Hotel. It was attended by more than a hundred representatives of the press and members of various organizations. Present in the receiving line was Andreeva. Since she had no knowledge of English, the meeting of hundreds of people she did not know was for her a painful experience.[33] Many years later Andreeva wrote A. Kaun, Gorky's biographer, that she considered her presence at the reception a great mistake and explained that she had no knowledge of it beforehand. This was the only time during the American visit that she was made to appear at an official function.[34]

The newspapers were still friendly towards Gorky on the 12th and the 13th of April (March 30 and 31). On April 14 (April 1), the outcome of his mission was pretty well decided by two photographs that appeared on the front page of the *World*. One was of Gorky and his "family," the other of Andreeva with the caption "[the] so-called Mme Gorky who is not Mme Gorky at all, but a Russian actress Andreeva, with whom he has been living since his separation from his wife a few years ago." It explained that Gorky was not legally divorced from his wife because of difficulties encountered with the Greek Orthodox Church. The Sunday papers reprinted the story published in *World*, with the result that Gorky and his party were evicted from three hotels and found themselves in the street, in the middle of the night, with their belongings piled up on the pavement in the rain. With the help of Leroy Scott, Gorky and Andreeva found temporary accommodation in the "A" Club and later moved to the home of Prestonia and John Martin, on Staten Island.[35]

There is little doubt that the story that appeared in the press on April 14 spelled the end of Gorky's mission, something of which both he and his friends were painfully aware. The consequences were not long in emerging. Messages began arriving from groups in New York and elsewhere, canceling meetings and dinners that had been arranged to boost the Gorky campaign. In Boston, Alice Stone Blackwell said, "I don't want to judge Mr. Gorky, but apparently his views on morality and ours somewhat differ."[36] The writer William Dean Howells canceled the dinner that he and Twain were sponsoring, and the latter withdrew from participation in the campaign.

Gorky wrote a letter to E. Peshkova on April 14 (or 18) (April 1, or 5), where he tried to explain the whole "incident" and asked her to send a wire to the American press to clarify the situation. By doing so, he continued, she would do a great service to the revolution. He explained the "incident" by reference to the attack by the press, the action of the Russian embassy, and the rival financial campaign of the SRs. The reply came in a cable, addressed to the editor of the *New York Herald*:

Today I received a letter from Aleksei Maksimovich Peshkov, Maxim Gorky, which confirmed the news communicated by the newspaper despatches about the reception accorded to him in the United States. I am appalled by the intrusion into the private and intimate life of a man, and amazed that the Americans, citizens of a free country, who have achieved such wide political freedom, are not free from prejudices which are dead in Russia.[37]

Signed "Ekaterina Peshkova," it appeared in the press on May 14 (May 1). But the cable was of no avail. As the smear campaign continued in the yellow press, Andreeva was referred to as "the actress," or "that woman Andreeva." On the same day that details of Gorky's private life appeared in the press, his socialist friends released a copy of a telegram signed by Gorky and addressed to W. D. Haywood and C. Moyer, two leaders of the Western Federation of Miners indicted for the murder of Frank Steunenburg, former governor of Idaho.[38] The telegram, sent in care of the

County Jail at Caldwell, Idaho, read as follows: "Greetings to you, my brother socialists. Courage! The day of justice and deliverance for the oppressed of all the world is at hand! Ever fraternally yours, Maxim Gorky."[39] In the hagiographic Soviet writings regarding responsibility for sending the telegram that in no small measure contributed to the failure of Gorky's mission, one finds an attempt to deny Gorky's responsibility.[40] Gorky's own explanation, in a letter written to K. P. Piatinskii is quite different:

I shall briefly explain the scandal of which you have heard. It was started by the newspaper *World* on the instructions of the Russian embassy. It was then "picked up" by the yellow press and the American press was "off and running!" I myself have helped matters by sending a telegram to the two unjustly imprisoned socialists whom the government wants very much to hang. This offended Roosevelt who at first had wanted to see me in the White House. The bourgeois were also offended.[41]

The anti-Gorky campaign in the press continued, but editorials of New York's better newspapers treated the story with moderation. Some turned to ridiculing those who, from an enthusiastic support of Gorky, turned against him overnight. Certain circles of the American society were outraged by the treatment of the distinguished Russian writer and revolutionary. Professor Frank Giddings wrote an article of protest in the *Independent* under the title "The Social Lynching of Gorky and Andreeva." He compared the treatment of Gorky with the lynching of three Negroes which took place in Missouri at the same time:

Maxim Gorky came to this country not for the purpose of putting himself on exhibition, as many literary characters have done at one time or another, not for the purpose of lining his pockets with American gold, but for the purpose of obtaining sympathy and financial assistance for a people struggling against terrific odds, as the American people once struggled, for political and individual liberty. . . . All was assertion, accusation, hysteria, impertinence in the way the papers have tried to instruct Gorky in morality.[42]

The strongest condemnation of Gorky's treatment by the American press was contained in a statement by H. G. Wells:

I do not know what motive actuated a certain section of the American press to initiate the pelting of Maxim Gorky. A passion for moral purity may have prompted it but certainly no passion for moral purity ever before begot so brazen and abundant torrent of lies. . . . In Boston, in Chicago it was the same. At the bare suggestion of Gorky's coming, the same outbreak occurred, the same display of imbecile, gross lying, the same absolute disregard of the tragic cause he had come to plead.[43]

For Gorky and Andreeva the episode was insulting. Gorky refused to give any explanation or denial regarding his relation with Andreeva and denounced the campaign waged against him: "That dirt is conspired by the friends of the Russian government"; he expressed the hope "that the best people of all lands will be with us."[44]

Liberal papers in Russia, outraged by the treatment Gorky was receiving in the United States, protested strongly. Gorky rejected the criticism of the Americans in an astonishingly moderate article that he sent to the liberal newspaper *XX vek* (Twentieth Century).[45] He was grateful for the interest shown and wrote that he regarded the "incident" as an expression of the class ideology of the upper stratum of bourgeois American society. Expressing his disdain for middle-class morality, he wrote that the phenomenon of the middle class, which considers itself to be the high priest of the moral order, was a universal phenomenon, and not characteristic of the United States alone.[46]

Among the American intellectuals, Mark Twain's desertion from the ranks of Gorky's supporters was a great loss to the cause. Twain made several pronouncements on the case, criticizing Gorky's behavior. In an article entitled "The Gorky Incident," he clearly defined his stand:

The efforts which have been made in Gorky's justification are entitled to all respect because of the magnanimity of the motive back of them, but I think that the ink was wasted. Custom is custom; it is built of brass, boiler iron, granite; facts, reasonings, arguments have no more effect upon it than the idle winds have upon Gibraltar.[47]

Commenting on the changed attitude of Mark Twain, Gorky wrote that there was no need to attack Mark Twain. "He is a wonderful person—but he is old and old people often cannot understand clearly the meaning of things."[48]

Gorky's report to Krasin throws more light on other factors that upset his mission. He wrote that the Russian embassy circulated a rumor accusing him and Andreeva of robbing the millionaire Savva Morozov of fifteen million (probably rubles) and then murdering him. Gorky mentioned also that he had promised to write fifteen articles about Russia for Hearst's *American* and that this preference given to the *American* had antagonized other newspapers.[49] In Russia, the newspaper *Birzhevye vedomosti* agreed with this interpretation, stating that the "incident" was caused by the rivalry between the Pulitzer and Hearst publishing houses.[50] An additional factor in the failure of Gorky's mission was the presence of the representatives of the SRs in the United States who were also campaigning for funds.

There was also the fear of Gorky's influence upon the American worker expressed in the press shortly after his arrival. An open letter signed "A gentleman" appeared in the *New York American*. It asked the following question: "Is there not every likelihood that he [Gorky] will do his utmost while here to fan the flames of discontent and sedition among our already restive proletariat?"[51]

In spite of great obstacles, Gorky tried to salvage his mission, appearing at meetings and writing articles, which were still being accepted by some American newspapers. In one of the articles, misleadingly entitled "To Replace and Punish Witte" and published in the *American*, April 25 (15), Gorky's criticism was of the Duma then assembling. He maintained that it was unrepresentative of the people and that the party that had the majority, the Kadety (Constitutional Democrat), was unable to find a solution to the peasant question, the most important question for Russia. The Russian people, continued Gorky, demanded a constituent assembly elected on the basis of the direct, equal, and secret ballot, the dismissal of S. Witte's cabinet, and punishment of those guilty of repression. Gorky predicted the imminent dissolution of the Duma.[52]

When on April 23 (May 6), 1906, the Fundamental Laws were proclaimed that curtailed the power of the Duma, Gorky contended in an interview that appeared in the *Boston Herald* that the tsar, by issuing the Fundamental Laws, had ruined all possibility of peaceful reforms in the country, if there ever had been such a possibility.[53]

Important to note was Gorky's disappointment over the lack of support from the Bolshevik faction of the Party that sent him on the mission.[54] There was some improvement when news of the developments in the Party and the country reached him through Krasin.[55] The latter forwarded the Protocols of the Fourth Party Congress of the RSDWP held in Stockholm, April 23 to May 8, and informed him of the events in the country, the unrest in the countryside, and the repressive measures taken by the government.[56] While still in the United States, Gorky received news of the death of his only daughter, Ekaterina (Katia). She was six years old. Personal grief added to the difficulties he encountered.

The Gorky mission to the United States was a failure, and no person was more aware of it than Gorky himself. Although he tried to raise his morale by writing to Krasin, Piatnitskii, Ladyzhnikov, and E. Peshkova that he would not give up the fight easily and that the campaign would still be financially successful, a note of disappointment is discernible in his letters.[57] He later wrote with regret that the total amount of funds raised did not exceed $10,000.[58]

And yet, not all was lost for Gorky during his stay in the United States. Seeing his mission failing, he turned to his literary work. The novel *Mat'* (Mother) is the most important work of that period.[59] Written on an upstate New York farm, it inspired and encouraged generations of revolutionaries. It exerted great influence on workers who believed that their sacrifices were worthwhile, for they would bring about a better tomorrow for all of mankind. In addition to the novel *Mat'*, Gorky wrote a series of sketches under the title *V Amerike* (American Sketches), which aroused a storm of protest. In these sketches he criticized the deplorable situation of the American masses, the enslavement of all creative instincts in man, and the transformation of the people into a machine-like mass. If one wants to become a socialist in a hurry, wrote Gorky, he should come to the United States.[60] Little wonder that the work came under fire.[61] In a letter to E. Peshkova, sent at the end of August, Gorky described the ever mounting resentment against him. "I am," he wrote, "the most terrible person in the country, [I am] an anarchist, bereft by nature of any moral principles, and astounding in my hatred of religion, order and finally, of mankind."[62]

In view of the controversy surrounding the reason for writing these sketches, Gorky's explanation contained in a letter to Ladyzhnikov is interesting. The sketches were written simply in order to earn some money from the American press, wrote Gorky: "What can you do? Americans read only what is written about America. These sketches are of no significance at all, but perhaps you could sell them to some German and French journals?"[63]

His favorable impression of America is evident in the letters he wrote to E. Peshkova and to his friends. "It is very interesting here, regardless of everything! What a life! A dream!"[64] In a letter to Andreev he commented that he was overwhelmed by the "amazing fantasy of stone, glass and iron; neither Berlin nor Paris could compare with New York."[65] His admiration was for such American traits as energy, the ability to work, and the desire to achieve. He wrote Piatnitskii, "What they do here, how they work, how much energy, ignorance, self-satisfaction. . . . I am marveling and cursing at the same time! I am bored, and I am happy, and the devil take it; it is very funny!"[66]

In the Russian conservative newspapers, such as *Vestnik Evropy* (Messenger of Europe), and *Rech'* (Speech), Gorky's writings concerning the United States were severely criticized. *Vestnik Evropy* wrote that "there was in these writings too much Gorky and too little America!" In *Rech'* it was stated that in the sketches *V Amerike* one can feel the strong pen, the noble soul, and the proud thought, and yet in all this one can sense this clumsy and dull man in whom the morality of a preacher had eclipsed the free brush of the artist![67]

On October 13 (September 30), Gorky and his party left the United States for Italy. A short note announcing his departure appeared in the *New York Times*:

MAXIM GORKY SAILS—HIS VIEWS ON AMERICANS TO BE PUBLISHED IN FORTHCOMING BOOK. Maxim Gorky, the Russian revolutionist, and his companion Mme Andreeva sailed for Naples on the steamship *Princess Irene* yesterday morning. They sailed as M. and Mme Peshkov, and both were averse to talking of their American experiences when seen by the reporters at the dock. Gorky said his views on this country would be contained in a book he is to publish, while Mme Andreeva said she had been misunderstood by the people of this country. That was all either actress or author would say.[68]

Gorky's stay in the highly industrialized United States deepened his resentment of economic inequalities present under the capitalist system. He wrote to E. Peshkova that the trip had made him a genuine revolutionary; previously he was only a reformer. The meaning of revolution had acquired for him new depth.[69] But he had failed as an emissary of the revolution. The causes of the failure were the scandal concerning his private life, his telegram to Haywood and Moyer, his exclusive contract with Hearst, and the disruptive activities by the Russian embassy. He consoled himself by turning to writing and then traveled to Italy where he stayed for a period of seven years. The time spent on the island of Capri has come to be known as the Capri period.

A rather sarcastic comment regarding Gorky, the revolutionary, came from the pen of the then president of the United States, Theodore Roosevelt. In a letter dated March 15, 1906, addressed to the writer Upton Sinclair, he put in doubt Gorky's contribution to the revolution in Russia. "The abortiveness of the late revolution in Russia sprang precisely from the fact that too much of the leadership was of the Gorky type, and therefore the kind of leadership which can never lead anybody anywhere save into a serbonian bog."[70]

NOTES

1. Gor'kii, *Sobranie sochinenii*, vol. 17, 9. See also *Letopis'*, I: 584; Akademiia Nauk SSSR, *M. Gor'kii v epokhu revoliutsii, 1905–1917 godov: materialy, vospominaniia, issledovaniia* (Moscow, 1957), 97–113. Gorky's adopted son, Zinovii Peshkov, was employed in the office of G. Wilshire, the millionaire socialist and owner of the *Wilshire Magazine*, before Gorky's arrival in New York. Since Wilshire was Gorky's host in New York, it is reasonable to assume that Zinovii took part in the organization of Gorky's trip to the United States. Zinovii Peshkov died in 1965, a French citizen, a decorated soldier, and in the last years of his life, in France's diplomatic service. He left his archives to the then Soviet government. The present writer had no access to these materials.

2. N. E. Burenin, "Poezdka A. M. Gorkogo v Ameriku," *Novyi mir* 6 (1940): 192. See also R. Ganelin, "M. Gor'kii i amerikanskoe obshchestvo v 1906 godu," *Russkaia literatura* 1 (1958): 201; A. Kaun, *Maxim Gorky and His Russia* (London, 1932), 569.

3. See M. N. Liadov and S. M. Pozner, eds., *Leonid Krasin: Gody podpolia* (Moscow, 1928), 247; "Daty zhizni i deiatel'nosti A. M. Gorkogo" *Krasnyi arkhiv* no. 5 (Moscow, 1936), 69; Tsentrarkhiv, *Revoliutsionnyi put 'Gor'kogo*, 103; *Arkhiv*, V: 172; *Andreeva: Perepiska, vospominaniia, stat'i*, A. P. Grigorieva and S. V. Shirina (eds). 2nd edition (Moscow, 1963), 611.

4. The appeal appeared in *L'Humanité* on January 21, 1906; it was also published in *Vorwärts*, the Belgian *Peuple*, and the Italian *Avanti*. The appeal circulated in Russia, and one copy, intercepted by the police, found its way into Gorky's police dossier. See Gor'kii, *Sobranie sochinenii*, vol. 23, 377, 452; Tsentrarkhiv, *Revoliutsionnyi put' Gor'kogo*, 104.

5. Gor'kii, *Sobranie sochinenii*, vol. 23, 377–380.

6. *Arkhiv*, V: 173; *Letopis'*, I: 584.

7. Gor'kii, *Sobranie sochinenii*, vol. 28, 407–408, 576.

8. M. M. Litvinov reported from Berlin on March 8 (21), that there were 5,000 francs left from Gorky's appearances at lectures and concerts. See *Letopis'* I: 591.

9. *Arkhiv*, V: 176–177.

10. Gor'kii, *Sobranie sochinenii*, vol. 28, 411.

11. The appeal was written in March 1906 and was sent to Ladyzhnikov with the request that it be forwarded to the United States and published there prior to his arrival. It appeared in the journal *Krasnoe znamia* 1 (1906), and in *L'Humanité*, 772 (April 9, 1906). See *Arkhiv*, VII: 136, 295; Gor'kii *Sobranie sochinenii*, vol. 23, 381–385.

12. Gor'kii, *Sobranie sochinenii*, vol. 23, 381–385. According to Lenin it was European capital that was saving the Russian autocracy; see Lenin, PSS IX, 372–373, 377–378; Gor'kii, *Sobranie sochinenii*, vol. 7, 522–523.

13. Gor'kii, *Sobranie sochinenii*, vol. 23, 386–391, 453–454; V. Lebedev, "Gor'kii v Amerike," *Sibirskie ogni*, no. 6 (1961), 74; *Letopis'*, I: 593. The letter, dated March 20 (April 2), first appeared in *Krasnoe znamia* 1 (1906): 17–22.

14. Gorky, *Articles and Pamphlets* (Moscow, 1951), 142.

15. *Letopis'*, I: 594.

16. C. Brinton, "Career of Maxim Gorky," *Everybody's Magazine* XII (1905): 464–467.

17. Brinton, "Career," 467.

18. The "A" Club had learned of Gorky's forthcoming visit from Ivan Narodnyi, who came to the United States from Russia a few months before Gorky's arrival. See Kaun, *Maxim Gorky and His Russia*, 583; *Arkhiv*, VII: 137, 396.

19. Cited in Kaun, *Maxim Gorky and His Russia*, 592.

20. E. Poole, "Maxim Gorky in New York," *Slavonic and East European Review* 22 (1944): 79.

21. "Gorky as Author and as Revolutionist," *Independent* LX (1906), 936; see also *New York Tribune* April 16, 1906, 1.

22. Quoted in Filia Holtzman, "A Mission That Failed: Gorky in America," *Slavic and East European Journal* 4 (1962): 233.

23. "Gorky as Author," 935–937. P. N. Miliukov was visiting the United States to deliver a series of lectures. His views on the political situation in Russia and the way to solve the problems were within the program of the Constitutional Democrats (*Kadety*).

24. Poole, "Gorky in New York," 79.

25. *New York Times*, April 11, 1906, 6; B. I. Burtsov, "Gor'kii i Zapad" in *M. Gor'kii: stat'i i pamflety* (Leningrad, 1949), 10.

26. *New York Times*, April 11, 1906, 6. See also Burenin, "Poezdka Gor'kogo,"

194; S. I. Brodskaia, "O deiatel'nosti Gor'kogo v Amerike v 1906 godu" in *Gor'kii v epokhu revoliutsii 1905–1907 godov*, 390; Lebedev, "Gor'kii v Amerike," 78.

27. *New York Tribune*, April 11, 1906, 1.

28. Poole, "Gorky in New York," 79.

29. Poole, "Gorky in New York, 80; *Arkhiv*, VII: 361.

30. *Literary Digest* 32 (1906): 599, cited in Ganelin, "M. Gor'kii:Amerikanskoe obshchestvo v 1906 godu," 205; Brodskaia ("Odeiatel'nosti Gor'kogo v Amerike," 390; Lebedev, "Gor'kii v Amerike," 85.

31. Poole, "Gorky in New York," 81.

32. Brodskaia, "O deiatel'nosti Gor'kogo v Amerike", 390; Lebedev, "Gor'kii v Amerike," 85; Kaun, *Maxim Gorky and His Russia*, 586.

33. *Letopis'*, I: 598.

34. Kaun, *Maxim Gorky and his Russia*, 585; Poole, "Gorky in New York," 79.

35. Poole, "Gorky in New York," 81–82; Lebedev, "Gor'kii v Amerike," 100; Brodskaia, "O deiatel'nosti Gorkogo v Amerike," 392; Ganelin, "M. Gor'kii: Amerikanskoe obshchestvo v 1906 godu," 207.

36. Cited in Kaun, *Maxim Gorky and His Russia*, 573.

37. *Letopis'*, I: 609, as quoted in Poole, "Gorky in New York," 82.

38. The Haywood-Moyer case began in December of 1905, when Frank Steunenburg, former governor of Idaho, was killed by an explosion of dynamite. Haywood and Moyer were accused of having paid one Harvey Orchard to kill Steunenburg and, in March 1906, were formally indicted for murder. For more details see J. G. Rayback, *A History of American Labor* (New York, 1966), 241–242.

39. Gor'kii, *Sobranie sochinenii*, vol. 28, 414.

40. Ganelin, "M. Gor'kii: Amerikanskoe obshchestvo v 1906 godu," 207.

41. *Letopis'*, I: 599.

42. F. H. Giddings, "Social Lynching of Gorky and Andreeva," *Independent* LX (1906): 976–978; Ganelin, "M. Gor'kii: Amerikanskoe obshchestvo v 1906 godu," 200.

43. H. G. Wells, *The Future in America* (London, 1906), 250–253.

44. *Times* [Buffalo], April 15, 1906; *Houston Chronicle*, April 15, 1906, quoted in *Letopis'*, I: 599.

45. Gor'kii, *Sobranie sochinenii*, vol. 23, 392–393. "Pis'mo v redaktsiiu" was first published in *Literaturnaia gazeta* 33 (June 15, 1938). See Gor'kii, *Sobranie sochinenii*, vol. 23, 454.

46. Gor'kii, *Sobranie sochinenii*, vol. 23, 392–393.

47. M. Twain, "The Gorky Incident: An Unpublished Fragment," *Slavonic and East European Review* 22 (1944): 37–38.

48. Gor'kii, *Sobranie sochinenii*, vol. 23, 393.

49. Gor'kii, *Sobranie sochinenii*, vol. 28, 417. It has been argued that no such agreement was made. Neither the *Evening Journal* nor the *New York American*, both Hearst papers, mentioned the contract. Had it been concluded, American journalism (being what it was) would have advertised it. See R. Zamula, "Maxim Gorky's American Visit and Sketches in Recent Soviet Interpretations" (unpublished

master's degree essay, Columbia University, New York, 1951). The argument cannot be accepted, since Gorky did commit himself to write fifteen articles for the Hearst papers and related such to Peshkova and Ladyzhnikov. See Gor'kii, *Sobranii sochinenii*, vol. 28, 427, 435; *Arkhiv*, VII: 177.

50. Burtsov, "Gor'kii i Zapad," 11.

51. *New York American*, April 13, 1906, editorial page.

52. An unpublished article by Gorky written in the United States is in the B. I. Nicolaevsky Archives, in the Hoover Institution on War, Revolution, and Peace, Stanford.

53. *Boston Herald*, May 30, 1906.

54. *Arkhiv*, VII: 139, 140, 141.

55. Akademiia Nauk SSSR, *Vtoroi period revoliutsii, 1906–1907 gody*, G. M. Derenkovskii, E. P. Voronin, A. V. Piaskovskii, K. F. Sidorov, and M. S. Simova (eds) (Moscow, 1961), 57–60.

56. *Protokoly s"ezdov i konferentsii vsesoiuznoi kommunisticheskoi partii bol'shevikov. Pervaia konferentsiia voennykh i boevykh organizatsii RSDRP* (Moscow, 1932), 252–257; *Letopis'*, I: 623.

57. Gor'kii, *Sobranie sochinenii*, vol. 28, 418.

58. *Lenin i Gor'kii: Pis'ma, vospominaniia, dokumenty* (Moscow, 1961), 222. Other sources indicate that perhaps the sum was higher. Y. M. Smirnov wrote in his reminiscences about Krasin that in July 1906 he received instructions from Andreeva to go to one of the villages on the Russo-Finnish border in order to transfer to Krasin (Nikitich) between 50,000 and 100,000 rubles earmarked for the Bolshevik faction. Smirnov further wrote that he did not find Krasin and instead transferred the money to Andreeva's sister, A. V. Krit, who had a *dacha* in Mustamiaki. See *Leonid Krasin: gody podpolia*, 256. V. Bogomolov, an active member of the RSDWP, wrote that in 1906 he saw Krasin often either in Mustamiaki or on the estate of Krit. The meetings took place for the purpose of transmitting money to "Nikitich," "which came," wrote Bogomolov, "from our finance groups, and especially from the United States, from Gorky and Andreeva." *Ibid*. Since the RSDWP had no accounting system until 1908, it is almost impossible to establish the exact amount raised by Gorky in the United States in 1906. Thus the question of funds raised by Gorky in the United States is still a matter of conjecture.

59. *M. Gor'kii: Materialy i issledovaniia*, III, 402.

60. Gor'kii, *Sobranie sochinenii*, vol. 28, 430.

61. Gor'kii, *Sobranie sochinenii*, vol. 28, 433.

62. *Arkhiv*, V: 183; Gor'kii, *Sobranie sochinenii*, vol. 28, 435.

63. *Arkhiv*, VII: 142, 144.

64. *Arkhiv*, V: 177. This letter, written on May 28 (15), is not included in the thirty-volume edition of Gorky's works.

65. *M. Gor'kii i Leonid Andreev, Neizdannaia perepiska* (Moscow, 1965), 267–268.

66. *Arkhiv*, IV: 202–203.

67. *Vestnik Evropy*, 12 (1906): *Rech'*, 206 (1906), quoted in Burtsov, "Gor'kii i Zapad," 26.

68. *New York Times*, October 13, 1906, 7.

69. *Arkhiv*, V: 183.

70. Upton Sinclair, *My Life in Letters* (Columbia, 1960), 11–12.

CHAPTER 5

CAPRI

The people, they are the creators. . . . In them dwells God in space between the stars. . . . And I saw her master, the omnipotent, immortal people. . . . And I prayed: Thou art my God, the creator of all the gods.

M. Gor'kii, *Ispoved'*, 308

The Capri period (1906–1913) marks a new and important phase in Gorky's political career. Influenced for a while by the remarkable personality of A. A. Bogdanov, he began to lean towards the left wing of the Bolshevik faction of the Russian Social Democratic Workers' Party (RSDWP). He was also one of the propagators of the ideology of *bogostroitel'stvo* ("god-building"), which, in essence, was an attempt to graft a religious superstructure upon Marxist ideology. This attempt met with resolute opposition from Lenin. Within the context of these developments stands the relationship between Lenin and Gorky, a friendship that reached its height during this period.

In October 1906, Gorky and his party arrived in Naples, where they were given an enthusiastic reception. Appearing at rallies and meetings, Gorky emphasized the idea of solidarity of the world proletariat and hailed the role of the masses in revolution, drawing examples from the events of 1905 and 1906 in Russia.[1] Gorky and Andreeva did not, however, remain in Naples, but instead settled on the isolated and picturesque island of Capri. It seems that the bitter memory of the New York scandal was still fresh in their minds. Gorky said that he would not want "the repetition of the ugly American story."[2]

In 1907 Gorky was introduced to Party politics at the Fifth Party Congress, where he was given a consultative vote.[3] He met Lenin there as well as other prominent members of the Party, such as G. V. Plehkanov, I. O. Martov, and L. D. Trotsky. Gorky described his meeting with Lenin thus:

When we were introduced, he shook me heartily by the hand, and scrutinizing me with his keen eyes and speaking in the tone of an old acquaintance, he said jocularly: "So glad you've come, believe you're fond of a scrap? There's going to be a fine old scuffle here."

I did not expect Lenin to be like that. Something was lacking in him. He rolled his r's gutturally, and had a jaunty way of standing with his hands somehow poked up under his armpits. He was somehow too ordinary, did not give the impression of being a leader. . . .

Before me stood a bald-headed, stocky, sturdy person, speaking with a guttural roll of his r's and holding my hand in one of his . . . beaming affectionately at me with his strangely bright eyes. He began at once to speak about the defects of my book *Mother*—evidently he had read it in the manuscript form which was in the possession of S. P. Ladyzhnikov [I. P. Ladyzhnikov]. I was hurrying to finish the book, I said—but did not succeed in saying why. Lenin nodded in approval: "Yes, I should hurry up with it, such a book is needed, for many of the workers who take part in the revolutionary movement do so unconsciously, and chaotically, and it would be very useful for them to read *Mother*, the very book for the moment."[4]

The meeting with Trotsky was most interesting and very friendly. The description of the meeting is quoted in Kaun's biography of Gorky:

On one of the first days of the [Congress], I was stopped in the church vestibule by a tall, angular man with a round face and high-cheek bones, who wore a round hat.

"I am your admirer," he said, with an amiable chuckle.

"Admirer?" I echoed in astonishment. It appeared that the compliment referred to my political pamphlets that had been written in prison. My interlocutor was Maxim Gorky, and this was the first time I ever saw him. "I hope it is not necessary for me to say that I am your admirer," I said, answering the compliment with another. In that period, Gorky was close to the Bolsheviks. With him was the well-known actress, Andreeva. We went about London together.[5]

Gorky seems to have had high regard for Martov, the Menshevik leader: "This amazingly attractive man spoke with the ardour of youth and was evidently most deeply affected by the tragic drama of dissension and the split [in the Party]."[6]

The congress had on its agenda questions concerning the relationship between the Bolsheviks and the Mensheviks, the attitude toward bourgeois parties, and problems of Party organization, but it did not accomplish much. The dissension between the factions was not resolved. A new Central Committee was chosen, consisting of fifteen members, of whom five were Bolsheviks and four Mensheviks. In addition, a new enlarged Bolshevik Center had been set up, consisting of fifteen members; and for the next few years, the Center, disguised as the enlarged editorial board of the Bolshevik newspaper, *Proletarii* (Proletarian), managed the affairs of the Bolshevik faction abroad.[7]

Gorky left the congress disillusioned with the wranglings in the Party, which he had observed for the first time in London. He was also called upon to help obtain a loan to provide funds for travel expenses of the delegates attending the congress.

In spite of the glowing reports in Soviet "Gorkiana" of the close relationship between the writer and Lenin, Gorky sided at that time with the left wing of the Bolshevik faction led by Bogdanov. Of Bogdanov, he wrote:

He [Bogdanov], will accomplish in philosophy the same kind of revolution Marx accomplished in political economy. His ideas are socialist and therefore revolutionary. . . . If he should succeed, we will witness the defeat of the remnants of bourgeois metaphysics, the disintegration of "bourgeois soul" and the birth of a socialist soul.[8]

It is difficult to understand what was meant by the "bourgeois" versus the "socialist" soul. One can also doubt Gorky's knowledge of either Marxian political economy or Bogdanov's theories. It seems that the bond between Gorky and Bogdanov was based on the belief in and concern for proletarian culture, and in the hope of reviving the revolutionary activity in Russia. At the same time, Gorky did not relent from attempting to bring about a reconciliation between Lenin and Bogdanov.[9] When this attempt failed, he, together with Bogdanov and A. V. Lunacharskii, established the Capri school for underground party workers despite Lenin's strong opposition.

Gorky supported Bogdanov's ideas with respect to tactics and believed that illegal, clandestine work was of primary importance in order to prepare the masses for an armed uprising. He wrote:

The quarrel which flared up between Lenin and Plekhanov on one side, and Bogdanov, Bazarov and others on the other, is very important and deep. Plekhanov and Lenin, though diverging on questions of tactics, both believe in and preach historical fatalism. The opposite side preaches a philosophy of action. To me it is clear on whose side there is more truth.[10]

Gorky's stand was a great disappointment to Lenin, who tried to keep the writer on his side in the struggle against Bogdanov's group. Moreover, Lenin needed Gorky's and Andreeva's help in the transshipment of *Prole-*

tarii to Russia, as well as Gorky's literary talents.[11] The importation of *Proletarii* was effected with Gorky's aid, but his literary contribution to the newspaper was minimal.[12] His first article was rejected by Lenin. Entitled "Razrushenie lichnosti" ("The Destruction of the Individual"), it contained ideas on religion and, according to Lenin, was therefore unsuitable for a socialist publication.[13]

To the disagreements on the question of tactics in the aftermath of 1905 came the doctrine of "god-building," which further deepened the rift between Lenin's and Bogdanov's groups. The term "god-building" was first coined by Gorky and could best be defined as a theory of the divinity of the masses. The literary critic Lunacharskii became the prophet of the new religion, and Gorky its popularizer. Lunacharskii's theories on socialism as the fifth religion of mankind were set out in his philosophical work *Religiia i sotsializm* (Religion and Socialism). Following L. A. Feuerbach, Lunacharskii puts forward the idea of *homo homini deus*, and in Lunacharskii's religion God disappears and is replaced by man.[14] Many years before the appearance of *Ispoved'* (Confession), where Gorky formulated his ideology of god-building, Andreev told him: "You speak like an atheist, but think like a believer."[15] A similar remark was made by Tolstoy in one of their conversations. Gorky had long rejected all organized religions. Yet he was not a materialist, and thus he could not be satisfied with Marx's ideas on religion. When asked to express his views about religion in a questionnaire sent by the French journal *Mercure de France* on April 15, 1907, Gorky replied that he was opposed to the existing religions of Moses, Christ, and Mohammed. He defined religious feeling as an awareness of a harmonious link that joins man to the universe and as an aspiration for synthesis, inherent in every individual.[16]

The novel *Ispoved'*, written in 1908, served as an exposition of these beliefs. In that work the people became the "god" of the new religion and, at the same time, "the god-builder."[17] The main theme of the work concerns religious faith, its distortion by the established church, and its deep roots in the people. The "god-builder" is the people that collectively possess mystical power.

Attempts have been made by B. Bialik, a Soviet critic, to acknowledge that the origins of the idea of "god-building" are to be found in the early writings of Gorky. In 1901, the idea found expression in a letter written to V. A. Posse, where Gorky, admonishing his friend for his religious leanings, wrote: "How can you accept something alien when you yourself are god and Kant. . . . only man exists."[18] In continuing his defense of Gorky's theories of "god-building," Bialik maintains that Gorky came to propagate these ideas in order to juxtapose them to the official religion and such renewed forms of the old as that of Tolstoy of the "god-seekers."[19] Commenting on *Ispoved'* he writes:

[A]nd yet there was in *Ispoved'* and in all of Gorky's pronouncements connected with the propagation of god-building one side which differentiated him from the other preachers of these false teachings. Gorky's attitude towards ancient religious forms . . . was closely tied with his attitude towards folk art, myths, and the heroic epos.[20]

Much earlier, Plekhanov expressed his views on "god-building" in an article, "O tak nazyvaemykh religioznykh iskaniiakh v Rossii" (On the So-called Religious Quests in Russia). He wrote that Gorky used his heroes as mouthpieces for the expression of his own ideas and that in view of the fact that his knowledge of socialist theory was limited, the attempt to clothe socialism in the chasuble of religiosity was even less successful than Lunacharskii's. Continuing his criticism, Plekhanov maintained that Gorky and Lunacharskii had turned humanity into a fetish and put upon it the stamp of divinity. He pointed out the contradiction inherent in their argument. Both started with the assumption of God as a fiction, yet ended by regarding humanity as a god. He admonished Gorky for repeating the mistake of L. A. Feuerbach in putting the stamp of religion on the relationship between people, which had nothing religious in them. Plekhanov had very little faith in Gorky's socialism. In order to understand Gorky's socialism, he wrote, one needed to comprehend only three things: truth has to prevail on earth, man should not rule over his fellow man, and these two beliefs are the reasons for the struggle against the bourgeoisie. Having pointed out the inconsistencies in Gorky's *Ispoved'*, Plekhanov concluded that Gorky was "a poor thinker and an unsuccessful propagator of the new truth."[21]

Non-Marxist writers regarded the ideas of "god-building" as proof of Gorky's religiosity and maintained that he could not be satisfied with the materialist philosophy of Marx.[22] "He had pinned on himself the label of social democracy and of a practical revolutionary and felt himself for a while to be a party worker. But a label can be pasted only to the skin and not the soul."[23]

Lenin, critical of the new religion, attacked Bogdanov and his group, but he was careful not to mention Gorky's name. The simple reason for this omission was that he needed funds and literary contributions for *Proletarii*. The situation changed in April 1908, following the appearance of *Ispoved'*, when correspondence between Gorky and Lenin ceased for over a year. Gorky was not ready to submit to Lenin's dictates.[24]

The strained relations between Gorky and Lenin continued. When in the fall of 1908 Lenin asked his sister to find a publisher for *Materializm i empiriokrititsizm* (Materialism and Empiriocriticism), his only "philosophical" opus, he wrote that he had little hope that *Znanie* would accept the manuscript. He was not far wrong in his assumptions, for Gorky, opposed to the publication of Lenin's work, wrote K. P. Piatnitskii, the editor of *Znanie*, that:

With regard to the publication of Lenin's work, I am against it, because I know the author. He is a very clever man, a wonderful man, but he is a fighter, and a chivalrous deed will only make him laugh. If *Znanie* should publish *that* book of his he will say: little fools—and the little fools will be Bogdanov, I, Bazarov and Lunacharskii.[25]

The Capri school for the training of underground party workers was organized in the fall of 1909. The idea of the school has been ascribed collectively to Bogdanov, Lunacharskii, Aleksinskii and Gorky; but it seems that the initiator was Aleksinskii, a Party member living in Geneva, who was concerned over the loss of party leadership in Russia as a result of arrests and exiles in Russia.[26]

The plan to educate Russian workers for party leadership had a special appeal for Gorky, who in a letter to Aleksinskii, wrote:

A1. A1. [Bogdanov] has written that you have prepared a plan for a foreign school for workers. Could you perhaps send me the plan? Has A1. A1. written to you of the possibility of your moving here? Would you let me know your views on the matter?[27]

He insisted that the school should be established on Capri and promised to find the necessary funds.[28]

After some difficulties, the school was organized. Thirteen "students" came from Russia, and a distinguished faculty was assembled, although neither Plekhanov, Lenin, Trotsky, nor any western Social Democrats attended.[29] Lenin's opposition to the school was unequivocal. He believed that it would serve the ideological and political objectives of the Bogdanov group. Bogdanov was accused of propagating a reactionary, idealist philosophy; both Bogdanov and Lunacharskii were expelled from the Bolshevik faction, and "god-building" was condemned by the enlarged editorial board of *Proletarii*.[30]

The censure by *Proletarii* had little influence upon the affairs of the school. By the beginning of August, the prospective students arrived at Capri.[31] Gorky was very enthusiastic about their arrival, and in a letter to Ladyzhnikov he wrote: "The people from Russia are wonderful. All of them are "centralists" [those who sided with the Central Committee against the Bolshevik Center functioning abroad]. They dislike *Proletarii* and the books for two rubles and 60 kopecks."[32] Gorky further stated that "[he] always valued highly the pleasure of being a heretic."[33]

The work at the school, "First Higher Social Democratic Propagandist-Agitator School for Workers," began on August 18 (5). In attendance were fifteen students, thirteen from Russia and two exiles who lived on Capri. There were also thirteen auditors.[34] The school was run by a *soviet* (council) composed of students and faculty, with decisions made by majority vote. The executive committee consisted of three students and two members of the faculty. In addition, students were represented on the faculty committee.[35] The objective of the school was to impart to the students theoretical knowledge and, at the same time, to train them in applying it.[36] To achieve this purpose, the program was divided into four main areas: party organization, party theory, philosophy of the proletarian struggle, and contemporary problems. Two lectures of two hours' duration were offered each day, the mornings being left free for assignments and the evenings for practical work.

Despite obstacles, the organizers succeeded in assembling a distinguished faculty: Bogdanov lectured on political economy and the history of social thought; Aleksinskii, on finance and the history of the labor movement in France and Belgium; and Lunacharskii, on the history of trade unions, international and German social democracy, and the history of art. Liadov lectured on the history of the Party; Desnitskii, on church-state relations; Gorky, on the history of Russian literature; and the future dean of Soviet historians, Pokrovskii, on Russian history.[37] In addition to formal instruction, Gorky took care to introduce the students to European culture, assisted by his friends, prominent artists and musicians.[38] Students were required to prepare reports, deliver addresses, and write newspaper articles. The intensive pace and the high standards set by the lecturers presented a problem for some of the students, Kosarev wrote: "Our first articles and addresses were in the majority of cases poor. In spite of the fact that we were chosen from among many, the selection was uneven. Some had adequate preparation; others came having completed only elementary school."[39]

The school was being criticized by Lenin and the Bolshevik Center.[40] They emphasized the importance of the ideological leadership of the center, and asked for the transfer of the school to Paris. The school council agreed, on condition that the internal autonomy of it be preserved. The Bolshevik Center rejected this offer, and the result was a split among the students. Five students declared themselves faithful to Lenin and his group and announced that according to the instructions of their local organizations, they were unable to continue their studies at Capri.[41] Expelled from the school, they left for Paris, where they attended lectures given by Lenin, L. Kamenev, and M. Liubimov, among others.

Lenin's main aim, to undermine the school, had been achieved. In his letters he tried to persuade Gorky not to take the Party strife too seriously and emphasized Gorky's importance to the Russian revolutionary cause as well as the cause of revolution everywhere.[42]

Gorky, for his part, was still trying to make Lenin come to Capri, to meet the remaining group of students. The letter, only recently released, conveyed an unflattering portrayal of Lenin. It read:

My dear Vladimir Ilich, I hold you in great esteem . . . moreover, I like you as a person. But you know, you are very naive in your relationship with people, and your judgement of them is . . . oh no, that won't do! It seems to me, at times, that everybody is for you nothing more but a flute, that you can play on it one time or another as long as it is pleasing you.
You value the individual [by the criterion] of whether he is useful to you in realizing your aims, views and tasks.
That kind of measure . . . will by necessity create around you some kind of void. This in itself is perhaps not very important, for you are a strong [individual]. The main thing is that this attitude will unavoidably lead you to the making of mistakes.[43]

He further elaborated on his stand regarding Lenin-Bogdanov break. He considered it as important as the Bolshevik-Menshevik split [of 1903]. As for himself, he identified with Bogdanov's ideology, and considered "the *Proletarii* as a dull, illiterate [*sic!*] paper, written by people who deep down in their hearts did not believe in the proletariat or in socialism."[44]

You know what, dear man? You ought to come here while the school is still in session in order to get acquainted with the workers, to talk with them. They are few, but they are worthy of your coming. It would be a mistake to reject them— even more than a mistake. Among them there are very serious people and they are certainly more sane than Mikhail [Vilonov]. They have good heads on their shoulders. Again, do not antagonize them. You can fight among yourselves—this is your privilege—but keep them out of it.[45]

The disagreements between Gorky and Lenin at the time of the Capri school led to a rumor of Gorky's expulsion from the RSDWP. An announcement to that effect appeared in the newspaper *Utro Rossii* (Morning of Russia), on November 20, 1909, in an article written by the writer L. A. Sulerzhitskii entitled "Ob otluchenii M. Gor'kogo" (On the Exclusion of M. Gor'kii). Gorky denied the rumor.[46] Lenin wrote in the article "Basnia burzhuaznoi pechati ob iskliuchenii Gor'kogo" (The Legend of the Bourgeois Press on the Expulsion of Gorky) that the accusations were malicious attempts to draw Gorky away from social democracy. "Comrade Gorky has tied himself through his literary works to the cause of the workers in Russia and in the world too strongly to answer the rumor with anything but contempt."[47] Still the question remains whether Gorky was ever a member of the Party. Or was it the Soviet hagiographical writings that made him one?
The studies on Capri ended in December of 1909. The success of the Capri school was limited in spite of the high standards set by the faculty.

Those students who returned to Russia were soon apprehended by the police.[48] Following the closure of the school, some of the faculty and a few of the students organized a distinct group within the Party, the *Vperëd* (Forward) group. In spite of his membership in *Vperëd*, Gorky persevered in maintaining his independence as a writer and a publicist.

The newly formed *Vperëd* group proceeded to plan a second school for underground party workers, and one was established in Bologna, running from November 1910 to March 1911. Gorky was invited to lecture there and was also asked for financial assistance.[49] He declined to come. Yet his refusal to lecture at Bologna did not mean that he dissociated himself from *Vperëd*.[50] The *Vperëd* group came under continuous fire in Lenin's pronouncements. In his view the only asset was Gorky's membership in the group.

There is no use hiding the fact . . . that M. Gor'kii belongs to the followers of the new group. And Gor'kii is without doubt the most outstanding representative of proletarian *art*. He has done much for it and will accomplish even more. Any faction of the Social Democratic party can rightly be proud of having Gor'kii in its midst. . . . In the field of proletarian art M. Gor'kii is a great *asset* despite his sympathy with machism and *otzovism*.[51]

Lenin did not miss any opportunity to entice Gorky away from the *Vperedists*. In the summer of 1910 he came to visit him on Capri, with the aim of securing his participation in a Bolshevik publication. He stayed for two weeks, the longest period the two men ever spent together.[52] The rapprochement with Gorky came at an opportune time for Lenin. The Bolshevik faction was trying to establish a newspaper in Paris and a journal and a newspaper in Russia. Funds were needed. On Lenin's request, Gorky made a financial contribution to these publications[53] and promised to write.

Lenin however, could not monopolize Gorky and his talents. For, at the time when Lenin was trying to enlist his full cooperation, Gorky was being persuaded by A. V. Amfiteatrov, a politically unaligned journalist, to participate in a new review, *Sovremennik* (Contemporary). Amfiteatrov's projected journal was to be socialist but not affiliated with any party.[54] In fact, Gorky's participation in publications affiliated with various political parties continued throughout his stay on Capri.[55] Lenin criticized severely Gorky's cooperation with Amfiteatrov.

I read today in *Rech'* an announcement about *Sovremennik*, which is to be published . . . with your continuous collaboration. What is the meaning of all that? "A large monthly" journal, with departments of "politics, science, history, public affairs,"—this is something entirely different than the *sborniki* aimed at the concentration of our best talents in the field of our literature. [Lenin must have been referring to the *Znanie sborniki*]. Such a monthly journal would have to have a fully determined, serious and consistent direction or it will . . . disgrace its contributors. . . .

A journal without a direction is an absurdity, foolish, scandalous and detrimental. . . . Amfiteatrov's journal . . . is a political step, a political undertaking. It lacks the awareness that a general sort of "leftism" in politics is insufficient, that to speak seriously about politics after 1905 without defining the attitude toward Marxism and social democracy is . . . impossible and unthinkable. It is bad. I am in a sad mood.[56]

Gorky tried to pacify Lenin by explaining to him the need for broader activity among the democratic circles. Lenin angrily replied:

You seem to tease me: "realism, democracy, activity!" Do you think that these are good words? These are *nasty* words, used by all bourgeois dodgers the world over, from our own Kadety [Constitutional Democrats] and SR's to Briand and Millerand here [France], Lloyd George in England, etc. . . . Bad. The words are nasty, and the content of *Sovremennik* promises to be SR-Kadet. Bad.[57]

Gorky, in turn, refused an invitation to lecture at the Longjumeau Party school founded by Lenin in 1911.[58] Gorky did not realize how far removed were his views from Lenin's on the question of Party unity. Lenin had no intention to arrive at an agreement with the Mensheviks of Martov's kind. As for Plekhanov, who left the Mensheviks in late 1910, Lenin did resume contacts with him. He welcomed Plekhanov's participation in the Bolshevik publications *Mysl'* (*Thought*), *Zvezda* (*The Star*), *Pravda* (*Truth*), and *Sotsial-Demokrat* (*The Social Democrat*) but hesitated to go beyond journalistic cooperation. Lenin was also aiming to effect a split in the Social Democratic Duma fraction. According to Lenin, the question of unification had to be abandoned; he did not want unity. In answering Gorky's letter on the renewed interest and participation of Vperedists in party organs, he wrote:

I would be ready to share with all my heart your joy over the return of the Vperedists if . . . your assumption is correct that "machism, god-building and all other tricks are gone for good." . . . If this is so . . . then I will eagerly share your rejoicing on the occasion of their return. But I wish to emphasize the *"if."* For up until now it is still more a wish than a fact . . . I do not know whether Bogdanov, Bazarov, Volskii (semi-anarchist), Lunacharskii, Aleksinskii are *able* to *learn* from the difficult experience of 1908–1911. Have they understood that *Marxism* is much more serious and profound than it seemed to them. . . . *If* they have understood, a thousand greetings to them, and all personal [ill feelings] . . . will quickly disappear. But, if they have not understood, if they have not learned, then please excuse me— "friendship is friendship and duty is duty" [a Russian proverb]. We will fight . . . against the attempts to abuse Marxism or to confuse the policies of the workers' party.[59]

In a letter to Aleksinskii, Gorky wrote that the Party squabbles were very hard on him.[60] He complained to Lenin that the leaders of the Party had written neither a book nor a pamphlet championing the cause of socialism, thus leaving the youth in Russia without guidance.

Lenin's stand on party unity was again shown at the Prague Conference held in January of 1912, which asserted the independence of the Bolshevik faction. Gorky was asked to attend and to assist financially with the founding of a Bolshevik daily in Russia. It is of little surprise that Gorky refused to come, his excuse being that his presence would endanger the conspiratorial work of the conference. Furthermore, he refused financial assistance for a Bolshevik daily, pleading financial difficulties.[61] The real reason behind his refusal was that he preferred to see the establishment of a journal to propagate socialist ideology, which, he wrote, had been forgotten by the theoreticians of the RSDWP in their factional struggles. "These Asiatic-like [uncivilized] actions have to be stopped, and it seems that only the practical workers can stop them by pointing out the material and moral harm which results from the uninterrupted and fruitless fight."[62]

Lenin emerged the winner in the controversy over the projected publication. In April 1912, the Bolsheviks began to publish the first legal Bolshevik daily paper *Pravda* (*Truth*) in St. Petersburg.[63] Reluctantly, Gorky promised support for *Pravda*.[64] It seems, however, that this support was limited to a sum of money and a few short stories. In the summer of the same year, Lenin moved to Cracow, to facilitate his contact with Russia and his work in editing *Pravda*.[65] He notified Gorky of the move; moreover, he shared with him some confidential information:

Well, things are brewing in the Baltic fleet! And (confidentially) I have received in Paris a special delegate, who was sent by a meeting of sailors and Social Democrats. There is no organization. One feels like crying! If you have any kind of connections with the naval officers, it would be important to do the utmost to arrange something. The sailors are in a fighting mood, but they may perish in vain again.[66]

Once settled in Poronino, near Cracow, Lenin tried to convince Gorky to join him there, even if only for a short time.

If it would only be possible for you to move closer. . . . If your health should allow it, you could move to one of the local resort places, something like Zakopane. . . . It would be closer to Russia, by two days. One could arrange that the workers come and we could again start a school for workers. The crossing of the border is not difficult; the transportation cost from Peter [Petersburg] would be 12 rubles. It would also be feasible to establish contacts with workers from Moscow and the South [Ukraine].[67]

In June 1913, he wrote Gorky of a conference of Bolshevik deputies of the Duma that was to take place at Poronino. Lenin repeated again his desire to establish a Party school there.

Please drop me a line whether you can come here (for a series of lectures or discussions or studies, as you may like), or not. It would be fine! Seven kilometers from here, (by rail), there is Zakopane—a very good resort. . . . If your health permits, come over for a while, won't you? After London [V Party Congress in 1907] and the Capri school, it would do you good to see some more workers.[68]

But Gorky did not go to Poronino. Furthermore, Lenin's efforts to meet with him in Berlin or Vienna in order to discuss matters connected with the closure of *Pravda* and the projected school in Poronino did not materialize.[69] It seems as if Gorky deliberately tried to avoid involvement in Lenin's party projects. Yet the two maintained their frequent correspondence until December 1913.

By December 1913, relations between Lenin and Gorky had broken off, not to be resumed until the fall of 1918.[70] The immediate cause of the break was the appearance of Gorky's article "Eshche o Karamazovshchine" (More about Karamazovism), which contained a critical evaluation of F. Dostoevsky's ideas and a bitter indictment of the Russian character, which he saw as frail, unstable, and inclined to senseless anarchism.[71] The article, which indicated preoccupation with "god-building," evoked a bitter answer from Lenin. He quoted it, commenting, "And 'godseeking is to be let go *for a while*'—(only for a while?) . . . 'It is a useless occupation: . . . Not having sown, one cannot reap. You have no God, you have *not yet*' (not yet!) 'created one. One does not seek gods, one *creates them*.'"[72] Elaborating further on the content of the ill-fated paragraph, Lenin wrote:

And so it seems you are against "godseeking" only "for a while"!! It seems that you are against godseeking *only* to replace it with god-building!! Is it not terrible! . . . Godseeking differs from god-building, or godcreating, or godconstructionism, etc., not any more than a yellow devil differs from a blue one. To talk about godseeking not in order to declare oneself *against all sorts* of devils and gods, against all sorts of ideological necrophilia . . . —but in order to show preference for the blue devil over the yellow devil, is a hundred times worse than not to discuss it at all. . . .

Any religious ideology, any idea of godkin, is an inexpressibly loathsome thing. . . . A million sins, mean tricks, acts of violence, and *physical* infections, are much easier discovered . . . and are, therefore less dangerous, than the *subtle* spiritual idea of godkin which is dressed up in "metaphysical" fineries.[73]

Turning reproachfully to Gorky, Lenin continued:

And you who know so well the "frailty and pitiful unsteadiness" of the Russian; (why Russian? Is the Italian any better?) *philistine* soul; you are tempting this soul with the sweetest of poisons covered up with candies and all sorts of coloured bits of paper!! This is terrible. . . . Is not god-building the *worst* kind of selfcontempt??

Anybody who occupies himself with the building of a *god* . . . *humiliates* himself
in the worst manner.[74]

The letter was signed "formally, Your V. Ulianov."

Gorky wrote in reply that he did not "understand" how the words "for
a while" had "slipped in," but at the same time, defended his ideas on God
and *bogostroitel'stvo*. Lenin in his answer pointed out Gorky's misinter-
pretation of ideas on religion and cited the influences of Bogdanov's philosophy, which Gorky obviously had never repudiated. He quoted Gorky's
letter and then elaborated on its content:

You are defending the idea of god and god-building. "God is a complex of ideas
formed by the tribe, the nation, humanity, which awake and organize social feelings, and aim to link the individual to society, and to bridle zoological individualism." It is obvious that this theory is closely bound with the theory, or theories
of Bogdanov and Lunacharskii. . . . It is not true that god is a complex of ideas that
awake and organize social feelings. This is the Bogdanov kind of *idealism*, which
obscures the materialistic origin of ideas. God is (historically and actually) first of
all a complex of ideas that have arisen from the oppression of man by external
nature and class yoke, ideas which have *consolidated* this oppression, and had *lulled*
to sleep the class struggle. . . . At present, both in Europe and in Russia, *any* defense
of the idea of god, however subtle and well intentioned, is a justification of reaction.
. . . The idea of god has never "linked man and society" but has always *linked* the
oppressed *classes* by their faith in the *divinity* of the oppressors. . . . I absolutely
fail to understand how you can call "the people's idea" of god "democratic." . . .
The idea that "god-building is a process of further development and accumulation
of social principles in the individual and society," is down right terrible!![75]

The letter was signed, "V. I."; Lenin stopped writing.[76]

During the Capri period, Gorky's political activity was closely interwo-
ven with his work as editor, journalist, and writer. The problems that occupied him were in essence the same as those he was concerned with before.
These were the nature of the Russian people, the differences between the
Russians and the peoples of the West, and the question of the role of literature in the process of social change. The problem of the Russian character, the dark and confused souls of the Russian peasants, and the
passivity of the Russians was a recurring theme in his letters to the Ukrainian writer M. M. Kotsiubins'kii and to Andreev.[77]

The misfortune of our country no doubt is in that we are poisoned by the thick,
heavy blood of the East, which awakes in us the urge towards a passive and empty
talk about eternity, space, self-perfection and all other "nonsense." . . . Besides, we,
as a nation, taught by our preposterous history, are incapable of a prolonged and
continuous effort. . . . We do not know how to believe and are torn between fanaticism and nihilism. This is in all of us, and this we have to fight as something
that hinders the growth and development of personality and reduces ability to act.[78]

He complained of the tendency of Russians to philosophize and to dream. "We waste our time on dreams about goodness, but do little about 'doing good' in practice." To the author I. D. Surguchev, he wrote, "We do not believe in the possibility of a good life here on earth, and hence 'self-destruction,' . . . escape from life into deserts and forests, nihilism and anarchism among the peasants, and periodical epidemics of suicides among the intelligentsia."[79]

Commenting on the difference between the intelligentsia and the people, Gorky maintained that this difference was a nominal one, the peasant having invented nihilism and anarchism before Pisarev and Bakunin. He blamed the political system of Russia for the birth of these propensities. One of his most severe indictments of the existing system is contained in his article "Pis'mo monakchistu" (A Letter to a Monarchist), in which Gorky condemned the Romanovs and gave a critical evaluation of the individual rulers. He concluded by reiterating his strong belief in the inevitability of revolution.[80]

Gorky was also concerned with the problem of Russia's many nationalities. He believed that the future of the Russian multinational empire depended on the successful resolution of conflicts among the nationalities. His position was that differences of nationality, color, and religion did not matter. When asked to express his opinion on the Ukrainian question, he wrote the article entitled "O russkoi intelligentsii i natsionalnykh voprosakh" (On the Russian Intelligentsia and the National Question), where he argued that for the intelligentsia, there was no difference between Great Russian, Ukrainian, or Yakut. He rejected the official line of centralized government, of *divide et impera*, and emphasized the idea of federalism based on full respect for the cultural heritage of each of the nationalities.[81]

As editor of *Znanie*, he continued to stress the purposes of literature which he had espoused in 1896: "to help man to understand himself, to fulfill his belief in himself, and to develop his striving after truth."[82] To a fellow writer, D. Aizman, Gorky wrote: "I do not have the right to offer my reader what seems harmful for him and will decrease his active participation in life."[83] His belief was that literature should serve as a vehicle of social protest and as a means to awaken the creative powers of man. He therefore was hostile to the pessimism and the decadence that were the main features of Russian literature after 1905. Numerous letters testify to Gorky's rigid adherence to the standards he had adopted in evaluating the works of writers who contributed to the *Znanie sborniki*. Among the contributors were his closest friends—Andreev, Skitalets, Kuprin, and others.[84] His criticism was best expressed in a letter to Ladyzhnikov:

There are many Russian writers here,—Veresaev, Aizman, Leonid [Andreev]. They are very dour people; they sit wrinkling their brows and thinking silently of the vanity of all things earthly, and the insignificance of man; they talk of corpses, cemeteries, toothaches, colds in the head, tactlessness of the socialists and other matters, all of which lower the temperature of the air, the body and the spirit.[85]

Moreover, since 1905, the ideology of revolutionary struggle had been a sacred cause for Gorky. He became increasingly intolerant toward those writers who abandoned the cause of revolution or departed from his ideas on the purpose of literature. He did not understand, nor did he want to understand, that after the defeat of the revolution of 1905, new literary trends had emerged and *Znanie* had lost much of its popularity.[86] His opinion of what should be done to remedy the situation of *Znanie* was influenced by his close association with the Bogdanov group. In order to emphasize the importance of revolution and to clarify the problems connected with it, he proposed changing the purely literary composition of the *sborniki* by including articles on philosophy. He wrote Piatnitskii shortly after the latter's visit to Capri in 1908:

You remember I spoke with you about the need for us to change the nature of the volumes by including articles on literary criticism and social philosophy. I consider it essential to do this right now. . . . It would be easy for me; I could organize a group of extremely valuable contributors: Lunacharskii, Voitlovskii, Bogdanov, Bazarov, to mention a few for the present, and many more.[87]

It was important, maintained Gorky, to discuss political and social issues in the *Znanie* publications, but Piatnitskii disagreed with Gorky's stand. He feared that such change would deprive *Znanie* of a considerable section of the reading public. The disagreements with Piatnitskii led Gorky to leave *Znanie* in 1912. His publishing affairs were now handled by the Ladyzhnikov publishers in Berlin.[88] In addition to articles written during the years of his stay on Capri, Gorky, with the slackening of his revolutionary activity, turned to the writing of works wherein he continued his analytical studies of the psychological and sociological aspects of pre-1905 Russian society, which he had begun in *Foma Gordeev*.[89]

The Capri period, 1906–1913, came to an end. All through the Capri years Gorky was involved in the affairs of the Bolshevik faction of the RSDWP, then beset by many problems, and where the disagreement between Lenin and Bogdanov led to a split within the Bolshevik ranks. For Gorky in the years immediately following 1905, the revolutionary cause was the supreme goal. Also, the ideas of *bogostroitel'stvo*, long latent in Gorky's philosophy, found their expression during the Capri period. In the factional struggle, he sided with Bogdanov against Lenin. The results were disappointing. Lenin succeeded in undermining the work of the Capri school, and the rift between the factions widened. Personal differences between Gorky, Bogdanov, and Lunacharskii alienated Gorky from the left-wing Bolsheviks, and his participation in *Vperëd* was limited. Gorky's continuous preoccupation with god-building constituted the immediate cause of the break in relations with Lenin. Lenin tried unsuccessfully to assume toward Gorky the role of a benevolent political mentor. He would have liked Gorky to espouse the cause of the workers and the revolution and pursue it within the frame of his faction. Realizing Gorky's intransigence, Lenin broke off relations. Gorky, on his part, could not understand the ideological discussions within the factions and refused to consider the split as final.

The long sojourn in the West affected Gorky's views on the peoples and cultures of Western Europe. He became painfully aware of the shortcomings of his own people; and as the ideas of revolution receded into the background, he saw education and culture as the best means to effect needed change.

Gorky's constant companion during the Capri years was Andreeva. For reasons that are not very clear, the relationship between the two deteriorated, and Andreeva left Capri in 1912. A short letter found in Gorky archives sent by Andreeva from Russia on October 3, 1913, reads: "[W]herever you should choose to live, with whom and how—I want to wish you all the best. For me there is nothing else that matters."[90] E. Peshkova was taking care of their son, Maxim, and Gorky was in close contact with her and watched over the education of the boy. They often went on holidays together.

In December of 1913, Gorky left Capri for Russia, determined to devote his time to writing and to the promotion of education and culture.

NOTES

1. *Letopis'*, I: 629–631; M. F. *Andreeva: Perepiska, vospominaniia, stat'ii*, A. P. Grigorieva and S. V. Shirina (eds.), 2nd edition (Moscow, 1963), 617–618; N. E. Burenin, "Tri mesiatsa na ostrove Kapri," *Gor'kii v vospominaniiakh sovremennikov*, 245–246. See also V. Rudnev, "Gor'kii revoliutsioner," *Novyi mir* 4 (1928): 169–170.

2. *Arkhiv*, IX: 20.

3. *Piatyi (Londonskii) s"ezd RSDRP (Aprel'–Mai 1907 goda), Protokoly* (Moscow, 1963), 456. For Gorky's participation in the work of the Congress, see also Rudnev, "Gor'kii revoliutsioner," 173–174.

4. M. Gor'kii, "Lenin in London, 1907," quoted in Krupskaia, *Memories of Lenin (1893–1917)* (Bournemouth, 1942), 300–301.

5. Quoted in A. Kaun, *Maxim Gorky and His Russia* (London, 1932), 392.

6. V. I. *Lenin i A. M. Gor'kii: Pis'ma, vospominaniia, dokumenty* (Moscow, 1963), 245; *Andreeva: Perepiska, vospominaniia, stat'i*, 96.

7. The newspaper *Proletarii* was established by the Bolshevik faction of the RSDWP after the Fourth Party Congress and appeared from 1906 to 1909, first in Finland and then in Geneva and Paris. Krupskaia, *Memories of Lenin*, 115, 126–127, 131: L. Schapiro, *The Communist Party of the Soviet Union* (London, 1960), 88–89.

8. *Arkhiv*, VII: 148.

9. All the reasons for the quarrel are by no means clear. For a recent discussion of Bogdanov's ideas, his role in the RSDWP, and his relationship with Lenin, see D. Grille's *Lenins Rivale* (Cologne, 1966). According to Grille, the primary reason for the quarrel between Lenin and Bogdanov was the rivalry for leadership in the Bolshevik faction. Lenin, maintains Grille, had used the question of differences in ideology as a pretext. S. V. Utechin maintains that the break between Lenin and Bogdanov came as a result of a dispute over the control of party funds and disagreements on tactics. See S. V. Utechin, *Russian Political Thought: A Concise History* (New York, 1964), 209–210. See also Schapiro, *Communist Party of the Soviet Union*, 107–12.

10. *Lenin i Gor'kii: Pis'ma*, 42.

11. *Lenin i Gor'kii: Pis'ma*, 15–16.

12. *Lenin i Gor'kii: Pis'ma*, 413; Gor'kii, *Sobranie sochinenii*, vol. 29, 67; *Letopis'*, I: 324–325.

13. *Lenin i Gor'kii: Pis'ma*, 27–31; *Letopis'*, II: 15–16.

14. A. V. Lunacharskii, *Religiia i sotsializm* (St. Petersburg, 1908), vol. 1, 145. Lunacharskii, in his eagerness to portray socialism as a religion, had included in his dogma the trinity, composed of productive energies (the Father), the proletariat (the Son), and scientific socialism (the Holy Ghost). See also A. I. Spiridovich, *Istoriia bol'shevizma v Rossii: ot vozniknoveniia do zakhvata vlasti 1883–1903–1917* (Paris, 1922), 196–200. For a detailed discussion of the idea of *bogostroitel'stvo*, see: Raimund Sesterhenn. *Das Bogostroitel'stvo bei Gor'kij und Lunacharskij bis 1909* (Munchen: Otto Sagner, 1982).

15. *M. Gor'kii i Leonid Andreev: Neizdannaia perepiska* (Moscow, 1965), 369.

16. *Letopis'*, I: 653, 656; Gor'kii, *Sobranie sochinenii*, vol. 29, 496. The comment in *Letopis'* regarding Gorky's answer to the questionnaire is that at that time he was under the influence of *bogostroitel'stvo*.

17. "Bogostroitel'stvo," *Filosofskaia entsiklopediia* (Moscow, 1960), vol. 1, 179.

18. Gor'kii, *Sobranie sochinenii*, vol. 28, 169–170.

19. B. Bialik, *V. I. Lenin i Gor'kii* (Moscow, 1970), 111.

20. Bialik, *V. I. Lenin i Gor'kii*, 17.

21. G. V. Plekhanov, *Izbrannye filosofskie proizvedeniia* (Moscow, 1957), vol. 3, 396. The article first appeared in *Sovremennyi mir* (St. Petersburg) no. 10 (1909): 164–200.

22. A. S. Izgoev, "Bogostroiteli," *Rech'* 25 (January 26, 1909): 3.

23. I. K. "Bogostroitel'stvo M. Gor'kogo," *Moskovskii ezhenedel'nik* 35 (1908): 5.

24. *Neizvestnyi Gor'kii* (Moscow, 1994) III: 24, 25, 44, 45.

25. *Lenin i Gor'kii: Pis'ma*, 42; K. P. Piatnitskii informed Gorky in a telegram of November 2, 1908, that the manuscript of *Materializm i empiriokrititsizm* was brought in for publication in *Znanie* and that Bonch-Bruevich and Bazarov had expressed their willingness to publish the book. *Lenin i Gor'kii: Pis'ma*, 417. (Emphasis in the original.)

26. Aleksinskii Collection, Columbia University, the Archive of Russian and East European History and Culture.

27. Letter of Gorky to Aleksinskii [n. d.], Aleksinskii Collection.

28. *Arkhiv*, IX: 311; *Letopis'*, II: 61, 64.

29. *Otchet pervoi vysshei sotsial-demokraticheskoi propagandistsko-agitatorskoi shkoly dlia rabochikh* (hereinafter cited as *Otchet pervoi*) (n.p., 1910): 1; S. I. Livshits, *Partiinye universitety podpolia* (Moscow, 1929), 11.

30. "Iz neizdannykh protokolov soveshchaniia rasshirennoi redaktsii *Proletariia*, Lenin i filosofskie diskussii 1908–1910 godov," *Literaturnoe nasledstvo* 1 (1931): 27–35.

31. *Otchet pervoi*, 2. For a vivid description of the school environment see A. V. Lunacharskii, *Sobranie sochinenii* (Moscow, 1964), vol. 2, 36–40.

32. *Arkhiv*, VII: 199; The reference to "books for two rubles and 60 kopecks" was made with regard to Lenin's *Materializm i empiriokrititsizm*.

33. Gor'kii, *Sobranie sochinenii*, vol. 29, 97–98.

34. The difference between the two categories concerned matters of administration rather than instruction. The auditors promised to leave for Russia at the termination of their studies at the school.

35. *Otchet pervoi*, 4.

36. Livshits, *Partiinye universitety podpolia*, 39.

37. *Otchet pervoi*, 7.

38. *Otchet pervoi*, 7.

39. *Otchet pervoi*, 7. The manuscript of Bogdanov's lectures, which is to be found in the Aleksinskii Collection, testifies to the high standards set by the lecturers of the Capri school.

40. The struggle against the school was conducted on the pages of *Proletarii* 47/48–50 and the supplements to 45–46; Livshits, *Partiinye universitety podpolia*, 48.

41. *Otchet pervoi*, 18; A. V. Lunacharskii, *Velikii perevorot; Oktiabr'skaia revoliutsiia* (Petrograd, 1919), vol. 1, 46–47. See also the minutes of a meeting of the school council held November 1, 1909, in the Aleksinskii Collection, Columbia University, the Archive of Russian and East European History and Culture.

42. Lenin, *Polnoe sobranie sochinenii* (*PSS*), XLVII, 219–220.

43. *Neizvestnyi Gor'kii* (Moscow, 1994), 25.

44. *Neizvestnyi Gor'kii*, 26.

45. *Lenin i Gor'kii: Pis'ma*, 46.

46. Gor'kii, *Sobranie sochinenii*, vol. 29, 99–100.

47. Lenin, *PSS*, XIX, 153. *Proletarii* sent a letter to *Utro Rossii* with a denial of the report.

48. Kosarev, "Partiinaia shkola na ostrove Kapri," *Sibirskie ogni* 2 (1922): 73, 75. Earlier, the *Okhrana* issued an order to all heads of their provincial departments to watch who would be leaving for the Capri school. Doc. 133289, July 12, 1909. Tsentrarkhiv, *Revoliutsionnyi put' Gor'kogo* (Moscow, 1933).

49. Livshits, *Partiinye universitety podpolia*, 67. See also letter addressed to Gorky in the Aleksinskii Collection, Columbia University, the Archive of Russian and East European History and Culture.

50. Gor'kii, *Sobranie sochinenii*, vol. 29, 141–42, 145; Livshits, "Partiinaia shkola v Bolon'e (1910–1911)," *Proletarskaia revoliutsiia* 3 (50) (1926): 117, 125; *Letopis'*, II, 165: The Soviet history of the Communist Party does not mention Gorky's name in the discussion of the Capri and Bologna schools. The disagreements between Lenin, Bogdanov, and Lunacharskii are discussed; but again Gorky's

name is omitted. See *Istoriia kommunisticheskoi partii Sovetskogo Soiuza, 1904-Fevral' 1917*, ed. by P. N. Pospelov et al. (Moscow, 1966), vol. 2, 269–290.

51. Lenin, *PSS*, XIX, 251. (Emphasis in the original.)

52. See *Lenin i Gor'kii: Pis'ma*, 231–232; Kaun, *Maxim Gorky and His Russia*, 425.

53. Lenin had initiated the publication of *Rabochaia gazeta*, which appeared in Paris from November 1910 to August 1912. In January 1912, *Rabochaia gazeta* was declared to be the official organ of the Central Committee (Bolshevik). See Lenin, *PSS*, XX, 438–390. The head of the secret service abroad reported to the police department that Gorky sent to the editorial offices of *Rabochaia gazeta* a very enthusiastic letter and 500 francs as subsidy for the paper. See *Letopis'*, II, 169; "Daty zhizni i deiatelnosti A. M. Gor'kogo," 74. *Zvezda*, a Bolshevik paper published legally in St. Petersburg from December 1910 to May 1912. Lenin enlisted Gorky's participation in the work of the newspaper. See Lenin, *PSS*, XX, 460–620. The journal *Mysl'* appeared in Moscow from December 1910 to April 1911. Lenin, *PSS*, XX, 470.

54. *M. Gor'kii: Materialy i issledovaniia*, I, 199–202.

55. While contributing to the Bolshevik *Pravda*, *Zvezda*, and *Prosveshchenie*, Gorky was also writing for journals such as the liberal *Vestnik Evropy*, and the Socialist Revolutionary *Zavety*. For Gorky's interest in *Zavety*, see Rudnev, "Gor'kiirevoliutsioner," 177–178. Lenin criticized in particular. Gorky's participation in the journal *Zaprosy zhizni*. See *Lenin i Gor'kii: Pis'ma*, 79.

56. Lenin, *PSS*, XLVIII, 3–5 (emphasis in the original.)

57. Lenin, *PSS*, XLVIII, 11. The cooperation with Amfiteatrov did not last long, for Gorky resented the single-handed leadership of Amfiteatrov. See *Letopis'*, II, 225.

58. For a detailed and interesting discussion of the Longjumeau school, see article by R. C. Elwood, "Lenin and the Social Democratic Schools for Underground Party Workers, 1909–1911," *Political Science Quarterly* LXXXI (1966): 370–391.

59. Lenin, *PSS*, XLVIII, 139–141 (emphasis in the original).

60. See letter to Aleksinskii written in 1912, in the Aleksinskii Collection, Columbia University, the Archive of Russian and East European History and Culture.

61. *Bol'sheviki*, M. A. Tsiavlovskii, ed., *Bol'sheviki: Dokumenty po istorii bol'shevizma* (Moscow, 1918), 95; *Letopis'*, II: 244–245; Gor'kii, *Sobranie sochinenii*, vol. 29, 222–223.

62. Gor'kii, *Sobranie sochinenii*, vol. 29, 222–223.

63. Schapiro, *Communist Party of the Soviet Union*, 129–130.

64. Tsentrarkhiv, *Revoliutsionnyi put' Gor'kogo*, 112; *Letopis'*, II: 270.

65. Lenin, *PSS*, XLVIII, 84.

66. Lenin, *PSS*, XLVIII, 84. The "again" was a reference to the event of 1905–1906.

67. Lenin, *PSS*, XLVIII, 139. See also *Letopis'*, II: 321.

68. Lenin, *PSS*, XLVIII, 200. See also Schapiro, *Communist Party of the Soviet Union*, 134.

69. Lenin, *PSS*, XLVIII, 204–205, 210–11. *Pravda* was closed in July 1913; the publication of the newspaper soon resumed under a new name, *Rabochaia pravda*. The final closure of the newspaper took place in July 1914.

70. Gorky's return to Russia was made possible by the amnesty, proclaimed in

connection with the 300th anniversary of the Romanov dynasty in 1913, for all accused under paragraphs 128, 129, 132 of the Criminal Code for criminal offenses committed through publications. *Letopis'*, II: 352.

71. Gor'kii, *Sobranie sochinenii*, vol. 24, 151–157.

72. Lenin, *PSS*, XLVIII, 226 (emphasis in the original).

73. Lenin, *PSS*, XLVIII, 226–227 (emphasis in the original).

74. Lenin, *PSS*, XLVIII, 227 (emphasis in the original).

75. Lenin, *PSS*, XLVIII, 231–233 (emphasis in the original).

76. Lenin, *PSS*, XLVIII, 233. For a recent discussion of Lenin's views on religion see the article by Bohdan R. Bociurkiw, "Lenin and Religion," in *Lenin the Man, the Theorist, the Leader*, ed. by L. Schapiro (London, 1967), 107–134. See also the work of M. I. Shakhnovich, *Lenin i problemy ateizma: kritika religii v trudakh V. I. Lenina* (Moscow, 1961), in particular Chapter 8, "V. I. Lenin o bogostro- itelstve," 490–526.

77. Gor'kii, *Sobranie sochinenii*, vol. 24, 136–137; *Arkhiv*, IX: 105–107.

78. *Gor'kii i Andreev*, 318–319; Gor'kii, *Sobranie sochinenii*, vol. 29, 192–94.

79. Gor'kii, *Sobranie sochinenii*, vol. 29, 221; Letopis', II: 348.

80. *M. Gor'kii: Materialy i issledovaniia*, I, 53–61. The article appeared in the paper *Budushchee* (L'Avenir) 6 (November 26, 1912): 2–3; It was written in answer to an article by Y. I. Breev, a publisher from Nizhnii Novgorod, who in 1910 wrote Gorky advising him to ask Nicholas II for permission to return to Russia.

81. *M. Gor'kii: Materialy i issledovaniia*, I, 64–72. The article was first published in the journal *Ukrainskaia zhizn'* (Ukrainian Life) 9 (September, 1912): 7–15. See also *Arkhiv*, VII: 204; Lenin, *PSS*, XLVIII, 162; *Gor'kii i Andreev*, 350; *Arkhiv*, IX: 132.

82. Gor'kii, *Sobranie sochinenii*, vol. 2, 195.

83. *M. Gor'kii: Materialy i issledovaniia*, II, 342.

84. Gor'kii, *Sobranie sochinenii*, vol. 29, 63; *Arkhiv*, IV: 268–269.

85. *Arkhiv*, VII: 159.

86. The circulation of the *Znanie sborniki*, which reached 41,000–80,000 before 1906, had fallen to 4,000 by 1907. See A. A. Volkov, *M. Gor'kii: Litraturnoe dvizhenie kontsa XIX i nachala XX veka* (Moscow, 1958), 304.

87. *Arkhiv*, IV: 225.

88. *Arkhiv*, VII: 210, 238.

89. Among the most important works written during the Capri period were *Ispoved'*, discussed previously; *Leto* and *Gorodok Okurov*, written in 1909; and *Zhizn Matveia Kozhemiakina*, written in 1910. Before leaving Capri Gorky began work on *Detstvo*.

90. Gorky Archives, Institut Mirovoi Literatury imeni M. Gor'kogo (IMLI) (Moscow), file KT, p. 34.

CHAPTER 6

WAR AND REVOLUTION

The Russian people have been wedded to Liberty.

M. Gor'kii, *Revoliutsiia i kul'tura*, 5

The practical maximalism of the anarcho-communist and vision-
aries from the Smolny is ruinous for Russia and, above all, for the
Russian working class. . . . They are sacrificing Russia in the name
of their dream of a worldwide or European Revolution. . . . And as
long as I can, I shall tell the Russian workers: "You are being led to
destruction! You are being used as material for an inhuman experiment!"

M. Gor'kii, "Nesvoevremennye mysli," *Novaia zhizn'*,
December 10 (23), 1917

The Revolution neither pities nor buries its dead.

I. V. Stalin, *Sochineniia*, III, 386

Gorky returned to Russia after an absence of close to eight years. The task
that he set for himself was to realize the ideas he had cherished to bring
Russia and its people closer to Europe. A member of the unique class of
the intelligentsia, he believed in the power of that class and its duty to lead
the people. The means were education and the promotion of culture. In his
ideology he was in essence a man of the eighteenth-century Enlightenment.
His aim was to make the people literate. He had connections; he was a

M. Gorky and V. Lenin at the Second Congress of the Communist International. Moscow, July 19, 1920. Reproduced courtesy of Gorky Archives of the Institute of World Literature, Moscow.

well-known writer accepted by some members of the intelligentsia, but criticized by others. The political was now in the background. He had his disagreements with Lenin during the Capri period and moved away from the *Vperëd* group. As one of his biographers wrote at the time, "he had lost his political orientation."

From the time of his return to Russia in December 1913 until his second exile in 1921, Gorky was both witness to and participant in events of great significance. First came World War I, followed by the revolutions of February and October, the Civil War, and Allied intervention. In reviewing Gorky's political activities during these years, it becomes obvious that he consistently maintained an independent stand. An illustration of this independence is his repudiation of the war on pacifist grounds. This alienated the intelligentsia, as well as wide sections of the Russian public who supported a "war to the victorious end." The same independence is seen in the position Gorky assumed between February and October of 1917. He cautiously accepted the February overthrow. During the period of the Provisional Government, he founded the independent paper called *Novaia zhizn'* (New Life). In October, he strongly opposed the Bolshevik coup d'état. Thereby Gorky forfeited any chance of assuming a leading role in the Bolshevik Revolution. In fact, he bitterly denounced the new regime. He finally arrived at a *modus vivendi* with the Bolsheviks. It was understood that Gorky would work to safeguard the cultural heritage of Russia, and he added a self-imposed task of protector of the intellectuals. Also, in attempting to influence the leaders in the Kremlin and Lenin in particular to ameliorate injustices of the "first proletarian government," he became the "great interceder."

Gorky returned to Russia after an absence of nearly eight years. As at the time of his departure in the spring of 1906, Russia at the end of 1913 was beset by many problems. The last capable prime minister, P. A. Stolypin, had been assassinated in September 1911; and since that time the government of Nicholas II had resembled a ship without a helmsman. Increasingly, power was passing to the court dominated by the "holy man," Georgii Rasputin. At the time of Gorky's return, the prime ministry was in the hands of the decrepit I. L. Goremykin. Yes, there was progress in implementing the reforms started by Stolypin, yet the situation in the countryside was far from satisfactory.[1] There was great instability in the cities. As Russia industrialized, the numbers and the dissatisfaction of the workers grew. Earlier, in 1912, the strike in the Lena gold mines was ruthlessly suppressed by the authorities, which provoked a wave of protest strikes in cities of European Russia. By 1913, more than 850,000 men stopped working, and by the spring of 1914 close to one and a half million men were on strike.[2] The central government was incapable of taking any decisive steps to remedy the situation.

The Russian Social Democratic Workers' Party (RSDWP) had sent both
Bolsheviks and Mensheviks to the Fourth Duma. There was a tendency
toward unity among the members of the Duma fraction, but Lenin was
against it and proceded to foster a split. The result of his actions was that
the Bolsheviks declared themselves a separate fraction.[3] The Bolsheviks
were in a difficult situation in 1913. The number of subscribers to *Pravda*
dropped; the Party suffered from a shortage of funds, and the work of the
underground organizations was disrupted. Gorky, who had repeatedly expressed his dislike of squabbles in the Party, showed on his return no eagerness to work actively for the RSDWP.

His arrival in the country came as a surprise to the tsarist police. He had
obtained a passport at the Russian consulate in Naples but was warned
that on his return he would be arrested.[4] Yet he somehow managed to slip
into Russia. His presence was noticed by a secret agent of the Okhrana in
St. Petersburg: "On the 31 of December [1913] . . . the famous immigrant,
Nizhnii Novgorod guildsman Aleksei Maksimovich Peshkov, arrived by
train from the station of Verzhbolovo and was put under police surveillance."[5] He settled in the country estate of Andreeva's family in Finland,
close to Mustamiaki, but travelled frequently to St. Petersburg. Although
he was not arrested, the case against him for the authorship of *Mat'* was
reopened and dragged on till May 1914, when it was closed "for lack of
evidence of criminal action on the part of the [writer]."[6]

His first impressions of Russia were recorded in a letter to the writer Amfiteatrov:
I do not know whether [returning to] . . . the fatherland is sweet for me or not. I
was greeted by the workers very warmly; Moscow alone greeted me seventy times.
. . . I am very moved. But . . . the intelligentsia does not like me. Not at all! . . . One
thing, however, I will say—Russia is a wonderful country![7]

Gorky was aware of the changes that had taken place during his absence,
and in writing to Plekhanov observed that though the differences were
considerable, he was not certain whether these were an improvement for
the better.[8] He decided to devote his time to work in publishing, education,
and cultural endeavors. In N. Valentinov's (N. V. Volskii) memoirs one
learns much about Gorky at the time of his return:

But I want to work in the open. We all agree that we need a revolution and that
we have to enlighten the people politically. This, however, is not enough. We have
to make the people literate; we have to teach them . . . respect for work and technical knowledge. . . . We are hateful and backward Asia.[9]

Gorky was fortunate to find a kindred soul in I. D. Sytin, the wealthy
owner of the largest publishing house in Russia and of the popular daily
Russkoe slovo (Russian Word). Sytin's aim was to educate and enlighten
the people by publishing books and textbooks and expanding wholesale

and retail sales of reading material. He was buying the editions of Gorky's works to give these to the subscribers of his popular journal, *Niva* (Cornfield). It was Sytin who provided financial support for Gorky's publishing house, *Parus* (Sail), where the journal *Letopis'* (Chronicle) was launched in December 1915.

Gorky's slogan was "Russia must become Europe." This meant that the Russians had to free themselves from the remaining vestiges of serfdom, they had to learn how to work, and they had to acquire knowledge to become educated. He expressed concern over the future of Russia and explained that a choice had to be made between the Asiatic pattern of despotism and a democratic form of government.[10] In trying to account for the backwardness of the Russians as compared with the Europeans, he wrote: "Our close proximity to Asia, the Mongol yoke, the organization of the Moscow state on the pattern of eastern despotism, and all kinds of similar influences could not but infect us with the basic traits of an eastern psychology."[11] Although he intended to confine his work to education and culture, there were contacts between Gorky and the Bolsheviks because of the latter's aim to keep him on their side. Soon after his arrival in 1913, the Bolshevik newspaper *Proletarskaia pravda* (Proletarian Truth) wrote: "We welcome the beloved writer on the occasion of his return to the motherland."[12] The welcome was followed by efforts to involve Gorky in the work of the Party, and in the spring of 1914 a Bolshevik member of the Duma fraction, A. A. Badaev, visited Gorky. According to Badaev, Gorky promised to help establish contacts and obtain funds for the Party.[13] Later in the summer, he was contacted by the St. Petersburg Committee of the RSDWP and in September donated 6,000 rubles "to revolutionary causes."[14] He was made responsible for the literary section of the Bolshevik journal *Prosveshchenie* (Enlightenment)[15] and, in collaboration with A. N. Tikhonov, was preparing a collection of works by proletarian writers.[16]

The war that broke out in the summer of 1914 came as a great blow to Gorky. For some time, he had been aware of the growing danger of an international crisis and had expressed his fears in letters to E. Peshkova. "Any day," wrote Gorky in September of 1912, "a giant slaughter can erupt in the Balkans. We will, no doubt, be involved and will be severely beaten."[17] Yet he seemed unprepared as many others for the events when they occurred.

I had been convinced for three years that a general European war was inevitable, and I thought that I was prepared for the catastrophe. But now that it has occurred, I feel depressed as if all that is now happening is unexpected. I fear for Russia, for our people, for its future; and I cannot think of anything else . . . one thing is clear—we are entering the first act of a world tragedy.[18]

There was a patriotic outburst in the country among all classes of the population. Even the workers accepted the war, and at first there were no strikes. The RSDWP was divided on the issue of war. G. V. Plekhanov accepted the war and wanted it to continue until the victory of the Western democracies was achieved. Iu. Martov wanted peace on the basis of self-determination, without indemnities or annexations. Lenin regarded the war as a bourgeois struggle for markets. By the fall of 1914, the Bolshevik Duma deputies, as well as many other members of the Party, were arrested; some of them were sent into exile to Siberia. The Russian Bureau of the Central Committee ceased to function, and the publication of *Pravda* was stopped in July 1914. Not till the summer of 1915, when a prominent Bolshevik, A. G. Shliapnikov, returned to Russia, was the Bureau reestablished.

Gorky was not caught up in the general martial enthusiasm. All his life he had wanted to see the triumph of reason over emotions and had confidence in the power of ideas, principles, and international solidarity. All this optimism vanished. In September 1914, shortly after the destruction of the Rheims Cathedral by the Germans, Gorky wrote Andreeva: "All this is so terrible that I am unable to express even one one-hundredth of my heavy feelings, which are perhaps best described in words such as world catastrophe, the downfall of European culture."[19]

Enraged over the events, he, with other men of letters, signed a protest against the barbarism of the Germans, blaming them for the war. Lenin from Switzerland sent a letter to Shliapnikov, where he severely criticized the writer: "Poor Gorky. How sad that he has disgraced himself by signing the despicable paper of the Russian liberals."[20] Gorky, unperturbed, wrote an "Appeal to the Population," in which he condemned the war and appealed to feelings of brotherhood and cooperation. As to the accusations of Gorky belonging to the camp of *porazhentsy* (the defeatists), B. N. Nicolaevsky, a prominent Menshevik, explained Gorky's position on the war thus: "Gorky, not being one of the *'porazhentsy,'* did not believe that Russia would be able to defeat Germany, was for a speedy end of the war and for peace without annexation or indemnities." He was not for a separate peace.[21] Lenin, not impressed by the "Appeal," nevertheless advised the Party to utilize it. "We have to *make use* of every protest (even if it is as timid and confused, *à-la Gorkii*)."[22]

The "Appeal to the Population" was only one of many protests written by Gorky at this time. A series of articles entitled "Nesvoevremennoe" (Untimely), in protest against the war and against the attempted defense of it by certain Russian writers,[23] was confiscated by the censor. Another article, "O sovremennosti" (On Contemporaneity), which appeared in the journal *Novyi koloss* (New Colossus), was also condemned, and the journal confiscated.[24] These articles, like his letters to friends in exile, focused on problems such as the indifference and passivity of the intelligentsia, the disastrous policies of the government, and the importance of imparting a social conscience to the peasants.

In the spring of 1915, together with I. P. Ladyzhnikov and A. N. Tikhonov, Gorky, supported by Sytin, organized the publishing house *Parus* (Sail).[25] The aim of *Parus* was "To clarify through its publications the unresolved contradictions of two world outlooks: the intellectual-empirical and the emotional-religious."[26] Among the projected publications was an encyclopedia of five volumes aimed to provide the workers with information in the fields of social and historical sciences.[27] The first issue of the journal *Letopis'*, a political-literary monthly, appeared later in the year.[28] The journal was designed to campaign against the justification of the war and to defend the idea of international culture against all manifestations of nationalism and imperialism. Gorky tried to secure the participation of the Russian scholar, K. A. Timiriazev, in the work of *Letopis'*. He wrote: "The aim of the journal is to try to introduce into the chaos of stirred up emotions the sobering elements of intellectualism—an aim that may be a bit utopian. . . . It is important to bring into the dark storm the elements of rational and critical attitude towards reality."[29]

The government, displeased with the criticism of its policies was about to close the journal when the February Revolution saved it for a while. Among the contributors to *Letopis'* were V. A. Bazarov, A. A. Bogdanov, A. V. Lunacharskii, N. V. Volskii, and N. N. Sukhanov. These men were either ex-members of *Vperëd* or Mensheviks (although Sukhanov at that time considered himself an unaffiliated Social Democrat). Lenin's criticism of *Letopis'* was expressed in a letter to Shliapnikov of October 1916. *Letopis'*, wrote Lenin, represented the ideas of the machists and *okists*,[30] whose political aims were most suspicious. As to Gorky, he could not be relied on, for, wrote Lenin, "In politics Gorky is always weak-willed and subject to emotions and moods."[31] Yet two considerations made Lenin anxious to publish in *Letopis'*. One was his desire to use the legal press for purposes of propaganda; the second was his own difficult financial situation. He wrote Shliapnikov:

As for myself, I will tell you that I need some income, otherwise I will perish, I swear!! Prices are devilishly high, and there are no means of existence! You must get money, by hook or by crook, from the publisher of *Letopis'* to whom I have sent my two pamphlets. . . . If nothing can be arranged, then I will not survive. I am very serious, very.[32]

Lenin had earlier approached Gorky with a request to publish his and Krupskaia's works:

I am sending you the manuscript of a pamphlet with a request that it be published.

I have tried to explain . . . new data about America which, as far as I am concerned, is useful for popularizing Marxism. . . . I hope that I have succeeded in explaining clearly this important data for the sake of the new stratum of the reading public in Russia which is growing and needs to be enlightened on the economic evolution taking place in the world. . . . Personally I am in great need of money and would request, if this should not inconvenience you, to hasten with the publication of the pamphlet.[33]

The letter was reservedly signed, "Respectfully, V. Ilin." A second letter followed where Lenin asked for the publication of Krupskaia's work, "Narodnoe obrazovanie i demokratiia" (People's Education and Democracy).[34] At the end of 1916, Lenin sent Gorky one more article for publication. This was the famous "Imperialism kak vysshaia stadiia razvitiia kapitalizma" (Imperialism as the Highest Stage of Capitalism). Having read it, Gorky evidently demanded the deletion of a passage criticizing Karl Kautsky. Lenin was enraged. He wrote Inessa [Armand]:

My manuscript on imperialism has reached Peter[sburg] and they write today that the publisher (and this is Gor'kii! Oh, the simple calf!) is dissatisfied with the sharp words against whom do you think? Kautsky! He [Gorky] wants to get in touch with me. It is both ridiculous and offensive![35]

The pamphlet appeared in 1917. The passage concerning Kautsky had been deleted.

Gorky's *Letopis'* was subjected to severe criticism for its so-called defeatist policies. In April 1916, the police department in Petersburg received an anonymous notice condemning the editors and the policy of the journal. *Letopis'* was accused of distributing proclamations and of collecting funds for nonphilanthropic causes. The notice contained information about clandestine meetings conducted by the members of the editorial board in which members of various revolutionary parties, among them Bolsheviks, participated. Gorky was accused of maintaining contacts with Russian émigrés in Sweden and Norway. A detailed investigation by the Okhrana found no proof for the accusations. The report of the Okhrana mentioned the "Russkoe obshchestvo dlia izucheniia zhizni evreev" (Russian Society for the Study of the Life of the Jews), which Gorky supported and championed through *Letopis'*. The society was established and maintained as a protest against the official policies of the tsarist government, which had continued the old tradition of making the Jews scapegoats.[36] The report emphasized that *Letopis'* had no influence in the Bolshevik circles and was not at all popular with the workers.[37]

Gorky's concern over the situation of the Jewish minority in the period of World War I was caused by severe repressions by the government against that minority. When in 1915 the Jews living in the Western Borders of Russia were accused of collaboration with the enemy and were forcibly moved further east, Gorky came to their defense by publishing articles and collecting funds to help the evacuees. More than helping, Gorky wanted also to find out the reasons of Russian anti-Semitism. In September 1915, Gorky, together with the writers L. Andreev and F. Sologub, published a collection of essays on the Jewish question entitled *Shchit* (The Shield).

Among the contributors were V. G. Korolenko, P. N. Miliukov, and Prince P. Dolgorukov. The second, a project rather unusual in its nature was a questionnaire drawn up by Gorky and Sologub, in order to learn of the views of his compatriots on the Jewish question. The replies received were published in *Letopis'*, No. 1, 1916, with Gorky's comments on the findings.

Letopis' became even more unpopular[38] after the publication of the controversial articles "Dve dushi" (Two Souls) and "Pis'ma k chitateliu" (Letters to a Reader).[39] The theme was a familiar one, for it was to be found in Gorky's letters and pronouncements made during the later period of his stay on Capri. According to Gorky, the Russians had two souls, one belonging to the "passive East"—the Asiatic soul—and the other to the "active West." As long as the influence of the East prevailed there was no hope for genuine progress. For Gorky, everything backward and passive was classified as Eastern-Asiatic. The West was synonymous with progress, civilization, and culture. The critics wrote that he was in error in regarding European culture as universal and for extolling its hegemony. The Marxists condemned Gorky's heretical views on the question of political and social reforms in Russia. According to Gorky, all classes had to participate in the work of reform, especially the economically strong merchant and industrialist class (in short, the bourgeoisie).[40]

Although the work in *Parus* and the publication of *Letopis'* took much of his time, Gorky was busy with two other projects. In cooperation with V. A. Miakotin and A. V. Peshekhonov, both members of People's Socialist Party, and E. D. Kuskova, a moderate socialist, he planned to establish a newspaper under the title *Luch'* (Ray).[41] The other project concerned the founding of a radical-democratic party that "would express the social and political interests of the masses of citizens who were tired of the Kadety (Constitutional Democrats) and who would not join the [left-wing] socialists."[42] As late as February 1917 Gorky still hoped to publish the newspaper,[43] but neither the newspaper nor the party ever materialized. On the eve of the February Revolution he wrote to V. Ia. Briusov: "The publication of the newspaper [*Luch'*] is being postponed indefinitely. I will not begin to list the causes, they are of little interest. . . . It is too bad that half a year of great effort was lost." He further elaborated on the projected newspaper and the radical-democratic party in April 1917:

Yes, I tried to establish *Luch'* with M. V. Bernatskii and M. T. Vinogradov whom I have held in great esteem for quite some time. *Luch'* was to be an organ of a radical democratic party. I took part in the work of the organizational committee, for I was convinced that such a party was necessary. . . . I had thought of organizing such a party as early as 1910 and I had discussed it with G. V. Plekhanov, who also considered the founding of it as necessary.[44]

In the months preceding the February Revolution Gorky devoted his time to the publishing of *Letopis'* and work in *Parus* and, as mentioned, tried to establish a new party and its organ. According to Gruzdev, "Gorky detached himself from the Bolshevik underground and lost the revolutionary orientation."[45]

V. M. Khodasevich, the niece of the poet V. F. Khodasevich, an artist and later stage designer, has left in her memoir the following description of Gorky, whom she met in 1916, in the editorial offices of *Letopis'*:

Before me stood a tall man of slender build, his head relative to his height, rather small. I was struck by the intense, very attractive, childlike, blue eyes. . . . There was nothing artificial about him, a simple demeanour, nothing that would harken of him being famous. . . . He was dressed in a grey well-fitting suit, a blue shirt and no tie [Gorky evidently all his life disliked ties].[46]

At that time Gorky lived in St. Petersburg, in an apartment on Kronverkskii Prospekt, No 23, with Andreeva. Soon the household expanded and until Gorky's departure in 1921 included a number of people who were close to him and who all lived in a kind of a commune. Among them were the infamous P. P. Kriuchkov, later lover of Andreeva; Maria Ignatienva Zakrevskaia Benkendorf, later M. Budberg; and the artist I. N. Rakitskii, who came to dinner and never left. V. M. Khodasevich with husband Dideriks moved in too. Others came and went.

By 1917 the criticism of Nicholas' government was increasing. Defeats at the front and economic disintegration at home resulted in a growing opposition to the inept policies of the tsar and his court. And the Revolution began. The Revolution, which had been considered for close to a century as the only solution for Russia, found the Russian intelligentsia unprepared and confused. Gorky too, was disconcerted. As early as January 1917, he wrote E. Peshkova of the ever-worsening situation in the capital, the paralysis of transport, and the threat of famine.[47] His letters written shortly after the beginning of the Revolution show little enthusiasm. He wrote that although the soldiers were now supporting the people, it was difficult to foresee the future stand of the army. "I am full of skepticism. . . . There is much that is absurd rather than great. . . . We will not turn back but will also not move too much forward . . . and there will be great bloodshed."[48] To his son Maxim he wrote:

Remember, the Revolution just began, it will last for a long time. . . . We won not because we are strong, but because the government (*vlast'*) was weak. . . . We have made a political Revolution and have to reinforce our conquest. . . . I am a social democrat, but I am saying and will continue to say, that the time has not come for socialist-style reforms. The new government has inherited not a state but its ruins. . . . It has to win the confidence [of the people] and be supported.[49]

Gorky's connections with various sections of Petersburg society made his apartment a meeting place for representatives of many factions. "Gorky's apartment in those days resembled general staff headquarters. . . . I remember Leonid Borisovich Krasin, Desnitskii, Tikhonov and others. Shaliapin used to come also. . . . Often people from the outskirts [of Petersburg] used to come without even introducing themselves."[50] One such meeting in Gorky's apartment is described in the memoir of the Menshevik O. A. Ermanskii. It took place before the events of February 23, with the participation of prominent members of the revolutionary parties. The reason for it was agitation to organize a demonstration by the workers with demands to be presented to the Duma. The demands were for a government that would have the confidence of the people. The idea of the demonstration originated with the Workers' Group of the Military-Industrial Committee. Present at the meeting were a member of the Social Democratic fraction of the Duma, the Menshevik Chkheidze, A. Kerensky from the SRs, Shliapnikov for the Bolsheviks, Ermanskii from the Menshevik Internationalists, and I. Iurenev of the *Ob'edinentsy*. The topic of discussion was the situation in the capital. Ermanskii writes, "In the course of discussion it transpired that none of the participants spoke of an imminent revolutionary outbreak."[51] The one who was able to bring some news was Gorky. He spoke of the mood of opposition among the military, and in particular in the upper echelons of the army. There were two more meetings of a similar nature but not at Gorky's apartment, for it was already under surveillance.[52]

According to N. N. Sukhanov, Gorky's first reaction to the momentous events of February 23 was indifference. This was followed by fear of chaos, anarchy, and disorder. Sukhanov thought that Gorky, a long-time member of the radical intelligentsia, would be an important asset to the cause if he could be persuaded to become active. There was an urgent need to write an appeal to the nations of the world, and Gorky was considered as the one most capable of doing it. Sukhanov succeeded in influencing him to undertake the drafting of this appeal. But to his disappointment, Gorky's draft resembled a dissertation. The Revolution was viewed only in its relation to culture, and political and social problems as well as the question of the war were ignored. In the end, the appeal was written by Sukhanov.[53]

Gorky's main concern was culture, its safeguard and its promotion. As early as March 4, he assembled in his apartment men of letters and of the arts, to organize a special commission with the aim of requesting that the Duma establish a separate department for the promotion of fine arts. On Gorky's initiative, *Komissiia po delam iskusstva* (Commission on the Arts) was established by the Provisional Government. Also, Gorky was reinstated as member of the Academy of Sciences, membership that had been denied him by the order of Nicholas II in 1902.

The Commission on the Arts sent an address to the Petersburg Soviet of

Workers' and Soldiers' Deputies offering its services in safeguarding historical monuments.[54] Further opportunity to voice his concern over safeguarding Russia's cultural inheritance came at a meeting of the Executive of the Petersburg Soviet on March 7. Gorky delivered an address, which was approved and published in the name of the Soviet.

> Citizens, the old masters are gone, leaving behind them a great heritage. It now ... belongs to the whole nation.
> Citizens, guard this inheritance. Guard the palaces; they will become palaces of your national art. Guard the paintings, sculpture, buildings—these are the embodiments of the fine things which gifted men have created even under the oppression of despotism, and which testify to the power and beauty of the human mind.
> Citizens, do not touch a single stone. Guard your monuments, buildings, old objects, documents—all these are your history, your pride. Remember that this is the soil from which your national art will grow.[55]

At the meeting, Gorky put before the Soviet a request in the name of the Petersburg artists to choose, as the place of burial for the victims of the March (February) Revolution, the Champ de Mars instead of the Palace Square.[56] Sukhanov gives in his work a vivid description of Gorky's appearance and the response of the Soviet. "After an ovation Gorky explained the matter, not very successfully, not concretely. . . . He was given due applause, but on the question whether the Soviet would review its decision about the place of burial, the vote was negative!"[57] This was Gorky's last attendance at the meetings of the Petersburg Soviet. Trying to promote the development of the sciences, he was instrumental in establishing the organization *Svobodnaia assotsiatsiia dlia razvitiia i rasprostraneniia polozhitel' nykh nauk* (Free Association for the Development and Dissemination of Exact Sciences).[58] The association continued to receive Gorky's support in the ensuing years.

His attitude toward the February Revolution was slowly changing. Fear and distrust gave way to cautious optimism.

The Russian people have been wedded to Liberty. Let us hope that out of this union new strong men shall be born in our land exhausted both physically and spiritually. Let us firmly believe that in the Russian man a bright flame of reason and will shall ignite forces that have been extinguished and suppressed by the centuries-old yoke of a police regime.[59]

Writing to the French author R. Rolland in March 1917, Gorky added a postscript. It read: "I congratulate you, Romain Rolland. . . . Russia has ceased to be one of the bulwarks of European reaction, our people have been wedded to liberty, and I hope that from this union will come many talented people for the glory of humanity."[60] He reiterated his belief in the power of knowledge and reason. "And up until today," wrote Gorky in

April 1917, "the Russian Revolution appears as a sequence of bright and joyful manifestations of reason." "The danger," continued Gorky, was that "with our inclination to anarchism we may easily devour the freedom."[61] He feared, he wrote, the unleashing of anarchical tendencies of the peasantry. Significantly, he called for cooperation of the bourgeoisie with the revolutionary democrats active in the country. In order to maintain order, he considered it inevitable, and not undesirable, that the bourgeoisie should move to the right; but he warned against doing it too hastily lest it repeat the mistakes of 1906. In an address to the Provisional Government and the Executive Committee of the Soviet, Gorky expressed his approval of the government's foreign policy. He called upon the government to conclude peace, "peace which would give Russia the possibility of an honorable existence among the nations of the world."[62]

Lenin's reaction to Gorky's address was not long in coming. In his fourth "Letter from Afar," entitled "Kak dobitsia mira" (How to Achieve Peace), he wrote:

One experiences a bitter feeling in reading the letter [Gorky's address] which is permeated with prevalent philistine prejudices. The writer of these lines often, during the meetings with Gor'kii on Capri, warned him against and reproached him for his political errors. Gor'kii answered these reproaches with an inimitable and disarming smile and a straight-forward statement: "I know that I am a poor Marxist. But then, we artists are all an irresponsible lot." One could not easily quarrel with that kind of a statement. There is no doubt that Gor'kii is a great literary talent who has brought much that is useful to the world proletarian movement. And will bring even more. But, why is Gor'kii meddling in politics?[63]

Gorky was apparently unperturbed by Lenin's criticism. Louis Fisher, the American historian and one of the biographers of Lenin, wrote of Gorky's popularity: "As a public figure, Gorky was at that moment probably better known and more loved than Lenin. The intellectuals, and many workers and peasants, whether or not they had read his stories, knew him. . . . Maksim Gorky was the man of the people who served the people in his own way."[64]

There is no evidence of Gorky's reaction to Lenin's return in April 1917 or his famous April Theses. There is no mention of a meeting between Gorky and Lenin before the fall of 1918. This was not surprising, given the disagreements of the 1909–1913 period. Valentinov writes, in his previously mentioned "Vstrechi s M. Gor'kim," that when asked whether he met with Lenin following his return from Switzerland, Gorky answered: "I have not seen Lenin and do not plan to see him."[65] Comments on Gorky's stand at the time are found in his 1930 reworked memoir of Lenin: "When Lenin, after his arrival in 1917 had published his theses, I thought . . . that he was sacrificing to the Russian peasantry the numerically insignificant . . .

but politically conscious group of workers and revolutionary intelligentsia. . . . But I was wrong."[66] But that was 1930. . . .

He wanted to enlist all those who favored socialist democracy in the work of the Provisional Government. With that purpose in mind he established, in April 1917, the daily *Novaia zhizn'* (New Life). Among his collaborators were members of the editorial board of *Letopis'*, ex-members of *Vperëd*, Mensheviks, and uncommitted Social Democrats. *Novaia zhizn'* was to replace the stillborn *Luch'*.[67] Gorky succeeded in obtaining funds for the projected newspaper from a number of sources.[68] His article entitled "Revoliutsiia i kul'tura" (Revolution and Culture) appeared in the first issue of the paper. He wrote of the frightful inheritance left by the monarchy and the necessity for constructive and creative work. He felt that the time had come for the people of Russia to prove to themselves and to the world their abilities, their capacities, and their genius.[69] Soon he began publishing there a series of articles entitled "Nesvoevremennye mysli" (Untimely Thoughts), dealing with current political, social, and cultural issues. The articles were criticized by some and praised by others.[70]

Novaia zhizn' occupied much of Gorky's time. It also presented many problems. One was the general policy of the paper. Sukhanov writes that in the period between the two Revolutions, *Novaia zhizn'* represented a group that was weakest in the Petersburg Soviet, but the newspaper had a large circulation and was used by many parties, including the Bolshevik, for a free expression of opinion. At one point, the future Bolshevik leaders D. B. Riazanov and L. D. Trotsky made an attempt at collaboration with the editors of the paper, but the leanings of the latter toward the Internationalists precluded that possibility.[71]

Gorky's main criticism of *Novaia zhizn'* in the first months of its publication was its overemphasis on politics, at the expense of fields such as philosophy and history. His ties with *Novaia zhizn'* affected his relations with people he met in the "Free Association for the Development and Dissemination of Exact Sciences" and in the literary circles and societies where he was active. These people, "bourgeois intelligentsia" according to Sukhanov, argued with Gorky about the newspaper, criticizing its policies. Manufacturers tried to demonstrate to him that the workers were criminal idlers who were destroying the national industry and national culture. Gorky was often impressed by their arguments and demanded that *Novaia zhizn'* throw light "on the other side of the problem."[72] Following the establishment of *Novaia zhizn'*, he was asked whether he also contemplated the creation of a new party. He replied: "At this moment, when our constitutionalists have turned into republicans, and the wide democratic masses are following the working class, I consider a radical democratic party perhaps unnecessary."[73] In a letter to E. Peshkova, he wrote that "Now I myself constitute a party. I do not know its name. In this party there is only one member—me."[74] Yet at the same time, writing in the paper *Rus-*

skoe slovo (Russian Word) he reaffirmed that he remained a Social Democrat.[75]

In the months after the February Revolution, Gorky's work in *Novaia zhizn'* and in various associations and societies that he established or led was, as is seen from his letters, not satisfying. In a letter to E. Peshkova of June 20, he wrote:

Tomorrow a meeting of the "Free Association" will take place in my apartment. . . . The day after [there will be meetings of] youth without party affiliations, then of the national theaters, then the [members] of the Museum of Fighters for Freedom, and on the 25th, a public meeting concerning social education in the Mikhailovskii Theater. . . . I live with a contradiction within myself, and see no other solution except to work for the promotion of culture.[76]

His agitation was described further in a similar passage:

I have never admired men who become petrified and fossilized under the pressure of the faith they profess. . . . I will say further that I regard myself in every group and party a heretic. In my political views there are many contradictions which I cannot and do not want to resolve. I feel that in order to maintain some equilibrium and peace of mind, I would have to kill that part of my soul which passionately . . . loves the living, sinful and . . . pitiful Russian man.[77]

Gorky's waverings were a symptom of a disease that afflicted the Russian revolutionary intelligentsia in the summer of 1917. Drowned in endless intellectual discussions, the intelligentsia was unable to come to grips with the problems facing the country. Thinking in terms of a priori blueprints for the restructuring of the political, social, and economic order in Russia, the intelligentsia accepted the bourgeois democratic stage of the Revolution. Lenin and his followers preached the idea of a socialist Revolution under the slogan "all power to the Soviets." His militant attitude and his assurances that his party was the only one capable of taking power was viewed with suspicion and ridicule. As the events in the country worsened, it became ever more obvious that the dual rule of the Provisional Government and the Executive of the Soviet of Workers' and Soldiers' Deputies could not last. The government passed gradually into the hands of A. Kerensky who lacked a definite policy on such crucial issues as war, land, and labor.

The incompetence of the Provisional Government combined with the Bolsheviks' propaganda provoked the uprising of July 2–5, 1917. The July Days began with the demand, put forward by soldiers of the Petersburg garrison and sailors from Kronstadt, that the Bolsheviks seize power. The Bolshevik leaders cleverly directed the masses toward the Tauride Palace, the headquarters of the Soviet. The Executive of the Soviet was asked to depose the Provisional Government and to replace it. The government had managed to gather reliable forces and succeeded in putting down the demonstrations and bloody clashes. By July 7, order was restored. The Bolsheviks had played a double role in the July revolt. Some of their leaders were arrested and Lenin fled to Finland. Gorky had no praise for the July Days.

One will forever remember the terrible scenes of madness which engulfed Petersburg on July 4. Here . . . running like a mad boar is a lorry thickly packed with . . . representatives of the revolutionary army. Among them a young man . . . cries hysterically: "Comrades, this is a socialist Revolution! . . ." I have seen a panicking crowd before . . . but I have never had such dreadful, devastating experiences.[78]

Yet despite the disgust at the Bolsheviks' responsibility for the July Days, the editorial board of *Novaia zhizn'* gave Lenin and Trotsky permission to publish articles in their paper.[79]

Following the July Days, Gorky was attacked and branded a traitor by V. L. Burtsev, a journalist and a member of the SRs. Lenin had been accused of spying for Germany, and Gorky's willingness to publish Lenin's article was considered evidence of his complicity. Burtsev published two articles, "Ili my ili nemtsy i te kto s nimi" (Either We or the Germans and All Who Are with Them) and "Ne zashchishchaite M. Gor'kogo" (Do Not Defend M. Gorky), in which he accused Gorky of treason.[80] Annoyed at Burtsev's slander, Gorky wrote a letter to the editor addressed *Burtsevu* (To Burtsev): "The yellow press played a scurvy trick on me and using the authority of your name, published a terrible slander against me. . . . I expected yesterday your denial of the slander, but you have not denied it. I demand a denial."[81] Gorky was censored by the left as well as by the right. Plekhanov's paper, *Edinstvo* (Unity), published an article entitled "Ne travite nashikh detei" (Do Not Poison Our Children), in which he criticized Gorky's "Nesvoevremennye mysli." Gorky had further angered Plekhanov's Mensheviks by sponsoring a collection to help the Bolsheviks arrested after the July Days.[82] It appears that during the summer months of 1917, Gorky alienated the right by his association with *Novaia zhizn'* and the left by his noncommittal attitude and his alliance with the Internationalists.[83]

In the country, a series of events occured that ultimately led to the Bolshevik coup d'état. After the July Days, Kerensky succeeded in strengthening his position, and there was a marked shift to the right on the part of the government. When General L. Kornilov was appointed commander-in-chief, the parties on the left began to fear the emergence of an army dictatorship. The general situation deteriorated, production almost stopped, and government finances were in a poor state, with inflation on the increase. Transport was disorganized, and the peasants, impatient over the procrastination of the Provisional Government on the question of land reform, began on their own accord to divide the landlords' estates. The failure of Kerensky's July offensive was proof that Russia was incapable of continuing the war. Kerensky's inept handling of the Kornilov Affair led ultimately to his own defeat. The Bolsheviks were moving swiftly into the foreground.

By September 1917, the Bolsheviks had obtained a majority in the Petersburg Soviet. Trotsky, released by Kerensky from prison, was elected chairman. Both Trotsky and Lenin thought that the time had come for the overthrow of the Provisional Government and the seizure of power by the Bolsheviks. Trotsky wanted the seizure of power to coincide with the meeting of the Second All-Russian Congress of Soviets, which was at first scheduled for October 20. Lenin maintained that power had to be seized independently of the Soviets.[84] Meanwhile the German advance toward Petersburg and the rumors that the government intended to move the capital to Moscow made the Petersburg Soviet decide to assume responsibility for the defense of the capital. On October 13, the Executive Committee of the Soviet established the Extraordinary Revolutionary Committee. The chairman of the Petersburg Soviet was, by virtue of his position, the head of the Revolutionary Committee. Thus the Government was outmaneuvered on the important matter of military control in Petersburg and the adjacent districts.

The armed uprising began on October 24, on the eve of the meeting of the Second All-Russian Congress of Soviets. Insurgent troops occupied all strategic points in the capital. On the night of October 25–26, the Government surrendered, and most of its ministers were arrested while Kerensky tried in vain to rally loyal troops in his support. When the Mensheviks and the Right Socialist Revolutionaries left the meeting of the All-Russian Congress of Soviets, the Bolsheviks obtained an absolute majority; the Bolshevik regime was quickly being established.

It is important to examine Gorky's stand during the crucial period leading to the coup d'état of the Bolsheviks and his attitude toward the October Revolution. He had spent part of the summer in the Crimea, far removed from the events just described. Returning to Petersburg on October 5, Gorky resumed his work in *Novaia zhizn'*. The policy of the paper was decisively against a Bolshevik insurrection. Upon learning of the decision taken by the Bolshevik Central Committee on October 16 to stage an uprising, Gorky wrote in *Novaia zhizn'* a prophetic editorial, "Nel'zia molchat'!" (One Must Not Be Silent!). In this, he warned of the danger of attempting a socialist Revolution in backward Russia.

Ever more persistent rumors are spreading of the forthcoming "action of the Bolsheviks" on October 20th. In other words, the abominable scenes of July 2–5 are going to be repeated. This means more lorries tightly packed with men armed with rifles and revolvers in hands trembling with fear; and from these guns they will shoot at shop windows, at people. . . . An unorganized crowd will crawl out into the streets poorly understanding what it wants, and under its cover adventurers, thieves and professional murderers will begin making the history of the Russian Revolution. . . . Who needs all this? The Centr[al] Committee of the S-D Bolsheviks is evidently not taking any part in the presupposed adventure, since up until today it has not confirmed the rumors of the forthcoming action, although it has not denied them. . . . The Central Committee of the Bolsheviks is duty bound to deny the rumors. . . . It [the Central Committee] has to deny them if it is in fact a strong and politically free organ, capable of leading the masses, and not a . . . weapon in the hands of shameless adventurers or fanatics gone mad.[85]

The reply to Gorky came in a condemnatory article published October 20, in *Rabochii put'* (Workers' Road) by I. V. Stalin.

As to the neurotics from *Novaia zhizn'*, we are at a loss over their demands. . . . *Novaia zhizn' is* deserting the ranks of the Revolution now for the second time. . . . They . . . were silent when the landlords and their officials drove the peasants to despair and hunger revolts. They . . . were silent when the capitalists . . . prepared . . . lock-outs and unemployment for the workers. They knew how to be silent when the counter-revolution tried to surrender the capital and withdraw the army. But these people "must not be silent" when the vanguard of the Revolution, the Petersburg Soviet, takes up the defense of the cheated workers and peasants! . . . The Russian Revolution has destroyed many authorities. Its strength lies in the fact that it does not bow before "great names." . . . A whole list of such great names was discarded by the Revolution. Plekhanov, Kropotkin, Breshkovskaia, Zasulich, and . . . all those old Revolutionaries who are distinguished only because they are old. We fear that the laurels of these "pillars" are disturbing Gor'kii's sleep. We fear that Gor'kii is drawn towards them, into the archives. Well, to each his own. The Revolution neither pities nor buries its dead.[86]

Gorky had not taken part in the events of October 1917, but he was not without personal anxiety, for his son, Maxim, was arrested as a Bolshevik and not been heard from for a week. He was subsequently released from prison.[87] Back in Petersburg by November 7, Gorky began his blistering attacks on Lenin's newly established dictatorship. These were to continue (with some moderation evident after the spring of 1918), until the closure of *Novaia zhizn'* in July 1918.

His first article following the Bolshevik coup, entitled "K demokratii" (Toward Democracy), concerned the case of the ministers of the former Provisional Government who were arrested, the corruption of the Bolshevik leaders, and the disappearance of the ideals of freedom and democracy.

Lenin and Trotsky and their followers already have been poisoned by the rotten venom of power. The proof of this is their attitude toward freedom of speech and of person and toward all the ideals for which democracy was fighting. Blind fanatics and conscienceless adventurers are rushing at full speed on the road to a social Revolution—in actuality, it is a road toward anarchy.[88]

Three days later, in another article, Gorky warned the workers against the system that was being established by Lenin:

Lenin and Trotsky and all who follow them . . . are dishonoring the Revolution, and the working class. . . . Imagining themselves Napoleons of socialism, the Leninists . . . are completing the destruction of Russia. Lenin is, of course, a man of extraordinary force; for twenty-five years he stood in the front lines of those fighting for the triumph of socialism; and he is one of the most prominent and striking figures of international Social Democracy; . . . Lenin is a "leader" and a Russian aristocrat . . . and therefore he considers it his right to perform a cruel experiment with the Russian people which is *a priori* doomed to failure. . . .

The proletariat is for Lenin the same as iron ore is for a metallurgist. Is it possible, taking into consideration the present conditions, to cast out of this ore a socialist state? Obviously, this is impossible; yet—why should not one try? What does Lenin lose if the experiment should not succeed? . . . Conscious workers who follow Lenin must understand that a pitiless experiment is being carried out with the Russian people which is going to destroy the best forces of the workers, and which will stop the normal growth of the Russian Revolution for a long time.[89]

Gorky declared that he could not identify with that section of the working class who followed their insane leaders:

Now when a considerable section of the working class, stirred by their rulers gone mad . . . is using oppression and terror against which the best among them had fought for so long. . . . I cannot be in the ranks of that section of the working class. . . . It is both shameful and criminal to frighten with terror and with pogroms men who do not want to take part in the mad jig of Mr. Trotsky which he is performing amidst the ruins of Russia.[90]

Though Gorky was allowed to continue the publication of his indictments of Lenin, Trotsky and their followers, articles began appearing in *Pravda* severely criticizing Gorky's desertion of the proletarian cause. Undaunted, Gorky answered:

Pravda writes: "Gor'kii started to speak the language of an enemy of the working class." This is not true. Turning to the conscious representatives of the working class, I maintain that fanatics and frivolous dreamers have stirred up among the working masses hopes which are unrealizable under present historical conditions. They are leading the Russian proletariat to defeat and destruction. . . . The article in *Pravda* ends with the following question: "When former . . . enemies come together at a celebration of all peoples, will Gor'kii, who so quickly deserted the ranks of genuine revolutionary democracy, be a welcome guest?" It is obvious that neither I nor the writer of the article will live to see the day of "that celebration." . . . And at a celebration where despotism of the half-literate masses rejoices over the easy victory, and where . . . the individual is oppressed, there will be nothing for me to do and for me this will not be a celebration.[91]

As the country was preparing for elections to the Constituent Assembly, Gorky came out in defense of the Kadety, who were being harassed during the electoral campaign. The Kadety, maintained Gorky, represented the will of hundreds of thousands of people and were the most educated section of the Russian society.[92] The greatest blow to Gorky, as to all who dreamt of the establishment of a constitutional government in Russia, was Lenin's dispersal of the Constituent Assembly in January 1918. The Bolsheviks had ruthlessly interrupted its work and then fired upon the crowd protesting the closure of the Assembly. Gorky wrote a bitter indictment of Lenin's action, comparing the events of January 5, 1918, with those of January 9, 1905:

On the 9th of January 1905, when downtrodden, tired soldiers were firing into the peaceful and unarmed crowds of workers, . . . people ran up to them and shouted . . . "What are you doing? . . . whom are you killing? They are your brothers, they are unarmed . . . they are trying to bring their grievances to the tsar! . . ." On the 5th of January [1918], the unarmed Revolutionary democracy of Petersburg— workers, officials—were peacefully demonstrating in favour of the Constituent Assembly. For a hundred years the best people of Russia lived with the hope of a Constituent Assembly. . . . In the struggle for this idea thousands of the intelligentsia perished, . . . and tens of thousands of workers and peasants. . . . Many of the "People's Commissars" have, during their political activity, impressed the working masses with the necessity of struggle for . . . a Constituent Assembly. *Pravda* lies when it writes that the demonstration of the 5th of January was organized by the bourgeoisie and by the bankers. . . . *Pravda* lies; it knows that the bourgeoisie has nothing to rejoice in the opening of the Constituent Assembly, for they are of no consequence among the 246 socialists . . . and 140 Bolsheviks. *Pravda* knows that the workers of the Obukhovo, Patronnyi and other factories were taking part in the demonstration. . . . And these workers were being fired upon. And *Pravda* may lie as much as it wants, but it cannot hide the shameful facts. . . . I am asking the "People's Commissars," among whom there must be honest people, if they understand that they will lose all that was won by the Revolution?[93]

Criticism of Gorky's "Nesvoevremennye mysli" continued to appear in *Pravda*. An attempt was made in one article, "Sotsial'naia revoliutsiia i M. Gor'kii" (The Social Revolution and M. Gorky), to explain Gorky's change in attitude toward the revolutionary cause. Gorky had lost faith in the revolutionary power of the peasantry and in the revolutionary spirit of the workers. Gorky did not see the beautiful face of the Revolution, but turned away from it. From a fierce advocate of the Revolution he had become a traitor to the cause. The author continued,

But Gor'kii is much too precious to our social Revolution, and therefore one has to believe that he will return to the ranks of its ideological leaders. He will rejoice over the Revolution and will assume the place which long belongs to him as the stormy petrel of the social Revolution.[94]

In answer, Gorky wrote that there was nothing to rejoice about. One could not rejoice over the fact that the Russian proletariat was being destroyed in a fratricidal war in the South and in the streets of Petersburg and that the intelligentsia was being terrorized by the "dark masses." "With whom are you going to make the Revolution? With the peasantry? With the soldiers? With the bayonet and the bullet? Do you really believe that Germany, England, France and Japan will allow us to fan the flame which will engulf us all?"[95] There was nothing to rejoice about, wrote Gorky, but the time was ripe to come to one's senses.

He continued the criticism of the newly established government. In a series of sketches entitled *V bol' nom gorode* (In the Sick City), he described the terrible famine in Petersburg. Famine was also spreading to the village, where peasants had stopped sowing because their seed had been requisitioned by the authorities. Beginning in January 1918, critical comments about Gorky and his newspaper appeared almost daily in *Pravda*'s column, *Obzor pechati* (Press Review). These comments concerned the stand of *Novaia zhizn'* on foreign and internal policies of the Bolsheviks. The articles became increasingly hostile to Gorky's newspaper. At one point, *Pravda* made insinuations about the financial sources of *Novaia zhizn'*. Gorky replied:

You want to know where *Novaia zhizn'* gets its money? *Novaia zhizn'* was founded by me with the financial assistance of E. K. Grubbe, who loaned me the sum of 275,000 rubles, out of which 50,000 was repaid. I could repay the rest if I knew where Grubbe resides. In addition, a part of my honorarium received from *Niva* [a journal published by I.D. Sytin] for the publication of my works, was invested in the newspaper. . . . I do not see anything shameful in the loan taken for the establishment of the paper. I consider the accusations against the paper as slanderous. For your information I want to add that in the period from 1901 to 1917, hundreds of thousands of rubles passed through my hands for the needs of the Russian Social Democratic Workers Party. Of this money my personal contribution amounted to tens of thousands [of rubles]. The rest was drawn from the pockets of the "bourgeoisie." *Iskra* was published on the money of Savva Morozov who did not loan the money but donated it. . . . V. I. Lenin is well aware of it as are other old members of the Party. Your slanderous and dirty tricks against *Novaia zhizn'* disgrace not my paper but yourselves.[96]

The opposition against *Novaia zhizn'* was mounting. When asked to make a final decision regarding the fate of the paper, Lenin answered that it was definitely necessary to suspend it. He felt that under the circumstances no intellectual pessimism should be allowed to threaten the Revolution. He did not, however, condemn Gorky.

Yet Gor'kii—is our man. . . . He is closely knit with the labour class and the labour movement, and he comes from the "lowly" himself. He will return to us beyond doubt. . . . Such things have happened to him before as in 1908. . . . He has long been afflicted by such political zigzags.[97]

Novaia zhizn' was closed on July 16, 1918. The Central Executive Committee of the Soviet passed a decree on November 4, 1917, giving the Bolsheviks control over all newsprint and wide powers to close down newspapers critical of the regime. Gorky's paper was published only for another eight months. For a while Gorky was unable to publish anything in the Soviet press. He could not even answer accusations made against him. It was at this point that a significant change occurred in Gorky's political orientation. At the time of the closure of *Novaia zhizn'*, he wrote E. Peshkova that he had decided to work with the Bolsheviks: "I intend to work with the Bolsheviks but on an autonomous basis. I am tired of the helpless academic kind of opposition of *Novaia zhizn'*."[98] Still full of pessimism over the situation, he ended the letter with the comment that "our Russian affairs are in a sorry state."[99]

One of the main reasons for his decision was concern for the survival of the Russian people. This was evident from his letters to E. Peshkova and articles in *Novaia zhizn'* written in the spring of 1918. The various cultural and educational institutions and associations that he had organized in 1918 were instrumental in drawing him into cooperation with the regime. He, in turn, called upon the intelligentsia to join him and wrote in April 1918: "My task is to unite the intelligentsia in the common cause of cultural work. I consider the timing right, for it is now possible to call upon all honest people to work towards the spiritual rebirth of our country."[100]

The summons to the intelligentsia provoked a cynical answer by the writer D. Filosofov, who rejected Gorky's call for cooperation with the Soviet Government.[101] Undaunted, Gorky persevered in his attempt. He bitterly criticized the tendency to brand as traitors those who were ready to work for the good of Russia.[102] Gorky's changed attitude was expressed in his appeal written in November 1918. In it he called upon the toiling masses of the world to follow the Russian people in their attempt to build a better life.

Follow us toward the new life which we are trying to build. Sparing no one and nothing, erring and suffering, with joy and ardent faith in success, we leave the judgment of our deeds to the honest appraisal of the future. Follow us in the struggle against the old order, and in the task of creating a new way of life. Follow us to freedom and the beautiful life.[103]

Gorky's decision to work with the Bolsheviks came at a time when the survival of the young state was in doubt. This was the period of Civil War and Allied intervention, the period known also as the era of War Com-

munism. As long as the fighting continued, no attention was given to domestic reconstruction. It was in this disastrous situation that Gorky began
his work. One factor that facilitated Gorky's cooperation with the regime
was the rapprochement with Lenin that came after the attempted assassination of Lenin. He came to see Lenin before the latter had fully recovered
from his wounds, and the occasion marked the beginning of the renewal
of personal contacts. Gorky suggested to Lenin that the Bolsheviks use the
talents of the intelligentsia in the interest of the survival of the proletarian
state. Lenin agreed it was to be on his terms:

Union of workers and intelligentsia? Yes! Not bad, not bad. Tell the intelligentsia
to come to us. . . . We have taken upon ourselves the colossal work of putting the
nation on its feet. . . . We are pointing . . . the way toward a better life. . . . Do I
dispute the fact that we need the intelligentsia? But you can see their hostility toward us. . . . And they do not understand that without us they are helpless and will
not be able to reach the masses. And it will be their fault if we should "break too
many pots" [if heads should roll].[104]

Until his departure in the fall of 1921, Gorky had a double task. He
became the curator of Russia's cultural inheritance and the "great interceder."[105] These activities took much of his time, and Gorky's career as
writer flagged. He became an unofficial minister of culture and an "organizer of public works for the starving intelligentsia."[106] These "public
works" included the establishment of the publishing house *Vsemirnaia literatura* (World Literature), aimed at publishing the world's great literary
classics in Russian.[107] The executive of *Vsemirnaia* consisted of Gorky's old
friends I. P. Ladyzhnikov, Tikhonov, and Z. I. Grzhebin. *Vsemirnaia literatura* was for Gorky an inexhaustible source of jobs; V. F. Khodasevich,
E. Zamyatin, V. Serge, and Maria Zakrevskaia Benkendorf (later known
as Moura Budberg), among others, found employment there. Gorky established a publishing house for cheap editions of Russian classics, another
for the publication of contemporary Russian works and a Workers' University in the Uritsky Palace. He was chairman of the *Ekspertnaia Komissiia
Narkomvneshtorga* (The Expert Commission of the Commissariat for Foreign Trade), established in February 1919, for the collection and evaluation
of antiques and antiquarian books.[108] By the order of the Council of Soviet
Commissars (of October 26, 1920), it was decided that the Commissariat
of Foreign Trade should organize abroad the sale of items that were selected for export by a special Expert Commission of the Petersburg Department of the Commissariat of Foreign Trade. From July 31, 1919,
Andreeva was the commissar of that commission and was empowered (with
Lenin's approval) to sell the antiques abroad for badly needed hard currency.

Gorky was chosen chairman of the society *Svoboda i kul'tura* (Freedom and Culture) that was to coordinate the work of all cultural-educational societies, clubs, and circles. He was chairman of the Presidium of the Executive Committee of the Union of Artists and deputy chairman of the Free Association for the Development and Dissemination of Exact Sciences. One of his enterprises was KUBU or *Komitet po uluchshenii byta uchenykh* (Committee for the Improvement of the Life of Scholars), which performed very important services during the trying years of War Communism. KUBU provided jobs for people in the professions and supplied them with special rations of food and shelter.

Of Gorky's work during this period one reads in the reminiscences of the writer Kornei Chukovskii:

We, the Petersburg writers, met with him during the first years of the Revolution. He took upon his shoulders all our troubles and needs. . . . I think that if one could collect the letters that Gorky wrote to various institutions on behalf of Russian writers, one would come up with at least six volumes. At that time he did not write novels or stories—only these endless letters.[109]

Chukovskii mentioned the great indebtedness to Gorky of many who were saved by him during those years of famine and disease. E. Zamyatin wrote of Gorky's help at the time when terror was used indiscriminately by the Cheka, established as early as December 1917.

It was common knowledge that Gorky was in close friendship with Lenin, and that he knew other revolutionary leaders well. And when the Revolution began to use terror. . . . Gorky was the last hope. . . . He wrote letters, swore on the telephone, and in more serious cases went to Moscow to see Lenin.[110]

Zamyatin mentioned an instance when he had asked for Gorky's help on behalf of one of his friends, arrested by the Cheka. Gorky, apparently unsuccessful in his appeal to Lenin, returned from Moscow and related that Lenin had told him, "It is time that you realized that politics is a dirty business and you had better stay out of it."[111]

Lenin did not grant all of Gorky's appeals. He told Andreeva in September of 1919, that with the likelihood of myriads of conspiracies, "It is better that scores and hundreds of the intelligentsia spend days or weeks in prison than that 10,000 should perish."[112] At times he did give prompt attention to Gorky's requests, and many were saved through Gorky's intercessions, among them Grand Duke Gavriil Konstantinovich Romanov and his wife. A further attempt at saving the lives of three other grand dukes ended in failure.[113]

The response of the Russian intelligentsia to Gorky's incessant care and intercedings was poor. In the eyes of many of them, Gorky's rapprochement with the Bolsheviks meant treason. The most outspoken enemies of Gorky were the writers E. Chirikov, D. Filosofov, and Zinaida Gippius. The latter, long before the Revolution, criticized the writer, whom she disdainfully called "the Negro in the silk top hat."[114]

Gorky, in spite of the fact that he succeeded in accomplishing much, was distressed by the new regime, and his unhappiness comes to light in the correspondence with Lenin and other Bolshevik leaders. The letters also reveal Gorky's naiveté and incomprehension of the basic features of the Soviet regime. Thus, in January 1919, Gorky asked Lenin whether the time was not right to resume the publication of *Novaia zhizn'*. Moreover, he thought that the Menshevik newspaper should also be published.[115] Was Gorky relying too much on his "closeness' to Lenin in making such requests?

In a recently released letter of September 6, 1919, written to Lenin, Gorky's disillusionment is clearly stated:

It looks like we have no hope to win and no courage to lose with honour if we resort to such barbarous and shameful actions as the destruction of the scholarly resources of our country. . . . I know that you will repeat the usual; this is a political struggle, those who are not with us, are against us, people who are neutral are dangerous, etc. . . . I, Vladimir Ilich, am on the other side, and prefer arrest, imprisonment, than taking part by being silent in the destruction of the best and valuable treasure of the Russian people. For me it became clear that the "reds" are the enemies of the people just as the "whites." Personally, I of course would rather be destroyed by the "whites," but the "reds" are also no comrades of mine. I would hope that you will understand.[116]

In the same vein was written the letter of September 16–19 (again, published only recently), where Gorky, mentioning the case of the professor of psychology A. A. Krogius,[117] arrested by the Cheka, expressed his indignation using rather strong language:

[T]he devil take you! One has to know that Krogius was never a member of the Kadet Party and that he is a *sincere* bolshevik. . . . In Russia, there are few brains, and we have few talented people, and too many scoundrels, adventurers and crooks! This our Revolution will last decades, where is the power that would lead it wisely and forcefully? . . . I don't believe in the peasant and regard him as an irreconcilable enemy of the worker and of culture.[118]

As to the Communists, Gorky had little regard for them either. He continued: "Oh, if you would only know, they are thieves, and within a year or two they will turn into despicable bourgeoise."[119]

In answer Lenin wrote:

The more I read your letter . . . the more I am convinced that the letter, the conclusions, and all the impressions, are morbid. . . . As in your discussions, so in the letter, it is the accumulation of your gloomy impressions which makes you to come to these conclusions. You start with dysentery and cholera and immediately some kind of bitterness emerges. . . . It appears that Communism is to be blamed for the poverty, the need and the disease in the besieged city. . . . You conclude that a Revolution cannot be made with the assistance of thieves. [It must involve] the intelligentsia. . . . Everything is being done in order to draw in the intelligentsia. . . . And *every month* in the Soviet republic the percentage of the bourgeois intelligentsia who are *sincerely* helping the workers and the peasants grows. . . . In Petersburg one can become convinced of this only by being politically oriented and having political experience. This you do not have. . . . You have put yourself in a position where *you are unable* to see the change in the lives of the workers and the peasants. . . . "Life has become loathsome. Differences deepen with communism." It is impossible to understand wherein the differences lie. . . . I have expressed my thoughts sincerely with regard to your letter. From my talks [with you] I have long come to these conclusions, but your letter augmented and crystallized the impressions which I had, I would not like to impose my advice. However, I cannot help but say: you should change your environment and your activities radically or life will surely become unbearable.[120]

He proceeded to assure Gorky that measures were taken to check on the arrests of members of the intelligentsia, of the "near Kadet type" (*okolo kadetskogo tipa*), although in general the actions of the revolutionary authorities were justified. Indicating that N. Bukharin and L. Kamenev had been chosen by the Central Committee to do the job, Lenin reminded Gorky of his statements made first in London during the Fifth Congress of the RSDWP, then on Capri in 1908, and at later dates, when Gorky admitted that "we artists are an irresponsible lot." That, emphasized Lenin, was the crux of the matter. Accusing Gorky of being under influence of the intelligentsia, Lenin remarked that, given the frame of mind the writer was in, there was little surprise in his statement that "the reds are the enemies of the people just as the whites." The logical outcome of that kind of thinking was leading to the faith in a "little god" (*bozhenka*) or, in a "father-tsar" (*tsar-batiushka*), reminding Gorky of the *bogostroitel'stvo* period Lenin never forgot. The letter ended again with the advice to change the environment.[121]

As the Civil War continued and the effects of War Communism became evident, Gorky's pessimism over the survival of Russian state and its people grew. In response to Maxim's views on the life that was being built in the spirit and by the methods used by the Soviets, Gorky voiced his scepticism and wrote about the danger looming ahead, the danger of the elemental forces of the village that would crush them all. Alluding to the failure of the world revolution, Gorky condemned the Western proletariat for that. That failure provided for the conditions that would lead to the defeat of the city by the peasant mass. His solution was in the alliance of the intelligentsia and the industrial class with the Bolsheviks, regardless of the sins and mistakes of the latter.[122] Even while castigating the government, Gorky could not see any alternative to it. The writer Victor Serge recalls a meeting with Gorky in the winter of 1919:

Maxim Gorky welcomed me affectionately. . . . His whole being expressed hunger for knowledge and human understanding, . . . never stopping at mere appearances, never tolerating any lies told to him. . . . All at once, I saw him as the supreme, the righteous, the relentless witness of the Revolution, and it was as such that he talked with me. He spoke harshly about the Bolsheviks: "They were drunk with authority," . . . "starting bloody despotism all over again"; all the same they were "facing chaos alone" with some incorruptible men in their leadership. . . . At present it was imperative to side with the Revolutionary regime, for fear of a rural counter-Revolution which would be no less than an outburst of savagery.[123]

Gorky, though disillusioned, continued his double task of "cultural minister" and "great interceder." He turned to Lenin when paper was needed for *Vsemirnaia literatura* or when workers were forcefully removed from the printing shop "Kopeika," or when it was necessary to increase the number of rations for the writers and scholars he was caring for, or when someone needed a visa to go abroad. Lenin, for his part, instructed Soviet officials to extend assistance and aid to Gorky whenever he needed it: "Comrades! I beg you earnestly, in all cases when Comrade Gorky turns to you with similar requests, give him every cooperation, and if there are any obstacles, hindrances or objections of one sort or another, be sure to inform me."[124] Still confident of his influence, Gorky wrote complaints addressed to other leaders of the Party. One of them, who later would cause him much grief, was G. E. Zinoviev, head of the Comintern and the Party boss in Petersburg. Pleading the case of unjustly arrested scholars, Gorky wrote: "[T]heir arrest is stupidity or something worse." He concluded: "Terrible things are being perpetrated presently in Petersburg which discredit the government, evoking against it hate and general contempt for its cowardice."[125] A second letter was dated June 3, 1919. This time Gorky interceded on behalf of the son of the writer E. K. Pimenova. He complained that "arrests were carried out in great numbers and in a sloppy manner. . . . It would be advisable to be more careful."[126] Zinoviev's answer was immediate, with the promise to investigate the matter and to see that justice is done. As to Gorky's complaint regarding the great number of arrests he wrote, "Yes, indeed, many arrests are carried out. . . . But what is to be done? We are facing the opposition of people like Count Palen, Benkendorf, Rodzianko. . . . Those who support them are, of course, the Entente powers. . . . We have to fight, be what may."[127] In a letter of October 1919, addressed to F. E. Dzerzhinskii, the head of the Cheka, Gorky questioned the continuing arrests of scholars, among whom was Prof. V. N. Tonkov, then president of the medical-military academy. He wrote: "I would like to inform you that I consider these arrests as acts of barbarism, as an attempt to annihilate the best brains of our country."[128]

During the years 1918–1921, Gorky's official contacts with the Bolshevik Party were few. These occurred at official celebrations and at meetings concerning the running of the societies and associations he was involved in. In April 1920 he attended the celebration of the fiftieth birthday of Lenin. In July he partook in the meetings of the Second Congress of the Comintern. Later in the year, he participated in the deliberation of the Central Committee over the policies of *Vsemirnaia literatura* and Soviet publications abroad.[129] Concerned over the shortage of books ("the book famine"), Gorky appealed in December 1920 to Lenin and to the Eighth All-Russian Congress of Soviets to retain for a period of time the private publishing companies. He described the poor performance of *Gosizdat* (State Publishing House), which was unable to satisfy the demand for books in the country, and came to the defense of Z. I. Grzhebin's publishing company, which was printing its books in Germany. The rationale for it was that the publishing industry was much advanced in that country, and that there was a possibility of competing with the emerging émigré community that would try to monopolize the publication of Russian books abroad. Gorky suggested as publisher Grzhebin; Russian works were published in Berlin and then imported into Russia. Not all in the operation was to Lenin's liking. In a meeting with Gorky held March 1920, when shown some of the works published by Grzhebin in Berlin, Lenin reacted rather angrily and informed Gorky that the treasury was too poor to spend hard currency on works that were of no importance. Also, other problems were arising. There were discussions in the central Committee regarding the cost of Grzhebin's publications as well as a suspicion that he was not altogether honest. Lenin, trying to avoid a confrontation with Gorky, sent a note to A. I. Rykov, with the instruction that a meeting be called of the "old" commission of the Central Committee, including Stalin and Trotsky, to discuss the validity of an earlier contracted agreement with Grzhebin's publishing house. Lenin indicated that if the *Gosizdat* should choose not to honor the agreement there would be an awful row, Gorky would withdraw from the contract, and the government would be in the wrong, for the decision once made could not be reversed.[130] Gorky still had some clout.

Bureaucracy was quickly growing in the newly established Soviet state, and the office of *Gosizdat* was giving Gorky many problems. One was the interference of a certain S. M. Zaks-Gladnev, who had an important position in the administration of *Gosizdat*. Gorky complained over the politics of Zaks-Gladnev and his office toward Grzhebin and him and wrote an angry letter addressed to Lenin:

I have done service to my country and the Revolution, and am too old to allow for the stupid and indifferent attitude towards my work. . . . I refuse to continue working in the enterprises established through my efforts, in *Vsemirnaia literatura*, the Grzhebin Publishing House, in the Ekspertnaia Komissia, in the KUBU, as well as in all other institutions. . . . I am tired of that muddle.[131]

Not much was done to remedy the situation. Here the enmity of the influential Central Committee member Zinoviev made Gorky's position more difficult. According to Khodasevich, Zinoviev, suspicious of Gorky's activities, ordered that Gorky's apartment be searched and threatened to arrest people close to him.[132] Gorky's mail was censored and food destined for the Home for Intellectuals (*Dom uchennykh*), which Gorky had founded, was requisitioned. Those arrested often fared worse when defended by him.[133]

By 1921, the relations between Gorky and Zinoviev worsened. According to Aleksinskii and Khodasevich, the reason was the ruthless suppression of the Kronstadt uprising. Gorky was much distressed over the events. He allegedly received documents that incriminated Zinoviev as the one who provoked the uprising. On Gorky's request, Lenin demanded an explanation from Zinoviev. The result was increasing animosity between Gorky and Zinoviev, who tried to use his influence against Gorky whenever he was able to.[134]

Sadly, in spite of his efforts, the "great interceder" failed to save the lives of the poets A. A. Blok and N. S. Gumilev, Blok, the symbolist poet and author of *Dvenadtsat'* (The Twelve), became dangerously ill in 1921, and Gorky tried to obtain a visa for him to go abroad. Even the persevering Gorky could not overcome the growing bureaucracy; and when the visa was finally granted, Blok was dead.[135] Gumilev, implicated in the "Tagantsev conspiracy,"[136] was shot by a firing squad in spite of assurances given to Gorky that his life would be spared.

Also unhappy with Gorky was L. B. Kamenev, whose wife quarreled with Andreeva over the chairmanship of *Teo*, the department that supervised the theaters in Russia. Olga Kameneva won the chairmanship of *Teo*, to the chagrin of Andreeva. Kameneva allegedly expressed her contempt for Gorky when she told Khodasevich that Gorky was forever covering up swindlers and that only the protection of Lenin prevented him from being arrested.[137] Yes, he could in some cases still count on Lenin, whom he visited in Moscow or in Lenin's country home in the town of Gorki, and to whom he continued to bring numerous complaints and requests.[138] In 1920, on the occasion of Lenin's fiftieth birthday, Gorky wrote the essay "Vladimir Il'ich Lenin."[139] It was to be a tribute to the leader of the Soviet state, but it proved to be an embarrassment to Lenin and evoked his severe criticism and that of the leaders of the Party. Reading the essay, one is not surprised at the reaction. It contained a dubious praise of the leader and an indictment of the character of the Russian people. The last paragraph read:

These lines speak of a man who had the temerity to start the process of an all out European social Revolution, in a country where a significant percent of the peasant class wants nothing more than to be satisfied bourgeois. That intrepidity many regard as madness. I began my work as the herald of Revolutionary spirit, with the praise of the madness of the brave. There was a time when sincere pity for the people of Russia has compelled me to regard that madness as almost a crime. But now that I see that people know much better how to quietly suffer than to work honestly and conscientiously, I am again singing the praise of the madness of the brave. And among those Vladimir Lenin—is first and the most mad.[140]

Lenin was angry. On July 31, 1920, on his initiative, the Politburo of the Central Committee passed a resolution that stated that the Politburo found most inappropriate the publication in the No. 12 of *Communist International* the essays by Gorky, in particular the editorial, because in the publications "there is nothing that is of communist ideology, but much that is anticommunist." The resolution further stipulated that under no circumstances should similar writings be allowed to appear in the *Communist International*.[141] In the explanatory notes one finds the following comment: "Gorky had given an inaccurate characteristic of the Russian national character, of the relations between the East and the West, and Lenin did not like these."[142] In the literature available, Gorky's response to these criticisms is not to be found.

From his letters to Lenin one sees that Gorky was writing from a position of strength, as an equal, not intimidated by the leader's authority and not hesitant to criticize the nature of his leadership and the state of the country following October 1917. The more one ponders over the tone of the recently published correspondence, the more obvious become the reasons for Lenin's insistence that Gorky leave. The aim to use the writer in the campaign to summon help abroad on behalf of the starving people was another important factor.

To the period 1920–1921, during which Gorky wrote little of literature, belongs the play *Rabotiaga Slovotekov* (The Plodder Slovotekov), in which he ridiculed the lazy and inefficient bureaucracy.[143] The play was staged on June 18; after three performances, following critical reviews in *Krasnaia gazeta* (Red Newspaper) of June 20, the play was taken of the stage.[144] In the play Gorky evidently had Zinoviev in mind, which was one reason that the performances were cancelled. Clearly, the idea of freedom of the press and of the word was not something the Bolsheviks were ready to preserve. Gorky, still under the cloud that descended upon him with the closure of his newspaper, *Novaia zhizn'*, suffered one more blow. The difficulties and disappointments were taking their toll, and he was ill. Bertrand Russell, who visited the Soviet state in 1920, relates on his visit with Gorky:

An extraordinary contrast to both these men [Lenin and Trotsky] was Gorky, with whom I had a brief interview in Petersburg. He was in bed, very ill and obviously heart-broken. . . . I felt him to be the most lovable, and to me the most sympathetic of all the Russians I saw. I wished for more knowledge of his outlook, but he spoke with difficulty and was constantly interrupted by terrible fits of coughing so that I could not stay. . . . Gorky has done all that one man can do to preserve the intellectual and artistic life of Russia. I feared that he was dying.[145]

John Reed (1887–1920), the American communist and author of *Ten Days That Shook the World*, not surprisingly had a different view of Gorky. In a letter to Upton Sinclair on June 1918, he wrote of Gorky's stand during the days following October 1917:

Gorky took an original and characteristic attitude. He violently opposed the suppression of the bourgeois and moderate socialist press. . . . He was horrified at the early arrest which occurred at the same time. But more than all else he was shocked at the bloodshed. Now everybody who was in Russia at the time knows that there was almost no bloodshed. . . . Gorky was wrong in his pronouncement and was under the influence of Marie Andreeva . . . who wants to manage things herself . . . who finds the Revolution disappointing.[146]

About the same time Gorky wrote to H. G. Wells, "You asked how I am getting on. I am working a great deal in the field of popular education, but I am not writing anything. . . . Life is difficult."[147]

There were more letters written to Wells in a similar vein throughout 1920 and 1921. They were old acquaintances. Wells had read Gorky's works in the early 1900s, when they were translated into English; and later they had met during the unsuccessful visit of Gorky to New York in 1906 (see chapter 4). Then again, the two met in London at the Fifth Congress of the RSDWP. Wells, at that time under the influence of Nietzsche's ideas of the superman, looked at Lenin and his followers as those able to bring salvation to mankind. In 1916 Wells's work *Mr. Britling*, depicting the cruelty of war, was translated into Russian and published in Gorky's *Letopis'*. In 1920, Wells came to visit Gorky in Petrograd. There he met one of Gorky's employees in *Vsemirnaia literatura*, the alleged countess Zakrevskaia-Benkendorf (M. Budberg). The meeting was important, and the event was to influence the relationship between the two writers in the future. In the meantime, Gorky would write to Wells of his problems and ask his assistance to mobilize the West to help the starving peoples of Russia. Another West European intellectual, who became a lifelong friend, was R. Rolland. The friendship began with Gorky's letter of December 1916, in which he invited Rolland to write a book on Beethoven for children. Gorky wrote of his aim to publish a series of biographies of great men for a children's library, and Rolland accepted the invitation, greeted Gorky warmly and expressed his wish to meet in the future. The correspondence continued for twenty years, and the two met for the first and last time in 1935.[148]

The state of Gorky's health and his difficulties in the country were a cause of worry for those close to him. Andreeva suggested in a letter to Lenin that Gorky be sent to the Caucasus for a cure in the company of Ladyzhnikov, his friend and co-worker in *Vsemirnaia literatura*:

So that Aleksei [Gorky] would have means of support, one could ask him to establish there a branch of the state publishing office; this would also explain to him the company of Ladyzhnikov. . . . Aleksei is in need of new impressions; if he should remain under the cloud of all that he now experiences he will go crazy. You yourself have frequently said that; such an assignment would distract him and would occupy him for a long while.[149]

Nothing came of Andreeva's suggestion.

In March 1921, Lenin in a letter to the Commissar of Health, N. A. Semashko, asked the latter to arrange a trip to Germany for several people who were in need of medical treatment and whom he obviously wanted out of the way. Gorky's name was included in the list.[150] Gorky was reluctant to leave Russia at a time when he felt that his work in many institutions and societies was important. He wrote Andreeva that he planned to postpone his trip until after the new harvest, but the harvest was still a long way away. Meanwhile, the food situation in the country deteriorated. The harvest of 1920 had been poor, and by February 1921 the rations of the workers in Petersburg had to be cut. The Kronstadt rebellion, the threatening famine, and peasant disturbances made it imperative to deal with the economic situation. The solution was the New Economic Policy (NEP), decided upon at the Tenth Party Congress, which was introduced on March 8, 1921. Lenin admitted that under the circumstances an immediate transition to a purely socialist economy was not possible. NEP was to be a temporary expedient to help restore the shattered economy of the country.

The NEP was successful, but not immediately. The reforms came too late to forestall the terrible famine of 1921–1922. In this difficult situation Gorky played an important role by appealing to influential people in Europe and the United States to aid the starving people of Russia. On July 6, 1921, he wrote the appeal "Chestnye liudi" (Honest People), which was addressed to the peoples of Europe and America. "Difficult days have descended upon the country of Tolstoy and Dostoevsky, Mendeleev and Pavlov, Mussorgsky and Glinka . . . and I hope that the intellectuals of Europe and America, having understood the tragic situation of the Russian people, will hasten to help with bread and medicine."[151] Gorky also sent personal appeals to Anatole France, H. G. Wells, Upton Sinclair, and other prominent men of letters. An appeal by the patriarch Tikhon was sent by Gorky to the archbishops of New York and Canterbury.[152] His appeal of July 6 to the Americans was answered by Herbert Hoover, who cabled on behalf of the American Relief Administration (ARA):

I have read with great feeling your appeal to Americans for charitable assistance to the starving and sick people of Russia. . . . We are today caring for three and one-half million children in ten different countries, and would be willing to furnish necessary supplements of food, clothing and medical supplies to a million children in Russia as rapidly as organization could be effected.[153]

There were some stipulations regarding technical procedures and a demand that Americans who were under arrest in Russia be released and given permission to return home.

Earlier in February 1921, by the decision of the All Union Central Executive Committee, a Central commission was established under the chairmanship of M. I. Kalinin to help in the relief effort.[154] At the same time, as the news of the catastrophic famine threatening the eastern provinces of European Russia became widely known, a group of concerned individuals from among the intelligentsia approached the government with a proposal to appeal to Western European countries and to the United States for assistance. The Soviet government, interested in projecting a friendly attitude toward the West and concerned over the magnitude of the disaster, agreed to the proposal. A decree of July 21, 1921, set up an All-Russian Committee for Aid to the Hungry, consisting of some sixty members. The president of the committee was L. Kamenev. Included were Rykov; Lunacharskii; Krasin; a few other Bolsheviks; two former ministers of the Provisional Government, Kishkin and Prokopovich, prominent members of the Kadety; and a large number of non-Party intellectuals. V. G. Korolenko was invited to be honorary chairman, and Gorky was to play an important role in view of the fact that his name was well known and respected in the West. The committee was to draw on funds from voluntary contributions and from a state subsidy; it was to collect supplies and funds abroad and to see to their distribution. That Gorky was to be the liaison between the committee and the government is indicated in a note written by Lenin to the Commissar of Agriculture, I. A. Teodorovich, on July 28, 1921. In it Lenin informed the latter that Gorky submitted a proposal for the establishing of such a committee and instructed Teodorovich to get in touch with Rykov, adding that the decision would be taken in the Politburo. Lenin thought of the feasibility of combining the two, "ours" [the Commission headed by Kalinin] and Gorky's.

Invited to be the honorary chairman of the committee, Korolenko in a letter to Gorky expressed his appreciation for the honor and indicated that he was ill, but would be ready to do his utmost to help the work of the committee. Included in the letter were his comments on the course the Revolution had taken. "We have put brakes on the course of our Revolution because we had not immediately recognized that at the basis of the Revolution had to be humanness."[155] He continued, "In our country in place of freedom all goes the way it did before: one oppression has replaced the other and this is our freedom."[156] In the end Korolenko resigned from the committee, giving as reason the deteriorating state of his health. He died in December of 1921.

It was not long before the oppressive hand of the regime had shown its power concerning the committee. Within a month the committee was dissolved, by a decree of August 27, 1921, and its leading "bourgeois" members arrested. When on August 20 the Soviet government had concluded an agreement with Hoover's American Relief Administration (ARA) for the organization of famine relief, it considered the work of the committee as superflous and even dangerous. The Bolsheviks were not about to tolerate an independent body in which many of the participants were members of the old order. Gorky, whose name was used by the authorities to summon help from the West and who had taken part in the work of the committee, felt betrayed. His anger was directed against Kamenev, the chairman of the ill-fated committee. Some of those arrested were exiled from Moscow and later allowed to leave the country; others were released.[157]

On August 24 Gorky sent a letter to E. Peshkova with the news of the dissolution of the local branch of the All-Russian Committee, announced by the Petrograd Soviet, that is, by Zinoviev, on April 23. "I stopped my work and sent to Moscow a declaration of my withdrawal as member of the All Russian Committee. . . . Today I was called to Zinoviev' office for the purpose of 'liquidating the incident.' . . . The arrests here are terrible. Hundreds are being arrested. Last night the whole city was buzzing with the cars of the Cheka."[158]

The failure of the committee and the duplicity of the authorities meant another defeat for Gorky.[159] Earlier, Lenin had written him a letter urging him to go abroad.

You are spitting blood and still do not want to leave!! This is both conscienceless and irrational. In Europe, in a good sanatorium you will cure yourself, and do three times as much work. . . . And here, there is neither medical treatment [available] nor work—only bustle. Purposeless bustle. Go away. Do not be stubborn, I beg of you.[160]

V. V. Vorovskii, the Soviet Ambassador to Italy, also wrote advising Gorky to go abroad. He mentioned the advantages of such a trip and emphasized the fact that Gorky's presence abroad would strengthen the interest of the peoples of Europe in the new Soviet state.[161] It seems that this was one of the reasons for Lenin's insistence that Gorky leave.

By the summer of 1921 Gorky's fear that the peasant would become master of Russia grew. As he observed the struggle between the workers and the peasantry, the threat of "the peasant tide engulfing everything" became for him ever more real.

In the struggle, which has been going on since the beginning of the Revolution, between the two classes [the workers and the peasants], the peasants have every chance of coming out victorious. . . . The urban proletariat was declining constantly for four years. . . . In the end, the immense peasant tide will engulf everything. . . . The peasant will become the master of Russia, since he represents numbers. And it will be terrible for our future.[162]

The cruelties of the Civil War intensified his feelings of disillusionment. Gorky wrote to Wells that he wished he had never lived to see "the revolting pictures of human stupidity and cruelty."[163] In 1921, the whole household on Kronverkskaia was on the move. Andreeva, assigned to the Trade Mission in Berlin as the chairman of the *Ekspertnaia Komissiia*, left with Kriuchkov. The artist I. N. Rakitskii, Gorky's friend, was to go too in order to advise on the sale of art objects and other items of value, in return for badly needed hard currency. Gorky's enterprise, *Vsemirnaia literatura*, was by the decree of the Central Committee made a department of *Gosizdat*, with Gorky responsible for its political and literary editorship as well as for the staff. There seems to have remained little of his previous independence.[164] In addition, there was Zinoviev's attitude toward Gorky. According to Khodasevich, Zinoviev was threatening with arrest people close to Gorky and was ordering searches in his quarters. Khodasevich goes as far as maintaining that Gorky was forced to leave Soviet Russia because of Zinoviev.[165]

The conditions in the country were deteriorating, famine was ravishing the population, and the regime's terror was on the increase. Lunacharskii, writing in 1925 on Gorky's state of mind at the time, remarked that the cause of Gorky's pessimism was his inability to accept the Revolution "at the time when the main features of the great Revolution were clouded by its unpleasant [*sic!*] details."[166] Gorky, remarked the literary critic Shklovsky, was perplexed, and so were the people around him. Further commenting on Gorky's affinity with Bolshevism he wrote: "Gorky's Bolshevism is ironic, a Bolshevism without faith in man. . . . By Bolshevism I do not mean membership in the political Party. Gorky never belonged to the Party."[167]

On October 16, 1921, Gorky left for Germany. Before leaving he wrote Lenin, "Leaving the country I am also leaving three institutions which I have organized that are dear to me and, I dare to think, are also of great importance to the state." He proceeded to enumerate the institutions: one was the *Ekspertnaia Komissiia*, for which he recommended the appointment of his friend, A. P. Dideriks as his deputy, for he was afraid that the valuables collected would be stolen during his three months of absence.

(From that comment it seems that Gorky planned to be away only till March of 1922.) The second was the committee for the improvement of the life of scientists and the *Dom Uchennykh*. He was leaving A. P. Pink- evich, whom he trusted, as replacement and asked Lenin to accept Pink- evich and to give him advice when needed. The third was *Vsemirnaia Literatura*, to be headed in his absence by A. N. Tikhonov, an old friend and former member of the editorial board of the closed *Novaia zhizn'*. The writer warned Lenin against the possibility of appointing some young and inexperienced people "whose energy was only equal to their ignorance" and who would try to interfere in the work of the institution.[168] A rider attached to the letter concerned the candidacy of Dideriks to head *Ekspert- naia Komissiia* and included a warning that if his appointment should not go through, Gorky would relinquish his responsibility for the work of the commission and the multimillion-ruble collection.

Lenin, insisting that Gorky leave Russia, had in mind using the name of the writer in order to mobilize public opinion and to ask for help in the West. "It would be good if you could write Bernard Shaw . . . and Wells that they should help in collecting funds for famine relief. . . . The starving people will get more. There is a great famine."[169] Gorky's answer, which came from St. Blasien, Switzerland, contained a detailed account of his plans for organizing the relief work in various countries. In the letter, Gorky tried also to advise Lenin on foreign policy. He asked him to con- sider seriously the question of Soviet-German rapprochement, thus an- ticipating in a way the future Rapallo agreement. He considered such rapprochement possible and desirable. He also invited Lenin to come to St. Blasien, where he could rest from his work of implementing the "old eco- nomic policy," as Gorky ironically called NEP.[170] The letter, dated Decem- ber 25, 1921, is the last available letter published in the Lenin-Gorky correspondence. Previously, on December 12, Lenin sent a letter to V. M. Molotov and the members of the Politburo of the Central Committee in which he asked that the Party or the Soviet should provide Gorky with financial assistance.[171]

The period of war and Revolution was crucial to Gorky's political career. He opposed the war on pacifist grounds and did not hesitate to express his views in his journal, *Letopis'*. Following the February Revolution, Gorky, satisfied with the overthrow of the Romanovs, advocated cooperation with the Provisional Government and wanted to see in Russia a democratic, constitutional order. His attacks on Lenin and his followers were motivated by his belief that the Russians were not ready for a socialist Revolution and by his fear of unleashing the elemental forces of the peasantry. His accomodation with the regime was neither treason (as some of the member of the intelligentsia viewed it) nor opportunism, but rather the result of deep concern for the fate of Russia and its people. He tried to fulfil the self-imposed role of "interceder" and to help save Russia's cultural inheritance.

NOTES

1. The question of the impact and the potential effects of Stolypin's reform is still a controversial issue. W. E. Mosse in his article "Stolypin's Villages," maintains that the reform made a very modest contribution to the solution of Russia's peasant problem. See *Slavonic and East European Review* 43 (1965): 257–274.

2. For discussion of the Russian labor movement for the period from 1905 to 1917, see Leopold Haimson, "The Problem of Social Stability in Urban Russia, 1905–1917" (Parts One and Two), in *Slavic Review* 23 (1964): 619–642; 24 (1965): 1–22.

3. L. Schapiro, *The Communist Party of the Soviet Union* (London, 1960), 134.

4. I. Gruzdev, *Gor'kii* (Moscow, 1960), 214.

5. Gruzdev, *Gor'kii*, 221.

6. *Letopis'*, II: 434.

7. Gor'kii, *Sobranie sochinenii*, vol. 29, 320–321.

8. Gor'kii, *Sobranie sochinenii*, vol. 29, 320–321.

9. N. Valentinov, "Vstrechi s Gor'kim," *Novyi zhurnal* no. 78 (1965) (N. V. Volskii), 124.

10. *Letopis'*, II: 400.

11. Valentinov, "Vstrechi s Gor'kim," 126.

12. *Letopis'*, II: 399. For evidence of the attempt to enlist Gorky's participation in the work of *Proletarskaia pravda* (Proletarian Truth), see "Pis'mo F. E. Rozmirovicha v Tse-Ka RSDRP," *Istoricheskii arkhiv* 4 (1959): 47.

13. A. A. Badaev, *Bol'sheviki v gosudarstvennoi Dume*, 7th ed. (Moscow, 1941), 324–325.

14. *Letopis'*, II: 445, 452.

15. *Letopis'*, II: 428, 432.

16. *Letopis'*, II: 420–421. See also Gor'kii, *Sobranie sochinenii*, vol. 24, 168, 169; and I. Eventov, *Gor'kii v Peterburge Leningrade* (Leningrad, 1956), 137–138.

17. *Arkhiv*, IX: 146.

18. M. Gor'kii. "Pis'mo I. M. Kasatkinu," *Novyi mir* 6 (1937): 16–17.

19. A. Ovcharenko, "Publitsistika M. Gor'kogo perioda pervoi mirovoi voiny," *Voprosy literatury* 3 (1961): 30.

20. Lenin, *Polnoe sobranie sochinenii* (*PSS*), XLIX, 24.

21. Hoover Institution, the Nicolaevsky Collection, Box 164.

22. Lenin, *PSS*, XLIX, 149 (emphasis in the original).

23. Gor'kii, *Sobranie sochinenii*, vol. 24, 158–163.

24. Tsentrarkhiv, *Revoliutsonnyi put' Gor'kogo*, 118.

25. *Letopis'*, II: 492.

26. *Letopis'*, II: 498.

27. *Letopis'*, II: 498.

28. *Letopis'*, II: 510.

29. Gor'kii, *Sobranie sochinenii*, vol. 29, 341. The publisher was A. N. Tik-honov, and the editor A. F. Radzishevskii. The journal was published with the close cooperation of Gorky. See V. Rudnev, *Gor'kii revoliutsioner* (Moscow, 1929), 104.

30. Lenin dubbed the Mensheviks, who were under the direction of the *Organizatsionnyi Komitet, okists*, from the initials OK. *V. I. Lenin i A. M. Gor'kii: Pis'ma, vospominaniia, dokumenty* (Moscow, 1961), 443. Machists—followers of the philosopher, Ernst Mach.

31. Lenin, *PSS*, XLIX, 300.

32. Lenin, *PSS*, XLIX, 300–302.

33. Lenin, *PSS*, XLIX, 170. The pamphlet was not published by Gorky. It appeared in 1917 under the imprint of the Party.

34. Lenin, *PSS*, XLIX, 182–183.

35. Lenin, *PSS*, XLIX, 340.

36. See article by M. Gor'kii, "Po povodu odnoi ankety," *Letopis'* I (January, 1916): 211, 220; Gor'kii, *Sobranie sochinenii*, vol. 29, 337, 346, 347. See also *Letopis'* II: 467, 468, 482; T. Yedlin, "Anketa po voprosu ob antisemitizme v Rossii," *Forum* 10 (1985): 184–226; M. Agurskii and M. Shklovskaia, *Iz literaturnogo naslediia: Gor'kii i evreiskii vopros* (Jerusalem, 1986). See also B. Paramonov, "Gor'kii: Beloe piatno," *Oktiabr'* 5 (1992). Paramonov's accusations of Gorky's anti-Semitism are totally unfounded.

37. Tsentrarkhiv, *Revoliutsionnyi put' Gor'kogo*, 120–22.

38. E. Chirikov, *Russkii narod pod sudom Maksima Gor'kogo* (Moscow, 1917).

39. See letter to V. Briusov in Gor'kii, *Sobranie sochinenii*, vol. 29, 354; M. Gor'kii, "Pis'ma k chitateliu," *Letopis'* III (March, 1916): 171–177.

40. M. Gor'kii, *Stat'i za 1905–1916 gg.*, 2d ed. (Petersburg, 1918), 206.

41. A. M. *Gor'kii i V. G. Korolenko*, Perepiska, stat'i, vyskazyvaniia (Moscow, 1957), 85–86; Gor'kii, *Sobranie sochinenii*, vol. 29, 376.

42. *Letopis'*, II: 523.

43. Gor'kii, *Sobranie sochinenii*, vol. 29, 379. See also *Arkhiv*, XIII: 162, 172.

44. M. Gor'kii, "O polemike," *Novaia zhizn'* 6, April 25 (May 8), 1917.

45. Gruzdev, *Gor'kii*, 221.

46. V. M. Khodasevich, "Takim ia znala Gor'kogo," *Novyi mir* 3 (1968): 11–66.

47. *Arkhiv*, IX: 191.

48. *Arkhiv*, IX: 194.

49. *Arkhiv*, XIII: 163–164.

50. E. G. Kiaksht, "V dome gde zhil Gor'kii," quoted in *Letopis'* III: 10.

51. O. A. Ermanskii, *Iz perezhitogo* (Moscow, 1927), 137. See also I. Yurenev, "Bor'ba za edinstvo Partii" (Petersburg, 1927) [B. I. Nicolaevsky collection], 13–14.

52. Ermanskii [B. I. Nicolaevsky collection], 13–14.

53. N. N. Sukhanov, *Zapiski o revoliutsii*, 7 vol. (Berlin, 1922–1923), vol. 2, 144–145.

54. *Letopis'*, III: 13.

55. Sukhanov, *Zapiski*, vol. 2, 160–161.

56. Sukhanov, *Zapiski*, vol. 2, 162–163.

57. N. N. Sukhanov, *The Russian Revolution, 1917*, edited and translated by

Joel Carmichael (London, 1955), 209. The burial, however, did take place on the Champs de Mars.

58. Akademiia Nauk SSSR, *Velikaia Oktiabr'skaia Sotsialicheskaia Revoliutsiia*, I, 416; *Letopis'*, 23.

59. M. Gor'kii, "Revoliutsiia i kul'tura, *Letopis'*, II–IV" (February–April, 1917): 307; M. Gor'kii, *Revoliutsiia i kultura: stat'i za 1917 god* (Berlin, 1920), 5.

60. *Arkhiv*, XV. *M. Gor'kii i R. Rollan: Perepiska (1916–1936)* (Moscow, 1995), 19.

61. *Gor'kii i Rollan.*

62. Lenin, *PSS*, XXXI; 48–49.

63. Lenin, *PSS*, XXXI, 49.

64. Louis Fisher, *The Life of Lenin* (New York, 1964), 325.

65. Valentinov, "Vstrechi s Gor'kim," 124.

66. *Letopis'*, III: 28; see also Gor'kii, *Sobranie sochinenii*, vol. 17, 25.

67. Quoted in *Letopis'*, III: 30.

68. See letter of B. A. Gordon, publisher, to B. I. Nicolaevsky of May, 1949. Nicolaevsky Collection, Box 137, Envelope 5. The Hoover Institution, Stanford.

69. M. Gor'kii, "Revoliutsiia i kul'tura," *Novaia zhizn'* 1, April 18 (May 1), 1917.

70. "Nesvoevremennye mysli" were not included in the thirty-volume collection of Gorky's work. In the West, one could read them on microfilm (Russian Library, Helsinki University, Finland) or in copies of the newspaper *Novaia zhizn'* (available in the Hoover Institution, Stanford). In 1995 there appeared in English the second edition of the work by Herman Ermolaev, *Maxim Gorky, Untimely Thoughts. Essays on Revolution. Culture and the Bolsheviks 1917–1918*. Earlier, in Russia a very detailed analysis and the text were published in Moscow, 1990. See, K. Vainberg, *Gor'kii M. Nesyoevremennye mysli: Zametki o revoliutsii i kul'ture* (Moscow, 1990).

71. Sukhanov, *Zapiski*, vol. 4, 185.

72. Sukhanov, *Zapiski*, vol. 4, 179.

73. Gor'kii, "O polemike."

74. *Arkhiv*, IX: 196.

75. Gor'kii, *Sobranie sochinenii*, vol. 29, 381.

76. *Letopis'*, III: 41.

77. Gor'kii, "O polemike."

78. Gor'kii, *Revoliutsiia i kul'tura*, 47–48.

79. Letopis', III: 44–45.

80. Letopis', III: 43. The articles appeared in *Russkaia volia* 159, July 7, 1917, and 161, July 9, 1917. See also *Arkhiv*, IX: 380–381. Previously Gorky was attacked in the press and accused of trying to mediate a separate peace. See N. Sukhanov, *The Russian Revolution 1917*. Joel Carmichel, ed., trans. (London, 1955), 865.

81. M. Gor'kii, "Burtsevu," *Novaia zhizn'* 70, July 9/22, 1917. See also *Arkhiv*, IX: 199, 200. To Gorky's defense came the Permanent Secretary of the Russian Academy of Sciences, F. S. Oldenburg, and the poet V. Ia. Briusov.

82. *Letopis'*, III: 47.

83. Gorky's popularity with the Internationalists was attested to by the fact

that he was selected as candidate in the forthcoming elections to the Constituent Assembly by the Poltava Internationalists' Committee. See *Letopis'*, III: 50.

84. See Schapiro, *Communist Party of the Soviet Union*, 168–170. It is important to note that Kamenev and Zinoviev, disagreeing with the Bolsheviks' decision to go ahead with the rising, had leaked the news of the plan to *Novaia zhizn'*. It was reported in the October 18 issue of the paper.

85. M. Gor'kii, "Nel'zia molchat'," *Novaia zhizn'* 156, October 18 (31), 1917. In *Letopis'*, the note on the publication of "Nel'zia molchat'" is followed by quotations from Gorky's works written in the 1930s: "I erred in 1917. I was afraid [then] that the dictatorship of the proletariat would lead to the dissipation and the destruction of politically conscious workers—Bolsheviks, the only Revolutionary force—and, that their destruction would destroy the idea of a social Revolution for a considerable period." (*Letopis'*, III: 52; Gor'kii, *Sobranie sochinenii*, vol. 24, 302, 342–433; *Lenin i Gor'kii: Pis'ma*, 309).

86. I. V. Stalin, *Sochineniia* (Moscow, 1946), III: 385–386.

87. *Letopis'*, III: 55.

88. M. Gor'kii, "K demokratii," *Novaia zhizn'* 174, November 7 (20), 1917.

89. M. Gor'kii, "Vnimani'u rabochikh," *Novaia zhizn'* 177, November 10 (23), 1917.

90. M. Gor'kii, "Nesvoevremennye mysli," *Novaia zhizn'* 179, November 12 (25), 1917.

91. M. Gor'kii, "Nesvoevremennye mysli," *Novaia zhizn'* 186, November 19 (December 2), 1917.

92. M. Gor'kii, "Nesvoevremennye mysli," *Novaia zhizn'* 194, December 6 (19), 1917.

93. M. Gor'kii, "9 ianvaria- 5 ianvaria," *Novaia zhizn'* 6 (220), January 9 (22), 1918.

94. "Intelligent iz naroda" [I. S. Blank], "Sotsialnaia revoliutsiia i M. Gor'kii" *Pravda* 5 (232), January 7 (20), 1918.

95. M. Gor'kii, "Intelligentu iz naroda," *Novaia zhizn'* 7 (220), January 11 (24), 1918.

96. M. Gor'kii, "Sotrudnikam 'Pravdy,' 'Severnoi Kommuny' i drugim," *Novaia zhizn'*, 127 (342), July 2, 1918. For Gorky's financial support of the RSDWP see the work of Nikolaus Katzer, *Maxim Gor'kij's Weg in die russiche Sozialdemokratie* (Wiesbaden, 1990).

97. *Letopis'*, III: 83.

98. *Arkhiv*, IX: 207–208.

99. *Arkhiv*, IX: 208.

100. *Letopis'*, III: 73.

101. *Letopis'*, III: 74, 75.

102. M. Gor'kii, "Nesvoevremennye mysli," *Novaia zhizn'* 86 (301), May 10, 1918.

103. Gor'kii, *Sobranie sochinenii*, vol. 24, 189. This appeal was read by Gorky on November 29, 1918, at a meeting in Petersburg. It was first published in *Petersburgskaia pravda*, November 30, no. 262. For the full text of the appeal see Gor'kii, *Sobranie sochinenii*, vol. 24, 186–189.

104. *Lenin i Gor'kii: Pis'ma*, 263.

105. Victor Serge, *Memoirs of a Revolutionary, 1901–1941* (London, 1963), 82.

106. E. Zamyatin, *Litsa* (New York, 1955), 89.

107. The agreement to establish *Vsemirnaia literatura* was concluded with the Commissar of Education, A. V. Lunacharskii. See *Letopis'*, III: 85, 88.

108. The Commission saved for the Soviet State objects of art, rare books, and document collections worth millions of rubles. Some of the treasures collected were kept in the country; others were sent abroad in exchange for hard currency, which was badly needed. *Lenin i Gor'kii: Pis'ma*, 64–65; A. M. Gak, "Iz istorii uchastiia A. M. Gor'kogo v rabote ekspertnoi komissii Narkomvneshtorga v 1919–1921 gg.," *Gor'kovskie chteniia* (Moscow, 1964), 222–233.

109. K. I. Chukovskii, *Sovremenniki: Portrety i liudi* (Moscow, 1962), 327.

110. Quoted in Zamyatin, *Litsa*, 92. Gorky's role in saving the intelligentsia during the difficult period from 1918 to 1921 is emphasized in the memoir literature found in the Alexinsky Collection, Columbia University Archives. See the memoirs of Count Boris G. Berg, Dr. I. I. Manukhin, and L. L. Sabaneev, among others.

111. Zamyatin, *Litsa*, 92.

112. *Leninskii sbornik*, XXXVI, 80.

113. V. Shklovskii, *Sentimental'noe puteshestvie* (Moscow, 1923), 244.

114. For a recent discussion of Gippius' criticism of Gorky, see the article by Temira Pachmuss, "Zinaida Gippius as a Literary Critic, with Particular Reference to Maksim Gor'kii," in *Canadian Slavonic Papers* VII (1965): 127–42.

115. Gor'kii, *Sobranie sochinenii*, vol. 29, 387–388.

116. *Neizvestnyi Gor'kii* (Moscow, 1994) III: 29–30.

117. A. A. Krogius, 1871–1933, Psychologist and author of many scholarly works.

118. *Neizvestnyi Gor'kii* III: 31.

119. *Neizvestnyi Gor'kii* III: 31–33.

120. *Neizvestnyi Gor'kii* III: 23–27 (emphasis in the original). See also *Andreeva: Perepiska, vospominaniia, stat'i*, 282–283.

121. *V. I. Lenin i M. A. Gor'kii*, 3rd edition (Moscow, 1969), 160.

122. *Arkhiv*, IX: 209.

123. Serge, *Memoirs*, 72–73.

124. *Lenin i Gor'kii: Pis'ma*, 211.

125. *Izvestiia TsK KPSS* I (January 1, 1989): 239.

126. *Izvestiia TsK KPSS* I: 240.

127. *Izvestiia TsK KPSS* I: 241. An interesting rider is attached here: a quote from a meeting of the Central Committee of the Bolshevik Party of September 11, 1919, concerning the case of the arrested scholars. The decision was taken to recommend that Dzerzhinskii, Bukharin, and Kamenev review the cases of those arrested during the latest wave of arrests, in case of difference of opinion, to refer the cases to the Central Committee.

128. *Izvestiia TsK KPSS* I: 241.

129. *Letopis'*, III: 186, 212, 225.

130. *Lenin i Gor'kii: Pis'ma*, 261, 263.

131. *Neizvestnyi Gor'kii* III: 33–34, 60.

132. V. Khodasevich, "Gor'kii," *Sovremennye zapiski* LXIII (1937): 267.

133. Khodasevich, "Gor'kii"; see also, G. Alexinsky, *La vie amère de Maxime Gorki* (Grenoble, 1950), 197. Alexinsky writes that Zinoviev's enmity toward Gorky was aggravated by the presence of Gorky's secretary, M. Budberg, whom

Zinoviev suspected of being a foreign agent. There were also disagreements between Andreeva and Zinoviev's wife, Z. M. Lilina. See *Andreeva: Perepiska, vospominaniia, stat'i*, 656.

134. Alexinsky, *La vie amère de Maxime Gorki*, 200; Khodasevich, "Gor'kii," *Sovremennye zapiski* LXX (1940): 139. See also Bertram D. Wolfe, *The Bridge and the Abyss* (New York, 1967), 104ff.

135. See *Neizvestnyi Gor'kii* III: 35–36, 58–59.

136. The so-called Tagantsev conspiracy involved a small group of intellectuals accused by the authorities "of drawing up a project for local self-government and monetary reform." The group was named after V. A. Tagantsev, the son of a well-known former member of the State Council and professor of criminal law. Sixty-one members of the group were executed, among them Tagantsev and the poet Gumilev. For more details see Wolfe, *The Bridge and the Abyss*, 122–123, 128–129. It is of interest to note that Professor Tagantsev intervened on Gorky's behalf in 1898 during his imprisonment in Tiflis. See Chapter 1. See also *Neizvestnyi Gor'kii* III, Letter 12, 38–39, 62–63. In the same letter Gorky complains over the arrest of old Bolsheviks.

137. Khodasevich, "Gor'kii," 136.

138. *Lenin i Gor'kii: Pis'ma*, 75–83.

139. The essay was first published in *Kommunisticheskii internatsional* 12 (1920): 1927–1936.

140. *Kommunisticheskii internatsional* 12 (1920): 1936.

141. *Lenin i Gor'kii: Pis'ma*, 258.

142. *Lenin i Gor'kii: Pis'ma*, 592.

143. *Letopis'* III: 170; P. Scheibert, *Lenin an der Macht* (Weinham, 1984), 325, n. 39.

144. *Letopis'*, III: 179.

145. Bertrand Russell, *The Theory and Practice of Bolshevism* (London, 1920), 38–39.

146. Upton *Sinclair, My Life in Letters* (Columbia, 1960), 208–213.

147. *Lenin i Gor'kii: Pis'ma*, 98–99.

148. *Gor'kii i Rollan*, 21.

149. Andreeva, *Pereptska, vospominaniia, stat'i*, 282–83.

150. *Leninskii sbornik*, XX: 353. Included in the list were also Tsiurupa, Krestinskii, and Korolenko.

151. *Letopis'*, III: 234.

152. *Letopis'*, III: 234.

153. H. H. Fisher, *The Famine in Soviet Russia* (New York, 1927), 51–53, 507.

154. *Lenin i Gor'kii: Pis'ma*, 586.

155. See *Pamiat'*, vol. 4 (Moscow, Paris, 1979–1981), 398.

156. *Pamiat*, 399.

157. For a recent account of the work of the All-Russian Committee for Aid to the Hungry, see N. Maksimov, "Komitet pomoshchi golodaiushchim" in *Pamiat'*, 382–386.

158. *Arkhiv*, IX: 212, 213.

159. Khodasevich, "Gor'kii," *Sovremennye zapiski* LXX (1940): 141. See also *Arkhiv*, IX: 211; Wolfe, *The Bridge and the Abyss*, 109–117. The Soviet version of the history of the All-Russian Committee for Aid to the Hungry reads as follows:

"On June 29, 1921, the Politburo of the Central Committee of RKP(b) reviewed the project of A. M. Gorky to establish an All-Russian Committee for Aid to the Hungry and adopted it in principle. It came into being on July 21, 1921, and existed parallel with the Central Commission for Relief of Famine established by the All-Union Central Executive Committee (VTsIK) on February 17, 1921. Bourgeois anti-Soviet elements (S. N. Prokopovich, E. D. Kuskova, N. M. Kishkin and others), who belonged to the All-Russian Committee, tried to use it for counter-Revolutionary aims. On August 27, 1921, after the refusal of the majority of the Committee to comply with the suggestion of Central Executive Committee to send people to organize help where most needed, the All-Russian Committee was dissolved." *Lenin i Gor'kii: Pis'ma*, 445.

160. *Leninskii sbornik*, XXXIII, 322.

161. *Letopis'*, III: 231.

162. Quoted in E. H. Carr, *The Bolshevik Revolution, 1917–1923* (London, 1952), vol. 2, 291, n. 1.

163. Gor'kii, *Sobranie sochinenii*, vol. 29, 392–393.

164. See *Letopis'*, III: p. 225: N. Berberova, *Zheleznaia zhenshchina* (New York, 1982), 146.

165. V. F. Khodasevich, *Nekropol': Vospominania* (Paris, 1976), 234.

166. A. V. Lunacharskii, *Literaturnye siluety* (Moscow, 1925), 154–55.

167. V. Shklovsky, *Sentimental Journey: Memoirs, 1917–1922* (Ithaca, 1970), 188.

168. *Lenin i Gor'kii: Pis'ma*, 215–216.

169. *Leninskii sbornik*, XXXIV, 428.

170. *Lenin i Gor'kii: Pis'ma*, 186.

171. *Lenin i Gor'kii: Pis'ma*, 217–218. See also Andreeva, *Perepiska, vospominaniia, stat'i*, 287, 288–289; *Leninskii sbornik*, XXXV, 332; *Lenin i Gor'kii: Pis'ma*, 407, 445. As a result of Andreeva's intercedings the Soviet government agreed to sign a contract for the publication of Gorky's works. *Letopis'*, III: 275.

A page from the manuscript of an unpublished story "Repetitsiia" (Rehearsal) 1925. Reproduced courtesy of Gorky Archives of the Institute of World Literature, Moscow.

CHAPTER 7

Gorky, 1921–1928

Gorky's second exile began in October 1921. The poor state of his health and reasons of a personal nature contributed to the decision to leave. There was also Lenin's prodding and constant attacks on him by the powerful Zinoviev. Gorky, the "conscience of the Revolution," was an inconvenient person, even more than other members of the intellectual elite who were sent abroad at the same time. Perhaps, as L. Trotsky would later write, Lenin had, in urging Gorky to leave, a "hidden agenda" holding that the writer, well-known and respected in the West, would be able to mobilize public opinion in support of the newly established socialist state and help its starving people.

He spent two and a half years in Germany. On his arrival in Berlin much was written about his reasons for leaving the Soviet state. It was thought that he could not find his place in the country of Lenin, that he did not really want to leave but that he was forced to, and that Zinoviev made life difficult for him. Others maintained that Gorky was angry for the closure of his newspaper *Novaia zhizn'*, in spite of his having done so much for the cause of the Revolution.

In his memoirs Khodasevich gave his views for Gorky's leaving:

Whatever the reasons were for the departure of Gorky from Russia in 1921, the basic fundamental reason was the same as that for all of us. He [Gorky] had thought of the Revolution as one that would bring freedom. . . . The Bolsheviks gave it altogether different features. When he realized his helplessness in changing anything in it [Revolution], he left and was very close to tear all his ties with the Soviet government.[1]

N. Berberova, like many others, blamed Zinoviev and Lenin: "Angry, at Zinoviev, at Lenin, at himself he went abroad."[2]

At the time of Gorky's arrival, there were close to 600,000 Russian émigrés in Germany, and the name "Gorky" was on everybody's lips. Gorky's attitude towards the émigré community was rather restrained. True, his home in Berlin was a meeting place for prominent people such as former ministers of the tsarist government, commissars from the government of Lenin, writers, artists, and community leaders of tsarist Russia and of the Soviet state. Gorky for his part refrained from making public appearances and statements and avoided the company of journalists. Although restrained in his dealings with the émigré community, he was unable to totally estrange himself from them. He knew that among the émigrés were many who, like himself, had left because they could not face the realities of the long-awaited Revolution. His stay in Germany was interrupted by a short sojourn in Czechoslovakia. By May of 1924, he moved to Italy and settled in Sorrento.

The contention that Gorky left financially secure is not borne out by evidence. On December 12, 1921, Lenin gave V. M. Molotov instructions to consult the members of the Politburo regarding financial assistance to Gorky. Lenin inquired of N. N. Krestinskii, who was attached to the Foreign Trade office in Berlin, regarding the matter of financial support for Gorky. Krestinskii reported that Gorky left Riga almost penniless and suggested including Gorky's name among those Soviet citizens who, because of many reasons, were sent abroad for a "cure" at the expense of the Party or government.[3] The notes appended to the letter indicate that a decision was taken to carry out Krestinskii's suggestion.[4] There was further communication between Lenin and members of the Party on the matter of financial support for Gorky. Andreeva from Berlin wrote Lenin on February 17, 1922, informing him of Gorky's poor health and asked that the decision regarding the publication of his works be speeded up. She mentioned the fact that whatever funds he had were spent and that the cost of living, particularly medical help, in Germany was very high.[5] According to official sources, the Politburo instructed the *Narkompros* (Commissariat of Enlightenment) to get from Gorky the rights to his publications, and the Berlin office of Foreign Trade was to formalize the deal and to fund Gorky immediately. And yet, not all is clear regarding the problem of Gorky's financial support at that time by the Soviet sources. In the work *Zheleznaia zhenshchina* (The Iron Lady), a biography of Gorky's secretary and close friend, the previously mentioned M. Budberg (also known as Moura, or Baroness Budberg), N. Berberova writes that Gorky received no financial support from the Soviet government at that time. The money, asserts Berberova, came from two sources: one was the income from the sale of his works abroad, and the other was money received from A. L. Parvus as the repayment of a loan long owed to Gorky. Between 1922 and 1924, the year of Parvus's death, a total of $25,000 was paid to Gorky. With the death of Parvus in 1924, that source of funds was no more.[6]

The correspondence between Lenin and Gorky continued till December 6, 1921. A letter to Lenin, published recently for the first time, tells more about the Gorky-Lenin relationship shortly after the writer's departure. Gorky expressed his concern over Lenin's safety, while adding some critical remarks regarding New Economic Policy (NEP) and the new ruling class:

Forgive me, if I say that I am very worried about you. I fear that some people would like to kill you (*kak by vam ne svernuli golovu*), for your New Economic Policy. There are many more idiots in Russia now than there were under the old regime; maybe the reason for it is that previously they were not seen or heard, now they are in power.

Here too, one finds mentioned for the first time Gorky's projected essay on the peasantry: "I intend to write an essay about the Russian people, that is, about our peasant . . . who, little by little, is swallowing the last bit of the Revolutionary potential of the Russian worker."[7] In answer, Lenin sent Gorky a short note in which he wrote of his fatigue, insomnia, and plans to go for a cure (*edu lechit'sia*). He continued:

I was asked to write to you: Would you write Bernard Shaw and ask him to go to the United States (*v Ameriku*), and to Wells, who is in the States now, to start a campaign to collect contributions in order to help the starving? It would be good if you would write them. The starving people will then get more. There is a terrible famine. . . . Regards, Lenin.[8]

Gorky informed Lenin that a substantial sum of money was collected in France and that he had urged Zinovii Peshkov, his adopted son, to send the money as soon as possible to Krasin. Gorky assured Lenin that he was doing all he could and that funds were also collected in Brazil and in Argentina, money and wheat. He was concerned that the work of relief was not coordinated and suggested appointing people in charge of the operation, recommending for the task Mariia Fedorovna and Mariia Ignatevna (M. Budberg), who, he wrote, was well educated and spoke five languages. He added: "She was a countess but—much can happen to people, especially to women."[9] The concluding remarks contain an invitation to Lenin to come and join him, to take care of himself, and to rest.[10]

The years spent in Germany were a re-introduction of Gorky to Western Europe after a break of eight years. But he was never comfortable in Germany, and his views on Germany and the Germans were ambivalent. He admired their ability to work hard and be efficient, but the pedantic attitude to life and all that comes with it was alien to him. He detested their exaggerated nationalism and had some harsh words to say about their phi-

losophers. It appears that he was not welcomed by certain circles of the
German society or/and government, and the German authorities were
watching over the writer. Also, members of the Russian émigré community
assembled in Berlin and in Paris did not spare efforts to criticize him for
his co-operation with the Soviet regime, which was considered treason to
the idea of democratic Russia.

Of himself in the new surroundings he wrote:

To write about myself is sort of boring. Of course I am being bitten and hunted
by fellow journalists . . . who implore me to share with them my old man's wisdom.
In the reputable press of our émigrés, I have read with sadness and envy that "Mr.
Gorky has sold his treasures: old silver, miniatures etc." The foreign press is treating
M. Gorky with kindness, interested in the "adventurer" . . . so are some foreign
ministers.[11]

His views on Germany not withstanding, he was full of admiration for
Europe:

And, in spite of it all, Europe—it is mighty! Beginning with Finland, that wonderful
country which the more you see the more you respect. What they do, these quiet
stubborn Finns! They have started the building of a new city for 150000 inhabitants
and are building it—just a dream! In Sweden they too work hard, and about the
Germans, it goes without saying.[12]

But the place he had in mind for a longer stay was Italy. During his stay
in Germany, Gorky and his entourage moved a number of times. From
Berlin, where he spent the spring and summer of 1922, to resort places of
St. Blasien (Switzerland) and Saarov, to Freiburg and Gunthersthal. As in
Petersburg, so in Germany; Gorky lived in a kind of extended family. There
were Maxim and his newly wedded wife Natalia, nicknamed Timosha, the
painter Rakitskii; following some months of anticipation, the "mysterious"
Moura (M. Budberg) arrived. The poet Khodasevich and his wife, the future poet, Nina Berberova came, and E. Peshkova was a frequent visitor.
Of Gorky during that period we read in Berberova's work: "Gorky belonged to a different part of the Russian intelligentsia. There was something
peculiar about Gorky . . . he had a native charm, a charm of a person who
lived a long difficult and wonderful life."[13] As to family matters, Gorky
reported to E. Peshkova of his meeting with Maxim. "He was," wrote
Gorky, "in good physical shape but his nerves needed a rest. The work of
a diplomatic courier was too demanding, and the constant travelling between Berlin and Rome had tired and strained him. The New Economic
Policy and Lenin's statements confused him . . . as it did many others, and
evoked in the young man some serious questions."[14] He informed E. Peshkova that he would look for a sanatorium in the Black Forest area for both

himself and Maxim and that the rumors of Maxim's addiction to alcohol were exaggerated.[15]

What were the activities he was engaged in? First came the care of his health, then the question of settling somewhere more permanently. There was time to reflect on the immediate past and on the means to express it. His views on Russia and its people following the Revolution are to be found in his letters and articles. As in the past, these contain many contradictions. In the journal *Novyi zhurnal* in 1976 a previously unpublished document of 1922 appeared, entitled "Gorky on Lenin and the Revolution." It contains a report submitted to the Foreign Minister of France, Mr. D. Peretti, on January 6, 1922, by Zinovii Peshkov. There one reads of a conversation between Gorky and Zinovii in which Gorky talked of the conditions in the Soviet state that were going from bad to worse. He spoke of chaos in the political, social, and economic life and of rulers who were able to stay in power by the force of arms. The village was isolated, and peasants cared only about themselves. The official information reaching the outside world had not a grain of truth in it, and the statistical data was false ["Potemkin villages"]. "As for Lenin, he had spent most of his life abroad and he did not know his own country: Russia is not of any concern to Lenin but as a charred log to set the bourgeois world on fire. The Bolsheviks' aim is but one: to start a world revolution." Yes, they talk about the abolition of the Cheka but at the same time are working to replace it by another. The population is passive and suffer privations, robberies, and violence in silence. Gorky described the situation as he saw it, offering no solution, no plan of action.[16]

In spite of the poor state of his health and the frequent moves, he turned to his literary work. To this period belong the following works: A chapter on V. G. Korolenko that was to be included in a major work under the title "Sredi intelligentsii" (Among the Intelligentsia). More significant, in view of the reaction to it, was the essay "O russkom krest'ianstve" (On the Russian Peasantry), first published (in part), in the Danish newspaper *Politiken* in Copenhagen in April 1922. Earlier, in January of that year, Gorky had written Ladyzhnikov: "I am sitting here and trying to write for newspapers about Russia, it goes slow."[17] And further: "I wrote an article on the peasantry and would like to have your advice—is it worthwhile to publish it? I must publish something. I have no rest from letters and telegrams with requests for articles."[18] He wrote Rolland on October 5, 1922: "I am sending you a little book steeped in great sorrow. It was not easy to write it, but it was necessary."[19] The essay, "O russkom krest'ianstve," was published in Russian and in German.[20] In the introduction Gorky wrote that he felt strongly about the peasant question in his country, but that this was an opinion, not an accusation. His arguments put forward there can be summarized as follows: the Russian people (read, the peasants) are by nature anarchists, still burdened by the legacy of serfdom, and are unable to work expeditiously and constructively in order to subject the forces of nature to the needs of the people. The Russian peasant is illiterate, ruthless, and hateful of the city; he is lazy and deceitful. In support of his arguments Gorky turned to history, mentioning the many jacqueries that ended in failure and left no imprint on the consciousness of the peasant. In essence, the Russian peasant remained as he was in the seventeenth century. He had learned nothing.

The experiences of the revolutionary period and of the Civil War showed that the peasant was not genuinely religious and reacted to the destruction of many of the churches and monasteries with equanimity. The discussions that he [Gorky] had had with representatives of that class convinced him that the people "see a lot but understand nothing" and find solution to all the problems in the destruction of the city, its inhabitants, technological inventions, and all that goes by the name of progress. The indifference to human suffering was another characteristic that came under the scrutiny of the writer. "They do not cry in Riazan' over the poor harvest in Pskov," answered one of his interlocutors.[21] And further: "It is a great misfortune, and many will die. But who? The weak, the infirm; for those who will remain it will be five times better."[22] Rejecting the worker and the intelligent, the Russian peasant recognized only himself and his community.

Why did Gorky write all this? No doubt he wanted to explain the reasons why the Revolution, that was once supposed to bring the better tomorrow, had brought instead violence and a brutal Civil War. After all, he said it before, in 1917, that the people of Russia were not ready for a socialist Revolution. He thought that "the tragedy of the Russian Revolution was played out, and was still continuing in the environment of semi-barbarians (*poludikikh*)" and that "the ruthlessness of the Revolution could only be explained by the ruthlessness of the Russian people."[23] He maintained that the accusations against the leaders of the Revolution were unjust. At the same time, he considered the politicians to be the most "sinful people of all the sinners," but this was because the nature of their activity dictated that they be guided by the Jesuit principle of "the aim justifies the means." He maintained that the Russian intelligentsia was that social stratum that worked for the benefit of the people and together with the worker paid a heavy price for it. The Revolution had accomplished the task of changing the old forms of peasant life. In the end, wrote Gorky, the hope was that the old semi-barbarian peasant would die out, and his place be taken by the young literate and conscious peasant—but one still suspicious of the intelligentsia, of the worker, of science, and of the city.

Two important points seem to be in order here. First, the reaction of the Soviet critics, and second, the consistency of Gorky's views regarding the peasant, the importance of the city, the role of the intelligentsia, and of the worker.

In Soviet Russia, one of the early responses to the work came in a poem written by the poet Demian Bedny and published in *Pravda* on July 22, 1922. Entitled *Gnetuchka* (Fever),[24] it ridiculed Gorky's thesis, maintaining that Gorky erred in his characterization of the peasant and of the nature of the Russian people. Gorky continued with his views as these were expressed in the articles published in *Novaia zhizn'*. Acknowledging later, in 1930, his "mistakes," Gorky explained that he was always concerned about the power of the illiterate village and the absence of social consciousness of the peasant. The masses needed leadership, which could only come from the intelligentsia in cooperation with the workers.[25] Since the essay was written shortly after his departure from Russia, the events of the Civil War were still very much on his mind. One would question his later retractions made under rather "difficult" circumstances.

The émigrés reacted angrily to the publication. His former friend, E. Kuskova, wrote a lengthy article entitled "Maksim Gor'kii o krest'ianstve" (Maxim Gorky on the Peasantry). Finding discrepancies and inconsitencies in his arguments, Kuskova, in juxtaposition to Gorky's thesis, put the blame for the events of the Civil War on the city, maintaining that it was the city and not the village that was guilty of the savagery. The famine, she continued, and its results were the fault of the politics of the government, of the infamous *prodrazverstka* (forceful requisition of grain) that drained the village of grain. It was the village that was toiling, while the city was busy with circuses. Kuskova concluded that it was wrong to generalize about a population of a hundred million on the basis of frightful but isolated episodes that occurred during the Civil War.[26] Criticism of the work came also from the pen of the émigré historian, S. P. Melgunov: "The Russian writer [Gorky], who not only was a sympathizer of Russian communism but had close ties with it, has put the responsibility not on the terrorist system but on the massess . . . [true], the Russian *narod* is ignorant and cruel, but it was not the psychology of the people that created the theories that were nurtured by the bolshevik ideology."[27]

While the work "O russkom krest'ianstve" evoked a storm of protest, Gorky's condemnation of the trial of the Socialist Revolutionaries met with even stronger reaction from the top leadership of the Party, including Lenin. In a recently published work on that trial, one reads: "The leaders of the PSR (Party of Socialist Revolutionaries) were condemned in 1922, in the greatest political trial ever held in communist Russia prior to the Stalinist era."[28] In official Soviet historiography the verdict as to the trial being a just trial remained unchanged till the period of glasnost'. Gorky was being chastized for his erroneous stand. Only this time one cannot find a recantation made by him; instead, one finds in the *Letopis'* quotes from foreign press apologizing for Gorky. Thus the French *L'Humanité* wrote that Gorky's views and his defense of the SRs were conditioned by the sensitivity of the writer and by the fact that being away from the country he did not realize that the SRs were agents of Western capitalism [*sic!*].[29] The German

Die Rote Fahne explained Gorky's and Anatole France's reaction to the trial as caused by the lack of clear political line and essentially as an emotional response.[30]

The trial of the Socialist Revolutionaries began on June 8, 1922, and lasted for a period of fifty days. On trial were thirty-four members of the SR Party, of whom twelve were the members of the Central Committee. They were accused of armed struggle against the Soviet state, of having carried out raids and terrorist activities, and of having maintained contacts with foreign states interested in the overthrow of the Soviet regime. The twelve, ten men and two women, were veteran revolutionaries, who had served long prison terms under Nicholas II for their struggle against the tsarist regime. Where was the truth? The SRs' active resistance against the Bolshevik regime began with the dispersal in January 1918 of the All Russian Constituent Assembly, where the SRs held a clear majority following the first free elections in Russia. During the Civil War the SRs controlled large areas of the country on the Volga and in Siberia. By 1919 when it looked as if the White movement under Kolchak, Denikin, and Yudenich was on the winning side, the SRs abandoned their armed struggle against the Bolshevik regime. By the decree of February 25, 1919, the Soviet government granted an amnesty to the members of the SRs. With the end of the Civil War, the victory of the Bolsheviks, and the inauguration of the New Economic Policy, the attitude towards former adversaries changed. In April of 1922, the Bolsheviks reversed their earlier decision and decided to put the SR leadership on trial for their activities in 1918.

The timing for the trial was not the best for the Soviet state. It coincided with the attempts made on the part of N. Bukharin and K. Radek, the representatives of the Comintern, to arrive at some agreement with the Socialist International and the Labor Parties in Europe, with the purpose being the acceptance of the newly established socialist regime in Russia by foreign socialists. In order to placate public opinion and win over the European socialist leadership, both Radek and Bukharin assured those concerned that the SRs would not be given the death penalty and that they would have the right to choose their own counsel. As it transpired, none of the assurances given were kept. Lenin's response to the concessions made by his commissars came in an article published in *Pravda* on April 11, 1922, under the title: "We Paid Too Dearly." He wrote, "Our representatives were wrong, in my opinion, in agreeing that the Soviet government will not apply capital punishment in the case of the forty seven SR's [the number was reduced before the trial] . . . and that the Soviet government would permit representatives of all three Internationals to be present at the trial."[31] To the defense of the accused came the members of the international socialist community. Among them were Emile Vandervelde and Arthur Waters of the Belgian Labor Party, Kurt Rosenfeld and Theodore Liebknecht of the German Independent Socialist Party, French communists

Boris Souvarine and J. Sadoul, and others. Their reception in Soviet Russia was far from cordial. Taking up the cause of the unjustly arrested SRs was the socialist émigré community, led by the Menshevik, Iu. O. Martov. It was Martov who conceived the idea to involve Gorky in the defense of the SRs. This was particularly important since many of the foreign defenders soon left the country as a result of harrassment by the authorities. With the Russian lawyers also leaving, the accused remained without effective defense. Martov's idea of winning Gorky's support was tied to the notion that Anatole France too would speak up on behalf of the unjustly tried SRs. France was a writer known world wide; he was a friend of Russia; he had donated his Nobel prize money to the famine relief fund and was a great friend of Gorky's. In 1905 France had come to the defense of the then imprisoned writer. On June 30, Martov approached the Menshevik B. N. Nicolaevsky, asking that he turn to Gorky for assistance and through him to Anatole France.

Gorky responded quickly to Nicolaevsky's request. He was insensed about the injustice meted out to the old revolutionaries. There was also a personal connection here that was not given publicity in Soviet sources, which was E. Peshkova's membership at one time in the Socialist Revolutionary Party. Although there is no available evidence that she approached Gorky to intervene, one cannot discard the possibility. On July 3, 1922, Gorky wrote two letters, one addressed to Anatole France and the other to A. I. Rykov, the actual head of state, since Lenin had suffered a stroke on May 26 and was almost totally incapacitated. The appeal to France was in a form of a telegram. It read:

Greatly esteemed Anatole France, The trial of the SR's has taken on a cynical character in order to prepare the public opinion for the execution of people who honestly served the cause of freedom of the Russian people. I very much request of you to turn to the Soviet authorities and point out to them the inadmissability of the crime. Perhaps your weighty word will save the precious lives of these Socialists. I am enclosing a copy of the letter which I have forwarded to one of the representatives of the Soviet leadership. Gorky.[32]

Gorky sent an angry letter to Rykov:

Aleksei Ivanovich, if the trial of the Socialist Revolutionaries will end with a death sentence, then this will be a premeditated murder, a foul murder. I beg of you to inform L. D. Trotsky and the others that this is my contention. I hope that this will not surprise you, since I had told the Soviet authorities a thousand times that it is sensless and criminal to decimate the ranks of our intelligentsia in our illiterate and lacking of culture country. I am convinced, that if the SR's should be executed the crime will result in a moral blockade of Russia by all of socialist Europe. M. Gorky.[33]

Anatole France's answer came on July 11.

Dear Citizen Gorky, I regret that I am unfamiliar with the matter you turned to me with, and which is of the utmost importance. I had had no opportunity to follow the proceedings of the trial taking place now in Moscow. I, as you, believe that the people in question had served the cause of liberation of the Russian people. I too, as you do, believe that their conviction will have a detrimental effect upon the fate of the Soviet state. With all my heart, dear Gorky, I join you in the appeal to the Soviet government, to one who serves in the trial in the capacity of prosecutor. [The reference here is to Piatakov]. With brotherly greetings, Anatole France.[34]

Lenin learned about the proceedings from Krupskaia on June 18 and earlier from Stalin, on June 11. Rykov informed him only in August, and Gorky's defense of the SRs became known to him at the beginning of September. Since August his condition had greatly improved, and he was permitted to read and to speak about politics. He wrote Bukharin:

I have read in *Sotsialisticheskii vestnik* [the publication of the Mensheviks in Berlin], the vile letter of Gorky. I thought of scolding him in the press on this SR's question, but decided that this would be too much. One has to ask for an advice. Are you perhaps in touch with him? Please give me your thinking on the matter. I have seen only a few of the newspapers (I have hardly seen the foreign press). It means that I know little of the "circumstances" [of Gorky's letters].[35]

On the same day Lenin sent a letter to Krestinskii. It read: "Comrade Krestinskii, Be so kind and forward the attached letter to com. Bukharin; choose a way that is reliable; I think that you will choose the best way [to send it]. Thanking you in advance, greetings to your wife, I press your hand. Lenin."[36] Lenin repeated the news that he had almost recovered and requested once again the original of Gorky's letter published in *Sotsialisticheskii vestnik* of July 20, 1922.[37] It is interesting that Lenin decided against publicly chastising Gorky, but thought that it was more advisable to discuss the matter with him. But by December 13, Lenin had suffered two cerebral thromboses and was pretty well incapacitated.

Gorky, in the tradition of his former appeals, took a strong stand in defense of the accused. On July 1, 1922, he wrote to Rykov, then the deputy chair of the Sovnarkom, condemning the Soviet government. Of interest are notes appended to the letter. One, written August 10, 1922, by Rykov read, "Send through the Secretariat to all the members of the Politburo." Trotsky's note read, "I suggest entrusting the editorial board of *Pravda* to publish an article on Gorky, the artist whom in politics nobody takes seriously; the article to be published in foreign languages too."[38]

It is evident from a letter to Ladyzhnikov that Gorky thought about writing Lenin in December of 1922,[39] but there is no evidence that he did. Pursuing further the cause of the SRs on trial, Gorky turned to L. Kamenev.

Only circumstancial evidence is available regarding that letter. The wife of F. Dan (sister of Martov) wrote Gorky that his letter to Kamenev was helpful in lightening the lot of the imprisoned SRs.[40]

The censure of Gorky for his open defense of the SRs came in an article by Sergei Zorin, the ideological watchdog, published in *Pravda* on July 18. In a poem by Demian Bedny published in *Pravda* on July 20, Gorky was called "the weeper for the Socialist Revolutionaries." The journalist N. Nurim wrote in *Krasnaia nov'* that all the prerevolutionary intelligentsia vacillated in the case of the SRs and that the best example was the "tactless and unwise move of Gorky." He continued: "It could not have happened otherwise. Not only are the SR's being tried but also those circles of the intelligentsia that considered October [the October Revolution], as a misunderstanding, as a preposterous prank of history."[41] A vitriolic attack on Gorky came from the pen of Karl Radek. Entitled "Maksim Gor'kii i russkaia revoliutsiia" (Maxim Gorky and the Russian Revolution), it was published in *Izvestiia*. Radek referred to letters that appeared in the press addressed to A. France and to Rykov. Gorky, away from the country, had lost contact with the developments and is surrounded by a clique of "hysterical literati." Gorky had misunderstood the Revolution and all that happened because, wrote Radek, he was a petit-bourgeois by birth and one who had lived part of his life among the lumpen proletariat. He was an enemy of the October Revolution because he feared that the peasant mass would destroy Russian culture. In conclusion, wrote Radek, one has to tell Gorky "that even a writer should not misuse his rights and be allowed to publish all kinds of rubbish."[42] The fact that such an article would appear in the organ of the government, authored by one belonging at that time to the upper echelons of the Party, was proof that Gorky was severely censored for his writings.

The verdict announced on August 7, 1922, was a death sentence for the twelve leading defendants. However, as a result of protests that came from abroad and were reported by Soviet embassies, the death sentences, although confirmed, were not carried out, and the executions were held in abeyance. Those who survived till the purges of the 1930s were executed on orders of Stalin. According to E. Peshkova, all the Socialist Revolutionaries who were on trial in 1922 perished.[43] By that time Gorky was dead. But in the months of July and August of 1922, his voice did tell the people of West European countries that injustice was done to old revolutionaries by the leaders of the first socialist state in history. Here was the old Gorky taking a stand in defense of justice.

Censured for his work "O russkom krest'ianstve" and for his open defense of the SRs, Gorky soon embarked on an enterprise that would bring him much frustration and would exacerbate his relations with the Soviet government. This was the attempt to found a literary-scientific journal in Berlin under the title *Putnik* (Traveller), later renamed *Beseda* (Colloquy).

Gorky conceived the idea shortly after his arrival from Russia although, according to Khodasevich, the initiative was V. Shklovsky's. As early as April 1922, Gorky wrote H. G. Wells about the projected journal: "It will be a monthly, about 25 printed pages, its aim, to acquaint literate Russians with the scientific and literary life of Europe. A publication absolutely indispensable for my countrymen."[44] At first Gorky thought of establishing two editorial centers: one in Berlin, and the other in Petersburg. Later, in May of 1923, he informed the office of *Glavlit* (Main Administration for Literary Affairs and Publishing) that *Beseda* would be published in Berlin. Both Soviet and West European writers were to publish their works there, free of censorship, and it was understood that the journal would become available for the reading public in the Soviet Union.[45] The publication of *Beseda* was entrusted to the publishing house *Epokha,* managed by two Mensheviks, Kaplun-Shumsky and D. Dallin. The editorial board consisted of Gorky, Khodasevich, A. Belyi, B. F. Adler, and F. A. Braun, a Baltic German and a former professor of anthropology at St. Petersburg, who left Russia after the Revolution and settled in Leipzig. Braun was the editor of the scientific part of the journal, and following Gorky's departure for Italy he became chief editor.

In the period between June 1923 and March 1925, seven issues of *Beseda* appeared. Gorky's frustrations with the undertaking were many. Contributions were lacking because Soviet writers were prevented by the censors from sending their works, some of the émigrés who would have participated were leaving Berlin, and others were not eager to publish in Gorky's journal. Few foreign contributors were ready to send their works to the projected *Beseda*. But the most important problem was the refusal by the Soviet authorities to allow the importation of the journal into the country. One source that sheds much light on that unsuccessful venture is the Gorky-Khodasevich correspondence. On July 23, 1923, Gorky wrote that a number of scholars from Russia were about to send their articles for publication, among them the Russian orientalist S. F. Ol'denburg, the noted sinologist V. M. Alekseev, and the writer S. N. Sergeev-Tsenskii.[46] Gorky had earlier approached his old friend Rolland for contributions and had written to Stefan Zweig and to Bernard Shaw asking for their works. It became soon apparent, wrote Khodasevich, that writers living in Soviet Russia were afraid to participate in *Beseda*, and only few of Gorky's foreign friends sent stories and articles.[47] A variety of topics and disciplines was included in *Beseda* as is evident from the letter of August 17, 1923, written to Khodasevich.

What have you got for the third number? [*Beseda*]. Will there be a poem of yours? Has Ellens' article been sent to the printer's? [Franz Ellens, a Belgian writer], Braun is giving us an article of his about language—11/2 sheets; Steindorf has one on Tutankhamen—two sheets with drawings; there are pieces on Far Eastern art and on German romanticism. Then there is an article called "Goethe and Goethe Scholarship in Modern Germany."[48]

Gorky's repeated requests for permission to import *Beseda* into Russia were turned down. Writing to E. Peshkova in September of 1924, he mentioned that "with '*Beseda*' they are still procrastinating."[49] He tried to hold on to the belief that the permit would be granted and at one point wrote to the Soviet writer, L. M. Leonov, that "*Beseda* has now been allowed into the country."[50] The information was inaccurate. Khodasevich comments in his notes that Gorky kept writing letters to Moscow and in his presence discussed the subject with Rykov when the latter, who at that time had taken the place of the sick Lenin, came to Saarov.[51] Kriuchkov assured Gorky that an authorization would come from Moscow and that he would be able to distribute a thousand copies in Russia.[52] When Gorky realized that the authorization was not forthcoming, he decided to resort to pressure and threatened to stop contributing to Soviet publications, which he actually did. In a letter to Nicolaevsky of September 1, 1923, he wrote:

I have yesterday refused the offer to participate in the journal *Zvezda* (The Star), in the almanac *Krug* (The Circle) and in the almanac *Atenei*, . . . because they do not allow *Beseda* into the country. I am in an akward situation vis-à-vis the foreign contributors invited by me to participate in *Beseda*.[53]

Gorky's son Maxim advised him to turn to "Il'ich." In answer, Gorky remarked that writing to Lenin would be useless, for he had suffered a stroke and lost the power of speech. The news came via newspapers and from E. Peshkova's letters.

By the spring of 1925, Gorky informed Khodasevich that *Beseda* was finished. He further elaborated:

[O]f whether or not to let *Beseda* into Russia, an extraordinary conference, attended by numerous wise and mighty men, was called. There were three who voted for admission: Ionov, Kamenev and Belitskii.[54] All the rest said, "Don't let it in—then Gor'kii will come back home." But he won't come back. He is stubborn too.[55]

In the end, the circulation of the journal was confined to the members of the émigré community. Gorky made one more attempt to revive *Beseda* under a new title, *Sobesednik* (Interlocutor), with the hope that this time he would succeed in getting it into Russia. Writing to Khodasevich on July 20, 1925, he informed him that he was in contact with the head of the Leningrad section of *Gosizdat* (State Publishing House), the previously mentioned Ionov, and that the latter had discussed with him the possibility of renewing the publication of the defunct *Beseda*. "The material would be collected abroad, i.e., in Sorrento, the publishing would take place in St. Petersburg . . . Ionov had put no restrictions, so far."[56] This is as far as it went. There was no further development, and the enterprise ended in failure.

The ambitious project of the journal failing and with criticism of his "O russkom krest'ianstve" unabating, Gorky's next publication, which appeared in 1924 under the title *Zametki iz dnevnika Vospominaniia* (From My Diary), evoked severe condemnation. *Vospominaniia* was a collection of short stories, vignettes of people and life in Russia before and after the Revolution and the Civil War. Here again, as in "O russkom krest'ianstve," one finds Gorky's severe indictment of his people and country. Yet the words of criticism are interspersed with comments that run counter to the tone of the work. Having drawn a dreary picture of life in Russia, Gorky comments, "I see the Russian people as exceptionally fantastically talented and unique. Even fools in Russia are original in their stupidity and the idlers indeed have in them the spark of greatness."[57] How is one to understand it? Was there in Gorky's thinking something harkening back to the ideology of the nineteenth century Slavophiles? asked one of the reviewers, I. Verov, answering the question in the affirmative.[58] Gorky, Verov continued, was a man divided, as an artist and as a person. The new Gorky of the 1920s is quite different from the "stormy petrel" who was so enthusiastically awaiting the storm. The new Gorky is a tired and a disillusioned man. He depicts life in Russia as full of ignorance and squalor, with people longing for something, lacking in purpose, and in a state of mind that could even lead to god-seeking. The types described in the work have little in them that is genuinely human, and Russia appears as a terrible, illiterate, backward, and Asiatic country. Gorky is leaning intellectually toward Marxism, toward European civilization, but, deep down, he is a petit-bourgeois walking with an undecisivly swinging gait. Verov continued his evaluation of Gorky, also criticizing his political orientation.[59]

A view of Gorky's life in Germany comes from the pen of an American journalist, Barret H. Clark, who visited Gorky in 1923, first in Saarov and later in Freiburg. One gets a picture of a very busy extended family, of warm hospitality accorded to those Gorky agrees to see, of his opinion of the Germans and the situation in Russia. From Clark's writings it appears that Gorky is pretty tired of the Germans and their "childish complaints" and that the economic and political situation (this was 1923), was "fast stripping off the thin veneer of their [German] civilization, and showing the dumb brute beneath."[60] On Russia, he had this to say: "Revolution never helps a bad situation—it usually only makes it worse. People suffer, rebel, fight for what they want or think they want, only to find that they are still as badly off as before, they substitute one set of chains for another."[61] He reiterated the ideas expressed in "O russkom krest'ianstve" and earlier, in his article on Lenin of 1920. The difficulty was "that the

Russian workers won't work. They have nothing to look for and they are without ambition."[62] He thought that the things were different in America, "where the worker doesn't lay off the moment he has enough money to fill his belly with food."[63]

Gorky's pessimism over the situation in his country was reflected in his letters. "The letters I get from Russia are far from good. There is some sort of a morass there, of weariness and depression."[64] Asked by the London PEN Club whether it would be feasible to establish in Russia an apolitical organization that would include both Russian writers living in Russia and those abroad, Gorky replied that "there exists a Soviet regime in Moscow which cannot allow any *apolitical* organization, for it does not recognize the existence of any persons not infected with politics from the cradle." "It was European literature," he wrote, "that could talk about everything, courageously and honestly."[65] When news reached him that N. Krupskaia had compiled a guide for libraries that instructed the removal of works by Western as well as Russian philosophers and writers, Gorky was furious. A strong condemnation of the index of "counter-revolutionary works" came in a letter to his friend and frequent correspondent Rolland. The portrait of Krupskaia as painted there is nothing short of iconoclastic when compared to the hagiographical panegyrics that appeared in Soviet works. He wrote:

The fact is that Lenin's wife is by nature not a very bright person, suffering from Basedov disease, and is therefore psychologically not very sound. She compiled a list of allegedly counter-revolutionary works and ordered these to be removed from libraries. The old woman considered works of Western European philosophers, thinkers, writers as well as Russian as counter-revolutionary. My first thought was to renounce my Soviet citizenship but then, it would not have changed much. . . . I wrote only letters to the "three big shots," but received no answer.[66]

The situation in Germany was becoming unpleasant. By 1923, the political climate was tense, and rumors of possible communist revolution were worrying Gorky. In September both he and Khodasevich decided to move to Italy. Gorky had fond memories of his previous seven-year sojourn on the island of Capri. The problem, however, was complicated by the question of an Italian visa. In addition, the newly appointed Soviet representative in Italy was N. I. Iordanskii, editor and literary critic, who, according to Khodasevich, Gorky suspected would keep him under close surveillance. It was decided to move to Czechoslovakia.[67] But Gorky was not happy in Czechoslovakia, where one of the conditions was that he not appear in public and where he was unjustly accused of being an anarchist. Leaving that country, wrote Gorky, meant also to leave behind the hostile letters that he was receiving.[68]

While Gorky was still in Marienbad, the news came in a telegram from

E. Peshkova that Lenin had died. It read, "Vladimir Il'ich is dead, cable the content of the inscription on the wreath." In reply, a short note was sent on February 11, 1924: "On the wreath write: 'farewell friend.' "[69] According Khodasevich's recollections, Moura (M. Budberg) made him [Gorky] write the obituary soon after the receipt of the telegram. Soviet authorities were obviously interested in Gorky's contribution to the outpouring of obituaries in memory of Lenin, for as soon as Gorky finished writing, there arrived, as if "per chance," the manager of *Mezhdunarodnaia Kniga* (International Book Co.), P. P. Kriuchkov. Aleksei Maksimovich was evidently told that it was expected of the "stormy petrel" of the revolution to write about the great leader. Gorky was asked to put aside his solemn promise not to publish in the Soviet Union and to allow the publication of the memoir. Kriuchkov took the manuscript to Moscow, where it later underwent strict censorship.

How was the memoir received? One is in difficulty to find an honest account except for the thorough and harsh analysis written by Trotsky in September 1924. He began his critique of the memoir thus: "Gorky's writings about Lenin are very poor"; although one could find in it some thin threads of brilliancy, many more are of "a banal psychological analysis." He continued hammering unrelenting at every phrase and metaphor of the memoir. Lenin was not, as Gorky writes, "one of the righteous"; it sounded false and was in bad taste. Some memorable details that were included were valuable for the understanding of Lenin's personality, conceded Trotsky, but for these one could forgive Gorky only "a quarter of all the banalities spread through the essay."[70] Trotsky pointed out the many contradictions inherent in Gorky's characterisation of Lenin and ridiculed the former's attempt to portray him as a kind of superman. He reminded Gorky that some of his appeals to Lenin on behalf of the "victims of the Revolution" were "indeed ridiculous." "It is enough to recall his . . . intervention in the defense of the Social Revolutionaries during the famous Moscow trial."[71] He mentioned Lenin's warm feelings toward Gorky and worry over his poor health. However, unlike the Soviet official hagiographical writings, he maintained that "in his [Lenin's] stubborn insistence that Gorky should go abroad there was also a political motive."[72] An explanation follows: Gorky was getting "hopelessly confused" during these difficult years, and had it not been for Lenin's insistence that he leave the country, he "might have gone tragically astray." Lenin needed a "straightened out Gorky," one that would not be influenced by those workers in the field of "culture" whom he defended. Also, the exposure to the capitalist world should have helped him find his bearings.[73] For Trotsky, Gorky was a sort of a culture's psalmodist, hence "his haughty attitude, his contempt for the intelligence of the masses, and also for Marxism."[74] He ended by criticizing Gorky's mistaken zeal in trying to save culture.[75] The criticism is as much of Gorky as it is

of Gorky's writings about Lenin. The interesting question that remains unanswered is Gorky's reaction to Trotsky's severe criticism of the memoir.

Still mourning the death of Lenin, Gorky received a letter of sympathy
from his friend Rolland. The letter read: "I think Lenin's death must have
created in you a flood of emotions and memories. We who have not known
this man personally . . . have felt the enormous void caused by the end of
this life."[76] In conclusion, Rolland asked of Gorky's views on both Lenin
and Trotsky. Gorky answered on March 3, 1924:

Yes, Lenin's death has hit me very hard, not to mention the immense and irreparable loss it is for Russia. I didn't think it would come so soon. I thought that the
story of the paralysis was fabricated by his political adversaries. . . . I loved him
with anger. I talked to him in strong words. . . . He understood what was behind
the words. He was a great Russian man. . . . I am proud to have known both him
and Tolstoy. . . . You ask me what I think of Trotsky. I don't know him well. I
believe he is a talented man, with a Semitic soul, passionate and revengeful. He is
intelligent, very well educated, courageous, as one of the Macabees. There is in him
a unique kind of beauty. . . . I am convinced that he is able to do something great,
if his temperament would not hinder him.[77]

Previously Gorky had tried to clarify to Rolland his attitude towards the
Soviets and elaborated on his relationship with Lenin.

I am considered to be a supporter of the Soviets, and Olar [French historian] writes
in his *Histoire des Soviets* that I have "joined" them. This is not entirely true. At
the beginning of [19]18, I understood that no other power for Russia was possible,
and that Lenin was the only person capable of stopping the process towards an
elemental kind of anarchy in the masses of peasants and soldiers. This does not
mean that I fully identified with Lenin. For years I quarelled with him pointing out
that his fight against Russian anarchism . . . has assumed the character of fight
against culture. I explained that by destroying the Russian intelligentsia he was
depriving the Russian people of its brain, and in spite of the fact that I love the
man, and he, it seems, he loved me too, often our conflicts brought about the hatred
of each other.[78]

The long-awaited Italian visa arrived with stipulations that he not engage
in politics. By the spring of 1924 he had moved to Sorrento, which was to
be his domicile for a period of nine years. "Today we moved to Sorrento,
and it will take a long time for them [the Soviet authorities?] to drag me
away from here, mark my words!" Although happy with the warm reception by the people who, he wrote, remembered him from ten years before,
he was aware that he was under surveillance, and his mail was "very attentively read." This was Mussolini's Italy.

Gorky's relationship with the émigré community was a troubled one. The émigré press continued its attacks against him, and Gorky was bitter about it: "[E]ach day opens wide its rotten maw and bellows infamies with poisonous breath. I swear that when I am alone by myself at night, I feel so discouraged that—if it were not so banal and ridiculous—I would shoot myself."[79] Earlier, in a letter to E. Peshkova, he wrote with tongue in cheek: "They say that I was bought by Loyd George. Everybody is buying me: the Jews, the Japanese, the English, and this gives me the right to consider myself indispensable to the enemies of Russia. I am very satisfied."[80]

When, in the Soviet Union, the Resolution of the Central Committee of June 1925 laid down principles of tolerance and restraint for Party policy on literature, Gorky was pleased.[81] One can say that 1925 marked the beginning of a change in Gorky's attitude toward his native country. With this change came the break with Khodasevich. According to the latter the reason for the break was Gorky's changed attitude towards the Soviet regime and his willingness to cooperate with it. Khodasevich, on leaving Sorrento in April 1925 and reflecting on Gorky's future, allegedly said, "He [Gorky] will not get the Nobel prize, Zinoviev will be demoted, the payments from Parvus will end and he will return to Russia."[82]

What were the thoughts of those who remembered Gorky first as the "stormy petrel" and then his "untimely thoughts"? Gorky's once-close friend, Lunacharskii, a member of the Capri school and later a colleague in the *Vperëd* group, wrote in 1925 of Gorky's long and distinguished career as a writer, but one whose stand on the Revolution of October was all wrong. Gorky, wrote Lunacharskii, was under the illusion that the February Revolution was carried out satisfactorily and that it was time to bring order into the country. He was frightened of the elemental forces of a twentieth-century *pugachevshchina*. Lunacharskii regretted Gorky's inability to write a work in praise of the Revolution. "Regrettfully," he continued, "not all revolutions have their Milton and Gorky did not make an effort to be one the Russian Revolution."[83] That both Trotsky's critique and Lunacharskii's pamphlet appeared free from the censor's pen and that they dared to criticize one who was to become a legend in his lifetime show the differences not only in degree but in kind between the publications of 1920s and those of the 1930s.

Not only were the latest works of Gorky discussed and criticized, but the nature of Gorky's political orientation and ties with the revolutionary movements were also under scrutiny. His participation in the revolutionary movements was not something sporadic and casual, but was motivated by Gorky's own experiences and the environment of prerevolutionary Russia.[84] An analysis of Gorky's views of Russia, the Russian people, and its history came also from the pen of the writer K. Chukovskii, who wrote that "The cruelty of the Russian people troubled Gorky. As did the slave like submission to fate, and a resigned attitude to ill-fate." According to Gorky, all the bad characteristics of the Russian people were a result of

"Asiatic, Eastern, Mongol influences." The influence of Asia was the source of all evil: of drunkenness, idleness, and becoming "superfluous" people, the likes of Oblomov, Onegin, Rudin, and others. The remedy, the panacea, was Europe (Western civilization).[85] He continued:

When we try to expound on Gorky's philosophical make-up, we have to realize that his is the philosophy of an artist, . . . abstract thinking is alien to him. . . . He is not a thinker, his creative work is instinctive. Gorky, the artist, is different from Gorky the publicist, and Gorky's style, in his publicist writings, is dry and banal. He admires only one class of the Russian society, the intelligentsia that strove to raise the Russian people from its stupor.[86]

Yet, in spite of his admiration and love of that class, Gorky remained an alien among them. Gorky, the autodidact, erudite person, lacked the culture of the likes of A. France, A. Herzen, and H. Heine, to name a few. Thus, his love of that class was pathetic. And so, Gorky, alienated from the village, had not come close to the city, was neither a burgher nor a peasant. He is a person without an address on the border of two worlds, one which is falling apart and the other that has not yet been built.[87] The constant struggle for existence that Gorky faced in his childhood and youth had fortified him for the hard road ahead and made him into a rebel against all that was violent, ruthless, and hypocritical. A revolutionary even before the Revolution, Gorky believed that he had to teach in order to provide solutions for the social ills that plagued Russia. "First he tried to cure us through the ideas of anarchism, then socialism and finally communism, convinced all along that he had the right answers and the best of remedies."[88] Unlike the hagiographical works of the 1930s, one finds here an attempt at an objective evaluation of Gorky's ideas as expressed in his literary and publicist writings.

Yet in response to the attack on Gorky by the émigré literati, Chukovskii came in defense of the writer and, in a letter addressed to the writer A. N. Tolstoy, who was abroad at the time, wrote: "If you should be seeing A. M. Gorky give him my regards. Our Russian émigrés are treating him abominably and he had done much for them."[89] One of those guilty of attacks on Gorky was the poet Zinaida Gippius, no friend of his even in the prerevolutionary period. She was joined in her denunciations by her husband, Dmitrii Merezhkovskii. Gippius, hateful of Gorky because she saw him siding with the Bolsheviks, was also accusing him unjustly of stealing valuable property in his capacity of chairman of the *Ekspertnaia Komissiia.*"[90]

The death of F. E. Dzerzhinskii in July 1926 and a personal letter of Gorky published in *Izvestiia* without his approval brought further criticism by the émigrés. Gorky's letter on the death of Dzerzhinskii read:

I am stunned by the death of Felix Edmundovich. I first met him in '09–'10 [1909–1910], and already then he made on me an impression of one pure of soul [sic!], and of solidity. I came to know him quite well in the 1918–1920 period, and have discussed with him matters of rather delicate nature. I have often burdened him with certain requests; thanks to his sensitivity and sense of justice [sic!], much good was done. He made me like and respect him. I can understand the sad letter of Ekaterina Pavlovna [E. Peshkova] where she wrote: "the wonderful man is no more, one that was . . . dear to those who knew him."[91]

   Anyone familiar with the record of the Cheka and Dzerzhinskii's leadership of that infamous institution could not be surprised at the reaction of the émigrés. Gorky, on his part, was indignant that his personal letter was made public without his consent. Nevertheless, the content of the letter remains. How is one to explain it? As mentioned earlier, in the period from 1918 to 1921 Gorky had devoted much of his energy to save people from the axe of the Cheka (see Chapter 6). It suffices to examine the content of letters written to Lenin with requests on behalf of one or another victim of the revolutionary terror. Also, it is well known that E. Peshkova was a personal friend of Dzerzhinskii while working in the Political Red Cross. Gorky would often ask her to intercede on behalf of his friends and many petitioners. There is circumstancial evidence that Dzerzhinskii did help Gorky in the case of M. Zakrevskaia-Benkendorf (M. Budberg) in 1920. Still, for all those acquainted with the reign of terror of Dzerzhinskii and his Cheka, Gorky's reaction is difficult to justify.
   Settled in Sorrento in 1924, he had many things to be satisfied with. To E. Peshkova he wrote: "Gorky is becoming a writer quite well known abroad, he is very much praised by three [writers]: in Austria by Stefan Zweig, in France by Romain Rolland, in Italy by D. Panini."[92] In the Soviet Union, *Gosizdat* signed an agreement to publish his works for a handsome sum. Some of his articles and short stories were appearing on the pages of Soviet periodicals, and royalties from these publications were an important source of income.[93] Close contacts with Kriuchkov, who later became his secretary and constant companion, Gorky's participation in a number of Soviet periodicals, the role of mentor to young and upcoming writers, were activities that drew Gorky closer to Russia. After 1925, he became more involved with publishing in *Krasnaia nov'* (Red Virgin Soil).[94] Gorky approved of *Novyi mir* (New World) and *Pechat' i revoliutsiia* (The Press and the Revolution), to name two. He had little good to say about the avant-garde journals *Lef* (Left), or *Novyi Lef* (New Left), and *Na postu* (On Guard). The attitude was reciprocal. Many of the avant-gardists were critical of Gorky, considering him "the man of yesterday." He was criticized for having left the country and having stayed abroad. One of the most outspoken critics was the poet V. V. Maiakovskii, who, in January of 1927, published in *New Lef* "A Letter of the Writer Vladimir Vladimirovich

Maiakovskii to the Writer Aleksei Maksimovich Gorky." It began: "It is too bad, comrade Gorky, that one does not see you here . . . while we are building our country."[95] In the first issue of *Na postu* appeared an offensive article entitled: "Byvshyi Glavsokol, nynie Tsentrouzh" (The Former Chief of Falcons, Now a Simple Grass-Snake), by one L. Sosnovskii.[96] Gorky's works were subject to critical reviews and articles.

Gorky, in spite of these criticisms, devoted much of his time to guide, supervise (to a degree), and advise new Soviet writers. Evidence of close contacts with some of the more promising comes in a letter to Rolland of February 22, 1927. Gorky was very impressed with the works of I. Babel', V. Ivanov, L. Leonov, and K. Fedin, who were, he thought, the most creative Soviet writers of the period. He often invited them to visit him in Sorrento.[97]

He had, however, his own ideas as to what literature should be. He was full of disdain for the writer who extolls the peasant. The village is still a problem, wrote Gorky, although there, too, is progress. He had faith in the great achievements of the Russian proletariat and was optimistic over the successes of the Revolution. Also, he insisted that the young writers be given freedom to write without dictates. He wrote, "The young writers should not be squeezed into a corner even in a Marxist one."[98]

In 1927, on the occasion of the tenth anniversary of the October Revolution, Gorky's article "Desiat' let" (Ten Years) was published in *Izvestiia* October 23, 1927.[99] In the article, Gorky criticized the West for its judgment of the Russians and the Soviet regime. Extolling the achievements of the ten-year rule of the Bolshevik Party, he emphasized the great strides made in the economy and in education and had praise for the growing grassroots democracy and tried to give an analysis of events of the ten years since the October Revolution.

Actually, the Bolsheviks had only six years of constructive work, he wrote. The Civil War destroyed the country and yet, at the same time, "sobered the people up from the many illusions and by it was changing their psyche."[100] And further: "My joy and my pride is the new Russian man, the builder of the new state."[101] This was not an article that was dictated, and it sounds sincere and is a harbinger of future publications written in similar vein in the 1930s. In a letter to a prominent Bolshevik, I. I. Skvortsov-Stepanov, he wrote again in praise of the Revolution and of all those who made it happen. The explanation for his original refusal to accept the October Revolution, he explained, was the fear that the workers would be swallowed by the anarchic forces of the peasantry and that the avant-garde of the proletariat would perish and Lenin and his Bolsheviks would be blamed. He continued: "I am a person that perceives events in life not by reason but by emotions, and this characteristic will always remain with me."[102] The letter was written on the eve of Gorky's first visit to Soviet Russia, which was planned for 1928.

How important for Gorky was the stay abroad? From N. Berberova's work, as well as from Gorky's extensive correspondence, one learns about his life in exile, of his literary output, and of his day-to-day existence. Berberova comments that he wrote better and different. The 1920s were a period of fruitful work for him because "he lived in the West and was free from political pressures because no one was dictating him what to write, and he was his own self. There was also a restful time following the events of the revolutionary years, and his personal life was happy."[103] In the six years from 1921(2) to 1928, Gorky wrote a cycle of his memoir–autobiographical work *Moi universitety*, stories, a number of literary portraits, and major works such as *Zametki iz dnevnika, Vospominaniia; Delo Artamonovykh* (The Artamonov Business), and the two volumes of *Klim Samgin*.

The futurist poet Nikolai Aseev visited Gorky in Sorrento in 1927 and left an interesting portrait of the writer, of his day-to-day life, and of the people around him. At the time of Aseev's visit, Gorky was fifty-nine years old. "Gorky," wrote Aseev, "is like a big tree well chiseled, towering over the small shoots of post-war humanity."[104] Aseev described the house of Gorky in Sorrento and the day-to day routine of the inhabitants of the villa *Il Sorrito*. Living with Gorky there was Maxim with his wife and two daughters, the painter Rakitskii, M. Budberg, "his closest friend," and a Swiss governess. Often as many as fifteen people came to dinner. After dinner, the company retired to the living room for music, singing, and conversation. Gorky was smoking a lot. A certain routine was followed in the household. Gorky's working hours began in the morning, and by 9:00 A.M. he was at his desk writing in longhand. At the time of Aseev's visit he was working on the third volume of *Klim Samgin*. Lunch was at 2:00 P.M. Gorky spent the afternoons working on his correspondence, as well as reviewing manuscripts sent to him from the Soviet Union by writers, poets, and playwrights. Aseev ends the chapter "Vstrechi s Gor'kim" full of wonder at the man he had met for the first time.[105]

And yet, was it really a period free from problems? The letters to E. Peshkova tell about concerns over Maxim. He and his family stayed with Gorky from 1922 on. In 1925, a daughter named Marfa was born. Two years later another daughter arrived, named Daria. Maxim seemed unable to use his creative abilities and his energy constructively. Gorky wrote about Maxim's love of fast vehicles, first the motorcycle and later the car. There were often excursions in the countryside and preoccupation with editing (for the enjoyment of Gorky's extended family) a satirical journal. It appears that at times Maxim's behavior was that of a child who never grew up. Gorky's love affair with Moura (M. Budberg) was not without grief either. She would often leave him and go to Estonia, allegedly to visit her children, who were being brought up by members of the Benkendorf family (her first husband's) and a devoted nanny. Because she was his translator, he depended on her knowledge of languages and thought highly of her abilities. Her trips, however, were not limited to Estonia. There were other destinations in her itineraries. She would go to meet with Wells and B. Lockhart and, what seems probable, to discharge her "duties." It is not clear whether she served the British, the German, or the Soviet intelligence.[106] Or, all three? M. Budberg stayed with Gorky until 1932, leaving a year before his final return to Soviet Russia in 1933.[107]

In Gorky's correspondence of that period one reads of her frequent absences and of Gorky's dissatisfaction and frustration over them. Thus he wrote to Khodasevich in February 23, 1923, from Saarov, that he is "in love, and very unhappily in love."[108] Further, when writing about his trip to Freiburg, he remarked: "[A]t the station in Berlin, while we were getting on the train, the Germans demanded a certificate of marriage from M. I. [Budberg] and me; said document did not prove to be in our possession, [Gorky was never officialy married to Budberg], and these pious Germans made us take separate compartments."[109] At times one reads of Gorky complaints over the moods of M. I. Trying to be humorous, Gorky informed Khodasevich that "I am going to buy a pistol, hammer its barrel first into the wall, and hang myself on the handle."[110] It seems that that kind of relationship between Gorky and M. Budberg was to continue.

Who *was* this M. Budberg? Also known as Moura, she was the former Maria Zakrevskaia-Benkendorf. Part of her past was told in the work *Memoirs of a British Agent* by Bruce Lockhart, who was the first secretary to the British Embassy in Petrograd during the Revolution and her intimate friend. But more information became available from two biographies of H. G. Wells written by his sons. One learns there that she was implicated in Lockhart's espionage activities in 1917 and was released by the GPU on condition that she would serve that institution as an informer. For that purpose she had been planted in Gorky's household by Zinoviev, who was rather suspicious of Gorky and his entourage. Gorky gave her a job in the publishing house *Vsemirnaia Literatura*. Feeling ill at ease regarding the GPU assignment, she told Gorky about her connection with that institution. Gorky made himself her protector. When in 1920 she tried unsuccessfully to cross the border to Estonia to visit her children and was caught and imprisoned, Gorky, through the offices of his first wife E. Peshkova, a friend of Dzerzhinskii, succeeded in having her released. She soon became Gorky's mistress. The same year she met H. G. Wells, who was visiting Russia at that time.[111] After a fleeting marriage to Baron Budberg, she was known as Baroness Budberg. In the work of N. Berberova, *Zheleznaia zhenshchina* (Iron Lady), more is said about M. Budberg, but not all the information is well documented.

In spite of contacts with writers, editors, and participation in a number of journals, as well as the contract with *Gosizdat*, Gorky was concerned over his popularity in his own country. Berberova makes the point that he listened anxiously to reports that "over there" they are now writing in the style of Maiakovskii, or Pil'nyak, and he was afraid that he would be forgotten.[112] The émigré press continued to be a source of annoyance, hurt, and hate. He decided to go back to the USSR, even if only for a visit.

There is little doubt that M. Budberg, E. Peshkova, and Maxim had contributed to the rapprochement with the Soviet government, which wanted him back. Gorky, on his part, could not have known that all through the years of emigration he was closely watched. From documents recently made available, it appears that Gorky had been under the surveillance of the GPU since 1922 and that a dossier on him was kept in the archives of Lubianka. His activities and his writings were carefully noted, his correspondence was scrutinized, and certain paragraphs were deleted from his letters before they were published.[113] A case in point is a letter sent from Marienbad on March 3, 1924, to E. Peshkova. The deleted paragraph read:

It is time, I think, to stop talking about my being under someone's influence. People should remember that I am 55 and have a very considerable experience of my own. . . . If I had really been susceptible to influence then long ago I would have submitted to Vladimir Ilych, who was superb at influencing others and today I would be dining on diamonds, running around with ballerinas, and riding about town in the best automobiles.[114]

People who were in one way or another in contact with the writer were also closely watched. Gorky's pamphlet "O russkom krest'ianstve," was severely criticized, as were his views on the October Revolution and his indictment of the Russian people and closeness to the anti-Bolshevik groups.[115] Gorky did not know all that. In V. Shentalinsky's recently published work, *Arrested Voices*, mentioned earlier, one finds letters sent to Gorky by anonymous writers, with very candid news regarding the new Russia. Gorky is being chastised by one signed only A. K. for his silence about the cruelties of the Bolsheviks: "Do you really feel no indignation at the cruelty of the ruling Party? Do you not feel obliged, exercising your authority and influence, to show that the Party, how loathsome and vile it is, to adopt such a casual disregard for human life?"[116] The author of the letter ends by mentioning the names of L. Tolstoy, Chekhov, and Korolenko, adding, "They would not have remained silent."[117] A letter of December 25, 1927, by one Adrian Kuzmin, contains very critical comments on Gorky's article "Desiat' let." One of the correspondents, aware of Gorky's forthcoming visit, advised him not to act like a VIP. "Do the opposite. Forget that you are a well known writer. . . . Go wherever your heart leads you as observer, as you did in your youth."

When Gorky, responding to the invitation by the government (read Stalin), decided to attend the celebration of his sixtieth birthday and the thirtieth anniversary of his literary career, he was coming to a country much changed from the one he had left in October 1921. At that time, he planned to be away for a period of three months to repair his poor health. He stayed in emigration for about six and a half years, but was not an émigré of the kind of I. Bunin or others like him. The years were peaceful, away from the horrors of the postlude of Civil War and the terror. He had time to reflect on events and, what was very important for him, to write. Ever concerned over the cultural life of his country, he tried unsuccessfully to found the journal *Beseda*, with the hope that it would enable the intellectuals of Soviet Russia to be in contact with Western culture and free them from the pen of the censor. He could use the freedom to speak up against injustices committed in the "first socialist state," as in the case of the trial of the SRs, in 1922. He was able to be in close contact with Western European writers, of whom Rolland became a very close friend, and with whom he could share his ideas and thoughts without the interference of the censor. Disappointed with the course the Revolution took, Gorky did not cut completely his ties with his country. The *pugachevshchina* and the destruction of the city and the intelligentsia he so much feared did not happen. The NEP (he was first against it) did give people some freedom, and material conditions improved. After all, this was the so-called golden period of Soviet power. Gorky soon resumed his vocation of adviser, corrector, and friend of upcoming young writers. He started to participate in a number of publications. Through E. Peshkova, his wide correspondence, and the foreign press, he was following closely developments in Soviet Russia. Visitors, among them members of the ruling elite, came and went. He was able to maintain a comfortable life style. He later wrote that, perhaps, he was "mistaken" in his judgment of 1917–1918 and after. There was some hope and excitement about the new kind of society being built by the Bolsheviks. Although informed of people's lives and work in the Soviet Union, Gorky did not know that he was under surveillance by the OGPU; he did not yet know Stalin; he did not realize that much of the achievements were of the "Potemkin villages" kind.

NOTES

1. V. F. Khodasevich, "Gor'kii," *Sovremennye zapiski*, LXX (Paris, 1940), 155.

2. N. Berberova, *Kursiv moi*, 2d ed. (New York, 1983), vol. 1, 197.

3. Akademiia Nauk SSSR. *V. I. Lenin i A. M. Gor'kii: Pis'ma, vospominaniia, dokumenty* (Moscow, 1969), 263. Hereafter refered to as *Lenin i Gor'kii: Pis'ma*.

4. *Lenin i Gor'kii: Pis'ma*, 587.

5. *Lenin i Gor'kii: Pis'ma*, 587.

6. N. Berberova, *Zheleznaia zhenshchina* (New York: 1982), 215. This is the only source where Parvus' repayment of the loan is mentioned.

7. *Neizvestnyi Gor'kii*, III (Moscow, 1994), 40–41.

8. *Lenin i Gor'kii: Pis'ma*, 218.

9. *Lenin i Gor'kii: Pis'ma*, 220.

10. *Lenin i Gor'kii: Pis'ma*, 221.

11. *Lenin i Gor'kii: Pis'ma*, 214.

12. *Lenin i Gor'kii: Pis'ma*, 215.

13. Berberova, *Kursiv moi*, 198.

14. Akademiia Nauk SSSR. *Arkhiv A. M. Gor'kogo*, IX (Moscow, 1939–1995), 213. Hereafter referred to as *Arkhiv*.

15. *Arkhiv*, IX: 213.

16. "Soobshcheniia i zametki" (Gorky on Lenin and the Revolution, 1922), *Novyi zhurnal* 124 (New York, 1976): 289–291.

17. *Arkhiv*, VII: 238. Mentioned in the letter to Lenin. See also letter to R. Rolland of October 5, 1922, *Gor'kii i Rollan*, 43, 351.

18. *Arkhiv*, VII: 238

19. *Maxim Gorky. Letters* (Moscow, 1966), 117.

20. "O russkom krest'ianstve" was published in Russian in 1922 in Berlin. Until the era of glasnost' it was not published in the Soviet Union.

21. Gor'kii, "O russkom krest'ianstve," 37.

22. Gor'kii, "O russkom krest'ianstve," 37.

23. Gor'kii, "O russkom krest'ianstve," 40–41.

24. This title has the sense of "Fever."

25. Akademiia Nauk SSSR. *Letopis' zhizni i tvorchestva A. M. Gor'kogo*, IV vols. (Moscow, 1958–1960), III, 276. Hereafter referred to as *Letopis'*.

26. E. Kuskova, "Maksim Gor'kii o krest'ianstve," in *Krest'ianskaia Rossiia* II–III (Prague, 1923): 211–214.

27. See S. P. Melgunov, *Krasnyi terror v Rossii, 1918–1923* (Berlin, 1924), 15.

28. Marc Jansen, *A Show Trial under Lenin* (The Hague, 1982), ix.

29. *Letopis'*, III: 285, 286.

30. *Letopis'*, III: 286. See also "Gorki für die Sozialrevolutsionäre," *Die Rote Fahne*, 317 (15 July, 1922).

31. V. I. Lenin: *Polnoe Sobranie sochinenii*, 5th edition, LV (Moscow, 1958–1965), XLV, 140–44.

32. Materials in Nicolaevsky Archives, the Hoover Institution (Stanford); *Russkii Berlin: 1921–1923*, L. Fleishman et al., eds. (Paris, 1983), 45.

33. *Russkii Berlin*, 45.

34. *Russkii Berlin*, 346.

35. *Lenin i Gor'kii: Pis'ma*, 264.

36. *Lenin i Gor'kii: Pis'ma*, 265.

37. *Lenin i Gor'kii: Pis'ma*, 267.

38. *Izvestiia TsK KPSS* 5 (1989): 243.

39. *Arkhiv*, VII: 243–244.

40. *Russkii Berlin*, 349. The letter was not available.

41. N. Nurim, "Protsess Eserov," *Krasnaia nov'* 4 (8), July-August (1922): 271–281.

42. See Karl Radek, *Portrety i Pamflety* (Moscow, 1927), 25.

43. Jansen, *Show Trial*, 178.

44. *Arkhiv*, VII: 72.

45. See "Maxim Gorky. Letters to Khodasevich," transl. by Hugh Mclean, *Harvard Slavic Studies* 1 (1953): 284–334.

46. "Letters to Khodasevich," VII, July 23, 1923.

47. "Letters to Khodasevich," VII, July 23, 1923.

48. "Letters to Khodasevich," IX, August 17, 1923.

49. *Arkhiv*, IX (1966): 237.

50. *Arkhiv*, IX: 401.

51. "Letters to Khodasevich," XIII, n. 2, September 27, 1923.

52. P. P. Kriuchkov (1889–1938) was from early in the 1920s a representative of the Soviet trade mission in Berlin and working in *Kniga* publishing house. In 1927 he was transfered to the office of *Mezhdunarodnaia kniga*. He was later moved to *Gosizdat* and was responsible for the publication of Gorky's works in the Soviet Union and abroad. As Gorky's secretary, he was the watchdog closely connected with the OGPU/NKVD. Accused of poisoning Gorky, Kriuchkov was shot in 1938. See *Arkhiv* XIV, for Gorky-Kriuchkov correspondece.

53. Letter to B. N. Nicolaevskii, quoted in *Russkii Berlin*, 398.

54. I. I. Ionov was the director of the Leningrad Branch of *Gosizdat*, the State Publishing House; L. B. Kamenev was a famous Bolshevik leader executed in 1936; Belitskii was a publisher and worked for *Gosizdat*.

55. "Letters to Khodasevich," XXVIII, May 1925.

56. Gorky's letter to Khodasevich. See *Novyi zhurnal* 31 (1952): 203.

57. Maksim Gor'kii, *Fragments from My Diary*, trans. by Moura Budberg (London: Penguin Books, 1940), 265.

58. I. Verov, "Maksim Gor'kii," *Novyi mir* 9 (1925): 148–150.

59. Verov, "Maksim Gor'kii," 150.

60. Barrett Clark, *Intimate Portraits* (New York, 1951), 21.

61. Clark, *Portraits*, 21.

62. Clark, *Portraits*, 21.

63. Clark, *Portraits*, 23.

64. "Letters to Khodasevich," Letter VI, July 4, 1923.

65. "Letters to Khodasevich," Letter XXII, July 1, 1924.

66. "Letters to Khodasevich," Letter XV, November, 1923; *Gor'kii i Rollan*, 88, 375. The letters were sent to N. I. Bukharin, A. I. Rykov, and L. B. Kamenev.

67. "Letters to Khodasevich," Letter XIII, September 27, 1923.

68. *Letopis'*, III: 368–369.

69. *Arkhiv*, IX: 232.

70. L. Trotsky, "The True and the False," in *On Lenin: Notes towards a Biography*, trans. by Tamara Deutscher (London, n. d.). The essay is translated from *Pravda*, October 7, 1924, 163. Not included in the Russian edition of the book.

71. Trotsky, "The True and the False," 167.

72. Trotsky, "The True and the False," 169.

73. Trotsky, "The True and the False," 173.

74. Trotsky, "The True and the False," 174.

75. Trotsky, "The True and the False," 176.

76. *Gor'kii i Rollan*, 91–93.

77. *Gor'kii i Rollan*, 93.

78. *Gor'kii i Rollan*, 88.

79. "Letters to Khodasevich," Letter XVI, August 23–24, 1924.

80. *Arkhiv*, IX: 219.

81. "Letters to Khodasevich," Letter XXI, July 20, 1925, n. 150; *Letopis'* III: 414.

82. Berberova, *Zheleznaia zhenshchina*, 181.

83. A. Lunacharskii, *Literaturnye siluety* (Moscow, 1925), 155.

84. Rafail Grigoriev, *M. Gor'kii* (Moscow, 1925), 105.

85. See K. Chukovskii, *Dve dushi Maksima Gor'kogo* (The Two Souls of Maxim Gorky) (Moscow, 1924), 34.

86. Chukovskii, *Dve dushi*, 62.

87. Chukovskii, *Dve dushi*, 69.

88. Chukovskii, *Dve dushi*, 37.

89. *Russkii Berlin*, 37.

90. *Sovremennye zapiski*, vol. 18 (1924); Zinaida Gippius, *Pis'ma k Berberovoi i Khodasevichu*, Erika Freiberg Sheikoleslami, ed. (Ann Arbor, 1978), 40–41. These accusations were unfounded. Similarly, Gippius's assertion that Gorky was guilty of refusing help to the writer V. V. Rozanov have also been proven false. ("Pis'ma A. M. Gor'kogo k V. V. Rozanovu i ego pomety na knigakh Rozanova," *Kontekst* [Moscow, 1978] 297–343). See also the critique by Gippius in T. Pachmuss, "Zinaida Gippius as a Literary Critic, with Particular Reference to Maxim Gorky," *Canadian Slavonic Papers*, VII (1965), 127–143.

91. *Arkhiv* IX: 409.

92. *Arkhiv* IX: 241–242.

93. In his letters to E. Peshkova and Kriuchkov, he refers frequently to financial problems: "Have you received money from *Ogonëk* and from *Gosizdat?* I have to know. From the latter you ought to get the sum of $500.00; from *Ogonëk*—I do not know how much" (*Arkhiv*, IX: 247). And further: "How much will *Krasnaia nov'* pay for the *Artamonovs'* (The Artamonov Business)? I must know because as far as my money matters go there is a kind of 'informality' " (*Arkhiv*, IX: 250). (This comment referred to the fact that during the 1920s there were strict regulations concerning the transfer of hard currency. *Gosizdat* owed Gorky money for the rights acquired to publish his works. The first publication of the first edition, in twenty volumes, was started in 1924, under the editorship of Gruzdev and Lunacharskii and was completed in 1928. Some of his works, in sixteen volumes, were published in Berlin by *Kniga*.)

94. The journal was established on the initiative of Krupskaia and the editor A. K. Voronskii, in February of 1921, with the support of Gorky. He took upon himself the editorship of the literary section of the journal and continued in the task till the departure from the country and later in emigration. Gorky was disappointed when Voronskii was relieved from his position of editor. The accusations against him were part of the witch hunt that started for some earlier than for others. The official explanation of Voronskii's dismisal was that he attached himself to the Opposition.

95. L. Spiridonova, "Konchaite svoe delo i pliunte v Sorrento," *Yunost'* 2 (1988), 79–83.

96. *Gor'kii: Sovetskaia pechat'*, kn. 2 (1965) (Moscow), 450.

97. *Letopis'*, III: 578; 131.

98. *Izvestiia TsK KPSS* 3 (March, 1989): 182; Letter to N. Bukharin, 1925.

99. See Gor'kii, *Sobranie sochinenii*, v. 24, 285–292; 552–553.

100. Gor'kii, *Sobranie sochinenii*, v. 24, 286.

101. Gor'kii, *Sobranie sochinenii*, v. 24, 293.

102. *Izvestia TsK KPSS* 1 (1989): 247–248. Letter to I. I. Skvortsov-Stepanov of October 15, 1927. See also letter of November 30, 1927, in which Gorky wrote against the preparations for his jubilee. Gor'kii, *Sobranie sochinenii*, vol. 30, 47–48.

103. N. Berberova, *The Italics Are Mine*, vol. 1 (London, 1991), 127.

104. Nikolai Aseev, *Vstrechi s Gor'kim*. Collected Works, vol. 5 (Moscow, 1963), 272.

105. Aseev, *Vstrechi s Gor'kim*, 271–291.

106. Anthony West, *H. G. Wells: Aspects of Life* (London, 1984), 74–75, 122–123, 143–147.

107. There are sources that mention her departure from Sorrento in 1932.

108. "Letters to Khodasevich," Letter II, February 16, 1923.

109. "Letters to Khodasevich," Letter III, June 13, 1923.

110. "Letters to Khodasevich," Letter XXV, August 10, 1924.

111. In the work by Wells' son Anthony, one reads: "In the course of few days that they [Moura and Wells] spent together in Moscow, Moura established a hold on my father's affections that was to prove unbreakable." More about M. Budberg's relationship with Wells is to be found in the A. West, *H. G. Wells: Aspects of Life* (London, 1984), 75; G. P. Wells, ed., *H. G. Wells in Love: Postscript to an Experiment in Autobiography* (London, 1984).

112. Berberova, *Zheleznaia zhenshchina*, 215.

113. V. Shentalinsky, *Arrested Voices* (London: 1996), 238.

114. Shentalinsky, *Arrested Voices*, 239.

115. Shentalinsky, *Arrested Voices*, 237; 242–243.

116. Shentalinsky, *Arrested Voices*, 245.

117. Shentalinsky, *Arrested Voices*, 246.

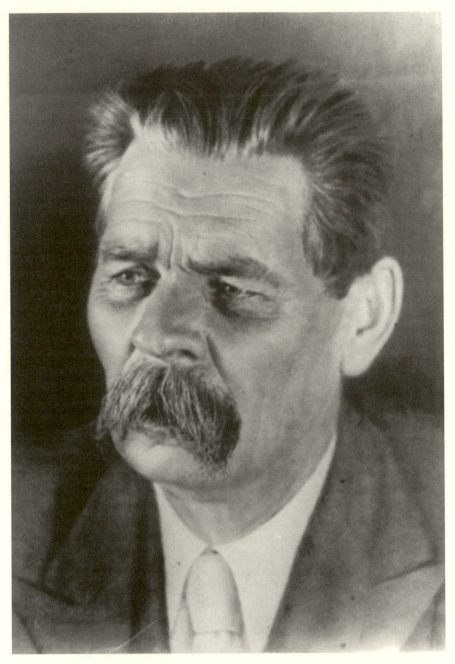

M. Gorky at the First Congress of Soviet Writers. Moscow, 1934. Reproduced courtesy of Gorky Archives of the Institute of World Literature, Moscow.

CHAPTER 8

Gorky, 1928–1936:
The Last Years

These are the times that try men's souls.

Thomas Paine

All interesting and useful work, all access to science, art, publishing
and education were in the hands of the state. The choice was either
death or adapting to the demands of authority. Adaptation was chosen for the most sincere of reasons—a wish to serve the people.

Andrei Sinyavsky, *The Russian Intelligentsia*

The period 1928 to 1936 began with Gorky's first visit to his country, now
ruled by Stalin, and ended with Gorky's death in June 1936. The over-
whelming reception accorded to the "first proletarian writer," the honors
and tributes could not but have impressed Gorky. He had, it seems, forgotten that in 1917 Stalin, furious over Gorky's criticism of the Revolution,
had relegated him to the "archives." In fact, in the years after 1928 Gorky
became the spokesman for Stalin's policies; he was on friendly terms with
the powerful Unified State Political Administration (OGPU) chief G. Yagoda and gave his *imprimatur* to what became part and parcel of the system, e.g., the forced labor camps, collectivization, and the trials of the
alleged "wreckers." In his writings Gorky glorified the achievements of the
Socialist state. At the same time, Gorky tried to promote culture within the
framework of the system, while also, when possible, becoming once again
"the great interceder" for those in difficulties with the authorities. The last

two years of Gorky's life, following Maxim's death in 1934, were the most tragic for his career, his family, and himself. Having decided that his place was in his native Russia, he returned to a country ruled by Stalin and the regime of "the Revolution from above." The motivations behind Gorky's return, his reactions to what he saw each time, and his final feelings about intellectual, political, and personal aspects of his life there remain difficult to ascertain with confidence even now; and in spite of newly released sources, certain questions still remain.

On May 20, 1928, Gorky, accompanied by his son Maxim, left Sorrento for a visit to the USSR after an absence of seven years. For a period of five consecutive years, with the exception of 1930, Gorky would divide his time between Sorrento and Moscow. He would leave in May and return in October. In 1933, his return was final. There were no more trips abroad, and the villa "Il Sorrito" was empty of its tenants. Gorky was coming back to the Russia of Stalin on the eve of the inauguration of the First Five Year Plan, at a time of feverish activity, the aim of which was to build "socialism in one country." At the beginning there were elaborate receptions, accolades, and other material rewards. After all, his approval for the measures taken to fulfill the Plans, regardless of the price, was required. Submitting to the dictates of the *"vozhd'"* [leader] Gorky, soon became a prisoner in his country, confined to a "gilded cage" with the "eye of the Inquisition on him." Gorky, who once said that "he had come to the world to disagree" and who had stood up to Lenin, was no match for Stalin and his ruthless and bloody dictatorship.

In light of what followed, which made the period 1928–1936 the most tragic of Gorky's life, we must ask why he went back. The invitation extended to him by Stalin was to come for the celebration of the thirty-fifth anniversary of his literary career and for the writer's sixtieth birthday. What did Stalin want from Gorky in the USSR? For Stalin, there was the prestige of a literary giant returning to a country where the government asserted that culture, literature in particular, was highly valued; more important, Gorky had been a friend of Lenin. Gorky might well become the propagandist of the achievements of the Soviet state and counteract the anti-Soviet activities of the émigré community. Also, Stalin wanted Gorky to write a biography of him. Gorky, clearly, had been invited back in order to serve the Revolution, the government, and ultimately "the boss," Stalin.

As to Gorky's motivations—here the views of the people closest to him shed some light on his decision. Much lay in Gorky's emerging and shifting vision of himself and his position in relation to what was happening in the USSR. To have made the decision that he did meant to some observers that he saw his rightful home there. In the recent publication of the Stalin-Gorky correspondence for the period 1929–1931, entitled: "Zhmu vashu ruku, dorogoi tovarishch" (I Press Your Hand, Dear Comrade), the editor simply says: "He did not want to remain away from the Soviet Union, and came to a tragic end."[1] Returning strained Gorky, it seems clear now, both physically and psychologically; nevertheless, returning to the USSR was attractive to him, apparently for political and perhaps for very personal reasons.

The influence on Gorky of E. Peshkova was important. She and Gorky were concerned over their son Maxim and his future. E. Peshkova wanted her son back in the USSR to get him settled. Gorky's reaction to her enthusiasm for her son's return, according to Khodasevich, was mixed. In a frank talk with this friend, Gorky confided: "Ekaterina Pavlovna was here to mix Maxim up, she wanted him back in Moscow." To Khodasevich's answer, "Let him go if he wants to," Gorky replied, "And when they (?) will finish them all, what will happen then? . . . I feel sorry for the fool. Besides, it is not only he that they are after. They think that I will follow him. And I will not go. Not on your life."[2] The year was 1925. By the time Gorky had decided to come back, in 1928, not much had changed regarding Maxim's problems, but Gorky's fears had by now become submerged. Now it was his own enthusiasm that carried the day; alas, as many scholars now fear, these enthusiasms would eventually help doom Gorky's son, whose future in Moscow depended more on his father's politics than on his own achievements, no matter how limited they were.

There were other factors. Gorky had never cut the ties with his country the way other émigrés did. He was never an emigrant in the usual sense. He continued his contacts with the young, upcoming writers in the Soviet Union, with whom he maintained a lively correspondence, whose manuscripts he read and commented on, and who came to him in Sorrento. It is as if he did not want to relinquish the role of mentor and teacher; besides, Gorky was concerned that his star was waning, what with new writers becoming popular. Was it that he did not want to spoil his biography of the first "proletarian writer," as Khodasevich would have it? Or was he concerned over the state of literature and culture in the Soviet Union, where he felt he was needed and could still make a contribution?

There were diverse professional pressures on Gorky at the time of his first return to his homeland. His last work, *Klim Samgin*, was about to be finished. He was receiving letters from people of all walks of life asking him to return. Some of that correspondence was, no doubt, a result of a well-organized campaign once Stalin decided to make Gorky come. Other letters seem to have been motivated by genuine desire for the return of the "stormy petrel." What were the other considerations? Berberova wrote of the financial problems. The income from royalties coming from the West was diminishing; the important source of funds for Gorky was now *Gosizdat* (State Publishing House), and his style of life demanded an income of about $10,000 a year. Like the complex professional imperatives, Gorky's personal reasons influenced his decision to come back.

The Western Europe of the 1920s was not the Europe of the Capri period. In between had been World War I, and much had changed. Gorky seems likely to have been disappointed at the political climate in pre–World War II Italy, particularly saddened by the failure of the socialist movements in Western Europe, and rather naively envious of those living in the "miracle" of the Communist state. In his writings Gorky had always emphasized the importance of work, and now he was impressed by the tempo of activity in Russia and by the progress made in the ten years after the October Revolution. M. Budberg was encouraging him to mend fences with the Soviet authorities, and an important obstacle to his return had been removed, since Zinoviev was no longer a threat after 1928. The struggle for power in the Party was over, and Stalin was now about to become the undisputed leader. Trotsky was in exile, soon to be expelled from the country, and many of the Bolshevik old guard were in disgrace. Politically, for Gorky, returning must have been attractive, for it seems probable that Gorky's irrepressible idealism would be served best by returning home, as he must have thought. In fact, some commentators connect the return of Gorky with the persecution of the oppositionists:

Among those actively opposed to the persecution of oppositionists, . . . was Maxim Gorky. Moreover, his great ambition was to assist in a reconciliation between the Party and the intelligentsia—to lead the Soviet regime, of which he had originally disapproved, into the social humanism he believed it capable of. It was partly for this reason that he had compromised himself by returning from Italy in 1928, and defending the regime against its external critics.[3]

This point of view, in the light of recently published sources, cannot be substantiated, but its possibility as an explanation of Gorky's desire to return cannot be ignored.[4]

Whatever the precise balance among these imperatives behind Gorky's decision to go to Moscow for the first time, the fact is clear: Gorky returned, and the USSR was ready for him, prepared by the government of Stalin to accord him the highest reception. Preparations to host the "first proletarian writer" were on the way prior to his arrival. From his letters to A. B. Khalatov, Stalin's plenipotentiary, one learns that Gorky was opposed to the fanfare that was being orchestrated. He wrote that he would refuse any kind of medals or awards.[5] In a letter to A. I. Rykov, dated December 10, 1927, Gorky repeated his desire to come quietly, to travel peacefully in the country, and asked that the celebrations be postponed for at least five years or until his departure.[6] In spite of his protestations, the campaign to honor the writer continued. The Moscow committee of VLKSM (Communist Youth League) was instructed to popularize Gorky's works.[7] In a resolution of March 29, the Council of People's Commissars officially congratulated Gorky on his sixtieth birthday and the thirty-fifth anniversary of his literary work. It read: "The Council of People's Commissars resolves to acknowledge the great service of Gorky for the workers,

the proletarian Revolution, and the Union of Soviet Socialist Republics."[8]
He was showered with congratulatory letters and wires coming from individuals and collectives.[9] By now, the government-sponsored campaign to
induce Gorky to return to the USSR, at least temporarily, was in high gear;
undoubtedly, the campaign's aim was Gorky's eventual permanent resi-
dence in the USSR as a literary and political prize, an icon for national and
international observers.

Arriving with Maxim in Moscow May 27, Gorky was met by the Party
and state luminaries K. E. Voroshilov, S. Ordzhonikidze, A. V. Lunacharskii, and M. M. Litvinov. Representatives of the writers' community were
also present. He found a warm reception from the people, too. To what
extent this was staged is difficult to determine. One can assume that for
certain elements of the population his return meant the return of an errant
son to his homeland, and for those opposed to the repressive regime there
was hope that some humanizing factor was returning with Gorky. In the
thinking of the Party, and of Stalin in particular, it was important to show
Gorky that his coming was a great event for the people. The government
raised at least part of the massive showing of respect for the returning
Gorky.

From the first, Gorky's initial return to the USSR was designed by Stalin's
people to be a great success, for the leader, the government, the political
and intellectual systems that were developing, and, of course, the writer.
There exists a memoir written by one P. Moroz, former head and War
Commissar in 1920 on the South Western Front and in 1930 in charge of
the enterprise Sevgresstroi near Sevastopol', as published in 1954 in *Sotsialisticheskii vestnik* (Socialist Herald). Moroz was Gorky's guide in 1928
during his trip through Northern Caucasus and had an opportunity to
observe Gorky's reaction to receptions staged for him and to talk to him
in confidence. Moroz wrote:

When the announcement came over the radio that Gorky was coming, and that the
inhabitants of the capital were called to greet the great writer in a manner that he
deserved, the call was answered with support that was not given to any other
undertaking of the Party or government. Many had a warm feeling toward the
writer, and the hope that they will find in him a savior. Everybody thought that
the "stormy petrel" of freedom . . . will not be silent.[10]

Moroz continued that Gorky said of the reception accorded him, "Such
grandiose reception can be staged only in two instances: either by the people who live in satisfying conditions, material, spiritual and political, or by
people who find themselves in deject poverty, material, political, spiritual,
and are enslaved."[11] Gorky seems to have been suspicious. Distrust of what
Gorky was seeing would surface rarely, but from time to time, he would
put aside officially desired elation about what he saw in his homeland;

Gorky's naiveté, real or pretended, would then be replaced by more critical examination.

Soon he would learn of the situation in the country from letters, which he would answer in articles (to be discussed) entitled "Mekhanicheskim grazhdanam" (For the Mechanical Citizens). But Gorky's comments made in the discussion with Moroz were substantially different from the answers contained in these articles. For in talking to Moroz he confided, "The forms of implementing measures of this kind of socialism will be, no doubt, very severe."[12] On Gorky's reaction to the visit to a collective farm, Moroz writes, "When asked by one A. A. Andreev who accompanied him in Rostov on the Don, what he [Gorky] thought about collectivization, he answered: 'All this collectivization should be build only on a voluntary basis, no coercion should be used. Only then would collectivization bring some good results.' "[13] And yet, very soon Gorky would clearly declare himself a supporter of collectivization without volition.

More light is shed on the official orchestration of Gorky's return in 1928 in the recently published diary of the writer Mikhail Prishvin.[14] Prishvin met Gorky in 1911, when the collection of the former's works was first published in Gorky's publishing house, *Znanie*. The two writers met rarely, but carried on a correspondence for many years. Called upon to attend a meeting with Gorky shortly after his arrival, Prishvin notes, on May 30, 1928, that he is in a quandary as to what he should say to Gorky about the new literature that is being written and about the writers.

If one would to tell Gorky everything, then, first of all, one would have to tell him that his jubilee was not organized by the people, the workers, the peasants, or admirers. It was all arranged by the government, just as all other Soviet celebrations are. The government could say today: "Kiss Gorky"—and all will do it. And when tomorrow, the order will come "to spit on Gorky," all will comply. . . . Julius Caesar never had a reception of the sort accorded to Gorky. . . . I begin to understand Gorky's state jubilee on the background of Russian history. . . . This jubilee is a striking document of the Russian peoples' obedience to the state bureaucratic system.[15]

In the entry of June 3, Prishvin tells of the reaction of rank-and-file workers to Gorky's arrival: "Russian Gorky has arrived," said one. Asked about the meaning of the statement, the man replied: "Well, there was the Italian, fascist Gorky, now it is the Russian, communist Gorky." An exchange of views followed:

Gorky, the writer, whose task was to observe and to write, left. Yes, he was capable of arousing the masses but when they heeded the call, he got frightened and left. . . . Gorky is now close to Stalin. Gorky takes the place of Ilich. . . . Of course, Ilich expelled him. . . . And now we are receiving him. Why? Ilich is probably turning over in his grave.[16]

There was also the acknowledgment from one of the interlocutors of the impact Gorky's works had on the lives of ordinary people. "Gorky! I was brought up on his writings. I am against the reception he is accorded now, undeserving. He left us, went to Italy, lived there with the fascists, now came the Russian Gorky."[17] A few short statements in Prishvin's diary indicate that Gorky understood the situation in the country. He told Prishvin, "I am a sly person. It is not that I will not use all that they have arranged for me." When one of the writers told him to go and see things on his own, he replied: "If so, I will see nothing."[18] Gorky was undeservedly confident, as we know now, and did not so easily deconstruct the "Potemkin villages" that Stalin presented for him, the criticism of intellectuals, and the official blinders he had to wear.

After his arrival, Gorky was invited to a appear at meetings and assemblies. In a speech delivered May 31, at the meeting of the "Plenum of the Moscow Council with the Professional and Party Organizations dedicated to the Social-political and Literary activities of M. Gorky," the writer extolled the achievements evident in all areas of life and in particular in the field of culture. He continued:

Why, then, comrades, is it sometimes bitter to read in the newspapers, when you abuse each other too harshly, too . . . mercilessly. . . . If every one of you would not be a good worker, then you could not have achieved all that you did. . . . I do not know, but one has to have a better approach. . . . No, one has to treat each other better.[19]

What was the rationale for those comments? Did he have in mind the struggle in the Party? The literary community? On June 6, he attended a meeting of workers' representatives (*Rabkory*) of the city of Moscow, chaired by Lenin's sister, M. I. Ulianova. Gorky, in answer to a question regarding his membership in the Party, replied:

If I should be asked to join the Party, I would consider it a great honor. But I think that it is more useful that I remain somewhere close to the Party, in the capacity of some kind of "partisan." For in that capacity I am being listened to by other people and quite attentively. I know and consider this approach more beneficial for the cause which you are engaged in, and which I will serve to the best of my ability for that is my duty.[20]

As mentioned earlier, the question of Gorky's Party membership has been a matter of debate by no means resolved. The late Valerii Tarsis, dissident writer, exiled from the Soviet Union following his release from a psychiatric hospital, met with the present writer in July 1982 in Bern, Switzerland. He maintained that Gorky was never a member of the Party. "Why," he remarked, "had Gorky been a card-carrying Bolshevik, his Party card would be on display in newspapers and journals." In a discussion regarding this question with the *gor'kovedy* (Gorky scholars) in Moscow, in December 1989, the present author was told that Gorky was a member of the Party, which he joined in 1905, but he did not renew his membership in 1917 and never rejoined it. Still, in letters and in articles that Gorky wrote on his return to the USSR, one finds much praise for the Party and its leadership. Addressing the workers of Sormovo, the industrial district of his native city, Niznii Novgorod, he said:

It seems to me that you treat the people who had taught the working class . . . to take into its hands political power in the country, with little confidence and attention. I am talking about the Party. I am not a Party member, I am not a communist, but I cannot honestly refrain from telling you that the Party is your brain, your strength, in reality your leader, a leader of a kind that the proletariat In the West, to its regret and grief [!] has not got.[21]

More about Gorky's visit and his activities comes to light in a work that appeared in 1994, entitled *Neizvestnyi Gor'kii* (The Unknown Gorky). Included there is the correspondence of Gorky and the then Deputy Chairman of the OGPU, Genrikh G. Yagoda. The letters belong to the period 1928–1936 and are an important source, published for the first time for the understanding of Gorky's stand on many issues. Both Yagoda and Gorky were natives of Nizhnii Novgorod. Yagoda's wife came from the Sverdlov family and was related to Gorky's adoptive son, Zinovii Peshkov (Sverdlov). Yagoda had no doubt been instructed to watch over Gorky, but the surveillance did not start with Yagoda. A file on Gorky had been kept in the archives of the OGPU as early as 1922.[22] In 1928 Gorky knew of Yagoda's position and influence in the Party and the government; and the year marked the beginning of the so-called friendship and the exchange of letters, with praise of labor communes of the OGPU and of the work of the "Cheka Men." Gorky was impressed with the communes for the young offenders run by the OGPU. The communes seemed to him a good solution for education through productive labor, which was allegedly the purpose of these institutions. In the short term, it appears that the staging for Gorky's visits was quite successful, although the whole of his trip was carefully managed and controlled.

In the four and a half months of his first visit to the Soviet Union, Gorky travelled widely. His impressions were later described in the articles entitled "Po Soiuzu Sovetov" (Around the Union of the Soviets).[23] Among the places Gorky visited was the Bolshevo labor commune near Moscow, established in the former Nikolo-Ugreshski Monastery. Here, enthusiastic about the visit, Gorky wrote the following in the guest book: "As for one who was considered in the past as 'socially dangerous' I say in all sincerity that here was established a very important enterprise."[24] Next came a meet-

ing with A. S. Makarenko, the head of one of the communes, and a visit
to one located near Kharkov and named after Gorky. He had nothing but
praise for the work done to rehabilitate the *"bezprizornye"* (homeless) par-
entless victims of the revolutionary era and the Civil War. He later wrote
an introduction to the book by M. S. Pogrebinskii, the director of the labor
communes, entitled *The Labor Commune of the OGPU.*[25] He praised
Makarenko's work *Putevka v zhizn'* (The Road to Life) and the work of
the Cheka men:

I will remind you of what is said in the *Road of Life* about the "Cheka men." Like
you, I rate highly and respect the comrades working in this area. In Russia, little
has been written about them, and that badly. . . . It would be good if you, who has
seen something of these security men, were to write a short sketch, or a story,
entitled *The Cheka Men.*[26]

What else did Gorky see and write during his stay? Mention is made in
a number of sources that he went about Moscow in disguise, visiting res-
taurants and tea houses to see for himself how the city lived.[27] As to his
efforts regarding publications, Gorky met with Krupskaia and members of
Gosizdat (State Publishing House) discussing the publication of Russian
classics and was one of the contributors to the journal *Nashi dostizheniia*
(Our Achievements). He left the country on October 12, 1928. A long
article appeared in *Pravda* on October 13, explaining that the reason for
his departure was the state of his health and the need to spend the winter
months in a warm climate. So that people would not be disappointed, the
article ended with the announcement that he would be "allowed" (by the
doctors, presumably) to return the following May.[28] How successful had
the visit been? It was definitely successful as far as Stalin was concerned,
and one source mentions that for Gorky it was financially successful. In a
wire sent July 20, 1928, addressed to the Secretary of State, Washington,
D.C., an official of the Legation of the United States of America in Riga
wrote:

Sir: With reference to the exploitation of the visit of Maxim Gorky to the Soviet
Union for propaganda purposes, I have the honour to report that the *Posledniia
Novosti*, Paris, July 1, 1928, reported that Gorky had sold certain publication rights
to the *Gosizdat* for $362,000. I have the honour to be, Sir, your obedient servant,
F.W.B. Coleman.[29]

After returning to Italy, Gorky wrote a number of articles published in
Pravda and *Izvestiia*, which were later included in his collected works.
"Mekhanicheskim Grazhdanam SSSR: Otvet korrespondentam" (To the
Mechanical Citizens of USSR: An Answer to the Correspondents) sheds
some light on the reaction by the rank and file to the writer's visit. He

wrote that he received over a thousand letters during the four-and-a-half-month stay, out of which close to two hundred were written by individuals with strong anti-Soviet views. He called them "mechanical citizens," meaning those who just by chance found themselves citizens of the Soviet Union and who wrote anti-Soviet, anti-working class, and indeed anti–the writer letters. These letters stated that Lenin was the Anti-Christ; the Bolsheviks were German spies; Lenin was a German spy; and Gorky, a friend of Lenin, was considered also a German spy; the old regime appeared to be an unobtainable heaven. Gorky's reply was to go back to his own past, to write of the sordidness of life during the "old regime" and to extol the new order. He finished by saying that only the Bolsheviks had the right answer:

I found the genuine revolutionary spirit only among the Bolsheviks, in Lenin's articles, in the speeches and the work of the members of the intelligentsia that followed them. I came close to them already in 1903. I did not join the Party and remained a "partisan" who was sincerely dedicated to the great task of the working class and in whose final victory over the "old world" I do not doubt.[30]

Later, in a letter to P. P. Kriuchkov sent from Sorrento, Gorky complained that the émigré paper *Rul* (Helm) "suspects" that he [Gorky] is sending the letters of the "Mechanical Citizens" to the GPU, adding: "and they [the émigrés] are not ashamed, the scoundrels."[31] The article "O Beloemigrantskoi literature" (On Literature of the White Emigration), published in *Pravda* on May 11, 1928, just before his departure for the Soviet Union, shows Gorky's attitude towards the émigrés and that his now-known views on the character of the Russian *narod*.[32] In the article Gorky did not hesitate to attack in harsh terms members of the literary intelligentsia of the White movement, Merezhkovskii, Gippius, and Filosofov, and leaders of the parties that lost to the Bolsheviks, A. Kerenskii, P. Miliukov and F. Dan, to name a few. As to his views on the *narod*, these had not changed since the publication "O russkom krest'ianstve," in 1922: The *narod* is cruel and even in its cruelty very talented, and the blame for its cruelty was the autocratic system of the tsars, oppressive and merciless. History is to blame. "One has to acknowledge . . . that no other European people was taught in such terrible university of blood, torture, cynical mass murders . . . as the Russian people were."[33] Gorky was proving to be an apologist for the Stalin regime, internationally as well as nationally, and perhaps unintentionally as well as intentionally.

The reaction to Gorky's return to the Soviet Union by the émigré community was not long in coming. In an article published in 1928, his one-time friend E. Kuskova called Gorky the "Obeskrylennyi sokol" (Falcon with Severed Wings) and wrote that:

Gorky was never only an artist, he was actively engaged in public life. . . . He had assumed a certain stand as a political figure. . . . In his teachings, in the complexity of his ideas, there was, no doubt, the spirit of the Russian pre-revolutionary times. Under Stalin he became the official registrar of the "splendid achievements of the new regime."

Kuskova ends her article with an ironic comment:

The Soviets are accepting Gorky and are asking him: You have erred, Maksi-mushka, in October? Never mind! We have also erred. We thought you to be a *sokol* (falcon), and we found that you are only a *kanareika* (a canary). A pleasant bird.[34]

But Gorky had left for Sorrento and resumed the style of life to which he was by now accustomed. Visitors came and went. He continued his correspondence with writers from the Soviet Union and Western Europe— Romain Rolland, Stefan Zweig, H. G. Wells, and others. Kriuchkov was more and more involved in the publication of Gorky's works, as well as being his financial contact with *Gosizdat;* he was the main consultant of the scientific and literary section of the journal *Nashi dostizheniia* and was asked to take on responsibilities regarding contributions to old and new journals. In the country the Five Year Plan had been decided upon. The peasants would soon be herded into the collectives, and Gorky thought of enlightening them about the life of the peasant in the West. He was at that moment in total support of the regime and in contact with Stalin.

That Gorky seems not to have realized fully the nature of the new order is evident in some of his letters written before 1929. In writing to Stalin, he recommends Karl Radek for editor of a new publication, *Za rubezhom* (Abroad), aimed at informing the people of the events in Western Europe and the world: "Radek's unorthodoxy in Party matters should not be an obstacle, for the task of the journal is very simple and clear."[35] At the same time it seems he did realize that something was not quite right in the Party and wrote that he felt a mood of disillusionment among the young. Mentioned were the letters previously dismissed by him in the article "Mekhanicheskim grazhdanam." His comments regarding the mood in the country were also based on letters appearing in the émigré press. Who was to blame for Gorky's unusual moment of wavering support for the regime? Gorky thought that the Party was not educating the young as to the changes that were taking place in society and, that the main reason was the struggle that was going on in the Party, fomented (Gorky's idea) by the *makhaevtsy*.[36] The struggle within the Party, which in any case had very limited human resources, resulted in "wretched" people being put in positions of authority, people who were against culture and the intelligentsia. More attention was to be paid to the cultural and political education of the youth, and the new life that was being created by the worker had to be written about. The successes of the First Five Year Plan had to be widely publicized, and the people of the USSR and the literati in particular had to be re-educated. In the same letter Gorky advocated an increase in anti-religious propaganda through the publication of anti-religious literature, scientific comments to the Bible, and the writing of a history of the Catholic church (why Catholic is not clear). Concerned with the education of the people, he urged Stalin to approve the proposal of writing a history of the Civil War, in order to enlighten the peasant in particular of the role of the White movement and the foreign intervention.[37]

For the second time, in May 26, 1929, Gorky left Sorrento for Moscow, this time in the company of his son and daughter-in-law. The accolades in honor of the writer continued. Gorky was chosen a member of the Central Committee of the Soviet of Deputies by the Congress. But more significant was his first open praise of the Chief Administration of Corrective Labor Camps (GULAG) established on the Solovetski Islands, in an old monastery. While the tributes paid to Gorky continued or even increased at this time, his blindness to the problems of his homeland under Stalin also increased, if we judge by Gorky's recorded impressions and his subsequent actions in support of Stalin. The report of this trip is contained in the cycle of impressions entitled "Po Soiuzu Sovetov," Part V, subtitled "Solovki."[38] He wrote, "I came here with Matvei Pogrebinskii, the organizer of the labor communes, the author of the work on the Bolshevo commune . . . a man who knew well the world of 'socially dangerous' (elements)."[39] Gorky was quite taken by the "clean barracks, big windows," and the "interesting" talks he had with the inmates. He had a chance to read some depositions that attested to the guilt of one of the men he met.[40] Gorky visited the women's quarters in the company of a guide who enlightened him as to the "crimes" of the prisoners. The cultural events, including a concert, were impressive. There was a library, a museum, and newspapers. Following a lengthy discourse on the importance of camps such as the "Solovki," Gorky came to the conclusion that "camps such as 'Solovki' were absolutely necessary, as well as the labor communes the likes of Bolshevo. Only by this road would the state achieve in the fastest possible time one of its aims: to get rid of prisons."[41]

By October 1929, Gorky was on his way back to Sorrento. He did not come to Moscow in 1930, returning only in May of 1931, and this too for a period of four months, but his ties with the country continued, and the exchange of letters with Stalin as well as with some of the writers reflected Gorky's views on the events of this period. The First Five Year Plan was well under way, the *kulaks* were being liquidated, and collectivization was forcefully being imposed. Gorky could not have been oblivious to the fact that the period from 1929 to 1931 was a very important period in the history of the Soviet Union. Stalin, having first destroyed the Left opposition of Trotsky and his followers, had now turned against the Right, led by N. Bukharin, A. I. Rykov, and M. A. Tomskii. The latter wanted the

continuation of the New Economic Policy (NEP) albeit with some modifi-
cations. All three were removed from the Politburo. With the Five Year
Plan officially approved at the Sixteenth Party Congress in April 1929, the
emphasis was on rapid industrialization and collectivization. To support
Stalin in his plans, three new members were appointed to the Politburo,
M. Kalinin, V. Molotov, and K. Voroshilov. From the onset the imple-
mentation of the Five Year Plan was fraught with many difficulties. The
deficiencies of the Plan were now blamed on the work of saboteurs
("wreckers"). It is little surprise that trials of the "wreckers" were staged.
First came the Shakhty trial, an open trial with A. Ia. Vyshinskii presiding.
The accused were engineers working in the coal industry and were con-
victed on trumped-up charges of sabotage and ties with the émigrés. Of the
fifty-three defendants, four were acquitted, five were executed, and the rest
were given prison terms of four to ten years. The pattern of defendants
admitting their guilt was to become the standard feature of these trials. In
the fall of 1930, a sabotage and espionage organization was "discovered"
in the food supply system, with Professor A. V. Riasantsev, formerly a
member of the Menshevik party, as head. This was a closed trial, and all
forty-eight defendants were shot. Soon after, on November 7, 1930, a political trial was held in Moscow. This time it was an open trial. A group
of technical specialists was accused of "wrecking" and of counter-
revolutionary activities as members of the *Prompartiia* (Industrial Party).
Among the accused were specialists prominent in their fields: L. K. Ramzin,
director of the Institute of Heat Engineering; I. A. Kalinnikov, deputy chairman of the production section of Gosplan (State Planning Commission);
and V. I. Ochikin, head of the Department of Scientific Research of the
Supreme Council of the National Economy (VSNKh). There were allegedly
two thousand members of that Industrial Party, most of them highly qual-
ified technical specialists. The reaction of the West European press and the
stand taken by Western socialists friendly to the Soviet Union and Stalin
was an important factor in that the death sentence imposed on leaders was
commuted to various forms of imprisonment. The last was of the Union
Bureau of the Committee of the Menshevik party. Most Mensheviks who
remained in the country held responsible positions in economic and planning institutions. They were now accused of wrecking, of having contacts
with the émigré Mensheviks, and of forming a secret bloc with the *Prompartiia* and the toiling Peasant Party, the purpose of which was to instigate
armed intervention from abroad and an insurrection in the country. They
were accused of ties with the Trotskyites and members of the Right opposition. Among the defendants were D. B. Riazanov, the director of the
Marx-Engels Institute; Professor V. G. Groman, of Gosplan; N. N.
Sukhanov, economist and writer; and A. M. Ginzburg, economist. Fourteen
of the defendants were sentenced to imprisonment ranging from five to ten
years. None survived the prison terms.

Repression struck not only the technical intelligentsia, but also military specialists.[42] This period saw the institutionalizing of the labor camps under the name GULAG, mentioned earlier. The trials served a propaganda purpose, and as an excuse for the failures in achieving the economic targets by blaming it all on *vrediteli* (wreckers). Stalin was interested that Gorky write a play about the wreckers. In the Stalin-Gorky correspondence of 1929–1931, mentioned earlier, the theme of the letters is the guilt of the act of sabotage and the guilt of the saboteurs. Yagoda supplied Gorky, on Stalin's orders, with materials for the projected play. Here "Gorky's socialist ideology merged with the Stalinism, ever-increasing in its strength."[43] Gorky, still naive about the results of government policies and far removed from the inner circle, seems simply to have believed what he was told; whenever he felt concerned about Stalinist policies, he would choose to overlook it. Thus, he became a "yes-man," in the main approving of all that was perpetrated by Stalin and his henchmen. Materials for the projected play *Somov i drugie* (Somov and the Others) were forwarded to Gorky in Sorrento.[44] Although the play was staged only in 1941 after Gorky's death, his belief and trust in what were trumped-up charges in all the just-mentioned trials was one more proof of his readiness to serve Stalin's goals. Gorky's comments on the trial of the *Prompartiia* come to light in a letter to Yagoda.[45] "I was pretty shaken by these skillfully organized acts of sabotage," he wrote Stalin, "but at the same time happy with the work of OGPU."[46] The extensive pattern of Gorky's support remains difficult for those sympathetic to the writer to accept. Arrested and soon to be tried were Gorky's friends and acquaintances, among them N. Sukhanov, L. Ramzin, and V. Groman. Concerned over the safety of Stalin and Yagoda, he wrote, "Having read of these adventurers who are on the hunt for you and Yagoda, I was appalled by the inadequate measures taken for the safety of our Party leaders."[47]

Although Gorky submitted few requests to Stalin, he did try to offer support in getting an exit visa for some writers, publication of the works of others, and alleviation of the fate of those imprisoned, often on requests from Rolland. But by and large in his articles he showed approval of Stalin's policies. In one, entitled "Gumanistam" (To Humanists), first published in *Pravda*, and *Izvestiia*, December 11, 1930, Gorky approved of the punishment of the forty-eight "criminals" mentioned earlier, who had allegedly organized the food famine in the USSR.[48] When the discussion of forced labor was on the agenda of the Sixth Congress of the Soviets and criticism of it appeared in the West, Gorky wrote the article "Po povodu odnoi legendy" (On the Legend), published in *Pravda* on March 11, 1931. There he denied what he called the calumnious accusations made in Western press of the use of forced labor in the USSR.[49] In addition to the open approval and justification of the regime's tactics, well documented in his letters, Gorky continued his efforts to publish journals and books glorifying the Soviet state and its achievements. It was necessary, he thought, to include history, and Gorky prepared for Stalin a detailed outline of a projected work on "The History of the Civil War."[50] His letters to Stalin show servility to and adulation of the leader. He wrote on November 12, 1931:

Be well and take care of yourself. Last summer, in Moscow [summer of 1931], I expressed to you my feelings of deep, comradely affection and respect. Please, allow me to repeat this. This is not a compliment, but a need to tell a comrade "I hold you in esteem, you are a good man, a determined [strong] Bolshevik." . . . I know how difficult things are for you.[51]

There are other surprises in the correspondence. One is the bitter criticism of his former friend and companion, the poet V. F. Khodasevich, who with his wife N. Berberova had stayed with Gorky when in exile for a period of three years. Their friendship went back to 1918.[52] Gorky's flattery of Stalin seems to have run away with him when, in a letter of December 1, 1931, concerned over Stalin's safety in case an attempt on his life should be made by the émigrés, he wrote:

Who could take your place, in case these scoundrels would succeed to kill you? Do not be angry, I have the right to be worried, and to advise. As a matter of fact, all the leaders of the Party, and the government should take a greater care of their safety.[53]

In his many pronouncements and publications he maintained that the main task of government was to educate the peasant, to forestall sabotage, and by force, if necessary, make people fulfill the Plan. For all those in the way there was to be an answer: Gorky's article "Esli vrag ne sdaetsia, ego unichtozhaiut" (If the Enemy Does Not Surrender, He Is to Be Destroyed) appeared in *Pravda* on November 15, 1930.

The Soviet people are aiming to build a new world order! In this new world order there is to be equality, equal opportunity to develop one's abilities, freedom to do it, and conditions propitious to that development.

The undertaking is difficult but possible. Within thirteen years of its dictatorship, the working class succeeded in winning the Civil War and in getting rid of the interventionists and the White armies.

The working class under the leadership of the Party will succeed in fulfilling the plans, as will the collective farmers.

Explaining the importance of fighting sabotage carried out by the enemies, he writes, "we still are in the midst of a Civil War. Thus, naturally, the conclusion is: if the enemy does not surrender, he is to be destroyed."[54] Once more, Gorky was blind to the suffering of the peasants and all opponents of the regime.

In fact, there are significant signs of Gorky's growing ties to the regime. His closeness to the OGPU through the friendship with Yagoda is painfully obvious from their correspondence, although the editor of the work containing the letters tries hard to exonerate the writer by emphasizing his (Gorky's) "hidden objectives." The editor maintains that Gorky actually intended to assist people in trouble with the OGPU. This attempt to rescue Gorky's reputation remains, in light of the scarcity of evidence supporting the view, unconvincing.[55] At the same time, the correspondence reveals a Gorky prodded (in some instances) by his friend, Rolland,[56] helping the Italian anarchist, Francesco Getsi, to leave the Soviet Union. Following was the case of the French communist Victor Serge, where both Rolland and Gorky were involved in getting him out of the Soviet Union.[57] The latter case dragged on and was resolved only in 1936. One reads in disbelief Gorky's letter to Yagoda of November 2, 1930, where he congratulates him and his subordinates for having served the working class well by uncovering those "guilty" of "wrecking" the Plan.[58] It appears that Gorky really believed or wanted Stalin and those observing his every move that he believed the depositions of the defendants and expressed disappointment for being absent at the trial.[59]

By 1931, there were over two million inmates in the labor camps, and close to seven thousand of the country's engineers were under arrest. The alliance of the Party and the noncommunist specialists came to an end. Earlier, in a letter to Rolland of October 30, 1930, Gorky tried to convince him of the guilt of those accused in the case of *Prompartiia* and the Mensheviks, as being saboteurs, and insisted that the confessions of the defendants were not obtained through the use of torture.[60] Gorky, manipulated by the OGPU was giving it a helping hand, as he had in a few earlier situations. It is evident that he praised the progress made in collectivizing the peasant, considering it to be very important and beneficial:

[F]ollowing the Party's decisive push towards collectivization—the social Revolution is assuming genuinely socialist character. This is an upheaval of geological proportions, and it is by far greater than anything carried out by the Party. What is happening is that the the kind of life that lasted for thousands of years is being destroyed, a system that produced a person particularly hateful, terrifying by an animal like conservatism and instinct of possessiveness.[61]

He continued: "The task is to re-educate them in the shortest possible time—this is an unbelievably difficult task. And yet, it is being accomplished."[62] In order to emphasize the magnitude of change that was taking place in the village, he wrote of the old foundations of peasants' lives that were being destroyed, hence the strength of their reaction. "One can construct anew a church that was destroyed and put in it any kind of a god [*sic!*], but when land disappears under one's feet, this can never be recovered."[63] Gorky's approval of the process of collectivization imposed on the peasant with the ruthless might of the Party can only be explained by his old distrust of the peasant and his readiness to submit to the Party's dictates.

N. Valentinov commented:

As terrible as it is to say, that barbarian operation could not make Gorky condemn it, because of his hatred of the peasant. Thus he could see in Stalin's actions a way to save Russia from the danger coming from the illiterate masses of the peasantry. It does not mean that there was an identification of Gorky's views with Stalin's, but it is here that they met.[64]

And yet, Valentinov, questioning Gorky's sensitivity, added: "A sensitive person could not have been with [i.e., supported] Stalin in the years 1928–34."[65] For Gorky, the uncultured, uneducated peasant, ruthless and vengeful, was to be changed by the collective through a campaign designed to educate him and make him into a cultured member of a cultured society. If private property was the cause, then the abolition of private property in land would ensure reform of the peasantry. Is it possible that Gorky was really unaware of the price already being paid for the transformation of both the individual and the peasant class?

Gorky must have been aware that the work of rewriting history had begun, but he did not oppose it. In 1930, the year when Stalin began building the cult of the leader, Gorky away in Sorrento was rewriting the memoir on Lenin that was published in 1924. The new version appeared under the title "V. I. Lenin." Some of the paragraphs of the original were reworded, others omitted. Lenin's laudatory comments on Trotsky, cited in the original, were now erased. Trotsky, expelled from the country and criticized for his ideas, was an inconvenient subject for praise. Eliminated also were the favorable remarks regarding the Jews. The last paragraph conveyed the idea of a glorious future under the leadership of Lenin's successors. Stalin's name was not mentioned. Millions of copies of the "new" "V. I. Lenin" were published, and generations of Soviet citizens were brought up with the "doctored" version while the 1924 original was buried in the archives.[66]

On June 5, 1930, Gorky was sending Stalin a letter where he wrote of the need to educate the village youth that lags behind in its political awareness. The solution? Addressing Stalin with the normal greeting "Dear Iosif Vissarionovich," he asked once again that a history of the Civil War be researched and published. "Beginning 1928, I have demanded that a history of the Civil War be published which is something needed for the political and socialist education of the peasantry."[67] It was an ambitious project that Gorky was determined to undertake. Accordingly, he suggested an editorial board: it was to consist of K. E. Voroshilov, A. S. Bubnov, and

M. N. Pokrovskii, as well as V. M. Molotov, S. M. Kirov, Ia. B. Gamarnik, and Stalin. The Central Committee of the Party ordered that materials be collected by Party members, Soviet, and military personnel entrusted with the collection of documents, memoirs, and biographies of active participants in the war. The first volume edited by Gorky appeared a year after his death; the last, the fifth, appeared in 1960. Gorky was taking upon himself the editorial work of the literary section. The organization of the new enterprise was to be given to Kriuchkov. A long list of names followed, mainly of writers who would be responsible for the style of the work and who, in the majority of cases, would have been familiar with the events of the Civil War in one or another place of action. The work when completed was to be placed in all Red Army libraries. Added to Gorky's requests was the project, mentioned before, of a newspaper for the peasantry. The objective of the proposed publication was to acquaint the peasant with life, politics, and the history and measures taken by the colonial powers in Asia and Africa in their repressive policy towards the peasant. The concluding sentence is interesting: "[The newspaper] has to acquaint the peasantry with the process of disintegration of the bourgeois states' organizations." The letter ends with a warm greeting: "All the best. I firmly press your hand."[68]

A few months following, Gorky received a letter from the writer L. M. Leonov, sent from Moscow, dated October 21, 1930:

We live in very difficult times. The *perestroika* is of a kind that nothing like it was happening since Jeremiah's times. All around us everything crumbles, there is a constant din in the ears, and small wonder that in the district of Volsk . . . they report that 65% of men are suffering from heart disease. There is no way back now. . . . The times are dangerous. About many things one cannot write. They want us to write about socialist competition, about the coming industrial-financial plan and so on. . . . Not this is needed for our literature.[69]

Leonov, in a barely veiled way, tried to tell Gorky what was going on in the Soviet Union. Gorky's answer was not long in coming, but to the queries and complaints expressed by Leonov he did not respond. His letter of November 8, 1930, was short. Having made some comments regarding cactus plants that Leonov was growing, Gorky ended the letter, excusing himself from a lengthier reply by the late hour and a cold.[70]

Sharing with Rolland his optimism on the new spirit and the progress made in the Soviet Union, Gorky wrote, "Here, thought and will have been miraculously revolutionized."[71] The collectivization process is praised, this time the progress in Central Asia, where "nomad tribes have avoided the phase of capitalism, and are passing from the nomadic life to socialist economy through the organization of livestock, cotton and grain collective farms."[72] Did Gorky not realize that this "marvelous development" cost the people of Kazakhstan about one third of their population and that it was wishful thinking to see a rosy picture of the new villages that were to "replace . . . the grimy Russian villages that were disappearing and their place being taken by towns with public bath-houses, theaters, mechanical bakeries, communal laundries, schools and infant creches, where woman would cease to be a domestic animal and the slave of her husband"?[73] This was the time when in some parts of the country famine had raised its ugly head, and millions of lives would be lost. To write that the *kulaks*, "former exploiters of the countryside," would join young Communist shock brigades in the "places to which they have been exiled" was naive to say the least.

On his return in 1931, Gorky settled in Moscow in the house given him by Stalin on Malaia Nikitskaia, No. 6 [now the Gorky Museum], built by the millionaire industrialist and Old Believer, P. P. Riabushinskii. There is evidence that Gorky tried to object to the elaborate headquarters. In a letter to Kriuchkov, dated March 1, 1931, sent from Sorrento, Gorky wrote of a rumor that a kind of palace or Christ Temple was being renovated for his use. He thought that it was all wrong and his settling there would be resented by people "who worked like crazy and lived in pigsties."[74] The correspondence and occasional visits with Stalin indicated that the relationship with the writer was rather businesslike and formal. Gorky turned to Stalin, as before, with numerous proposals regarding new publications to further the development of culture, but also to extol the achievements of the Soviets. The meetings of the Leader (*vozhd'*) with the writer were widely publicized. One such event was Stalin's visit on October 11, 1931, in the company of the then Commissar of Defense, K. E. Voroshilov, when Gorky read his short story, *Devushka i smert'* (Death and the Maiden). Stalin praised the work, allegedly commenting that it was greater than Goethe's *Faust*.[75]

Stalin's continuing efforts to win over Gorky to serve his goals were not limited to occasional visits, letters, and the use of the writer as mouthpiece for Soviet propaganda. Gorky was important for Stalin to enhance his own position and to give support and approval of his plans to realize "socialism in one country." So far Stalin seemed to have succeeded. Gorky gave his approval to collectivization, and he sided with the Party in the trials of the so-called "wreckers." He was friendly with the deputy chief of the OGPU, Yagoda; and his friendship with Rolland made it possible for Gorky to minimize the impact of the campaign waged in the émigré press against the Soviet Union. There was, however, a special assignment for Gorky as far as Stalin was concerned. Stalin wanted Gorky to write his biography. He wanted it to be written in the style of the memoir Gorky wrote about Lenin, in order to show that he, Stalin, was worthy to wear the mantle of the great Revolutionary. The biography was important for the Stalin cult that was being built. The story of the projected biography that was never written began on December 19, 1931, when Stalin's personal secretary, I. Tovstukha, sent Gorky materials consisting of memoir literature on Stalin and his participation in revolutionary movements. There being no response from Gorky, on January 22, 1932, A. B. Khalatov, a literary functionary of Stalin, sent to Sorrento an inquiry whether additional materials were needed for the biography.[76] At the same time Gorky was reminded that the jubilee of the fortieth anniversary of his literary career was about to be celebrated. The Gorky legend of "the first proletarian writer" and supporter of Stalin and his regime had its start just at the moment when Stalin was demanding and, one may assume, expecting a hagiography for a new saint.

The fate of the biography is also mentioned in the work of A. Orlov, Stalin's secretary, who, following a successful escape from the Soviet Union, wrote the work *Tainaia istoriia stalinskikh prestuplenii* (The Secret History of Stalin's Crimes). Orlov writes, "I was sitting in the office of Ia. Agranov. Into the office entered M. Pogrebinskii." It appeared from the talk that Pogrebinskii had just returned from Gorky's villa. "Somebody spoiled it all. . . . Gorky refuses to talk about the book [the biography]."[77] First there was a rewritten Lenin memoir, and now there was to be a biography that would do the same. By this time, Gorky could not have missed the fact that Stalin wished him to become the apologist for the regime, the Revolution, and "the boss" who had hand-picked Gorky for this unsavory role. Whatever we can say to Gorky's discredit, he never produced the biography. Gorky offered several reasons for not fulfilling Stalin's expectations. In a letter to Lunacharskii, he suggested with irony that the Bolshevik leaders write their own autobiographies for the use of the young generation.[78] In answer to another assignment suggested by Khalatov, Gorky wrote on January 23, 1932, that he could not write a "literary work" on the fifteen years of achievements of Soviet power. "This is not my task, besides, I have no time for such a difficult work. No, look for somebody else, and, better yet, for others. . . . This task can be tackled only by a collective effort. . . . I have too much to do without it."[79] Even at the very moment when Gorky was proving reluctant to follow Stalin's directions in regard to the biography, honors were increasing. Perhaps they were partly intended as a spur to write the biography, as well as to repay Gorky for other support and to meet the public's enthusiasm for Gorky's works.

The year 1932 marked the fortieth anniversary of Gorky's literary work. Here was an opportunity for Stalin and the Party to further the "Gorky legend." On September 17, 1932, the Presidium of the Central Committee of the Party passed a resolution, "On Measures to mark the fortieth Anniversary of Maksim Gorky's Literary Work." It was decided to establish an Institute of Literature named after A. M. Gorky.[80] After that particular honor, Gorky became the recipient of more honors and gifts. In addition to the house on Malaia Nikitskaia No. 6, he was given a villa in Gorki, near Moscow, and a summer home in Tesseli, the Crimea. An announcement of the publication of his collected works appeared in press. Gorky's name was used to rename streets, towns, cities, and institutes. His native city, Nizhnii Novgorod, was now Gor'kii; the region had become the Gor'kii province (*Gor'kovskaia Oblast'*); and a number of schools, factories, and collective farms bore the name of the writer. The renaming of the Art Theater in Moscow has an interesting twist. It appears that one of the literary functionaries, Ivan Gronsky, tried to object to having the Moscow Art Theater renamed Gorky's Art Theater, maintaining that the history of that theater is associated with the name of another writer, Anton Chekhov. Stalin's answer was, "That does not matter. Gorky is a vain man. . . . We must bind him with cables to the Party."[81] There is evidence that Gorky attempted to refuse the honor. When writing letters and reflecting on the change of name of his native city, Gorky remarked, "It is not pleasant to write 'Gor'kii' instead of 'Nizhnii Novgorod.' "[82] But he could not fight it.

Gorky's assistance was sought by Stalin in bringing Soviet culture and, first and foremost, literature under the control of the Party. His *imprimatur* was important in legitimizing the gigantic enterprises that were part and parcel of the Five Year Plans. As to the control over literature—it seems that Gorky proposed for himself the post of oraculum as to whom would be published and what works were acceptable, by maintaining contacts with Soviet writers all through the years of emigration from the middle of the 1920s on. This task he took very seriously, and he did not hesitate to criticize the official line when necessary and while it was possible. This was true till the early 1930s. Thus, in 1931, he wrote that the state of Soviet literature during the First Five Year Plan was of poor quality. For the period from 1928 to 1931, maintained Gorky, seventy-five percent of works published were "very bad books." That he was often disagreeing with the governmental powers in judging a writer's work or the writer unjustly can be illustrated in the case of Boris Pil'nyak, who was censored for having published his work abroad. Pil'nyak was not a favorite of Gorky, yet angry over the treatment of Pil'nyak by the authorities he wrote:

We have formed a stupid habit of dragging people up the bell-tower of fame and throwing them down into the dirt and filth after a little while. I won't give examples of such absurd and brutal treatment of the people; they are known to everyone. They remind me of the lynchings of petty thieves in 1917–18.[83]

His article "Trata energii" (The Waste of Energy) was published in *Izvestiia* in September 1929, stating that it was unwise to antagonize those who were capable of helping in the very difficult but great undertakings (fulfilling the Plan). He maintained that as far as the state of literature was concerned, too much harmful emphasis was put on the concept of "class enemy," and that in most cases the culprits were shady characters and self-seekers.[84] In a letter to Yagoda, dated January 22, 1930, Gorky commented on the collection of poems written by the members of the Units of the

Political Border Police (under the jurisdiction of the OGPU). Yagoda sought Gorky's approval to have the work published in the journal *Litucheba* (Literary Studies), one of the journals he participated in. Gorky refused, as he was concerned that if the work were to be published, the "manufacturing of very poor literature will begin and the doors will be opened to losers and graphomaniacs."[85] His attempts to maintain certain standards of the new Soviet literature were made in the face of Stalin's determination to subject it to control by the Party.

In order to contextualize Gorky's efforts, one has to remember that in the 1920s, during the period of the New Economic Policy, the arts had enjoyed a certain measure of independence. There were numerous literary organizations and groups, and among these the Russian Association of Proletarian Writers (RAPP) became the arbiter of Soviet literature. At the head was Leopold Averbakh, brother-in-law of Yagoda. Averbach's rule was in essence a literary dictatorship. This was the time when Pil'nyak was censored and Evgenii Zamiatin was attacked for the publication of his famous work, *We*, a satire on the totalitarian system. The latter was lucky to get the support of Gorky, and he emigrated.[86] Gorky's apparent decision to act more freely in the 1930s pales when we remember the independence of writers in the 1920s. In the 1930s, under government attack, independence quickly disappeared; thus Gorky's moments of free speech may seem surprisingly brave to modern readers. In contrast, however, we have the sad picture of Gorky's general support of the regime that had carefully planned and brutally implemented these restrictions on writers.

In 1932, RAPP was abolished, and measures were taken to make the writer subservient to the needs and the demands of the Party. Details regarding Gorky's position on the question of the disbandment of RAPP and his role in the literary struggle at the time, as well as his relations to the decisions of the Central Committee of the Party on literature, come to light in the recently published article by N. N. Primochkina, "Likvidirovat' slovo zhestokoe: Gor'kii protiv postanovlenia TsK."[87] Gorky's support was important. A well-known writer with authority in his native land and well respected in the West, distant from the "modern" and the "obscure," he was needed to legitimize Stalin's credentials as cultural leader. On April 23, 1932, a decree was passed by the Central Committee, "On the Reconstruction of Literary-Artistic Organizations." An organizing committee was established by the Orgburo of the Party commissioned to realize the task of establishing what was later to become the Union of Soviet Writers. With it was formulated a new artistic canon. In spite of the importance that Stalin attached to Gorky's participation, he was not invited to a joint meeting of the "organizing committee" and the Central Committee's commission. Did Stalin not trust Gorky anymore? Was he suspicious of the writer's vacillations? This was 1932. The biography Stalin so much wanted to see written was obviously not to be. The French Communist Henri Barbusse would write it, the most laudatory work on the Soviet ruler ever to be written. Gorky, however, would help Stalin's regime formulate and spread the restrictive writing policies of the 1930s.

On October 26, 1932, a meeting was held at Gorky's mansion on Malaia Nikitskaia No. 6 that was to decide on "literary policies for years to come." The meeting is described thus:

Tables covered with white cloths filled the dinning room. The curtains were drawn, and the chandeliers glittered. The room was full and the place of honor were occupied by the Kremlin leaders. Stalin, Molotov, Voroshilov, and Kaganovich. . . . Around the tables sat about fifty writers who were rather more restrained in their behavior. Akhmatova, Mandelstam, Pasternak, Platonov, Bulgakov, Babel, Bely, Kluyev and Pil'nyak were not present.[88]

It is well known that some of those absent at the time were the very talented Soviet writers. On the agenda was the question of the artistic canon. Gorky's idea, voiced in a previous meeting with the writers, was that the aim should be to "unite realism and romanticism in a third form designed to depict the heroic present in brighter tones and speak of it in more elevated and dignified manner." After much discussion, the artistic canon was defined as "Socialist Realism," the name suggested by Ivan Gronsky, the principal spokesman on literature. The term was officially adopted in 1934. At that 1932 meeting, Stalin's famous/infamous dictum was heard: "Writers were to be engineers of human souls."[89] Emphasizing the importance of "these engineers," Stalin allegedly said that "the production of souls [sic!] was more important than of tanks." It is important to note that "every fourth participant [writer] at that meeting, was in the Gulag or was silenced within a period of a few years."[90]

The year 1932 marked the height of Gorky's popularity with those in power. He was the one who still had access to the *khoziain* (boss); he addressed his letters with the familiar "Iosif V." or "Dorogoi I.V." Stalin would help to speed up the publication of some old journals and approve new ones. This was also the time when a group of Leningrad scientists embarked on the project to establish an institute of experimental medicine, Soviet Institute of Experimental Medicine (VIEM) that Gorky favored.[91] After 1932 the relations became rather tense. Stalin's moods became even more erratic after the tragic death of his second wife, N. A. Allilueva.[92]

In May of 1933, Gorky and his family left Italy for the USSR. Did Gorky know at that time that he would never again come back to Western Europe? It does not seem so. Writing about his departure from Sorrento, Berberova comments:

In May of 1933, the villa in Sorrento was closed. Gorky's archive for the period 1921–1933, containing correspondence with Bukharin, Piatakov and others, often critical of Stalin and the regime, was divided. One part was shipped to Moscow, the other was given to Maria Ignatievna Budberg (Moura).[93]

Here one finds the source of the story of the "mysterious valise," which M. Budberg was supposed to have brought to Moscow in June 1936 when she came to bid good-bye to the dying Gorky. The valise with materials that Gorky could not take with him on his return has not yet been discovered.

There were reasons for Gorky's return in 1933. These concerned his personal life, the future of Maxim, and the role he could see himself still playing in contributing to the growth and development of culture. Also, conditions in Western Europe would not have been encouraging for Gorky or for any socialist, revolutionary Communist, or artist opposed to Modernism, Impressionism, and other movements. The year 1933 marked the coming to power of Hitler and the Nazis in Germany. Gorky often mentioned in his letters and pronouncements the possibility of war. There was pressure from the authorities in the Soviet Union [read Stalin] who wanted him back in the country for good but, as will become evident, on Stalin's terms.

The personal factor was important. The woman closest to him, M. Budberg, had left already, in 1932, to join her lover, H. G. Wells, in London. In recent scholarship little has been written about Gorky's love affairs. M. Budberg's name is mentioned only seven times in volumes III and IV of *Letopis'*, where in a cursory manner she is identified as his secretary and translator. To explain Gorky's relationships with women it is perhaps appropriate to quote the following statement by Professor V. Ivanov, the son of the writer Vs. V. Ivanov, a friend of Gorky's: "The complexity of the love affairs in Gorky's household goes beyond that which can be, at this time, discussed with any certainty."[94] There are, however, quite reliable sources regarding the Budberg-Wells relationship.[95] She was a very important person in Gorky's life, and her leaving must have been a blow to him. She had come to say "good-bye" in May 1933 when the boat *Jean Jaurès*, that was taking Gorky and his entourage back to the USSR, docked in Istanbul. Interestingly, other people who wanted to meet Gorky were on the ship when it docked there. The present writer, working in the Houghton Library in November 1985, met with Mr. Jean van Heijenoort, the last of Trotsky's secretaries. He mentioned the attempt made by him and one Pierre Frank, a French communist, to see Gorky on board the *Jean Jaurès* in dock. Both he and Frank were sent by Trotsky, then in exile in Prinkipo, to ask for Gorky's intercession in the case of Christian Rakovsky, Trotsky's friend, then in difficulties with the authorities. The attempt was unsuccessful. Met by Peshkov, Gorky's son, they were told of the writer's indisposition; Peshkov promised to convey the request to Gorky. The incident was also reported in Heijenoort's work *With Trotsky in Exile from Prinkipo to*

Coyoacán. There he mentions the presence during the meeting of two "guardian spirits cocking their ears, trying to follow the words."[96] Visits by M. Budberg to the Soviet Union before June 1936 were never mentioned in the Gorky sources; they became known only after the period of glasnost'.[97] It has come to light in the two biographies of H. G. Wells written by his sons and in the materials found in the Lubianka's archives.[98] Distressed over the difficult relations with M. Budberg, Gorky was also concerned about Maxim's way of life, which was one more factor in his decision to leave Sorrento. In a letter to E. Peshkova of February 3, 1932, he wrote:

I am not writing . . . because I am busy and also because there is nothing to write about. There is little that is good, and about the bad, one does not feel like writing.

Here all is more or less okay. . . . I am concerned over Maxim's state of health. He is very nervous and tires easily. All his organs are functioning well but his nerves are strained. He stopped drinking wine, he smokes less; it was extremely difficult to make him give up wine and tobacco. Lipa [Olimpiada Chertkova, nurse and friend of the family] is giving him massages . . . and this helps. He is quieter and more alert. But you know what I am afraid of [??]. I am trying to persuade him to leave for Moscow and not wait for me, I may yet succeed. He should undergo there medical examination and try to get well. Such are things.[99]

Gorky wanted to believe that in Moscow Maxim would be able to establish himself and to provide for his young family. The country was on the move, and the second Five-Year-Plan was on. Little did he suspect that within a year Maxim would die under suspicious circumstances and Yagoda, the head of the now NKVD (People's Commissariat of Internal Affairs), would tighten the noose around Gorky and those close to him.

Having decided to return and to continue serving Stalin and social realism, Gorky's goal, as late as 1933, was still to foster the development of culture and education in the country. He had initiated the publication of numerous journals, was working on the history of the Civil War, and was planning a series of collective works aimed to enlighten the people of Russia, and of the world, about the achievements of the Soviet regime. One of the projected series was a collection of documents and articles under the title *Istoriia fabrik i zavodov* (The History of Factories and Mills). His extensive correspondence with writers and artists was proof of close connection with them and of the fact that his *imprimatur* of their works was important. Thus, in April 12, 1933, Gorky wrote from Sorrento to the playwright A. N. Afinogenov, whose play *Lies* Gorky had reviewed. Gorky indicated that he understood the regime well and that, although the play was interesting, it could only be staged at a close showing before a picked audience.[100] Included were comments regarding the Party and his relation with it:

I am not a Party member and I know little of the internal doings in the Party. But, I have known the *Bolshevik* type for a period of thirty years. Yet, I will never be able to give an accurate portrayal of him. . . . The difficulties that he encounters are to be found in the past which he is trying to destroy. His merits are in the present, in his work of building the future.[101]

Further proof of Gorky's close watch over the state of literature comes in a letter to Kriuchkov, dated March 18, 1933, still from Sorrento. "I get the books,—I am mad. What sort of rubbish is being published! I will write about it. Pasternak complaints that *Glavlit* (Main Administration for Literary Affairs and Publishing) rejected his *Okhrannaia gramota* (Charter of Immunity)—a work of literature, no doubt—and the stupid nonsense of [one] Petrov-Vodkin was published. . . . Devil take them! When will intelligent people be in charge of our literature?"[102] Gorky was also aware of the internal problems in the Party. On January 20, 1933, he wrote to A. I. Rykov, who was being criticized for his Rightist deviation. He expressed his satisfaction with Rykov's address at the Plenum of the Central Committee and Central Control Commission, of January 7–12, 1933, where the two "deviationists" Rykov and M. A. Tomskii were persuaded to recant and were warned about the consequences if they continued their oppositionist stand. Gorky, concerned over stability in the Party, congratulated Rykov for the "Bolshevik courage," emphasizing the importance of their recantation for the good of the Party and the world revolutionary movements.[103]

Shortly afterward Gorky sent Rolland a long letter, dated January 30, 1933, in answer to questions raised by Rolland concerning the deterioration of the quality of life in the Soviet Union as reported in the French press. Gorky, explaining the causes of shortages of food, housing, and basic needs, put the blame on the peasant. He argued that the peasant, whose expectations were rising, was envious of the better life of the city; and he blamed the *kulaks* for fomenting dissatisfaction in the countryside as well as the "internal enemies" of the Soviet power, the remnants of the old bourgeoisie that was in close contact with the émigré community. And, *voilà*, the peasant and the "enemies of the people" were culprits, guilty of the problems that faced Soviet leadership. Gorky never mentioned the man-made famine that was taking a heavy toll of the inhabitants of Ukraine, the Northern Caucasus, the Volga area, and Kazakhstan. He informed Rolland that he was leaving Sorrento for Odessa; elaborating on his new projects, he wrote: "Back in Moscow, I will take on the reorganization of literature for children. Then we will establish an institute for the study of world literature and European languages. There is lots of work waiting for me in Moscow."[104] Clearly, it is fair to say that these were priorities, and he was returning to a country ruled by Stalin and his clique, where the trend was towards complete enslavement of the population.

The diary of Prishvin mentioned earlier contains an entry written shortly before Gorky's return, in which he severely censures Gorky and describes in detail the grim reality of life in the Soviet state:

Yes, Gorky built his "jubilee" on the backs of Tolstoy, Chekhov. . . . And now, when Russian truth and justice had vanished, when people in the cities are dressed in rags, and on the collective farms there is no sugar to get even on a holiday, and children have seen no cookies or cakes, our father is arranging a jubilee for himself.[105]

It is inconceivable to assume that Gorky did not realize that the situation in the country was as described by Prishvin. He was also aware of the opposition within the Party ranks against Stalin. It seems that he was concerned over stability in the Party and this explains his previously mentioned letter to Rykov congratulating him on his admission of error, his and Tomskii's. But conspiratorial groups in the Party were emerging in the early 1930s as well. One group was led by I. S. Syrtsov and B. Lominadze, previously loyal to Stalin. Their critique of the achievements of the first Five Year Plan led to their expulsion from the Central Committee, but without further repressions.[106] Another group was organized by M. I. Riutin, Moscow district Party secretary, whose program contained a bitter indictment of Stalin and his policies and argued the need for his removal.[107] That Gorky was aware of the Riutin case is evident from his letter to Yagoda, dated November 20, 1932. "My mood is apprehensive, in my dreams I hear Riutin, Riutin . . . ,"[108] indicating his concern over the danger of the conspiracy.

The White Sea–Baltic canal should have shaken Gorky's confidence in the regime and might also have warned him of crimes to come later in the 1930s. Regrettably, he gave his *imprimatur* to the project. The White Sea–Baltic canal was aimed at connecting the Baltic with the Northern Seas to become the most important artery of the Northern regions. Plans had been drawn up in 1931, and the work was finished by mid-July 1933. The canal named so proudly after Stalin was built with forced labor, under horrible conditions, but Gorky wrote Rolland that the prisoners, builders of the canal under the supervision of the GULAG, were socially dangerous elements, counter-Revolutionaries, wreckers, *kulaks*, and thieves. He praised the effort made to re-educate them and mentioned that many were ready to move on to the next assignment, the building of the Moscow-Volga canal.[109] On August 17, 1933, Gorky, in the company of a group of 120 writers, went to see the finished canal; and in January of 1934, the book *Belomorsko-Baltiiskii kanal imeni Stalina* was published in Russian, with the English translation, *The White Sea Canal*, appearing in 1935. It was a collective effort of thirty-four writers, all extolling the outstanding feat. The editors were Gorky; L. Averbakh, the then head of RAPP, soon to be dissolved; and S. G. Firin, of the OGPU, Yagoda's second in command. The content of Gorky's address at the site was included. He spoke of the great service of the OGPU in reforming prisoners: "I am happy and touched by what has been said here, and what I know—I have been watching the GPU reform people since 1928. . . . You have done a great thing—a very great thing!"[110]

Gorky, who in 1906 had had the courage to write an open letter addressed to the government of France asking that no loans be given to the government of Nicholas II, who in 1917–1918 wrote the well-known articles under the caption *Untimely Thoughts*, and in 1922 came out openly defending the Left Social Revolutionaries then on trial and unjustly accused of treason, now allowed his name to be included with that of L. Averbakh and S. G. Firin, glorifying the GULAG.[111] The late Andrei Sinyavsky in the work *The Russian Intelligentsia* cites the case of well-known writers who signed letters written in 1937 that called for the destruction of "the enemies of the people."[112] Among them were Pasternak, Platonov, and Vs. Ivanov. Gorky then was no exception. Did Gorky misunderstand the events or miss seeing the unjustices being perpetrated there, or did he not wish to admit that such wrongdoings were official government policy, Stalin's approved strategies, and the communist society's possibilities? Was he afraid to recognize these affairs, or was he naive, extremely so, believing all that he was told by the government and only protesting when things involved friends who were also writers? Or did he know everything, evaluate every improper action correctly, but lack the courage to speak out? The writer V. Shentalinsky writes that Gorky on his visits to Russia was surrounded tightly by a cordon of the Lubianka's servants, especially after he returned for good in 1933. Gorky's house was linked by a direct line to Yagoda's office.[113] From 1933, the meetings with Stalin were on official occasions only. The fact that Gorky was not allowed to leave the Soviet Union after 1933 contributed to a cooling of relations between the two.

Yet one sees Gorky, once "the great interceder," now a lesser interceder, trying still to help some people in difficulties with OGPU (later NKVD). Here the contact with Yagoda was useful. The work was not always easy, and often the cases he tried to defend took a long time. Rolland's prodding, his connection with the left intellectual elite in the West, and the pressure of public opinion there contributed to Gorky's success. In particular, Rolland and Gorky were of assistance to foreigners who were unjustly sent to penal exile or imprisoned by the OGPU. One was the writer V. V. Bianki. Gorky intervened on behalf of the historian E. V. Tarle, the literary critic M. Bakhtin, and the scholar A. A. Semenov; and he succeeded in getting an exit visa for E. I. Zamiatin, famous for his anti-totalitarian novel *We*, mentioned earlier. Thanks to Gorky's efforts, L. B. Kamenev, the old Bolshevik in disgrace, was appointed director for a while to the publishing house *Akademiia*. Gorky tried to intercede on behalf of K. Radek and N.

Bukharin and took up the cases of the Italian anarchist Getsi and the writer Victor Serge. Thus Gorky's intellectual and political lives during this period sometimes moved in different directions, as if the writer were in a tragic drama.

Even Gorky's residences in the USSR mirrored his position, for they were far removed from the dwellings of workers or peasants; and the artists whom he wished to lead, and sometimes to save, were not in his proximity no matter where Gorky stayed. After 1933, Gorky lived his private life in splendor with his extended family in the house on Malaia Nikitskaia No. 6. There was also a summer home in the village Gorki, from Rolland's description a very impressive building, and a house in Tesseli, on the Crimea. The Moscow domicile was a busy one. Staying there was his son Maxim, his wife Natalia Alekseevna, nicknamed Timosha, their two daughters Daria and Marfa, and a governess. In addition, there were others who stayed with Gorky during the years spent in the West, for example, the artist I. N. Rakitskii and Olimpiada Chertkova, a nurse (fel'dsher) by profession, an old friend of the family, who was taking care of Gorky during the last years of his life. E. Peshkova was a frequent guest. An important resident was Kriuchkov. His room on the first floor, adjacent to Gorky's study, indicated the importance of his presence. A friend of Yagoda, connected with the OGPU, Kriuchkov was in charge of Gorky's publishing and financial matters. A staff of employees, many of whom were in the service of OGPU, watched over the comings and goings of the inhabitants of the house. In the USSR, Gorky's private life in homes of splendor and isolation could not be completely private, any more than the less showy homes of other people there.

In fact, the wealthy, pampered life did not protect Gorky from the sordid machinations of Stalin and his spies. In 1934, Gorky suffered a heavy blow in the untimely death of his son. Maxim was thirty-six years old. He had stayed with father since 1922. He had been in charge of Gorky's vast correspondence, accompanying him at official functions and helping with translations. His interests seem to be travel and technological innovations; he also liked to paint. Except for a short assignment as diplomatic courier in 1920–1921, however, he does not seem to have had any job experience. Maxim was captivated by the nature and landscapes of the northern regions of Russia and traveled there frequently. In a letter to Rolland dated September 8, 1932, Gorky wrote that he was enclosing photographs taken by Maxim on the island of Vaigach, situated behind the Arctic Circle, where he was spending the summer among prisoners working in the lead mines, supervised by the employees of the OGPU. Gorky wrote of the work, the conditions of life and the rewards for those engaged in this arduous task.[114] Maxim's wife, Natalia Alekseevna, wrote: "[T]o great regret, Maxim could not and did not apply himself systematically in order to become a professional. He was constantly with Aleksei Maksimovich

[Gorky]. There were difficulties and frequent moves, all this took a great deal of time, and was in the way of serious work."[115] There have been unanswered questions about that death ever since it was reported that Maxim died on May 11 of 1934, allegedly of a severe case of pneumonia. He was buried the very next day. Was there fear of an autopsy that would have thrown some light on the cause of his sudden death? As in the case of Gorky's own death in 1936, a number of interpretations exist regarding the circumstances of Maxim's death. In a letter to his granddaughters on May 10, sent from Gorki, Gorky writes that he would have wished to come to be with them, but that he was sick and that their father also was ill. "He had caught a cold at the airport and is sick in bed, coughing."[116] The explanation to the letter reads: "M. A. Peshkov died May 11 of pneumonia." The memoir of Maxim's wife contains a slightly different version:

In April of 1934, Ekaterina Pavlovna [E. Peshkova] with Marfa and Daria, left for Tesseli. Aleksei Maksimovich was ill and decided to remain for a while in Gorki. I and Maksim remained with him. . . . Maksim fell ill. He caught a cold on a fishing trip. From the first day of his illness the temperature rose to 40° C. The doctor . . . diagnosed it as a serious case of pneumonia . . . Maksim died on May 11 and was buried on May 12.[117]

The discrepancy is evident here. We know that Gorky wrote that Maxim caught a cold at the airport, whereas his widow mentioned a cold caught on a fishing trip. I. M. Koshenkov, superintendent of the home on Malaia Nikitskaia No. 6, wrote of the involvement of Yagoda in bringing about the death of Maxim Peshkov. Kriuchkov and Yagoda were accused in 1938 of murdering Maxim Peshkov.[118]

Whatever the circumstances of Maxim's death, there can be no question that this father took the passing very hard. In answer to Rolland's letter of condolences, Gorky wrote on May 26:

The blow is indeed heavy and unnervingly outrageous *idiotsko oskorbitel'nyi* . . . Maksim was healthy and strong and died a difficult death. He was gifted. He had a unique kind of talent, on the like of Hieronymus Bosch. He was interested in technology and was listened to by specialists and inventors. He had a sense of humor and was an able critic. But he was weak-willed; he squandered his energies and did not succeed in developing any of his talents. He was thirty-six years old.[119]

Gorky's state of mind and his behavior following the death of his son are described in the memoir of his daughter-in-law.

At first he attempted to continue with work and to participate in public life as if nothing had happened. Within three months after Maksim's death he was taking part in the proceedings of the Congress of the Union of Soviet Writers. But one sees another side of Gorky, the father who could not come to terms with the fact that the son, who was with him for many years, was no more. The loss broke Gorky. When alone, he could not read. He paced the floor of his room at night, his eyes were not laughing anymore. He planned to write about Maksim, to issue a collection of his drawings and paintings, but could not make himself do it. The time did not heal his wound. While earlier he could talk about Maksim with me and the girls, he remained later alone with his grief and only occasionally would mention his inability to write about his son.[120]

In the memoir of Valentina M. Khodasevich, an old friend of Gorky's, we read:

After the terrible tragedy of Maksim's death on May 11, 1934, Aleksei Maksimovich, though he had the courage to continue living, was not anymore a person, but an institution established by him, and now in spite of all obligated to continue working.[121]

Kriuchkov was now the one who would give permission to visit with Gorky, and frequently very friendly and respectable people were turned away.[122] Thus the realities of life in the USSR were compounding the pressures on Gorky; as the 1930s passed, Gorky's life there was becoming unsupportably painful and limiting. This must have shocked, surprised, and frightened the writer.

The last two years of Gorky's life in the USSR were the most difficult and tragic. On the one hand, through the means of propaganda he had become an icon, albeit a tarnished one. He was being used by Stalin to meet visiting foreign dignitaries and members of the Western intellectual elite, some of whom were his friends. His participation was required at the First Congress of Writers, which laid the foundations of the Union of Soviet Writers. Of significance here is a recently published letter to Stalin, written August 2, 1934. It was composed on the eve of the First Congress and begins with Gorky informing Stalin that he is enclosing the draft of his address prepared for the forthcoming opening of the Congress, along with a request for its perusal and possible corrections. There follows a lengthy critique of some of the writers being considered as suitable candidates for membership in the Presidium of the projected union. The standards of Soviet literature, wrote Gorky, were to be preserved, and no compromises with mediocrity was admissible. He submitted names of writers deserving membership and asked for Stalin's intervention in the matter.[123] The Congress would prove crucial in the development of the doctrines associated with socialist realism and to the "re-education" of artists and the reshaping of art in the USSR.

At the Congress, the decision was taken to make the canon of socialist realism the guiding idea in literature and, later, in all of the arts. The opening remarks were delivered by A. A. Zhdanov, Secretary of the Central

Committee of the Communist Party of the Soviet Union (CPSU), whose idea of what Soviet literature was to be like was summed up in the following statement: "Soviet literature must know how to portray our heroes, it must be able to look into our tomorrow."[124] Among the participants at the Congress were Karl Radek and N. Bukharin, soon to disappear in the great purge. The key address, entitled "Soviet Literature," was delivered by Gorky.

For the writer, who only three months earlier had buried his son, the task must have been a difficult one. His address was long and repetitive but did show great erudition. He told those who were present there that Western literature was in decline and that much of the literature of Russia of the nineteenth century had been influenced by bourgeois Western culture. He spoke of Bolshevism as the single most powerful and motivating idea, one that was to guide the works of writers and their art and that the new literature should remain individual in its form and Socialist-Leninist in its fundamental governing ideas. "Gorky emphasized the significance of Soviet literature in world literature, showed the ideological peculiarities which distinguished it from the literature of the bourgeois, gave an appraisal of its present state, and outlined the task of further development."[125] But he also spoke of the task of the Writers' Union "not to restrict individual creation, but to furnish it with the widest means for continued powerful development."[126] In spite of the fact that the Congress was under close scrutiny by the Party, there was a kind of euphoria among the participants.[127] History did not justify the optimism and belief in a new, better future for Soviet literature and its writers.[128] Gorky's address was rather disappointing, wrote one critic, for according to Gorky, the writer was now instructed to describe an ideal reality, to gild the "Potemkin villages" erected by the state.[129] Gorky himself had insufficient enthusiasm for the Union, it seems, for he would move to terminate his role in the organization, because of fears either for his future or for the future role of intellectual life in the society around him. Probably both worries contributed to Gorky's decision. The times were that trying, after all. Not long after the Congress was over, Gorky, dissatisfied with the policy of Zhdanov and the participation of writers whom he did not respect, wrote a letter to the Central Committee of the Party. In it Gorky maintained that writers the likes of Panferov, Ermilov, Fadeev, and Stavsky among others, were unworthy of membership in the Union of Soviet Writers. This being the case, Gorky asked to be relieved of the duties of chairman of the board of the Union of Soviet Writers.[130]

The year 1934 did not end auspiciously. Along with the death of his son, Gorky was mourning the death of S. M. Kirov, the Party boss of Leningrad and a member of both the Politburo and the Secretariat, a long-term protege of Stalin and one of his close associates, murdered December 1, 1934, in Leningrad. Gorky knew Kirov, had met him a number of times, and often came to him with requests. Kirov, it is now believed by some and questioned by others, was murdered on Stalin's orders. An able administrator, he had emerged as a serious competitor to Stalin's rule and had to go. In a letter to the writer K. A. Fedin, dated December 2–25, Gorky wrote: "I am depressed over the murder of Kirov, I feel completely shattered and bad. I very much loved and respected the man."[131] Gorky had found affinity with Kirov's views, in particular as far as the foreign policy of the USSR was concerned. According to R. Tucker, the American historian and biographer of Stalin, Gorky, when appearing at the Moscow Party Conference that preceded the Seventeenth Party Congress, spoke of the dangers of Hitler's Germany and the fascist ideology.[132] Kirov's views on Soviet foreign policy met here with Gorky's. Following Kirov's murder, Gorky sent a telegram on December 4, with the caption *Bol'she bditel' nosti* (More Vigilance), published in *Pravda*, No. 333. It read:

A wonderful person was murdered. He was one of the outstanding leaders of the Party, an ideal example of a proletarian, a master of culture. I share with all my heart the grief of the Party, and the grief of all honest workers. I cannot help but say: The success of the enemy speaks not only of his villainy, but also of our inadequate vigilance.[133]

As to the perpetrators of the crime, Gorky had no doubts, at least for the public record; in an article published in *Pravda* he wrote: "The enemy must be exterminated ruthlessly and without pity, paying no attention to the gasps and groans of the professional humanists."[134] Once more, Gorky buried his doubts and came to the defense of the regime, even when it meant demonstrating public distrust of "professional humanists."

An interesting detail on the postlude of Kirov's murder came to light in a recently published article. Gorky was in the Crimea when the murder occurred. According to the source, a car with armed guards approached Gorky's house, obviously with the aim of protecting the writer, though there was no explicit statement made about the identity of the threat to Gorky. Since Gorky was not in danger, it looked as if "The Boss was protecting not him [Gorky] from someone, but himself from him. God forbid that the old man [Gorky] should take it into his head to do something strange, such as going somewhere, or making a public statement that the Boss would not like him to make."[135] Gorky might have appeared to some to be Stalin's potential enemy, perhaps to the boss himself; but Gorky acted as if he were not aware of this awful possibility. Either unaware of this threat or unwilling to show that he was aware of it, Gorky continued to be stalked by forces of death, sorrow, and tragedy.

Soon after the murder of Kirov, V. Kuibyshev, a member of the Politburo, died suddenly, allegedly of a heart attack. The situation in the country was unsettling, and Gorky came under criticism in the press. On

January 28, 1935, an attack on Gorky, supposedly for his literary articles, was published in *Pravda*, No. 27, written by the writer F. I. Panferov.[136] It appears that the real reason for the attack was Gorky's refusal to write an article condemning individual terror, as ordered by Stalin and conveyed to Gorky by Yagoda. Gorky's reply read: "I condemn not only individual, but state terror too."[137] Relations with Stalin were distant and meetings rare. Also, the frenzy of arrests and executions that followed Kirov's murder could not help but influence Gorky's relations with Yagoda. Gorky sought to distance himself form his "friend." In their correspondence there are few letters written after 1933. In one, dated November 8, 1934, Gorky informed Yagoda that in accordance with Stalin's orders conveyed to him by A. S. Shcherbakov, the History of the Civil War had to include the history of the Cheka and its fight against counter-Revolution.[138] A letter dated July 29, 1935, contained Rolland's communication of the news of the protest by the International Committee against Anti-Proletarian Persecutions in Russia and against the reign of terror following the murder of Kirov.[139]

An opportunity for Gorky to leave for the West came in 1935. He was invited to participate in the International Congress in Defense of Culture being organized by Henri Barbusse and I. Ehrenburg. The Congress was to take place in Paris. Perhaps the best indication that Gorky did plan to attend comes from a letter he sent Rolland in answer to the latter's news of his forthcoming visit to the USSR. Gorky wrote that in view of his commitment to participate in the Congress he was not certain that he would be in Moscow at the time of Rolland's arrival. Shortly afterward, he turned to Shcherbakov, his intermediary now in communicating with Stalin, with the request that the latter inquire of Stalin about the possibility of meeting Rolland during his visit.[140] Gorky received the passport to go abroad on June 8, but the trip did not materialize. In the official press the explanation given was that he could not go because he fell ill with bronchitis. The Congress met June 21–25.[141] Gorky's greetings were read by one of the members of the Soviet delegation.

In June 1935 Rolland, accompanied by his Russian-born wife, Maria Pavlovna Kudasheva, came to the USSR for a visit and stayed for almost a month. The two friends, whose contacts had begun in 1916 met for the first time. Rolland kept a diary of that trip, which has recently been published in a Russian translation. In the introduction to Part One of the diary, the editor T. Motyleva makes the following comments: "In these pages that are now open for us, there is much of the naive. Some of the observations are rather inadequate, but there is no doubt in the sincerity of the trusting, albeit at times also perspicacious writer which redeems its shortcomings."[142] Rolland had come at a bad time, when repressions and arrests were the order of the day. The first meeting took place on June 29, when the Rollands came to visit Gorky in his Moscow house. Rolland described Gorky thus:

He is tall, taller than I, big, not a very handsome countenance, a duck shaped nose, thick, light color mustache and brows, a crew cut, big hands and feet. Rather thin. He is dressed in a white shirt. His light blue eyes are full of kindness and sadness. When he gave me a hug, I noticed that he is taller than I by a head.[143]

Rolland was fortunate that he had a competent translator in his wife, from whose family in Russia he learned much of the life of ordinary citizens and of the general situation in the country. He was wined and dined by the powers that were and was able to meet the intellectual elite of Moscow. Finally he had the opportunity to observe the life led by his friend of many years. He was shown and/or told of many "Potemkin villages." Yagoda, the constant "guest" in Gorky's house, assured him that censorship was abolished in the Soviet Union; but Rolland knew better, for his letters were usually opened by the censor. Rolland also learned from Yagoda that a labor camp near Moscow with 200,000 inmates in the care of OGPU provided excellent conditions for the inmates and that the communes for the homeless (*bezprizornye*) were so well run that very few would leave before being fully rehabilitated. On his part, Kriuchkov, the "nanny," was informing Rolland that the war in the village [read collectivization] was caused by the *kulaks*.

At the beginning of the visit, it seemed that Yagoda won Rolland's confidence. The latter wrote of Yagoda's pleasant appearance, his quiet demeanor, and his gentle look; but Rolland soon discovered Yagoda's deceit when the case of Victor Serge came up for discussion. Rolland had devoted much time and energy to getting Serge out of the Soviet Union, and he raised the question of his release with Stalin. Rolland's meeting with E. Peshkova and with Maxim's widow, upon the women's return from a European tour at the time of his visit, seems to have been extremely important. From E. Peshkova, Rolland learned of Gorky's present situation, and she was able to tell him of the conditions in which Gorky was spending what was to be the last year of his life. She told Rolland that she was against the people who surrounded Gorky, but she had to hide it. Her work in the Red Cross gave her no possibility now to help those in difficulties with the authorities. She had nothing good to say about Yagoda and was critical of him and of his activities. She also spoke of Gorky's displeasure with her work in the Red Cross; Gorky had maintained that "one should not interfere with the affairs of state."[144] Was Gorky afraid that his former wife and friend of many years would risk her freedom and that of her granddaughters by continuing her work in the Red Cross?

One learns much about Gorky from Rolland's diary. Although the two friends had to communicate through a translator and were seldom alone, the reader gets a picture of Gorky's way of life, of his surroundings, and of his state of mind. At the outset, Rolland writes with regret that in spite of Gorky's statements that it was important to discuss openly the many problems of life in the Soviet Union, an open discussion never took place and that their conversations were less informative and lacked the sincerity present in their correspondence. In view of the fact that a sincere and open discussion was impossible under the circumstances, Rolland had to resort to guesswork and base his impressions on Gorky's utterances, his reactions to people and events. Rolland was surprised at the lavish life style Gorky led, the magnificent home in Moscow, and the beautiful villa in Gorki. He did not go to the Crimea. Having seen the poverty, the scarcities, and the hard life of the people, Rolland was taken aback by his friend's indifference to all that. The extravagant entertainment provided for him and the other guests of the political elite of the country was criticized by Rolland; Gorky, wrote Rolland, did not seem to enjoy the crass style of the dinners, lunches, and banquets. One such banquet, with Stalin and the top brass of the Party in attendance, Rolland described as tiring and tedious. The mood at the table was tense, and Gorky, defying the order of his doctors, was drinking. Stalin and Gorky engaged in a battery of rather silly arguments. Gorky's life seemed to have taken an unhappy, even potentially disruptive and dangerous turn by this time.[145]

Gorky, wrote Rolland, appeared tired and had told him that the circle of his friends was growing smaller all the time. He was critical of many; even the late Korolenko did not escape his criticism. Gorky, commented Rolland, had obviously forgotten all that Korolenko had done for him. He was never alone but at the same time was very lonely. Trying to explain Gorky's actions and moods, Rolland wrote:

Gorky put his heart and soul in the Revolution, dedicated himself to the idea of Leninism-Stalinism, and with enthusiasm and optimism accepted the Five Year Plans. . . . It seems, however, that the chorale is there to deafen a groan which comes from his inner self. I have felt a deep sorrow hidden in him, yes.[146]

He continued:

The Revolution brought with it a moral dilemma. At first, he rejected it, shaken by its cruelty. He ran away to Italy, the beautiful but useless [sic!] Italy, that became for him a kind of an opiate. [How many people worked to make him return, asks Rolland, and answers it himself.] Gorky was tempted to return and having watched Russia from afar, it looked to him very glamorous. After the return he found many changes. This was not the Russia of the Civil War, but Russia of pharaohs. Surrounded by honours he devoted himself to the great cause, albeit seeing the mistakes, the suffering and even the inhumanity of the cause. . . . I cannot be fooled, his life is being lived as if on the surface of the sea, and not in its depth. Gorky

... is a weak, very weak man in spite of his looks of an old bear. ... Poor old bear! Surrounded by fame, and luxuries that he does not enjoy! ... It seems to me that if the two of us were left alone, and the language barrier would be no more, he would give me a hug and would quietly cry for a long while.[147]

The concluding comments at the time of parting with his friend read:

Until today I see Gorky's face before my eyes, approaching our car. He is pale, his eyes express sadness and kindness. He is a very kind and weak man. He is acting against his nature, and makes great efforts not to condemn the actions of his powerful political friends. There is, in his soul, a fierce struggle that nobody knows about.[148]

This was one of those times that try men's souls, as the American Revolutionary writer Thomas Paine had put it about his own age; and Gorky was certainly among those tested by the times in which he found himself. In Gorky's case, the test was increasingly moving the writer toward an uncharacteristic quietude, almost a silencing of his voice. Within a year of Rolland's departure, Gorky would be dead. What was this last year of the life of the "old bear" like? Gorky spent most of the time in Tesseli and only occasionally travelled to Moscow, or/and the village Gorki. The efforts of Kriuchkov to isolate him were very successful; even some of his remaining close friends had difficulties in meeting with him. The writer M. Prishvin came to visit during his brief stay in Moscow and was at first turned away by Kriuchkov. "Prishvin pushed his way past Kriuchkov and entered Gorky's study. Informed of what had just happened, Gorky said, 'Why, don't you realize that I am under house arrest?' "[149] Ilia Shkapa, who worked in the editorial office of the journal *Nash dostizheniia*, wrote about his visit with Gorky on September 20, 1935. Alone with Shkapa, Gorky turned to him and said: "I am very tired. ... I would like to spend some time in the country-side, just to stay there for a while, as in the olden days. ... No such luck. They surrounded me with a kind of a fence. There is no possibility to cross over it. ... No moving forward or back! All this is something I am not accustomed to."[150] Shortly after that meeting, Shkapa was arrested and spent twenty years in the GULAG.

In spite of all, Gorky, the "institution" as V. M. Khodasevich referred to him, continued working. He was trying to finish part four of the *Life of Klim Samgin;* continuing his participation in the journals *Kolkhoznik* (Collective Farmer), *Nashi dostizheniia*, and *SSSR na stroike* (USSR under Construction); and commenting on works of literature that were sent for his perusal. He tried to speed up the publication of the history of the Civil War that he had begun to work on and of which part one, dealing with the period from 1914 to October 1917, was published in 1935. He was also working on the projected *Istoriia fabrik i zavodov* (History of Factories and Mills).[151]

In March 7–10, 1936, the French writer André Malraux came to Tesseli for a visit in company of M. E. Kol'tsov and I. Babel. Kol'tsov wrote in a memoir published in 1938: "We visited Maksim Gor'kii together with Malraux, who came from Paris to inform on the project of publishing a new encyclopedia. . . . He was not well, but this did not cause him to interrupt his work schedule."[152] In the file on I. Babel, found in the archives of Lubianka, is the deposition of Babel regarding the visit with Gorky during Malraux's visit. There he painted a very somber picture of the lonely, isolated, and depressed Gorky.[153]

Following the visit by Malraux, Gorky sent Stalin a letter (only recently published), in which he shared with him his impressions of the visit. Gorky wrote at length of Malraux's role in the intellectual life of France and beyond, of his prestige, and of his concern for human rights. Continuing in that vein, he conveyed to Stalin Malraux's concern over the severe criticism heaped on the young D. Shostakovich for his opera *Lady Macbeth of Mtsensk*, a work that Gorky said had been well received in the country and abroad. The composer was not deserving of the treatment meted out to him by the critics, wrote Gorky. Here, too, as in 1934, when Gorky defended the standards of Soviet literature, he came to the defense of creative art and the talented composer. The letter was written in a forceful albeit polite tone. This was March 7–10, 1936, two months before his death, and the "old bear" had spoken up.[154]

An indication of the close surveillance of Gorky by the NKVD in the months preceding his death comes from a letter dated March 21, 1936, by K. P. Piatnitskii, a friend and former publisher of *Znanie*. In the letter Piatnitsky complained that his archive containing Gorky's letters and documents was seized by Yagoda. He asked for Gorky's assistance in retrieving these. In Gorky's answer, dated April 8, he wrote, "Of course I do not know who ordered to have the documents taken. . . . Following your letter to Ekaterina Pavlovna [it is obvious that Piatnitsky complained to her too], I immediately turned to the Commissar of the Interior asking to return these papers to you."[155]

On May 26, Gorky left Tesseli for Moscow, and on June 1 he fell ill with influenza. From June 6 on, in *Pravda* and *Izvestiia*, official bulletins began appearing with details of the writer's health. Gorky died in Gorki on June 18. An official medical report was published in *Pravda*, No. 167, June 19. It contained a detailed summary of his illness and stated that "the death occurred as a result of a cardiac arrest and paralysis of the lungs."[156] Cremation took place on June 19, and the urn with the ashes was placed in the Kremlin Wall.[157]

Gorky's funeral in Red Square in Moscow was attended by Stalin, other dignitaries of state, and a crowd of 800,000. Attending the funeral was the son of the writer Prishvin. On his return he related that the funeral had taken place earlier than expected, only a day after cremation. Many came to pay their respects, and as a result of overcrowding people got hurt in the procession. "Gorky," commented the older Prishvin, "was taken from us by the state, and the funeral, the most intimate thing for a person, his funeral, was appropriated by the state."[158] The French writer André Gide, visiting in the USSR at the time, attended Gorky's funeral and later wrote of his impressions: "I saw the Red Square during the funeral of Gorky. I saw an unending crowd slowly moving behind the catafalque. A quiet procession, solemn, intense. Who was Gorky to these people? A friend? A brother? On all faces even of little children one could see numbness full of sorrow."[159] Immediately after Gorky's death his archive was seized by members of the NKVD. Mentioned in a number of publications is Yagoda's reaction to the material found. Expressing his anger he allegedly said, "No matter what you feed the wolf he always yearns to be back in the forest."[160] In his work Shentalinsky mentions "a little known document of Gorky's last days. A note found there reads 'end of novel, end of hero, end of the author.' "[161]

During the last of the three show trials staged in Moscow March 8, 1938, among the twenty-one accused were Bukharin, Rykov, Rakovsky, and Yagoda. Kriuchkov and Yagoda were accused of the murder of Gorky, Gorky's son, Kirov, and Kuibyshev. In the case of Gorky, the doctors who attended him, L. Levin, Stalin's personal physician, Professor Pletnev, and doctor A. I. Vinogradov were also among the defendants. As the doctors were rehabilitated, but not Yagoda or Kriuchkov, the official verdict still stands, meaning that Gorky's death was apparently due to three different things: natural causes, which the official certificate states as the reason; murder by Yagoda and Kriuchkov, which the trial of 1938 declared was the reason; and the orders of Stalin, which the 20th Party Congress later decided was the reason for the actions of Yagoda and Kriuchkov. In fact, other speculations abound in the literature on Gorky made available recently.

One of Stalin's biographers, the late American historian R. H. McNeal, seemed to doubt Stalin's complicity, noting that there was no need to get rid of Gorky, for he was under control in the years 1935–1936 and was still a propaganda asset. McNeal dismisses the possibility that Gorky would have been able to protest at the trial of Zinoviev-Kamenev, had he still been alive.[162] The British historian Walter Laqueur, in his work, *Stalin: The Glasnost Revelations*, writes with reference to the "Gorky tragedy": "[T]here is sufficient evidence that Gorky was quite aware to his last days what went on around him, and he certainly knew his Russia infinitely better than the Rollands and the Feuchtwangers. Suspicions about the circumstances of his death were voiced under *glasnost'*; the full truth about the last months of his life may never be known."[163] A detailed account of the causes and circumstances of Gorky's death, with materials taken from the Gorky archives of IMLI and memoirs of the period immediately following Gorky's death, as well as of a later date, is contained in the article by V. S. Barakhov (head of IMLI and a well-known "gor'koved"), "M. Gor'kii. Posledniaia stranitsa zhizni" (M. Gor'kii. The Last Page of His Life). The author concludes: "The memoirs of the contemporaries as well as recently made available materials concerning the rehabilitation of the doctors, provide an opportunity to cite a number of arguments in favor of the version that Gorky died of natural causes. Yet, it would be too early to assume that all is clear and the case closed."[164] In the biography of Stalin by the American political scientist Robert C. Tucker, one reads:

Exactly how Gorky died remains a subject of speculation. Published eyewitness reports by persons who attended him in his final days indicate that he died a natural death, yet in commenting on these reports the keeper of the Gorky archive in Moscow's Gorky Institute of World Literature wrote that it would be premature to say that the case has been conclusively clarified.[165]

An article published in 1993 by Professor V. Vs. Ivanov contains interesting memoir material on Gorky and his life in the 1930s, as well as insights into the Gorky-Stalin relationship. Ivanov's thesis as to the causes of Gorky's death can be summarized as follows: Gorky's close relationship with Yagoda was aimed at the removal of Stalin, with the help of Kirov and Gorky's son Maxim, who were all involved in the plot. This startling thesis cannot be substantiated for lack of documentation.[166] Shentalinsky, who had the good fortune to locate the Gorky File in the archives of Lubianka, comes to the conclusion, given the documents available, that Gorky died of natural causes:

A photocopy of the medical record of Maxim Gorky, retrieved from the bottomless depths of the Lubianka archive, lies before me. . . . The correct diagnosis was made in good time. The best doctors . . . took the most decisive measures to save the writer's, already hopeless, worn-out-and-illness-shattered-organism.[167] [On] the final page in the medical history is listed the clinical diagnosis. . . . There followed the signatures of four doctors: Lang, Konchalovsky, Pletnyov [Pletnev] and Levin.[168]

The tributes of Gorky's contemporaries in the USSR and abroad reveal that, in spite of Gorky's collaboration and complicity in the excessess of the Stalinist period, Gorky still carried weight at home and in Europe, especially among left-leaning writers and those critics who had long before valued highly Gorky's literary works. Expressions of sympathy began appearing in the Soviet press immediately after Gorky's funeral. These were sent by the many organizations Gorky had participated in. The writers wrote of their appreciation of his life and work, and Krupskaia wrote of the friendship between Lenin and Gorky.[169] From his Swiss abode, Rolland sent a letter, dated June 20, entitled "Grief Overtook Me," which was published in *Pravda* the same day. It read:

The grief that overtook me on the news of the death of my dear friend, brother in arms, one who was my comrade for a period of twenty years, makes it impossible, at this point, to write an article about him. . . . I recall his rich life akin to his native Volga, a life borne out in his works. I recall his youthful ardour, sparkling enthusiasm when he spoke of the new world in the building of which he was taking part. I recall his goodness and sorrow hidden in its depth.[170]

The letter ended with high praise of the achievements of the Soviet state and a call to treasure the name of the writer.

The German writer Thomas Mann wrote in the *Internationale Literatur* an obituary, entitled "Beileidstelegram zum Tode M. Gorkijs." It was short, but said a great deal: "A great Russian has passed on with Maxim Gorky, a great humanist and socialist, very esteemed intermediary between the values of the Past and the will to the Future."[171] Alexei Tolstoy's appreciation of Gorky's life and work was expressed in the following passage: "For the artist who was able to mirror the revolutionary era so thoroughly and so truthfully as Gorky, for one who led humanity to the creation of the liberated world there are no two dates of his historical being, birth and death, but only one date, birth."[172] Fedor Shaliapin, also a friend of many years, learned of the death of Gorky while on his way from New York to Le Havre. He sent the obituary to P. Miliukov's newspaper *Poslednie novosti* in Paris. It was entitled "Chto zhe byl za chelovek Aleksei Maksimovich Gor'kii?" (What Kind of a Person was Aleksei Maksimovich Gor'kii?). It read:

Whatever one would tell me about Aleksei Maksimovich I, without a shadow of doubt know that all his thoughts, feelings, doings, merits, mistakes, all these had only one root, Volga the great Russian river and its groans . . . when Gor'kii marched forward, he marched toward a better future for the people, and when he erred and perhaps went off the road that others considered to be the right one, he too was marching towards the same goal.[173]

Published in the *Spectator* on June 26, 1936, was the obituary "Maxim Gorkij" written by the prominent British historian E. H. Carr.

Political theory was not in his temperament. "You a socialist!" exclaimed Tolstoy to him once. "You are a romantic, and romantics must be monarchists!" It is no wonder that Lenin found him unorthodox, and that despite his literary distinction and his generous contributions to Party funds, he was never admitted to the inner council of the revolutionaries . . . posterity will not place Gorky with Dostoevsky, Chekhov and Tolstoy, but we will remember him as an honest painter that knew in colours legitimately heightened with a dash of romance; the rising school of proletarian writers will find that they are indebted to Gorky.[174]

Trotsky's obituary for Gorky appeared July 9, 1936. It read:

Gorky died when there was nothing more that he could say. This makes it easier to come to terms with the death of a remarkable writer, who for a period of forty years exerted great influence on the development of Russian intelligentsia and the working class. . . . In the revolutionary years Gorky assumed the task of the "director of culture." Rejecting October, he left in 1921 having done much to save and preserve culture in the years 1918 to 1921. . . .

We say good-bye to him without a note of intimacy and an exaggerated praise, but with respect and gratitude. This great writer and great man has entered forever into the history of our people that was now blazing new historical paths.[175]

For Trotsky Gorky was the "satellite of the Revolution."

The requiems published in honor of Gorky indicate that his place in history was secured as one of Russia's great writers and one that championed the anti-fascist cause. The tragedy of Gorky was that while recognizing the danger of the rising fascism in Germany and critical of Mussolini, he did not understand or did not want to accept the reality of the Stalinist totalitarian regime. Gorky's fate was but one example of the destruction of the individual whose idea was to enlighten and to teach in the spirit of freedom of thought and universal sympathy.

The question can be asked, how far can one go in blaming Gorky for the compliance and inability to stand up to Stalin? And how does one equate it with Gorky's fight against the tsarist regime of Nicholas II and later his opposition to Lenin's Revolution? Gorky's arguments against the Bolsheviks, published on the pages of *Novaia zhizn'*, insisting that the country and its people were not ready for a socialist revolution, were prophetic. In the 1920s and 1930s Gorky appeared weak-willed, for like many of the intelligentsia he was not able to oppose Stalin. Or was Gorky still hoping against hope that Socialism would triumph in the end? One will never know, but it is clear that personal, intellectual, and political pressures on him were combining in this period to produce actions that seem indefensible. The country had changed in ways that would limit freedom even for a celebrated writer, and would make independence difficult or impossible. Acquiescence to the demands of the state, surveillance by the secret police, interference in one's movements, threats to one's writing colleagues, and dangers to oneself and one's family—could Gorky have foreseen these awful realities of the 1930s? Freedom was in conflict with duty and coercion. The artist was, in fact, in conflict with the political person inside Gorky, and the family man would suffer as a result. Gorky's socialist dream had turned into a grossly distorted reality, and before Gorky's suffering and death, his work would also become distorted and cruelly insensitive to those around him in the collectives and GULAG. Nothing could compensate for all that this period of the returns to the Soviet Union would cost Gorky. "End of novel, end of hero, end of the author."

NOTES

1. "Zhmu vashu ruku, dorogoi tovarishch," T. Dubinskaia-Dzhalilova i A. Cherneva, eds., *Novyi mir* 9 (1997). From the introduction, 167.

2. V. F. Khodasevich, "Gor'kii," *Oktiabr'* 12 (1989): 187.

3. R. Conquest, *The Great Terror: A Reassessment* (New York, 1990), 72–73, 84–85, 98, 99. See also Robert H. McNeal, *Stalin: Man and Ruler* (New York, 1988), 146, 355 n. 43; Walter Laqueur, *Stalin: The Glasnost' Revelations* (New York, 1990), 26–27; Anna Larina Bukharina, *Nezabyvaemoe* (Moscow, 1989).

4. See *Neizvestnyi Gor'kii*, III (Moscow, 1994); Akademia Nauk SSSR. *Arkhiv A. M. Gor'kogo*, XV; *M. Gor'kii i Rollan. Perepiska* (1916–1936) (Moscow, 1995); Hereafter referred to as *Gor'kii i Rollan*; "Zhmu vashu ruku," 167–183; Shentalinsky, *Arrested Voices* (London, 1996), 226–279.

5. See *Letopis'*, III: 582.

6. *Izvestiia TsK KPSS* (1989), I: 213–214.

7. *Letopis'*, III: 593.

8. *Pravda* 76, March 30, 1928.

9. See *Letopis'*, III: 595 ff.

10. See D. Shub, "Maksim Gor'kii i kommunisticheskaia diktatura," *Mosty* 1 (1958): 245.

11. Shub, "Maksim Gor'kii," 245.

12. Shub, "Maksim Gor'kii," 246.

13. Shub, "Maksim Gor'kii," 247.

14. "Vekselia, po kotorym kogda-to pridetsia rasplachivatsia. Mikhail Prishvin o Maksime Gor'kom," *Druzhba narodov* 6 (1993), 230.

15. Prishvin, "Vekselia," 231.

16. Prishvin, "Vekselia," 231.

17. Prishvin, "Vekselia," 231.

18. Prishvin, "Vekselia," 232.

19. Gor'kii, *Sobranie sochinenii*, vol. 24, 369.

20. *Letopis'*, III: 623.

21. Gor'kii, *Sobranie sochinenii*, vol. 24, 401.

22. Shentalinsky, *Arrested Voices*, 222–240.

23. Gor'kii, *Sobranie sochinenii*, vol. 17, 210–232; *Letopis'*, III: 786.

24. "In the Monastery," *Izvestiia* 157, July 8, 1928; see *Letopis'*, III: 623.

25. *Letopis'*, III: 657.

26. "Letter to A. S. Makarenko," October 5, 1935, in *Maxim Gorky, Letters* (Moscow, 1966), 176.

27. From Maxim's letter to his wife. N. Peshkova's Arkhive. See *Letopis'*, III: 634.

28. *Letopis'*, III: 673.

29. The National Archives of the United States, the microfilm collection, Wash-

ington, DC. Microfilm 316, Roll No. 96, Item 861.44, Dispatch No. 5460. How reliable this information is was impossible to determine. It is known that there was an agreement with *Gosizdat* in 1924.

30. Gor'kii, *Sobranie sochinenii,* vol. 24, 439.

31. *Arkhiv,* XIV: 486.

32. See Gor'kii, *Sobranie sochinenii,* vol. 24, 345 and 558–559.

33. Gor'kii, *Sobranie sochinenii,* vol. 24, 345.

34. E. Kuskova, "Obeskrylennyi sokol," *Sovremennye zapiski* XXXVI (Paris, 1928), 310.

35. *Izvestiia TsK KPSS,* No. 3, March 1989. Letter 11, November 27, 1989, p. 186. Radek was at the time criticized for his deviations; see Stalin's answer in *J. V. Stalin, Works,* vol. 12 (1955), 180–183.

36. The movement of *Makhaevism* originated with V. Makhaevskii-Vol'skii (1867–1926). According to his theory the intelligentsia is the main source of workers' oppression and even after the Revolution continues to exploit the proletariat. The Bolsheviks fought against *Makhaevism.* It is of little surprise that Gorky, whose faith lay in the intelligentsia leading the people and not exploiting it, was against *Makhaevism* and its influence. See *Socialist Realism without Shores,* Thomas Lahusen and Evgeny Dobrenko, eds. (London, 1997), 66, 74.

37. *Izvestiia TsK KPSS,* No. 3 (1989), 186.

38. Gor'kii, *Sobranie sochinenii,* vol. 17, 202–236.

39. Gor'kii *Sobranie sochinenii,* vol. 17, 236; M. S. Pogrebinskii (1895–1937), head of the OGPU, Nizhnii Novgorod region, and organizer of the labor communes of the OGPU. He committed suicide in 1937. Pogrebinskii left a letter addressed to Stalin. It read: "On one hand, I tried to turn criminals into honest people, and on the other I was forced . . . to put a label of a criminal on the honest Revolutionary leaders of our country." *Neizvestnyi Gor'kii* III: 193. In connection with the visit to Solovki and Gorky's meeting with the inmates, there is a story of a suitcase containing notes written by the inmates that he, Gorky, secretly collected. The suitcase, it said, was vandalized, and its contents burned. See *Neizvestnyi Gor'kii* III: 165.

40. Gor'kii, *Sobranie sochinenii,* vol. 17, 216–217.

41. Gor'kii, *Sobranie sochinenii,* vol. 17, 236.

42. For a detailed discussion of these trials, see R. Medvedev, *Let History Judge* (New York, 1972), 111–137.

43. "Zhmu vashu ruku," 167.

44. "Zhmu vashu ruku," 173–174. See also Nadeshda Ludwig, *Maxim Gorki: Leben und Werk* (West Berlin, 1984), 267–269.

45. *Neizvestnyi Gor'kii* III: 175, 198.

46. "Zhmu vashu ruku," 174, 175. What is interesting in the comments appended to Stalin's letters is that Stalin "corrected" some of Gorky's statements in the articles that were to be published.

47. "Zhmu vashu ruku," 176.

48. "Zhmu vashu ruku," 177, 179. Gorky refused participation in the literary publication of the "International Union of Writers Democrats," explaining it by the fact that among the leaders were Thomas Mann and Albert Einstein, who protested the violation of human rights in the Soviet Union.

49. Gor'kii, *Sobranie sochinenii,* vol. 25, 437–446.

50. "Zhmu vashu ruku," 186–188. Volume one appeared in 1941.

51. "Zhmu vashu ruku," 189.

52. "Zhmu vashu ruku," 190–191.

53. "Zhmu vashu ruku," 191–192. See the explanatory note to the letter on p. 192 regarding the circumstances that prompted Gorky to write it. Evidently, in *Die Rote Fahne* (October 1931, no. 31), the German communist newspaper, an article appeared with the news about a number of terrorist organizations in Poland, Romania, and Czechoslovakia that planned to kill Litvinov, Stalin, and one Dovgalevsky. The article translated by M. A. Peshkov is in the A. M. Gorky Archives, Moscow. See "Zhmu vashu ruku," no. 4, 192.

54. Gor'kii, *Sobranie sochinenii*, vol. 25, 226–230.

55. *Neizvestnyi Gor'kii* III: 163.

56. *Gor'kii i Rollan*, 165 ff.

57. *Neizvestnyi Gor'kii* III: 172.

58. *Neizvestnyi Gor'kii* III: 173–174. See also letter to N. Bukharin, December 11, 1930. *Istochnik* 1 (1994): 12.

59. Gor'kii, *Sobranie sochinenii*, vol. 25, 210.

60. *Gor'kii i Rollan*, 170–171.

61. *Izvestiia TsK KPSS*, No. 7 (1989): 215.

62. *Izvestiia TsK KPSS*, No. 7 (1989): 215.

63. *Izvestiia TsK KPSS*, No. 7 (1989): 215.

64. N. Valentinov, "Vstrechi s Gor'kim," *Novyi zhurnal* (New York, 1965), 135.

65. Valentinov, "Vstrechi s Gor'kim," 135.

66. *Letopis'*, IV: 35–36; *Arkhiv*, XIV: 492–493. The revised "Vladimir Lenin" appeared now as "V. I. Lenin" in a separate edition published by *Gosizdat* in 1931.

67. *Izvestiia TsK KPSS*, No. 7 (1989): 216.

68. *Izvestiia TsK KPSS*, No. 7 (1989): 216.

69. *Perepiska Gor'kogo*, v. 2 (Moscow, 1986), 302–303.

70. *Perepiska Gor'kogo*, v. 2, 304.

71. *Maxim Gorky, Letters* (Moscow, 1966), 314–315; *Gor'kii i Rollan*, 197–198.

72. *Gor'kii i Rollan*, 197–198.

73. *Gor'kii i Rollan*, 197–198.

74. *Arkhiv*, XIV: 176, 496–497.

75. *Letopis'*, IV: 154.

76. *Arkhiv*, X (1): 260.

77. Ia. Agranov, deputy of G. G. Yagoda and an old friend of Stalin. Later purged; A. Orlov, "Tainaia istoriia Stalinskikh prestuplenii," *Ogonëk* 50 (December 1989): 22. According to some sources, Gorky, after his return in 1933, submitted to pressure and tried to work on the biography, supplied with materials from the Central Committee. In the end, he gave up, "pleading inability to fulfill the task on the requisite high level." See Robert C. Tucker, *Stalin in Power: The Revolution from Above, 1928–1941*, 335. Tucker gives as sources: *Politicheskii dnevnik*, II, 1965–1970 (Amsterdam, 1975), 217, citing *M. Gor'kii i sovietskaia pechat'*: *Arkhiv Gor'kogo*, X, book I, 216; V. Kostikov, "Illuzion shchastiia," *Ogonëk* 1 (30 December–6 January, 1990): 14.

78. *Perepiska*, vol. 2, Letter to Lunacharskii, 335.

79. *Arkhiv*, X, book 1: 161.

80. Now the Maxim Gorky Institute of World Literature of the Russian Academy of Sciences.

81. See Shentalinsky, *Arrested Voices*, 257.

82. See V. Ivanov, "Pochemu Stalin ubil Gor'kogo," *Voprosy literatury* 3 (1993): 127.

83. Gor'kii, *Sobranie sochinenii*, vol. 30, 289.

84. Quoted in Harold Swayze, *Political Control of Literature in the USSR: 1946–1959* (Cambridge, MA, 1962), 147.

85. Swayze, *Political Control*, 147.

86. E. Zamyatin, *Litsa* (New York, 1955), 89.

87. *Seria Literatury i iazyka*, tom 54, 2 (1995): 3–14.

88. Shentalinsky, *Arrested Voices*, 257.

89. See McNeal, *Stalin: Man and Ruler*, 154, no. 65.

90. Shentalinsky, *Arrested Voices*, 259.

91. *Letopis'*, IV: 243.

92. *Letopis'*, IV: 317.

93. N. Berberova, *Kursiv moi*, 2d ed. (New York, 1983), vol. 1, 229–230.

94. Ivanov, "Pochemu Stalin," 103.

95. G. P. Wells, ed., *H. G. Wells in Love* (London, 1984); A. West, *H. G. Wells: Aspects of Life* (London, 1984); William Harrison, "H. G. Wells' View of Russia," *Scottish Slavonic Review* 7 (Glasgow, 1986).

96. See Heijenoort, *With Trotsky in Exile from Prinkipo to Coyoacán* (Cambridge, 1978), 40–41.

97. Berberova, *Zheleznaia zhenshchina* (New York, 1982), 273.

98. Shentalinsky, *Arrested Voices*, 524.

99. *Arkhiv*, IX: 283–284.

100. *Gor'kii i Sovetskie pisateli: Neizdannaia perepiska* (Moscow, 1963), 31–34.

101. *Gor'kii i Sovetskie pisateli*, 31–34.

102. *Arkhiv*, XIV: 504. K. S. Petrov-Vodkin (1878–1939), painter and writer.

103. *Izvestiia TsK KPSS* 7 (1989): 219–220; *Gor'kii i Rollan* 471–472.

104. *Gor'kii i Rollan*, 265–266.

105. Prishvin, "Vekselia," 235.

106. L. Schapiro, *The Communist Party of the Soviet Union* (New York, 1960), 391.

107. *Izvestiia TsK KPSS*, 9–12 (1991).

108. *Neizvestnyi Gor'kii* III: 187.

109. *Gor'kii i Rollan*, 274.

110. *White Sea Canal*, M. Gorky, L. Averbakh, S. G. Firin, eds. (London, 1935), 338.

111. A. S. Solzhenitsyn, *Arkhipelag GULAG*, vol. 3 (Paris 1974), 78–101.

112. Andrei Sinyavsky, *The Russian Intelligentsia* (New York, 1997), 7–8.

113. Shentalinsky, *Arrested Voices*, 255.

114. *Gor'kii i Rollan*, 233. It is quite clear that the place was one of the GULAG camps. Maxim spent the summers of 1931 and 1932 there. In the explanations to the letter, mention is made of Maxim's interest in trips to the area, but nothing is said about his working there (*Gor'kii i Rollan*, 464; *Arkhiv*, XIII: 281). Was it that

Maxim met and was befriended by some of the OGPU officials working there who later, on "somebody's orders," helped to get Maxim out of the way?

115. *Arkhiv*, XIII: 236.

116. *Arkhiv*, XIII: 207.

117. *Arkhiv*, XIII: 207.

118. *Arkhiv*, XIII: 296–297. According to the official version, M. A. Peshkov (1897–1934) died of pneumonia. However, on the evidence of the superintendent of the home on Malaia Nikitskaia No. 6, I. M. Koshenkov, at home they suspected that M. A. Peshkov was "made to catch a chill" on the order of G. G. Yagoda, and then "new methods of cure" were used. See *Gor'kii i Rollan*, no. 1, 489. It was widely known that Yagoda was courting Maxim's wife, trying to win her favors. Quoted in Shentalinsky, *Arrested Voices*, 266, is the American Ambassador in Moscow Joseph Davies: "Yagoda was in love with Peshkov's wife and everyone knew it." Shentalinsky, *Arrested Voices*, 262–276.

119. *Gor'kii i Rollan*, 284–285.

120. *Arkhiv*, XIII: 297.

121. V. M. Khodasevich, "Takim ia znala Gor'kogo," *Novyi mir* (1968), 59.

122. Khodasevich, "Takim ia znala," 60.

123. See "Dva pis'ma Stalina," prepared for publication by V. S. Barakhov, *Literaturnaia gazeta* 10 (March 10, 1993): 6.

124. *Soviet Writers' Congress, 1934: The Debate on Socialist Realism and Modernism* (London, 1977), 9, 22.

125. See John and Carol Garrard, *Inside the Writers' Union* (New York, London: 1990), 42–43. See also Gor'kii, *Sobranie sochinenii*, vol. 27, 296–353.

126. Garrard, *Writers' Union*, 67.

127. See comment of Danish Communist Martin Anderson Nexø, a delegate at the Congress, in Garrard, *Writers' Union*, 43; on the euphoria regarding the importance of Party's leadership in the work of the Union of Soviet Writers see Sinyavsky, *The Russian Intelligentista*, 6–7.

128. Sinyavsky, *The Russian Intelligentsia*, 8.

129. Garrard, *Writers' Union*, 42–3.

130. See *Izvestiia TsK KPSS* 5 (1990): 217–218. The letter was dated August 30–September 1, 1934.

131. Gor'kii, *Sobranii sochinenii*, vol. 30, 369.

132. Tucker, *Stalin in Power*, 250–252, 258–296.

133. *Letopis'*, IV: 428.

134. See Shentalinsky, *Arrested Voices*, 262. Shentalinsky comments that Gorky's statement was made at the time of arrests and executions without trial of those allegedly guilty of complicity in the murder of Kirov.

135. Vadim Baranov, "Da i net Maksima Gor'kogo," *Sovetskaia kul'tura* (April 1, 1981); quoted in Tucker, *Stalin in Power*, 363.

136. See *Letopis'*, IV: 446; Schapiro, *The Communist Party of the Soviet Union*, 402–403; Tucker, *Stalin in Power*, 302. The letter by F. I. Panferov was entitled "Otkrytoe pis'mo A. M. Gor'komu."

137. *Neizvestnyi Gor'kii* III: 190.

138. *Neizvestnyi Gor'kii* III: 191.

139. *Neizvestnyi Gor'kii* III: 192.

140. *Letopis'*, IV: 482.

141. *Letopis'*, IV: 494. Gorky's address to the Congress, "Obrashchenie kongresu," was read by a member of the Soviet delegation. Gor'kii, *Sobranie sochinenii*, vol. 27, 449–450, 574.

142. "Moskovskii dnevnik Rollana," *Voprosy literatury* 3, 4, 5 (1989). The diary contains valuable information and comments on the situation in the country and on some of its leaders including Stalin and gives a picture of Gorky in the declining year of his life. It covers the period from June 22 to July 21, 1935. Excerpts from the work appeared first in the journal *Europe* in March 1960. The text published in *Voprosy literatury* is based on a typescript given by Rolland's wife to the Gorky Archives at IMLI (Insitut mirovoi literatury imeni M. Gor'kogo). The typescript and copies of the original are deposited there.

143. See "Moskovskii dnevnik Rollana," *Voprosy literatury* 5: 157.

144. "Moskovskii dnevnik Rollana," *Voprosy literatury* 4: 40.

145. "Moskovskii dnevnik Rollana," *Voprosy literatury* 5: 157.

146. "Moskovskii dnevnik Rollana," *Voprosy literatury* 5: 154.

147. "Moskovskii dnevnik Rollana," *Voprosy literatury* 5: 179.

148. "Moskovskii dnevnik Rollana," *Voprosy literatury* 5: 183.

149. See Tucker, *Stalin in Power*, 363, quoted from *Gor'kii i Stalin, politicheskii dnevnik* 37 (October 1967), 58, in Stephen F. Cohen, ed., *An End to Silence* (New York, 1982), 76.

150. I. Shkapa, *Sem' let s Gor'kim* (Moscow, 1966), 363–384. Tucker, in *Stalin in Power*, writes that as late as 1988, Shkapa, then over 90 years old, still maintained that Gorky was murdered on Stalin's orders (364).

151. For details on the project, see *M. A. Gor'kii i sozdanie istorii fabrik i zavodov* (Moscow, 1959).

152. *Letopis'*, IV: 575–576.

153. See Shentalinsky, *Arrested Voices*, 269; for a detailed outline of Gorky's work, meetings, and concerns during the last months of his life, see *Letopis'*, IV: 586–593.

154. "Dva pis'ma Stalinu," *Literaturnaia gazeta* 10 (March 10, 1993): 6.

155. *Arkhiv*, IX: 362–363.

156. *Letopis'*, IV: 600–601.

157. In Shentalinsky's *Arrested Voices*, we read that Gorky in his will asked to be buried in the Novodevichi cemetery by the grave of his son. E. Peshkova's attempts to carry out his wish were unsuccessful (276).

158. Prishvin, "Vekselia," 237.

159. Quoted in Iu. Annenkov, *Dnevnik moikh vstrech: Tsikl tragedii* (New York, 1966), 53.

160. Shentalinsky, *Arrested Voices*, 276. Also quoted in *Letopis'*, IV: 599.

161. Shentalinsky, *Arrested Voices*, 275. It is not clear whether the document mentioned was found in the Lubianka file on Gorky.

162. See McNeal, *Stalin: Man and Ruler*, 206. McNeal maintains that Gorky's "relatively non-partisan image" played a major role at the Anti-Fascist First International Congress for Writers for the Defence of Culture.

163. Walter Lacqueur, *Glasnost Revelations*, 195.

164. V. Barakhov, "M. Gor'kii. Posledniaia stranitsa zhizni," *Vorposy literatury* 6 (1990): 191.

165. See Tucker, *Stalin in Power*, 364.

166. See V. Ivanov, "Pochemu Stalin ubil Gor'kogo," *Vorprosy literatury* 1 (1993): 91–134.

167. Shentalinsky, *Arrested Voices*, 271–272.

168. Shentalinsky, *Arrested Voices*, 274.

169. *Letopis'*, IV: 601.

170. *Gor'kii i Rollan*, 329–330.

171. Quoted from *Internationale Literatur* 9 (1936) in *Mit der Menschheit auf Du und Du: Schriftsteller der Welt uber Gorkij*, Herausgegeben von Ralf Schroder (Berlin, 1969), 83–85.

172. *Mit der Menschheit*, 84.

173. Quoted in E. Kuskova, "Tragediia Maksima Gor'kogo," *Novyi zhurnal* 38 (New York, 1954), 244.

174. E. H. Carr, "Maxim Gorkij," *Spectator* 156 (June 26, 1936): 1178.

175. Written in Norway July 9, 1936, and published in *International Review*, September–October, 1936; translated in Leon Trotsky, *Portraits: Political and Personal* (New York, 1977), 160–163.

CHAPTER 9

Gorky: For and Against

"What sort of man was Maxim Gorky, then?" ("Chto-zhe za chelovek byl Maksim Gor'kii?") wrote Shaliapin, the famous singer, on the death of his one-time friend. The question for over half a century remains unanswered.

The "for and against" of Maksim Gorky began with the appearance of his short stories and plays, which very early in his writing career brought him fame and wealth. He became the most widely read writer, and his publications went through several editions in a short period of time.

Gorky's arrival on the literary scene coincided with the rise of capitalism in Russia when the *signum* of the times was the protest against the political and social order. The heroes of his early works were the *bosiaki*, the outlaws, daring, generous in spirit, and juxtaposed to the self-satisfied members of the *meshchanstvo*. The theme of struggle and the call for revolt in Gorky's works frightened the establishment, and he came under strong criticism by writers and literary critics. Thus the writer D. S. Merezhkovskii, commenting on Gorky's stories, wrote that although Gorky was not a Tolstoy or a Dostoevsky, only by reading his writings could one understand "the times" and be able to answer the question, "Whither Russia?" In the early biography of Gorky by the writer N. I. Stechkin, Gorky is compared to the eighteenth-century rebel Emelian Pugachev, whose reign of terror came to be known in Russian history as *pugachevshchina*. But there were also voices in praise of the artistic talent of Gorky. In the "for Gorky" camp was N. Mikhailovskii, as was V. G. Korolenko.

On his part, Gorky, the intelligent, rejected the concept of good and evil that prevailed in his environment and put forward his idea of the individual's responsibility for his moral behavior. The origins of Gorky's outlook were to be found in the eighteenth-century Enlightenment. Gorky inherited the intellectual tradition adopted by Westerners (Western-educated intelligentsia), which was over a century old. He was captivated by the idea that education and art make man better and lead to infinite progress for mankind. This belief in the power of education and culture remained with Gorky all his life, and he devoted his talents and his energy to the aim of making his people literate and bringing them closer to Europe.

For L. Trotsky, Gorky (whom he never counted among the revolutionaries) was "culture's psalmodist" (psalm singer who in the Orthodox liturgy assists the officiating priest). N. Sukhanov in his work *The Russian Revolution* wrote of Gorky's understanding of the revolution in terms of culture.

Gorky travelled a long and confusing road along the many ideologies that abounded in the Russia of Nicholas II. From populism he, disillusioned with the peasant, put his faith in the growing might of the urban worker and the Marxist party. By his own admission he was a bad Marxist; when chastised over his political waverings, he would add, "We artists are in essence an irresponsible lot." In an article "O polemike," published in his newspaper *Novaia zhizn'* in 1917, Gorky wrote that he had no sympathy for people who stiffen under the pressure of a belief or an ideology. "I count myself everywhere a heretic," he wrote. Gorky's cooperation and assistance to the Russian Social Democratic Workers' Party (RSDWP) was motivated by his faith in Lenin as leader.

All through his political career, Gorky seemed to have been drawn to personalities rather than to identify himself with one or another ideology. First was the priest Gapon, whom Gorky admired for his ability to organize and lead the workers. Then was Lenin. Rapprochement with him came following the Revolution of 1905, where Gorky took an active part. However, his involvement in the affairs of the Party did not last. Gorky turned toward the left wing of the Bolshevik faction, and his hero was its leader the philosopher A. A. Bogdanov. A new ideology, that of "god-building" (*bogostroitel'stvo*), caused a break with Lenin and brought a torrent of criticism. Gorky's socialism was questioned, and his future as a writer was put in doubt.

The prelude and the postlude of the Revolutions of February and October 1917 were trying times in Gorky's political career. Having accepted the February Revolution with the hope that it would bring about a constitutional and democratic Russia, he condemned the Bolshevik coup d'état. He was chastised by the Bolshevik leaders for his desertion and blamed by the opponents of the now established Soviet regime for the Revolution. Many maintained, and do to this day, that the Revolution was Gorky's offspring (*detishche*). This view of Gorky the revolutionary is connected with his literary works, such as the poems *Pesnia o burevestnike* (Song of the Stormy Petrel), prophesying the coming storm (the revolution); *Pesnia o sokole* (Song of the Falcon), which contains the often quoted slogan, "*Bezumstvu khrabrykh poem my pesniu*" (We sing the song to the madness of the brave); and the novel *Mat'* (Mother), which was to become a kind of a Bible for the revolutionaries. One can debate this contention. In his statements at the time, Gorky was adamant that Russia was not ready for a socialist revolution and that he feared the unleashing of the elemental anarchic forces of the peasant.

Gorky did not believe in the Bolshevik victory, but when it came, he decided to remain in the country. His goal was to save Russia's cultural inheritance and to protect its intellectual elite. Criticized by many and praised by few, even in his courageous stand against the policies of the Bolsheviks and their leaders Lenin and Trotsky, Gorky persevered in his task of saving Russia's cultural inheritance and members of the intelligentsia. It was to Gorky that Lenin turned with a request to mobilize the public opinion of the Western world to help the starving people of Russia. Gorky's second and allegedly voluntary exile was to a large measure conditioned by the fact that he had now become a persona non grata for Lenin and the Party.

In his second exile Gorky was not spared criticism. The "for and against" continued. The émigrés had their own ideas of Gorky's cooperation with the Bolsheviks. The Soviet authorities were angry over his publications, in particular the essay "O russkom krest'ianstve," as were the émigrés.

The death of Lenin and the subsequent developments in his country found Gorky unprepared for the Revolution's new face. In exile in Sorrento he turned to his vocation, that of a writer, and made a successful comeback. Watching from afar the changes that had been taking place in the Soviet Union, Gorky rather naively perceived these to be for the better and in 1927 wrote the essay "Desiat' let" (Ten Years), in which he extolled the achievements he thought had been attained during the ten years of Bolshevik power.

Gorky returned to the USSR in 1928 after an absence over six years. The response to his return by a member of the émigré community, his former friend E. Kuskova, entitled "Obeskrylennyi sokol" (The Falcon with Severed Wings), marked the beginning of the debate that has since become known as "whither Gorky?" The question of the "why" is as important as the "whither." Why did Gorky decide to heed the invitation to come? Why did he become a spokesman for Stalin and his worst policies, and why did Gorky now betray the ideas that he had hitherto held dearly—freedom, liberty, and the rights of the individual? It is in that period of his life that one looks for signs of what has become known as *tragediia Maksima Gor'kogo* (the tragedy of Maxim Gorky). This became the title of Kuskova's article, which was published in 1954, eighteen years after Gorky's death.

Earlier, the émigré writer Mark Aldanov published the article "Iz ikonobortsa on stal sovetskoi ikonoi" (From Iconoclast He Became a Soviet
Icon).[1] In that article Aldanov writes of the role played in Gorky's life by
Lenin, who was at one time important in shaping Gorky's political stance.
Aldanov, unlike other émigrés, mentions Gorky's help to the intelligentsia
in the difficult period of the postlude of the Revolution. An interesting
observation by Aldanov refers to the fact that neither Lenin nor Stalin ever
offered Gorky even a ceremonial position in the government, a fact that
speaks in favor of Gorky but also indicates the irony of Gorky's position
in the USSR, where he was both honored and at times ignored. In Stalin's
Russia, Gorky became, writes Aldanov, the official "scribe" of the peoples'
"*vozhd'* " (leader). Aldanov does not go so far as to address the "why,"
and the present study still finds the question of Gorky's personal motivations difficult to answer.

With the opening of the archives and the publication of materials on and
by Gorky that were buried for many years, the debate "Gorky, for and
against" has recently gained renewed momentum. Many of the sources at
last published in Russia are incorporated in the present work, but some
materials are still in the archives. The authors of available publications,
often repetitive in their arguments, are divided into two camps. One camp
argues that Gorky betrayed his ideals and holds him responsible in great
measure for the disasters that befell his country, blaming in turn Gorky's
love for fame and the good life that Stalin offered him in exchange for his
services.

Writers of the other "camp" defend Gorky by asserting that, as some
maintain, he did not know what was hidden behind "the Potemkin villages" shown to him and that he believed, or wanted to believe, that the
socialist system was and would always be forging ahead towards a better
future for the people. Also important to this camp is the fact that the system
provided a defense against rising fascism in Europe. From this viewpoint,
Gorky helped defend the USSR against the fascist tide. In between the two
camps we find those who explain the tragedy of Maxim Gorky by an analysis of Gorky's humanism, which they believe led to contradictions in himself and ultimately to his tragic end.

The article of the literary critic Pavel Basinskii entitled "Logika gumanizma: ob istokakh tragedii Maksima Gor'kogo" (The Logic of Humanism:
On the Origins of Maxim Gorky's Tragedy) is interesting in this debate.[2]
Basinskii writes that the tragedy of Gorky has its source in contradictions
inherent in European humanism, which holds two opposing ideas: one idea
is moral and religious, not subject to the rule of reason of the ordinary
mortal; the other idea is that of secular humanism, in which, to simplify
for summary, the individual decides on the meaning of his or her life.
Gorky's humanism, writes Basinskii, was in its origin religious and not
secular. The influence of Western ideas postulating the possibility of making man better and by the same token making the world a better place

prevailed in Europe, Basinskii argues; and reason took the place of God in the thinking of intellectuals, among whom Basinskii places Gorky. In this view, Gorky accepted the idea that God is dead and that ancient religious verities need not guide the search for a demonstrably improved society; the price of that acceptance may, of course, be participation in a moral tragedy. As a way out of the end of religious belief and the obvious need for social reform, Gorky attempted to "build" God, Basinskii says. Gorky's idea of "god-building" was the rationalizing of God as a "collective" and thus the national soul is brought as sacrifice. The soul is identified with the East, Reason with the West. The question is that of a choice. Gorky's tragedy lies in that he chose Reason and lost his soul.

Whether Basinskii provides the correct interpretation or not, it is clear that Gorky lived his life as many others do, with contradictions within himself. In fact, Gorky wrote that he was fully aware of these contradictions but that he could not and did not want to resolve them.

To put all the blame on Gorky for the Revolution that failed is to do him an injustice. Gorky opposed the Revolution. His return to the Russia of Stalin, all other reasons aside, was motivated by his love for his country and his people. Gorky did know what was happening and yet, by and large, was in support of Stalinist policies. The émigré historian David Dallin in his work *Forced Labor in Soviet Russia*, while writing about the construction of the Belomor Canal, mentions the trip made by writers to the site and the book that was published glorifying the great feat. "No doubt, only a few of the authors believed what they wrote, . . . the rest, they were merely carrying out orders. . . . Maxim Gorky belonged to the first group. He was a strange mixture of great literary talent and childish naivete."[3] Dallin writes further that Gorky until his death wanted to believe that the Soviet regime was in the process of establishing a community of human brotherhood.

Gorky died in the totalitarian state of Stalinist Russia, the most oppressive and ruthless state in the history of the Russian people, a regime that can be compared only with the reign of Ivan the Terrible in the sixteenth century. Gorky realized too late that if indeed there was no way (or even a need) to resolve all the contradictions in his country and his life, he was left with no way out, except tragedy. The "whither" has become clear; the "why" remains to intrigue future scholars of Maxim Gorky.

NOTES

1. Mark Aldanov, "Iz ikonobortsa on stal sovetskoi ikonoi." Written in 1941. First published in Russian in *Literaturnaia gazeta* 12 (March 24, 1993): 6.

2. Pavel Basinskii, "Logika gumanizma: Ob istokakh tragedii Maksima Gor'kogo," *Voprosy literatury* 2 (1991): 129–154.

3. David J. Dallin and Boris I. Nicolaevsky, *Forced Labor in Soviet Russia* (New York, 1947), 242–243.

Glossary and Abbreviations

GLOSSARY

artel'	artisans' cooperative
bezprizorny	homeless
boevye druzhiny	fighting detachments
bogostroitel'stvo	God-building
bosiaki	outlaws
bureglashatel'	herald of the oncoming storm
glasnost'	openness
gor'kovedy	Gorky scholars
Gosudarstvennaia Duma	State Duma
khoziain	boss
kulaks	rich peasants
meshchanin	burgher
meshchanstvo	burgher class
mir	peasant commune
narodovol'tsy	members of the People's Will Party
oblast'	province
obshchestvennik	social reformer
Okhrana	tsarist secret police

perestroika	restructuring
prodrazverstka	forceful requisition of grain
pugachevshchina	peasant rebellion in the eighteenth century
raion	district
skaziteli	narrators of folk-tales
veche	popular assembly in ancient Russia
vozhd'	leader
vrediteli	wreckers, saboteurs
zemstvo	local government

OFFICIAL ABBREVIATIONS AND ACRONYMS

Cheka	*Vserossiiskaia Chrezvychainaia Komissiia po Bor'be s Kontrrevoliutsiei, Sabotazhem i Spekuliatsiei* (All-Russian Extraordinary Commission to Combat Counter-revolution, Sabotage and Speculation)
Comintern	*Kommunisticheskii Internatsional* (Communist International)
Glavlit	*Glavnoe Upravlenie Literatury* (Chief Administration for Literary Affairs and Publishing)
Gosizdat	*Gosudarstvennoe Izdatel'stvo* (State Publishing House)
Gosplan	*Gosudarstvennaia Planovaia Komissiia* (State Planning Commission)
GPU	*Gosudarstvennoe Politicheskoe Upravlenie* (State Political Administration)
GULAG	*Glavnoe Upravlenie Lagerei* (Chief Administration of Corrective Labor Camps)
Kadety	*Konstitutsionnye Demokraty* (Constitutional Democrats)
KPSS	*Kommunisticheskaia Partiia Sovetskogo Soiuza* (Communist Party of the Soviet Union)
KUBU	*Komitet po uluchshenii byta uchenykh* (Committee for the Improvement of the Life of Scholars)
Narkompros	*Narodnyi Komissariat Prosveshcheniia* (People's Commissariat of Enlightenment)
NEP	*Novaia Ekonomicheskaia Politika* (New Economic Policy)
NKVD	*Narodnyi Komissariat Vnutrennykh Del* (People's Commissariat for Internal Affairs)
OGPU	*Ob'edinennoe Gosudarstvennoe Politicheskoe Upravlenie* (Unified State Political Administration)

Politburo	*Politicheskoe Buro* (Political Bureau)
Proletkult	*Proletarskaia Kul'tura* (Proletarian Culture)
Prompartiia	*Promyshlennaia Partiia* (Industrial Party)
Rabkory	*Rabochie Korrespondenty* (Worker Correspondents)
RAPP	*Russkaia Assotsiatsiia Proletarskykh Pisatelei* (Russian Association of Proletarian Writers)
RSDWP	Russian Social Democratic Workers' Party
TsK	*Tsentral'nyi Komitet* (Central Committee)
TsKK	*Tsentral'naia Kontrol'naia Komissiia* (Central Control Commission)
VIEM	*Vsesoiuznyi Institut Eksperimental'noi Meditsiny* (All-Soviet Institute of Experimental Medicine)
VLKSM	*Vsesoiuznyi Leninskii Kommunisticheskii Soiuz Molodëzhi (Komsomol)* (Communist Youth League)
VSNKh	*Vysshyi Sovet Narodnogo Khoziaistva* (Supreme Council of the National Economy)
VTsIK	*Vsesoiuznyi Tsentral'nyi Ispolnitel'nyi Komitet* (All-Union Central Executive Committee)

BIBLIOGRAPHICAL ABBREVIATIONS

Arkhiv	Akademiia Nauk SSSR. *Arkhiv A. M. Gor'kogo*, 15 vols. (Moscow, 1939–1995)
Letopis'	Akademiia Nauk SSSR. *Letopis' zhizni i tvorchestva A. M. Gor'kogo*, 4 vols. (Moscow, 1958–1960)
PSS	V. I. Lenin, *Polnoe sobranie sochinenii*, 55 volumes. Fifth edition (Moscow, 1958–1965)

CHRONOLOGY OF GORKY'S LIFE

1868	Aleksei Maksimovich Peshkov born in Nizhnii Novgorod on March 18.
1871	Death of Gorky's father, M. S. Peshkov.
1876	Mother remarries.
1877	Gorky is enrolled in parish school.
1878	Leaves school. In the records: "Left school because of poverty."
1879	His mother dies.
1879–1884	Gorky is sent away from his grandparents' house to fend for himself; begins the apprenticeship years.
1884	Leaves for Kazan' to enter university. Introduction to the populists (*narodniki*).
1887	Attempts suicide.
1888	With Romas the populist, tries to work educating peasants. The experiment fails.
1889	Asks Tolstoy for a grant of land to establish an agricultural commune; fails in the attempt. Accused of revolutionary propaganda. Gorky is arrested and then released from prison.
1890	Meets V. G. Korolenko.
1891	Stays in Tiflis. A member of one of the populist circles.

1892	His first story, "Makar Chudra," is published under the pseudonym Maksim Gor'kii (Maxim Gorky).
1895	In Samara. Works for the *Samarskaia gazeta* (Samara newspaper) as a copywriter. Writes "Pesnia o sokole" (The Song of the Falcon).
1896	Marries his first wife, Ekaterina Pavlovna Volzhina.
1897	Birth of his son, Maxim.
1898	The first volume of his short stories is published. Under police surveillance for clandestine revolutionary activities. Starts correspondence with A. Chekhov.
1901	Arrested and then released from prison. Birth of his daughter, Katia (Ekaterina). Meets the actress M. F. Andreeva, who became his second wife. Writes "Pesnia o burevestnike (The Song of the Stormy Petrel). Participates in Marxist circles.
1902	Writes "Na dne" (The Lower Depth). Nicholas II blocks Gorky's appointment to the Imperial Academy of Sciences. Gorky provides financial support to the RSDWP.
1903	Meets the millionaire Savva Morozov, Gorky donates money for Lenin's *Iskra* (The Spark).
1905	"Bloody Sunday." Participates in the revolutionary events. Arrested and incarcerated in the St. Petersburg Peter and Paul Fortress. Released following international protest against his imprisonment. Flees Russia.
1906	Goes to the United States with Andreeva to collect money and to win support for the revolution. Writes the novel *Mat'* (Mother) and the play "Vragi" (Enemies). Death of his daughter Katia. Unable to return to Russia, he travels to Italy, settling on the island of Capri.
1907	Participates as a delegate with a consultative vote in the Fifth Party Congress of the RSDWP in London. Meets with Lenin.
1908–1909	With A. Lunacharskii and A. Bogdanov, Gorky founds the Capri school for underground Party workers. Writes *Ispoved'* (Confession).
1909	Disagrees with Lenin over the idea of "bogostroitel'stvo" (God-building).
1910	Joins the *Vperëd* group of the RSDWP.
1913	Publishes the article "Eshche o karamazovshchine" (More about Karamazovism). Breaks with Lenin. Returns to Russia.
1914	Outbreak of World War I. Gorky settles with M. F. Andreeva in St. Petersburg.

1915	Founds the publishing house *Parus* (The Sail). Publishes *Letopis'* (Chronicle), a political-literary journal.
1916	Publishes the article "Dve dushi" (Two Souls). Becomes a member of the Society for the Study of the Life of the Jews.
1917	The February Revolution occurs. Gorky founds the newspaper *Novaia zhizn'* (New Life). Writes against Lenin, the Bolsheviks, and the October Revolution in his articles "Nesvoevremennye mysli" (Untimely Thoughts).
1918–1921	Acts as guardian of Russia's cultural inheritance. Gorky makes peace with Lenin and the Bolshevik regime. Assumes the role of "the great interceder."
1921	Leaves the Soviet state. The second exile begins.
1922–1924	Lives in Germany and Czechoslovakia. Writes the essay "O russkom krest'ianstve" (On the Russian Peasantry). Active in defense of the Socialist Revolutionaries on trial.
1924	Death of Lenin. Gorky publishes the memoir "Vladimir Lenin." Settles in Sorrento, Italy, with his son and daughter-in-law.
1925	Maintains contacts with writers and publishers in the Soviet Union.
1927	Attempts to establish a *modus vivendi* with the regime of Stalin. Writes the essay "Desiat' let" (The Ten Years).
1928	Gorky's first return to the Soviet Union. The public celebration of his sixtieth birthday.
1929	Gorky's second return to the Soviet Union. Visits the Solovki labor camp.
1930	Revises the memoir "Vladimir Lenin."
1931	Gorky's third return trip to the Soviet Union.
1932	Gorky's fourth return trip to the Soviet Union. The celebration of the fortieth anniversary of his literary work. Gorky is showered with honors and rewards.
1933	Leaves Italy for the last time, accompanied by his son, Maxim and family.
1934	Death of his son Maxim. The First Congress of the Union of Soviet Writers.
1936	Gorky dies on June 18 and is cremated on June 19. His ashes are put in the Kremlin Wall.

Selected Bibliography

ON SOURCES OLD AND NEW

No major biography of Maxim Gorky is available to date in any language. The famous writer who left a rich legacy of literary and publicistic works, who wrote about 20,000 letters, and was well known and respected in the West is still awaiting his biographer.

The political role that he played in the crucial period of Russia's history was, until the period of glasnost', a taboo subject to be discussed only within rules imposed from above. The reasons for the conspiracy of silence was that, beginning with 1928 and Gorky's return to Stalin's Russia, he had become an icon. A "Gorky myth" was created, and anything concerning the writer was to be discussed according to the canon established by Stalin and the Party. Gorky was hailed as the first proletarian writer, Lenin's friend, a committed Bolshevik who erred in 1917–1918 but later recanted, and who from the late 1920s was a faithful follower of Stalin and his policies. Many of the sources that would have shown a different Gorky were soon relegated to the archives and were not accessible.

The work *Gor'kii-revoliutsioner*, written by V. Rudnev (Bazarov) and published in Moscow in 1929, in which the writer discussed Gorky's revolutionary road as it was (*wie es eigentlich gewesen*), soon disappeared from circulation, when the writer was purged in the Menshevik *chistka* in 1931. The publication of the Okhrana file on Gorky, entitled *Revoliutsionnyi put' Gor'kogo* (Tsentrarkhiv, Moscow, 1933), was an important source of information of Gorky's political affiliation to 1917. The copy became available in the West, as were other works by Gorky and about him. The case of the "celebrated" essay, "O russkom krest'ianstve," published in Berlin in 1922, is perhaps the best example of a forbidden work that became known in Russia only during the period of glasnost'. In 1987 it appeared in the émigré journal *Sintaksis* in Paris. Similar was the fate of the essays/articles known under the title "Nesvoevremennye mysli," which appeared on the pages of the newspaper *Novaia zhizn'* (April 1917–July 1918). There were other letters and notes that were hidden or published with many "white spots," all to preserve the "Gorky myth."

Still, within the limits put by the Party on the Gorky publications, a number of important series of works by Gorky and about him were published. *M. Gor'kii: materialy i issledovaniia* (4 vols., Leningrad, 1934–1951), contained articles and archival materials written by known scholars in the field or in literature. Soon to follow was the edition of *Sobranie sochinenii v tridtsati tomakh* (Moscow, 1949–1955), an important edition marred by rules of selectivity, but with useful notes and indices. The next important compilation was the work *Letopis' zhizni i tvorchestva A. M. Gor'kogo* (4 vols., Moscow, 1958–1960), a year-by-year chronicle of Gorky's life and works, but again excluding some events or names of people the writer was in contact with. Thus, one would look in vain in the index for an entry on G. Yagoda or N. Bukharin. M. Budberg, Gorky's steady companion (his mistress?) for a period of about thirteen years, is mentioned a few times in a cursory manner, and "O russkom krest'ianstve" never existed.

In the same period, another series was inaugurated that contains much interesting material: Gorky's wide correspondence with many of his friends, writers, and family members and some essays—all supplemented by copious notes, but not without the red pen of the censor. This is the work *Arkhiv Gor'kogo* (vols. I–XV, Moscow, 1939–1995).

In the freer environment of the "Thaw" under Khrushchev (1954–1964), several one-volume biographies and monographs were published. More of Gorky's letters became available, although with the sign of the censor's pencil still evident. I. Gruzdev, Gorky's biographer, wrote the first volume of what could be assumed to have been a multivolume work about Gorky. Entitled *Gor'kii i ego vremia, 1868–1896* (Moscow, 1960), it was well researched and very readable. Regrettably, there was no sequel. Instead, another one-volume work (a general account of Gorky's life and work) was authored by Gruzdev.

Further, during that somewhat more liberal era, two important books were published. *V. I. Lenin I A. M. Gor'kii: Pis'ma, vospominaniia, dokumenty* was first published in 1961 in Moscow. It later went through two more editions, the last appearing in 1969. The memoirs and letters of Gorky's second wife, M. F. Andreeva, were published in two editions in 1961 and 1963. They were edited by A. P. Grigorieva and S. V. Shirina, and entitled *Mariia Fedorovna Andreeva: Perepiska, vospominaniia, stat'i*.

During the same period more of Gorky's correspondence was released. *Gor'kii i sovetskie pisateli: Neizdannaia perepiska* was published in Moscow in 1963. And in 1968, on the occasion of the centenary of Gorky's birth, a decision was taken to issue a new edition of Gorky's complete works; to date only twenty-five volumes have appeared, under the general title *M. Gor'kii: Polnoe sobranie sochinenii. Khudozhestvennye proizvedeniia v dvadtsati piati tomakh* (Moscow, 1968–1976).

In the West, Gorky was well known as the writer of stories and novels that showed a different Russia from that of L. Tolstoy or A. Chekhov. His autobiographical trilogy was very popular, as were his plays. He lived part of his life in Western Europe, travelled to the United States, and became persona non grata in

1905 when his imprisonment evoked strong protests and the tsarist government was compelled to yield. Gorky was freed and later left the country for a period of seven years. The earliest work based on Gorky's writings was E. T. Dillon's *Maxim Gorky: His Life and Writings* (London, 1902). The biography by Alexander Kaun, an American professor of Russian literature and an admirer of the writer, was perhaps the best biography in English written at this time. His *Maxim Gorky and His Russia* (London, 1932) was based on a series of interviews with the writer, with whom he had spent time in Sorrento. Kaun made use of sources pertaining to the period of World War I and the prelude and postlude to the revolutions of 1917. Kaun's letters addressed to Trotsky, deposited in the Trotsky Papers and housed in the Houghton Library in Cambridge, Massachusetts, have not been published to the knowledge of the present writer and make for very interesting reading.

The 1960s brought a revival of interest in Gorky, in his life, his work, and the still unsolved question surrounding his death. It is worth mentioning that all through the 1920s and 1930s articles about Gorky appeared on the pages of newspapers and journals written and published by émigré communities in France, Germany, and later the United States. Hotly debated in the articles were Gorky's return to the Soviet Union and his compliance with Stalin's policies.

A revived interest in Gorky in the West came at the time of the "Thaw" in the Soviet Union. There were more contacts with Soviet scholars and some better conditions for doing research. Among the published works was Irwin Weil's *Gorky: His Literary Development and Influence on Soviet Intellectual Life* (New York, 1966), a valuable addition to the literature on Gorky the writer. B. D. Wolfe, the well-known American political scientist, authored the work in which Gorky's ideology and political activity were discussed: *The Bridge and the Abyss: The Troubled Friendship Maxim Gorky and V. I. Lenin* (New York, 1967). It was based on sources available in the Boris Nicolaevsky Archive at the Hoover Institution (Stanford University), on the Lenin-Gorky correspondence, and on the essays and articles by Gorky published in his *Novaia zhizn'* in 1917–1918. Wolfe's conclusion that there was no friendship or understanding between Lenin and Gorky was sound enough. About the same time Herman Ermolaev brought to the attention of his English-speaking audience a translation of the much discussed (in the West) "Nesvoevremennye mysli." It appeared under the title *Maxim Gorky: Untimely Thoughts. Essays on Revolution, Culture and the Bolsheviks, 1917–1918* (New York, 1968; second edition New Haven, 1995).

Things changed with the advent of the period of glasnost' (1985–1991). New materials were released from archives and became available to the general public. There arose the possibility of communicating with the West and learning of sources that had become accessible. An important role in this exchange of information on Gorky was played by the intellectual émigrés of the "Fourth Wave." Gorky divested of the myth appeared as a real person, with all his inconsistencies and vacillations. He became "human." Writers, literary critics, and journalists availed themselves of this new freedom and were able to write without the eye of the "inquisition" upon them. Now they could take sides in their interpretations of Gorky's role and his significance in the history of Russia and the Soviet Union.

The following is a short list of works on and by Gorky published in the years 1982–1997 that added valuable information on the subject.

Agurskii, M., and M. Shklovskaia. *Iz literaturnogo naslediia: Gor'kii i evreiskii vopros.* Jerusalem, 1986.

Barakhov, V., and L. Spiridonova, eds. *M. Gor'kii i R. Rollan: Perepiska 1916–1936.* Moscow, 1995.

Barakhov, V. S., S. V. Zaika, and V. A. Keldysh, eds. *Neizvestnyi Gor'kii.* Vol. 4. Moscow, 1995.

Baranov, V. *Gor'kii bez grima.* Moscow, 1996.

Barret, A., and B. Scherr, eds., trans. *Maksim Gorky: Selected Letters.* Oxford, 1997.

Berberova, N. *Kursiv moi.* 2nd edition. London, 1991.

Burlaka, D. K., and Iu. V. Zobnin, eds. *Maksim Gor'kii: Pro et Contra.* St. Petersburg, 1977.

Katzer, N. *Maxim Gor'kijs Weg in die Sozialdemokratie.* Wiesbaden, 1990.

Kjetsaa, G. *Maksim Gor'kii: Sud'ba pisatelia.* Moscow, 1997.

Sesterhenn, R. *Das Bogostroitel'stvo bei Gor'kij und Lunacharskij bis 1909.* München, 1982.

Spiridonova, L. M. *Gor'kii: Dialog s istoriei.* Moscow, 1994.

Vainberg, K. *Gor'kii M. Nesvoevremennye mysli: Zametki o revoliutsii i kul'ture.* Moscow, 1990.

The subject of Gorky in Stalinist Russia was discussed in works that appeared in the West in the period of glasnost'. Listed here are some of the important books found useful in the writing of the present work:

Agurski, M. *Ideologiia natsional-bolshevizma.* Paris, 1980.

Conquest, R. *The Great Terror: A Reassessment.* New York, 1990.

Fleishman, L., et al. *Russkii Berlin.* Paris, 1983.

Garrard, J., and Carol Garrard. *Inside the Writers' Union.* New York, 1990.

Lahusen, T., and Dobrenko, E. eds. *Socialist Realism without Shores.* London, 1997.

McNeal, R.H. *Stalin: Man and Ruler.* New York, 1988.

Shentalinsky, V. *Arrested Voices: Resurrecting the Disappeared Writers of the Soviet Regime.* Translated by John Crowfoot. London, 1996.

Sinyavsky, A. *The Russian Intelligentsia.* New York, 1997.

Tucker, R. *Stalin in Power: The Revolution from Above, 1928–1941.* New York, 1990.

A flood of information by and about Gorky appeared in well-known journals such as *Novyi mir, Oktiabr', Voprosy literatury, Novaia i noveishaia istoriia, Druzhba narodov,* and *Sovetskaia kul'tura* and in the weeklies, in particular *Literaturnaia gazeta* and *Ogonëk.* For the historian the resurrection in 1989 of the "forgotten" monthly *Izvestiia TsK KPSS* was of special importance. There, in the section "Iz arkhivov partii," is found the correspondence of Gorky with the leaders of the Party in the years 1921 to 1936. These were never previously published.

Listed here are some of the interesting essays and articles of importance to the present work that were published between 1988 and 1997:

Aldanov, M. "Iz ikonobortsa on stal sovetskoi ikonoi." *Literaturnaia gazeta*. No. 12. 1993.

Barakhov, V. S. "Dva pis'ma Stalinu." *Literaturnaia gazeta*. No. 10. 1993.

Barakhov, V. S. "Gor'kii kotorogo my ne znaem." *Literaturnaia gazeta*. No. 10. 1993.

Barakhov, V. S. "Posledniaia stranitsa zhizni." *Voprosy literatury*. No. 6. 1990.

Barakhov, V. S. "Tragediia M. Gor'kogo v interpretatsii sovremennykh kritikov." *Neizvestnyi Gor'kii*. Vol. 4. Moscow, 1995.

Barrat, A, and E. W. Clowes. "Gorky, Glasnost' and Perestroika." *Soviet Studies*. No. 6. 1991.

Basinskii, P. "Logika gumanizma: Ob istokakh tragedii Maksima Gor'kogo." *Voprosy literatury*. No. 2. 1991.

Basinskii, P. "Strannyi Gor'kii." *Literaturnaia gazeta*. No. 17. 1993.

Dubinskaia-Dzhalilova, T., and A. Cherneva eds., "Zhmu vashu ruku, dorogoi tovarishch: Perepiska Maksima Gor'kogo i Iosifa Stalina." *Novyi mir*. No. 9. 1997.

Ivanov, V. "Pochemu Stalin ubil Gor'kogo?" *Voprosy literatury*. No. 3. 1993.

Khodasevich, V. F. "Gor'kii." *Oktiabr'*. No. 12. 1989.

Kostikov, V. V. "Iliuzion shchastiia." *Ogonëk*. No. 1. 1990.

Kostikov, V. V. "M. Gor'kii i emigratsiia: Neizvestnye stranitsy istorii." *Novaia i noveishaia istoriia*. No. 1. 1990.

Kostikov, V. V. "O fenomene Lokhankina i russkoi inteligentsii." *Ogonëk. Luchshie publikatsii 88 goda*. Moscow, 1989.

"Moskovskii dnevnik Rollana." *Voprosy literatury*. Nos. 3, 4, and 5. 1989.

Motyleva, T. "Maxim Gorky's Tragedy." *Moscow News*. No. 4. 1990.

Orlov, A. "Tainaia istoriia stalinskikh prestuplenii." *Ogonëk*. No. 50. 1989.

Paramonov, B. "Gor'kii, beloe piatno." *Oktiabr'*. No. 5. 1992.

Prishvin, M. "Vekselia po kotorym kogda-to pridetsia rasplachivat'sia." *Druzhba narodov* No. 6. 1993.

Saraskina, L. "Strana dlia eksperimenta." *Oktiabr'*. No. 3. 1990.

Spiridonova, L. "Konchaite svoe delo i pliunte v Sorrento." *Iunost'*. No. 2. 1988.

Yedlin, T. "Anketa po voprosu ob antisemitizme." *Forum*. No. 10. München, 1985.

Gorky was one of the most widely published writers in the Soviet Union, and it is natural that a vast literature about him as writer and about his works would be published. S. D. Balukhatyi, one of the early experts on Gorky, lists some seven thousand articles and books about the author published between 1893 and 1932. This figure was multiplied many times over in the years following, when every book, article, and essay was recorded and published. Listed here are only a few of the many available works.

Balukhatyi, S. D. *Kritika o M. Gor'kom. Bibliografiia statei i knig: 1893–1932.* Leningrad, 1934.

Brodskii, N. L., ed., *M. Gor'kii. Rekomendatel'nyi ukazatel'*. Moscow, 1949.

Kaleps, B. *Bibliographie Maksim Gorkij 1868–1936*. Billings, 1963. A multilingual
    bibliography of works by and about Gorky.

Muratova, K. *Seminarii po Gor'komu*. Leningrad, 1956. A compendium of articles
    and books.

Clowes, E. W. *Maxim Gorky: A Reference Guide*. Boston, 1987.

PRIMARY SOURCES: LOCATIONS

The main depository of sources on Gorky and by Gorky in terms of manuscripts,
letters, and documents is the Gorky Archive at the Gorky Institute of World Literature (IMLI) in Moscow. The archive was established in 1937 by a decree of the
Presidium of the Council of People's Commissars. Today collections housed in state
agencies and institutions are being transferred to the Gorky Archive. Recently the
papers from the *Presidentskii arkhiv*, the former archives of the Central Committee
of the Communist Party of the Soviet Union (TsK KPSS), have become the latest
important acquisition. It is assumed that with time much of the materials will be
published.

In the West the main locations of works by and about Gorky are libraries and
universities in the United States and Europe. In the Library of Congress one finds
a rich collection of journals and newspapers published in Russia and in the West
in the prelude and postlude of the revolutions of 1917. Deposited there are the
originals of Gorky's letters to the poet V. F. Khodasevich for the years 1922–1925,
with comments by Khodasevich appended in 1939. These were translated and edited by H. McLean and entitled "The Letters of Maksim Gor'kij to V. F. Khodasevich, 1922–1925" and published in *Harvard Slavic Studies*, vol. 1 (Cambridge,
MA, 1953).

A very valuable source of primary material is the B. I. Nicolaevksy Archive at
the Hoover Institution, Stanford, California. Nicolaevsky, an émigré and prominent
member of the Menshevik Party, was a great collector of documents, letters, memoirs, and newspapers of the revolutionary period. The Gorky-Nicolaevsky correspondence, notes, and memoirs of participants in the events of 1917 and after are
to be found there. An important collection of prerevolutionary newspapers and
journals published in Russia and in the Western press is available in the New York
Public Library.

Columbia University, New York, is the curator of the Archive of Russian and
East European History and Culture, where one can find the Aleksinskii Papers. G.
Aleksinskii, a member of the RSDWP, was at one time a friend of Gorky and a
participant in a number of undertakings, including the organization of the Capri
School for Professional Revolutionaries in 1909.

The University of Illinois at Champaign-Urbana has in their Slavic Library collections of microfilms and some original materials pertaining to Gorky. The H. G.
Wells–Gorky correspondence is deposited there.

The Russian Library of Helsinki University in Finland is rich in prerevolutionary
journals and newspapers. The Houghton Library in Cambridge, Massachusetts, is

the depository of the Trotsky Papers. There is in the collection the unpublished correspondence of A. Kaun, Gorky's biographer, and Trotsky.

The preceding list is not a complete reference to all the unpublished materials concerning Gorky, but the present writer used them for most of the research pertaining to Gorky's political activities.

INDEX

About the Author

TOVAH YEDLIN is Professor Emerita in the Department of Modern Languages and Cultural Studies and the Division of Slavic and East European Studies, University of Alberta, Canada. In addition to her translations and articles, Professor Yedlin is the editor of *Women in Eastern Europe and the Soviet Union* (Praeger, 1980).